THE HISTORY OF MUSEUMS

Printed and bound by
Antony Rowe Ltd., Chippenham, Wiltshire

MUSEUMS AND
ART GALLERIES

Thomas Greenwood

ROUTLEDGE/THOEMMES PRESS

This edition published by Routledge/Thoemmes Press, 1996
Reprinted in 1998

Routledge/Thoemmes Press
11 New Fetter Lane
London EC4P 4EE

The History of Museums
8 Volumes : ISBN 0 415 14872 3

This is a reprint of the 1888 edition
Reproduced by kind permission of
The Trustees of the National Library of Scotland.

Routledge / Thoemmes Press is a joint imprint
of Routledge and Thoemmes Antiquarian Books Ltd.

British Library Cataloguing-in-Publication Data
A CIP record of this set is available from the British Library

Publisher's Note

The publisher has gone to great lengths to ensure the
quality of this reprint but points out that some
imperfections in the original book may be apparent.

THE BIRMINGHAM ART GALLERY.

MUSEUMS

AND

ART GALLERIES.

BY

THOMAS GREENWOOD, F.R.G.S.,

AUTHOR OF

" Free Public Libraries," " Eminent Naturalists," etc.

——————

London:

SIMPKIN, MARSHALL AND CO.,

STATIONERS' HALL COURT, E.C.

—

1888.

LONDON:

PRINTED BY THE NATIONAL PRESS AGENCY. LIMITED,

WHITEFRIARS STREET, E.C.

PREFACE.

THE subject upon which this book treats is almost without a literature. Several books on some of the pictures in the leading Galleries have been written, but the chief of these are now out of print. Taking the subject in its entirety, all that has been published are fugitive articles in Reviews and Magazines, or an occasional paper read before the British Association. The most practical and comprehensive sketch upon Museum work which has yet appeared is the Report of the Committee appointed by the British Association, for the purpose of preparing a Report upon the Provincial Museums of the United Kingdom. This Committee consisted of nine eminent gentlemen, with Mr. F. T. Mott, of Leicester, acting as Secretary, and to whose efforts that excellent Report is largely due. Within a compass of thirty-two pages this Committee have given an invaluable document for the interior working of Museums.

I have endeavoured to cover other ground, and to treat the subject from a popular standpoint. This book does not claim to be a scientific treatise on the objects and specimens usually found in Museums, or a disquisition on the works of art contained in Art Galleries. The undertaking has grown out of *Free Public Libraries,* a work which kindly critics say has given a distinct impetus to the movement. These three classes of institutions—Public Libraries, Museums, and Art Galleries—are inseparably associated.

Many Curators have given the warmest encouragement in the work, and I would express my indebtedness to them, and to my old tutor, the Rev. W. Urwick, M.A., for useful suggestions.

Among the main points I have had in view during the progress of this work are the following :—

First and foremost, the urgent necessity for the appointment of a Minister of Education, whose Department shall be responsible for the utilisation for the people of the British Museum, South Kensington Museum, and other national institutions supported out of the public funds. The same Department to keep itself in touch with all the Museums, Art Galleries, and Free Public Libraries of the country, and from time to time to publish works relating to them. Many intricate points are constantly arising, and such a Department would be able to answer these as they occur. There is too much isolation in the present methods of management in these national institutions, and until there is some Department absolutely responsible there will neither be economy in expenditure or the fullest measure of utility accruing out of them. The term economy is used, not in the narrow and captious sense which it so frequently means, but in the sense of securing the maximum of value for national money expended. It is worthy of note here that the

Leader of the House of Commons, in reply to a question on July 9th, 1888, said that the placing of the British Museum, the National Gallery, and South Kensington Museum under one governing body would involve dealing with separate trusts, and the Government were not prepared to give any pledge on the subject.

As the British Museum, South Kensington Museum, and the National Gallery are maintained by public money to which the whole nation contributes, the provinces as well as London should more largely share, by means of loans of objects, and in other ways, in the advantages attaching to these national institutions. It is also very essential that these institutions, scattered throughout the country, should take a distinct place in the nation's educational work, and that the poorer institutions receive Government aid. Government officials abroad, such as Governors-General, Consuls, Agents, officers of gunboats and other vessels belonging to the nation, as well as the large army in the merchant service, should be encouraged to enlist their practical aid in the acquiring of specimens and objects for distribution among the Museums in various parts of the country.

The need for some feasible arrangement among Curators for the exchange of duplicates is pressing. At present this is done only to a limited extent. This will be accomplished by the formation of an Association of Curators, and towards the formation of such an Association active steps have been taken within the past few months.

These institutions have ceased to be luxuries, and

should be considered as absolutely necessary for the
welfare of every Municipality throughout the country.
Gaols and workhouses are provided as a matter of course,
and why should not Museums and Free Libraries be
looked upon as of equal importance ? These institutions are calculated to take a high place in the
educating of the people in the duties and privileges of
citizenship. Even on the ground of being economical
investments, every Municipality should possess its
Museum and Free Library. There is unmistakable
proof that crime is decreasing, and this may be largely
attributed to the presence, in many of the large towns,
of the institutions for which I am pleading.

The conviction has impressed itself deeply upon me
during inquiry into this subject that it is only the
rate-supported Museums which are doing really useful
work. Museums supported by subscriptions and voluntary donations are in a state of decrepitude and decay.
Many of them are almost ready to close their doors
from lack of public support and interest. Ultimate
failure in many instances can only be avoided by giving
the Museum an entirely new lease of healthy life by
the adoption of the Public Libraries and Museums
Acts, and making each existing Museum the nucleus of
such an effort.

Municipalities could, by the adoption of the
Public Libraries or Museums Acts, begin first with
a Museum, but it appears that, in the majority of
cases, it is wiser and more politic to begin with a Free
Library, and let the Museum grow out of this work.
The Lending and Reference Libraries, with cheerful

newsrooms well supplied with the leading periodicals, appeal to a larger number than does the Museum, and so the work becomes popularised and prepares the way for a Museum being established. If the success of the Library is assured, generous gifts of money or kind are much more likely to flow in for the sister institution, when it is in process of organisation.

We may, as a nation, congratulate ourselves that we are not behind other nations in the excellence of these institutions, although in point of number we may, perhaps, be outstripped. Taking a general survey, we are in advance in some departments, rather than behind the corresponding institutions of Europe and America.

It is not commendable to us, as a nation, that there has been, comparatively, a paucity of large-hearted gifts of money and of private collections to these institutions. Some Museums and Art Galleries have fared exceedingly well in this direction, but others have had little for which to thank donors. I trust this work may lead to the awakening of a new interest on the part of the public in Museums and Art Galleries, and that in the future there will be many noble and generous bequests to record.

20, Lordship Park,
  Stoke Newington,
    London, N.
September, 1888.

CONTENTS.

CHAPTER VIII.

CHAPTER IX.

CHAPTER X.

CHAPTER XI.

CHAPTER XII.

CHAPTER XIII.

CHAPTER XIV.

CHAPTER XV.

CHAPTER XVI.

CHAPTER XVII.

CHAPTER XVIII.

CHAPTER XIX.

CHAPTER XX.

CHAPTER XXI.

CHAPTER XXII.

CHAPTER XXIII.

CHAPTER XXIV.

CHAPTER XXV.

CHAPTER XXVI.

CHAPTER XXVII.

CHAPTER XXVIII.

LIST OF ILLUSTRATIONS.

MUSEUMS AND ART GALLERIES.

CHAPTER I.

INTRODUCTION.

WE have to deplore, as a nation, that the Education Act of 1870 came so late. Even those who, politically, opposed the late W. E. Forster, in the efforts he for some fifteen years carried on, now see, and are not unwilling to acknowledge, that we should not now have so many arrears in education to overtake, had that Act been passed twenty years earlier, or even less, before the time when it was placed upon the Statute-book.

Had this been the case we should not now have to lament so great a paucity in the number of Museums and the impoverished condition in which many of them exist at the present time. These institutions, it is safe to assert, would have long ago formed part, along with

B

similar institutions, of our national system of education, and no Municipality would have been considered complete without its Museum and sister institution of a Free Library.

The only adjuncts to a Municipality which are at present, in too many instances unfortunately, looked upon as absolutely indispensable beyond street improvements, drainage, lighting, and waterworks, are a gaol and a workhouse, with their concomitants of police, magistrates, and a share in a lunatic asylum and the national hangman. We are most lavish in our expenditure under these heads, but when we come to the expenditure for education, with the institutions which should necessarily spring from the parent stem, our national niggardliness becomes painfully apparent, and we resort to rigid retrenchment. If a few millions are required for an impossible and useless railway in a desert, or for powder and shot to blow away into space, or if a number of thousands of pounds are to be spent in finding a political partisan a place at a foreign court where his services are from the first of a shady and doubtful necessity, up go the thumbs of a large section of our legislators, and the money is forthwith voted. But let the object be a few extra thousands for the British Museum, the endowment of research, Board Schools, or Free Libraries, down go the thumbs, and strangulation forthwith proceeds. A new torpedo is considered of greater value than a hundred Museums, and the next list of pensions must be passed because the preceding lists have gone merrily on, until the nation begins to stand aghast at its annual bill, and wonders at what point it is likely to reach high-water mark.

The coming power of the future will spend, it is hoped, less for the baser elements of humanity, inevitable as much of this outlay may be, and will be more disposed to aid in every possible way whatever tends to promote or enhance the education of youth and the general culture of the people.

Even taking all into account in London and the United Kingdom and Ireland, the number of Museums is under 200, and many which are included in this estimate should really not be in the list, for, although they have been established with worthy aims, they hardly deserve the name. In not a few towns a casual inquiry from a passer-by of average intelligence as to the whereabouts of the local Museum would cause him to hesitate before replying and, ultimately, all that can, perhaps, be ascertained is that he believes there is a Museum somewhere in the town, but he has forgotten the name of the street in which it is situated. Should the inquirer be interested in things antiquarian or geological, and be persistent in his determination to find the local Museum, he will perhaps, in the smaller towns, eventually drop upon it only to find it situated in some narrow and unfrequented street, or some out-of-the-way yard where the chief ornament is a pump. When the enthusiast has mounted the stairs, and congratulates himself upon having discovered the object of his search, his joy will in far too many instances be short-lived, for immediately he casts eyes on the cases he finds dust and disorder reigning supreme. Confusion worse confounded will be frequently his first thought, and the *olla podrida* condition of almost everything will make him eagerly echo the poet's words :—

> " Oh, for the wizard hand of patient skill
> To bring forth beauteous order from this pile
> Of rich but wild confusion ! "

Or say with Dryden :—

> " Set all things in their own peculiar place,
> And know that order is the greatest grace."

The orderly soul of the Museum student will quake at the sight of a Chinese lady's boot encircled by a necklace made of shark's teeth, or a helmet of one of Cromwell's soldiers grouped with some Roman remains. Another corner may reveal an Egyptian mummy placed in a mediæval chest, and in more than one instance the curious visitor might be startled to find the cups won by a crack cricketer of the county in the collection, or even the stuffed relics of a pet pug dog.

This is not by any means overdrawn; but that order and system is coming out of chaos in many Museums is clear. This is especially the case in those which are the property of the citizens, inasmuch as they are established under the Museums Acts or the Public Libraries Acts, and so are rate-supported institutions with an administration by a governing body which is elective. Responsibility in this way to the local community invariably prevents much fossilism or foolish proceeding on the part of the committee. Museums are springing up in various parts of the country, and are becoming institutions of far-reaching utility, and the pride of all intelligent citizens.

The main objects of a Museum may be classed as follows, although this need not necessarily apply to every Museum :—

1st.—That it provide rational amusement of an elevating character to the ordinary visitor.

2nd.—That it be in the fullest sense an educational institution easily accessible to all classes.

3rd.—That it provide a home for examples of local objects of interest of an antiquarian, geological, or other character.

4th.—That a section of it be a commercial Museum containing specimens of manufactures resembling those produced in the immediate locality.

5th.—That it be one in a series of institutions whose object shall be to further the education of the many, and the special studies of the few.

This is of a sufficiently comprehensive scope, and I am quite aware that Professor John Ruskin, for whom I have the most profound respect, as these pages will show, would not sanction one-half the number. Still, in this work-a-day life, with its multitudinous interests and the increasingly pressing burdens of life, utilitarianism as applied to these institutions should be scrupulously borne in mind on the one hand, and strictly good value for money invested, if the institution be rate-supported, on the other.

Mr. Ruskin's influence on the age has been marked and beneficial. To many he is known only as an art critic, but to others he is known as an idealist with regard to Museums. More than any other public man he has laid bare many things which other people conceal. He has taken the world into his confidence, and has shown himself the frank, true, and earnest man which he calls us to be. He has often said startling things, but underneath and blending with these there has been an evident predominant desire, that there should be a beautiful England, filled with people living beautiful lives, in unison with the beautiful objects by which they may be surrounded. He has placed at the door of humanity hard thinking and hard work, and has enriched his age and generation, and all the generations to follow, with words and thoughts which have burned themselves into an immortal existence.

"A Museum is," he says, "be it first observed, primarily, not at all a place of entertainment, but a place of Education. And a Museum is, be it secondly observed, not a place for elementary education, but for that of already far-advanced scholars. And it is by no means the same thing as a parish school, or a Sunday-school, or a day school, or even—the Brighton Aquarium.

Be it observed, in the third place, that the word
' School ' means ' Leisure,' and that the word ' Museum '
means ' Belonging to the Muses,' and that all schools
and Museums whatsoever, can only be, what they claim
to be, and ought to be, places of noble instruction,
when the persons who have a mind to use them can
obtain so much relief from the work, or exert so much
abstinence from the dissipation, of the outside world as
may enable them to devote a certain portion of secluded,
laborious, and reverent life to the attainment of the
Divine Wisdom, which the Greeks supposed to be the
gift of Apollo, or of the Sun ; and which the Christian
knows to be the gift of Christ."

The designation of Museum is now a generic phrase,
and it has always been so.   It comes from the
Greek *Mouseion*, the name originally given to a
temple devoted to the Muses, and was also applied
by the Greeks to philosophical schools or colleges,
and frequently again to halls set apart for the
study of music.   On the Continent the term *Musée* is
still used in a somewhat wider sense than we in
England use Museum ; but it is noteworthy that
although the art of delighting by sound has long been
called emphatically Music, we never apply the name
Museum to a concert hall.   It has remained for our
American cousins to drag the term Museum down to a
very low level.   On the other side of the Atlantic
no good-sized town would be considered complete without its " Dime Museum," where every description of
monstrosity, natural and otherwise—usually otherwise
—can be seen for a modest fivepence.   The most
extraordinary make-believes which a deluded public
ever paid their money to see are to be found in
these collections.   In one of these places " The Wild
Man of Siberia ; caught with great difficulty while
fleeing from his pursuers," chained in a cage, and

" made up " in a most terrific way, turned out to be a harmless negro.

When the revival of learning set in, the early Museums contained principally coins, sculptures, and gems. There is, however, no record that anything similar to the Museums of modern times existed among the ancients. The casual reader knows full well that in the houses of the wealthy Romans there were collections of statues and paintings, but these were frequently intended for splendour and effect rather than for the promotion of art.

The name, however, soon ceased to be limited to collections of antiquities, sculptures, and paintings, and was used to embrace collections illustrative of Natural History and other sciences, which now form a chief part of the treasures of many of the greatest and most celebrated Museums.

Not only Professor Ruskin but others may be disposed to question the wisdom of a Museum providing amusement as well as instruction. Still although amusement might be the primary object in visiting a Museum on the part of many there is, as a rule, so much to be seen that it would be almost impossible for anyone to visit an institution of this kind, of average merit, without receiving impressions or learning something to carry away, about which to talk with associates and friends. Life presses hardly upon so many, that a craving for mental relief in looking upon something grotesque or comical, viewed from one standpoint, may be excusable, and the sense of the ridiculous is so deeply rooted in the British mind that often humour is quickened by an object which is in itself capable of conveying serious and important lessons.

The educational character of Museums is only now becoming generally recognised, and the usefulness of a Museum in this respect does not depend entirely so much

on the number or intrinsic value of its treasures as
upon the proper arrangement, classification, and naming
of the various specimens in so clear a way that the uninitiated may grasp quickly the purpose and meaning
of each particular specimen.

The effect of a walk through a Museum on the minds
of even very young children is that of awe and speech-
less wonder. I was particularly struck with this
during a visit to the Harvard Museum at Cambridge,
Massachusetts, the seat of the University of that name,
on a public holiday in the spring of 1886. I had not been
long in the Agassiz Rooms of the Museum when in
trooped a group of youngsters of both sexes, numbering
about a dozen. The eldest could not have reached ten
and the youngest could not have been more than three
years old. There was no hall-keeper to turn them out,
and no voice said them nay, and they went from case
to case, hand in hand, pointing now and again at
some of the objects which specially attracted their
attention. They spoke little, but their eyes were
full of unspoken words. The eyes of some of them
glistened in a way not to be forgotten, for it is well
for the world that children have not learned the art of
concealing their pleasure. At least two of the youngsters
were without shoes and stockings, it may have been
from choice more than from necessity, as the day was
warm, but the fact remains, and I could not refrain
from expressing my admiration for the governing body
of any Museum which displayed such catholicity of
mind as to permit children so young, unaccompanied by
elders, to go in and out of the rooms without let or
hindrance.

Every locality has a fund of interest attaching to it of
either a botanical, geological, or antiquarian character ;
and what more natural home could there be for specimens collected by field naturalists' and other societies,

than a local Museum? A new interest in life and
in a given district may thus be excited, and pursuits be
awakened calculated to convey invaluable and life-long
lessons.

The fourth purpose of a Museum set forth is one of
growing importance with each succeeding year, and
a local Museum affords the most appropriate centre for
illustrations of the industrial arts, their raw materials,
models of the machines employed, the various processes of manufacture, and the completed products.
Too much prominence cannot be given to this
matter, and in the chapter dealing particularly with
that section its importance will be urged upon Municipalities and other governing bodies.

The fifth purpose of a Museum named is becoming daily more and more patent in its necessity.
There is at present, in too many instances, no
cohesion among Museums and kindred institutions
which links together the interests and constitutes them
one of an important group of buildings, not necessarily
in one locality, around which shall centre the intellectual life of the town.

There is need for one central institution which
shall be looked upon as the head, and to which
missionaries, colonists, travellers, and the generously
disposed shall be invited to send specimens, to
be distributed in turn to provincial or other Museums.
Such a central institution, again, should provide a
place of exchange for duplicates—one of the pressing
requirements of Museums at the present time. A
central Museum fulfilling these and other needs
should be thoroughly in touch with the spirit of the
times and vigorously administered by a responsible
chief, holding a post analogous to that of the Post-
master-General, or the President of the Local Government Board. That South Kensington is capable of

occupying such a position is very clear, but he would be a bold man who would assert that it does so at the present time.

The main point, however, to which I desire to direct attention in these pages is the pressing need for some special State assistance or Municipal grants to Museums and Art Galleries. It is a well-known fact to all who have read much upon the matter that in other countries with whom we have now to compete in the business world Municipal grants are given to similar institutions in the most liberal—nay, it may be said lavish—manner. The result has been to place in the industrial centres of the Continent men of considerable ability, who have obtained their experience by visits to our own and other countries. In the training of these men the local Museum or Technical School has occupied an important place.

The rationale of Art Galleries may be epitomised under a few leading heads, the first of which is that they place us in direct communication with some of the best thoughts and feelings of highly-gifted people, and this by means of the quickest of the five senses. Pictures, again, not only give us the records of the past and the present, but help us to gain an intimate knowledge of some of the best lives lived by men and women. As a third point, there may be given the fact that there is always something more to be learned from a picture than the picture itself can tell us. Pictures and other works of art cultivate the wholesome habit of finding out information for ourselves, and so we become accustomed to follow out the suggestiveness conveyed to our minds by the picture. Pictures thus become powerful aids in education, as well as giving pleasure and restfulness to the mind.

Art is essentially democratic in its character. There is universally a liking for the beautiful ; the eye of the most ignorant will turn naturally to the pretty and beautiful, and be repulsed from the ugly and grotesque, if the two are side by side. There can, of course, be no universal standard of beauty, and it would be the few, and not the many, who could, with the limited place which art has at present in education, give an intelligible reason why they considered a thing beautiful.

A true enjoyment of pictures and beautiful things can be brought about only by making art less uncommon, and in the diffusion of works of art. Art-education does not mean simply the teaching of every one to draw, but instructing both young and old in the appreciation and enjoyment of that which is beautiful. The education at present in vogue has too much rigour and severity in it, too much inculcation of painful duty. Art occupying its proper place in education would produce a leavening influence on these tendencies, and would lead men and women throughout the length and breadth of the land to delight in those things which give pleasure and recreation to the mind through the eye. Art should not be approached as something unusual or accidental —something for the aristocratic few, and not for the many. It exercises a vast influence in life, and its full effect in the elevating and refining of mankind can only grow out of its filling a distinct place in education all through life.

I have sent out to every Museum in Great Britain, whose existence I have been able to ascertain, a series of questions, and in response to the following question, "*What do you consider the best means of extending the work of Museums generally, and of increasing their individual utility?*" a considerable number of Curators have expressed an opinion, and the salient parts of some of these suggestions are worth quoting.

Mr. W. W. Midgley, of the Bolton Museum, suggests annual conferences of Curators; the establishment of a workable system of exchange of duplicate specimens; Museums should be in the hands of the Town Councils; and, most important of all, they should be free.

Mr. J. J. Ogle, of the Bootle Museum and Free Library, says:—(1) Some sort of association for Curators. (2) The extension of "pictorial mounting" of objects. (3) The introduction of typical living animals where possible. (4) Periodical addresses by the Curator and others on the specimens. (5) The extension of the "economical aspect" of Museums, i.e., the exhibition of silks with the silk-worms; of furs made up with the fur-bearing animals; of manufactured goods by the side of the uncommon metals, &c. (6) References to books on the classes of animals, attached to descriptive labels of such classes.

Mr. B. Lomax, of the Brighton Museum, regrets that the public apathy is so difficult to overcome. He would like to see well written manuals of the contents of Museums, and suggests a close association with the schools of Science and Art, and with the Board schools.

Mr. W. A. Taylor, of the Hanley Museum, advises the extending of their scope and range, and that they be more cosmopolitan in their organisation. He urges the delivery of lectures on objects in the local Museum. Individual Museums, he thinks, can become more useful by making a speciality of exhibiting objects having a direct bearing on the trades and industries of the district.

Mr. James Yates, of Leeds, urges the developing of a Technical Section illustrating the manufactures, &c., of each town.

Mr. Thomas J. George, of the Northampton Museum, makes the following suggestions:—(1) To secure a Curator whose whole time can be given up to the Museum. (2) To confine it to articles both natural and artificial, being productions of the town and neighbourhood or county. (3) To have each article labelled in the simplest as well as in a technical manner; to have good diagrams. (4) To hold a kind of evening soirée, when some collection will be explained by competent persons.

Mr. J. Woolman, of the Watford Free Library, says that one of the best things he has known in connection with Museum work is half-hourly explanations by the Curator at certain times and days on particular classes of exhibits. He is of opinion that to make a Museum merely a curiosity shop is not worth striving for, but when by such aids as lectures it is the means of instruction, it is likely to accomplish its object—raise the moral and intellectual tone of the people.

Mr. C. C. Jones, of the Welshpool Museum—which is now to form part of the Free Library work, the Acts having been adopted in 1887—refers to a point important and vital to the immediate subject in hand. He believes that the best means of extending the work of Museums is for collectors to yield their private collections to the Public Museums, where they can be inspected by all, including themselves, instead of simply being content with looking at them in their private repositories. By such a step as this the donor merely takes the public into partnership with himself, and gives them, without depriving himself, all the advantages and enjoyments he had hitherto retained to himself. These are wise words, and may they have their effect. He goes on further to say that he thinks the law of treasure-trove should be altered, and any antiquity found should belong, not to the finder or to the Crown, but to the local Museum of the district. All will agree with him when he says that such articles so discovered belong to the public, which is fairly represented by the local Museum.

One answer from the Curator of a subscription Museum comes from one of the largest towns in the country. He urges that the first essential is adequate financial support. The Museum of which he has charge does not get this and is not likely to, unless it is taken over by the Municipality, and converted into a Free Museum—a very desirable proceeding. Beyond this he considers that all first-class Natural History Museums should be affiliated with the British Museum of Natural History, South Kensington. The mutual help they could give each other is very considerable. By affiliation he means direct subordination, and, to a certain extent, " State endowment," as well as donations of specimens; the local authority might be left to arrange the routine details, but important matters should be only carried out by this authority after consultation and under the direction of the central authority; in this case, the Trustees of the British Museum. At least one students' room should be provided at every large Museum, adjoining the Curator's.

The replies from the Curators of general and private Museums all follow very much in the same strain. Perusing all of them very carefully, it is impossible not to be convinced that Curators, as a body, are deeply in touch with the aims and objects of Museums, and would willingly adopt any methods likely to increase their individual and general utility.

CHAPTER II.

THE RELATION OF THE STATE TO MUSEUMS.

HE influence of Mr. Herbert Spencer on the thought of the age is unmistakable, and his political philosophy is permeating the efforts towards reforms which on all sides are looked upon as necessary; the difference resting only in the degree with which parties view a possible and necessary change, in order to adjust a law or series of laws to the requirements of the time. Mr. Herbert Spencer considers that Museums and literature should be provided for the public in a way accessible to them is highly desirable. But when we begin to lay on the public shoulders the cost of what they say is not vital but merely desirable, where is this, he asks, going to stop? And he further charges us with being committed to State Socialism to bring about social amelioration by force.

Every thoughtful mind which has read Mr. Herbert Spencer with a desire to do him justice can scarcely ·fail to have received so much mental stimulus that to feel oneself differing from a master, not so much in the general principles laid down as in the application of a particular principle to a particular department of the work of the State, is not an agreeable position.

It is impossible not to feel the force of his statements in *The Coming Slavery*, in *The Man versus The State*, and with much that he says about the State monopoly in letter carrying, telegraphs, and telephones many are in full accord. This, however, does not prevent such from differing from him when he says:—" The changes made, the changes in progress, and the changes urged will carry us not only towards State ownership of land, and dwellings, and means of communication, all to be administered and worked by State agents, but towards State usurpation of all industries, the private forms of which, disadvantaged more and more in competition with the State, which can arrange everything for its own convenience, will more and more die away; just as many voluntary schools have in presence of Board schools. And so will be brought about the desired ideal of the Socialists." But may it not be reasonably asked why should the action of the State be limited to what is necessary to the material existence of a nation, and rigidly excluded from what ministers to its higher life? What divine right has property that no demands should ever be made upon it for the latter purpose? And why may not we use the organised forces of the community to do that which it is desirable in the interests of the whole community should be done? No school of thought condemns the establishment and maintenance of the British Museum and the National Gallery out of national taxation; why, then, should it be called " State Socialism " for a local community to support its own Museum or Public Library out of its local taxes?

As to the questions of State ownership of land and dwellings; the first is already too patent as exemplified in the State land under the control of the Ecclesiastical and Charity Commissioners, but with regard to the second count there is not much danger of the State becoming the landlords of huge industrial dwellings. State usurpation, again, of existing means of communication and all industries, is receiving considerable check at the present time rather than an impetus, as judged by the dismissal of workpeople from the dockyards and clothing factories, and the marked tendency of public opinion to prevent the State from interfering with particular industries.

Does not the line of demarcation lie here ? That the State cannot compete with private enterprise when it comes to the building of ships, making rifles, guns, or clothing. The disadvantages arising chiefly from costly and inefficient management, without an individual pocket to suffer from depreciation in stock and plant, is becoming acutely recognised. Where the State has sought to come into competition with industries of any kind it has egregiously failed in every department. This is unwise and impolitic State Socialism which cannot be too effectually scotched.

But in all educational matters and affairs relating to the public health and safety, if this be State Socialism for the Municipality to take these under its control, it has been an inestimable boon to the people, and a diminution of the first category of State Socialism, and an enlargement of the second class may well be advocated. Mr. Herbert Spencer has not asserted anywhere that the Education Act of 1870 has not worked most beneficially for the good of the country although it may have caused the disappearance of a few voluntary schools. The utter deadness of many of the voluntary schools so closed was universally apparent.

The recognition by the two leading political parties in the State that unwise and impolitic State Socialism is a possibility and a danger against which to be on the alert, is a sufficient safeguard for our national welfare. The mischief lies, not in the tendency for the State to do in the future what the people should do for them-

c

selves, but that up to 1832 the people were not allowed the choice of doing anything for themselves, but had to accept without voice whatever laws were passed contrary to their best interests. The privileged classes, up to that time, placed upon the Statute Book so many laws of a distinct State Socialistic character that the reading of political history up to that time is one of the saddest records of human selfishness that we have in all the range of literature. The fear is, not that we may, as a nation, go in too much for State Socialism, but that we may fail, or, at all events, be so long in undoing the unjust State Socialism of bygone generations.

There is no more marked characteristic of our national life than the self-dependence of the people, which has been the outcome of Municipal Corporations. Where these Corporations are the strongest and most vigorous, there must we look for the highest sense of the duties of citizenship and the most self-reliant populations. It is again in these Municipalities, such as Birmingham, Liverpool, and Leeds, that the most has been done for the education of the people, either in the way of Board Schools, Museums, or Free Libraries. The same Municipalities have the best street lighting and street cleansing arrangements, and the Police Force are under the most perfect control. Surely this fact should dispel the fear that the energies of the poor in the way of self-help may be relaxed, and the rich become apathetic to their higher duties, by the spread of Museums and kindred institutions, supported out of the same funds as are the local Police and the street lighting and cleansing.

It may be asked, what is a Corporation? There are various kinds, but we are here concerned with the Corporation as a body politic elected by the people, and responsible to them. The word is used as equivalent to incorporated joint-stock companies, where the whole of the citizens are shareholders and are banded together for a common purpose, that purpose being the commonweal of the entire local community.

The one vital principle which surrounds Corporations is that they are gifted with perpetual life. They may well have been in some laws designated immortal, although in some cases their privileges have run only for a definite number of years, but during that period, when well organised, they cannot die, notwithstanding all the original members are withdrawn, for they are continued by succession. A Corporation has, in fact, been compared to a stream which maintains its identity throughout all the continuous changing of its parts. Men come and go, Acts of Parliament are passed and become often a dead letter, to swell the number of much similarly cumbrous stuff already on the Statute Book, but the Corporation lives on. In many of our Municipal Corporations all the men who were elected representatives when the charter was first granted have gone over to the majority, but the tide of corporate life is not stayed; yea, rather, time has consolidated and added strength.

This is the main reason why no private enterprise can possibly do for Museums, Free Libraries, and Education what the Corporation can do, and it is on this rests the plea for Municipal Museums, Free Libraries, and Universities, which shall be the property of the citizens, administered by their own elected representatives, and forming an integral part of their local life.

The term ratepayer is a designation altogether too cramped and obnoxious; the general use of the name *citizen* would be an infinitely better and more appropriate one. There can scarcely be a more pressing matter of importance at the present time than that of infusing into the minds of the people a high sense of the duties and privileges of citizenship.

It is a happy and healthy characteristic of public life in this country that in the midst of controversies which go down to the roots of our national existence, our statesmen of all parties are regarded by their country-men as men of light and leading, whose views on subjects of general and non-political interest are entitled at all times to respectful hearing and attention. This same characteristic is evident in Municipal life, and men of opposite politics meet and discuss matters for the general good. Around what institutions could local life better gather than Museums and Free Libraries? There is too much sentimental patriotism, too much lip patter about love of country, and far too little of the real thing itself. National patriotism is an excellent thing, but so also is local patriotism, and no institutions are more likely to cultivate the latter quality than these.

The State has not done everything for the people that it is called upon to do when it has provided a gaol, a work-house, a lunatic asylum, a policeman, and a share in the common hangman. State Socialism has done far too much in providing throughout the length and breadth of the land workhouses, and we have, by our system of Poor Law, done more to pauperise our people than we have ever done to raise them. The Church and the State have gone hand in hand to stifle the spirit of self-dependence, the one in its everlasting stream of blankets and soup, and the other in affording what no other nation in the world has afforded, the right to demand food and shelter in case of destitution.

Why, again, should our pauper life be so heavy a tax on the thrifty and rich? Why is it not made more self-supporting either in farm labour or other ways? Not that its being brought into competition with the labour out of its doors is advocated, but surely in the raising of food, and in the making of their own clothing, there is ample scope for such productive labour.

Oh ye great British nation, with all your wealth and boasted common-sense, how long is this national waste of money and force to go on and the nation idly look on, content with an occasional futile protest? If the Liberty and Property Defence Association were not merely a body for the defence of landlords' privileges, here is a splendid scope for national usefulness instead of remaining content with uttering shrieks over so-called (by them) Socialistic Acts like the Public Libraries Acts and Museums Acts.

The higher life of the citizen has received too little attention, and the lower and baser life seems to have absorbed all the sympathy and care of the authorities. But we have touched the fringe of better days, and soon no Municipality or local governing body will be considered complete unless it has under its administration a Museum and a Free Library, as well as a workhouse, a prison, and the preservers of law and order. It is for the provisions for this higher national life that I plead, and do very earnestly urge upon Municipalities the need of giving the fullest and best attention to this question.

The fact should be emphasised that the Municipality can do for the people in the way of Museums what cannot possibly be done by private enterprise. It may be unhesitatingly asserted that in fullest usefulness, economical management, and best value for money invested the existing Municipal Museums are far and away before the private institutions of this nature.

The utmost rate permitted is at present a penny in the pound on the rateable value. Although in some cases this is barely enough, we must rather look at the enlarging of the sources from which local rates are obtained. This is, of course, a large subject, and one which cannot be adequately discussed here, but it is in this respect that the nation should look to the State to aid indirectly these institutions by the passing of such laws as shall bring about this widening of the, at present, narrow circle upon whom local rates are assessed. That those departments are the land upon which the town stands and other property which does not bear, and never has borne, its quota of local taxation, goes without saying.

In course of years we shall possibly see a new source available for national educational purposes, and particularly for the aiding of Museums, and that is a million or two of the enormous national wealth now under the control of the Ecclesiastical Commissioners, invested, and the interest annually expended in such a purpose as indicated, and this, it may be hoped, by a voluntary act than otherwise. Is such an idea chimerical? Here is untold wealth, the property of the nation, going on accumulating at compound interest, and receiving an unearned increment of untold value, and of which the nation is ignorant. Is there to be no limit to this? Surely it is not the dream of an enthusiast that some of this people's wealth shall at some time or other become available for people's institutions as represented by Museums and Free Libraries.

A further way in which the State may reasonably be looked to for aid, is in giving an impetus to an inquiry of what is being done by the Museums of other countries by means of a special committee of inspection and inquiry. It is lamentable that when we turn to Government publications referring to Museums and Free Libraries, they are of the most trumpery and utterly worthless character. A half-sovereign would buy copies of the entire lot, if the annual Blue-book containing the

Report of the Committee of the Council of Education be excluded.   Notwithstanding the smallness of the amount, the money would be well worth what would be obtained for the outlay.   Let anyone so desirous verify this by ordering through Eyre and Spottiswoode all the Government publications and Blue-books referring to Museums and Free Libraries, and see the character of the literature he will receive.   By way of contrast let him order all the Blue-books and returns referring to torpedoes, guns, rifles, and ships, and see what he will pay for the cart-load of books he would have when his order was executed.

This meagreness contrasts greatly with the books published by the Bureau of Education of the State Department at Washington, and the publications of the German Government of a similar nature.   To the former reference will be made more fully in the chapter dealing with the American Museums.

May it not with good reason be urged upon members of Parliament the necessity of taking the fact stated seriously to heart and urging the House to do more than it has ever yet done in promoting the welfare of these institutions.   But not in the form of a Royal Commission, for these are very costly, and it is an open question whether the sum total of practical good is at all commensurate with the enormous cost of such Commissions. The Reports of the Royal Commission on Scientific Instruction and the Advancement of Science, appointed in 1870, have probably been seen by few.   The last of the Reports appeared in 1875-76, and most of the suggestions put forward by those who were examined are still being digested.   Put briefly, the Commission acknowledged very emphatically that they had received strong evidence that it is the interest and within the proper function of the State to give efficient aid to the advancement of knowledge, even in those cases where such knowledge is not directly required for State purposes, and that some of the most decided expressions of opinion to this effect are those of statesmen, whose views, owing to their official experience and their intimate knowledge of the exigencies of Parliamentary Government, are entitled to great weight on points involving increased grants of public money. Surely in this conclusion, to which the Commission arrived, there is granted the principle of State aid to these institutions.

The expedition of the *Beagle* and the *Challenger* did more for Natural Science than had ever before been done by the Government, and the results have far more than repaid the nation for the comparatively small outlay incurred. It is questionable whether we should ever have had the ripe Charles Darwin to endow a world with a new set of ideas and principles had it not been for his share in the expedition of the *Beagle*.

England has done its share at Arctic Exploration for the present. Can we not do more for Natural Science ? The following points are respectfully urged upon our legislators :—

1. The despatching of a Government boat on an expedition with the following objects in view :—

  (*a.*) The obtaining of specimens of Natural History, such as shells, birds, fossils, mineralogy, &c., from coast and inland places.

  (*b.*) The obtaining of specimens of native products, art, and industries likely to be useful in Commercial Museums.

  (*c.*) To give a report of the Museums of North and South America, our own Colonies, India, Greece, China, Japan, and Egypt.

  (*d.*) To obtain from such Museums antiquities, works of art, duplicates, casts, &c.

(*e.*) The specimens, which could not fail to be numerous, distributed among Municipal (or rate-supported) Museums.

(*f.*) The issuing of full and comprehensive reports of each section of the expedition.

Two of the Royal yachts might be turned to good account by being put to such a use as this.

We are becoming accustomed to the periodical scares over our national defences and the condition of our army and navy. John Bull is beginning to see that it is merely a cry for more money by the daughters of the horse-leech—the two branches of the service. The cost of Government reaches now from £90,000,000 to £100,000,000 a-year, and it is not unreasonable to expect that a much larger slice of this huge sum might be put to educational purposes.

<hr />

CHAPTER III.

THE PLACE OF MUSEUMS IN EDUCATION.

THE most casual observer of educational methods could not fail to notice that the receptive mind of a child or a youth learns from an infinite variety of sources. We all know that we begin at one end of education, but there is no period in life of the most aged where the other end is reached. Frequently, again, that information which does not absolutely form part of the ordinary process of education, but which comes from unexpected quarters, is of as great a service in the development of the mind as any set lessons can possibly be. Whatever becomes suggestive to the mind is of educational value. That Museums have from their very nature the very essence of this suggestiveness is patent. It may be true that of themselves alone they are powerless to educate, but they can be instrumental and useful in aiding the educated to excite a desire for knowledge in the ignorant. The working man or agricultural labourer who spends his holiday in a walk through any well-arranged Museum cannot fail to come away with a deeply-rooted and reverential sense of the extent of knowledge possessed by his fellow-men. It is not the objects themselves that he sees there, and wonders at, that cause this impression, so much as the order and evident science which he cannot but recognise in the manner in which they are grouped and arranged. He learns that there is a meaning and value in every object, however insignificant, and that there is a way of looking at things common and rare, distinct from the regarding them as useless, useful, or merely curious. These three last terms would be found to be the very common classification of all objects in a Museum by the uninformed and uninitiated.

After a holiday spent in a Museum the working man goes home and cons over what he has seen at his leisure, and very probably on the next summer holiday, or a Sunday afternoon's walk with his wife and little ones, he discovers that he has acquired a new interest in the common things he sees around him. He begins to discover that the stones, the flowers, the creatures of all kinds that throng around him are not, after all, so very commonplace as he had previously thought them. He looks at them with a pleasure not before experienced, and talks of them to his children with sundry references to things like them which he saw in the Museum. He has gained a new sense, a craving for natural knowledge, and such a craving may, possibly, in course of time, quench another and lower craving which may at one time have held him in bondage—that for intoxicants or vicious excitement of one description or another.

The craving for intoxicants or excitement is often as much a result as a cause. The toilers have few things to occupy their mind, and frequently in their home surroundings much cheerlessness and discomfort. Life is for very many a hard daily grind for mere existence, with little or no relief from the daily round of the struggle to make ends meet. These, and other conditions under which so many live, cannot fail to produce tastes and likings which are not qualified to tend in the uplifting of the mind and the desires by which their life is governed.

It is only those who come closely in contact with the more intelligent of the working classes, who know the nobility of character and the earnest reaching out towards higher things to be found among them, who can be familiar with the intense longing to have within their reach institutions such as Museums, Art Galleries, and Free Libraries, to which they can have easy access. That such as these use the institutions which already exist is most amply and conclusively proved by the ocular demonstration of those who have visited the Museums in any of the large towns of the country.

The nation should never forget that some of its greatest benefactors have belonged to this class of intelligent working men. James Watt, the engineer, Hugh Miller, the stonemason geologist, Stephenson, the collier-railway projector, Arkwright, the weaver-inventor, and scores of others who could be named. Where, indeed, should we have stood as a nation had it not been for the sturdy common-sense of the intelligent and thrifty working classes ?

Until very recently the great defect of our system of education has been the neglect of educating the observing powers—a very distinct matter, be it noted, from scientific or industrial instruction. The confounding of the two is evident in many books which have from time to time been published. There are not a few who seem to imagine that the elements that should constitute a sound and manly education are antagonistic; that the cultivation of taste through purely literary studies and of reasoning through logic and mathematics, one or both, is opposed to the training in the equally important matter of observation through these sciences that are descriptive and experimental. There is considerable inconsistency in any such idea, and educational leaders are now universally recognising the need there is for not giving too much attention to one class of mental training to the exclusion of the rest. Equal development and strengthening of all are necessary for the constitution of a well ordered mind.

A consensus of opinion is now apparent that this method is erroneous, and the Universities are taking the lead by emphasising to a less degree the merits of a purely classical education. The conductors of private schools, again, are beginning to see the great need which exists for a practical acquaintance with the leading Continental languages, and the Board school curriculum is rapidly becoming to mean a year or two devoted to technical instruction and manual training. It is almost impossible to satisfactorily and effectually to conduct the latter without the aid of Museums, and these institutions are destined to occupy a most important place in this respect. Specimens of raw materials with labels clearly defining their properties and uses, and the relation that one kind of raw material bears to another kind, are now, in many instances, looked upon as indispensable scholastic aids.

The Manchester Exhibition of last year was particularly useful in this respect, for there were many sections in which the various stages of the raw material up to the perfected article were shown, and it may safely be stated that no Exhibition of modern times possessed in this way a wider and more real educational value than the very successful one held in Manchester in 1887. The silk, chemical, pottery, and other sections were especially complete in this respect. The number of models of an almost infinite variety in these departments had a value attaching to them as a means of instruction, which could not fail to be useful to the many thousands of the youth of both sexes who visited the buildings at Old Trafford.

Vast collections of objects, whether in Museums or Exhibitions for educational purposes, do not always accomplish the object in view. Doubtless the vastness of the collections in some of our own Exhibitions in London, and those which have been held in other cities, has been very impressive, but it may be gravely questioned whether any mind has carried away many useful impressions from the infinite multitude upon which he has had an opportunity of looking. The general mental state very frequently produced by such a numerous display is that of distraction. There is such a condition of mind as picture drunkenness or Museum drunkenness, and this should be carefully guarded against. There should be in Museums and Art Galleries a more extensive use of folding screens, so that anyone so disposed could shut themselves off from the crowd while they study a case or a picture minutely. A few striking objects well and carefully studied are infinitely better and of greater educational worth than a number of things at which there is only a casual glance.

Modelling, whether in cardboard, wood, or clay, is an invaluable means of cultivating and developing the manipulative skill of youths. All know how readily a boy will take to the construction of a boat, or a girl to dress a doll, and in this lies the indication that most young people will take as readily to modelling as the boys do to cricket and the girls to their skipping ropes.

Charles Kingsley, addressing working men, with reference to their requirements, says : "We must acquire something of that industrious habit of mind which the study of Natural Science gives. The art of seeing, the art of knowing what you see, the art of comparing, of perceiving true likenesses and true differences, and so of classifying and arranging what you see, the art of connecting facts together in your own mind in chains of cause and effect, and that accurately, patiently, calmly, without prejudice, vanity, or temper."

The late Ralph Waldo Emerson, writing on the same subject, says: "Manual labour is the study of the external world." This kind of manual labour should be taught in schools. Children's habit of collecting and arranging objects of interest should be encouraged. The study of a single branch of natural science, such as constructive botany, may be made the means of cultivating habits of neatness, order, and skill. The analysis of plant forms would illustrate the application of geometry to ornamental purposes, and open up wide fields for the development of decorative taste and manipulative skill. But cramped by the restrictive rules of our result system, these sources of useful culture are neglected ; and, therefore, our children are turned out of the educational mill imperfectly prepared for the further processes necessary to qualify them for taking their part in the struggle for existence.

All this proves the necessity for Museums having the closest possible connection with elementary as well as advanced education. The uses of constructive botany, as referred to in the short quotation from Emerson, are especially helpful as a suggestive study to the mind. For this branch of education Museums are the best text-books which can be provided, but in order that specimens in these branches of natural science be properly and usefully studied they require to be explained by competent teachers. It is in this respect that practical and efficient Curators can be of the greatest service in giving short and informal explanations of some of the specimens in their Museums.

As far back as 1853, there was delivered at the Museum of Economical Geology, in London, a lecture by the late Professor Edward Forbes, on the Educational Uses of Museums. In one part of this lecture he spoke as follows : " In their educational aspect, considered apart from their educational applications, the value of Museums must in a great measure depend on the perfection of their arrangement, and the leading ideas regulating the classification of their contents. The educated youth ought, in a well-arranged Museum, to be able to instruct himself in the studies of which its contents are illustrations, with facility and advantage. On the officers in charge of the institution there consequently falls a heavy responsibility. It is not sufficient that they should be well versed in the department of science, antiquities, or art committed to their charge. They may be prodigies of learning, and yet utterly unfitted for their posts. They must be men mindful of the main end and purpose in view, and of the best way of communicating knowledge according to its kind, not merely to those who are already men of science, historians, or connoisseurs, but equally to those who, as yet ignorant, desire to learn, or in whom it is

desirable that a thirst for learning should be incited."
Among the most useful Museums are those which
are made accessory to professional instruction, and
there are many such in the country, but almost all
confined to purposes of professional education, and
not adapted, or open to the general public. The
Museums of our Universities and Colleges are, for the
most part, utilised in this way, but the advantages derived
from them are confined to a limited class of persons.

This educating the children in the schools in the
elements of natural science is most essential, especially
in country districts. When a person reaches mature age
without knowing anything about Natural History objects,
they find it is then too much trouble to investigate
these subjects. But by getting at them when young, by
simple and forcible illustrations, they are bound to
carry it forward with them to a certain extent, and if
there should come a time when they are in a position
to give time to study, the first they will take up
and pursue with patience will probably be some
subject of this nature, merely for the pleasure of the
study. On the other hand, if they have no inclination
to work, they will not forget the pleasant hours they
spent when they sat listening to some explanation of
an object so familiar, which will create a tendency to
put their hands to the bottom of their pockets and act
feelingly. If children could be taught to see God
in Nature and the wonders which He controls,
without cramming the brain with so much theory,
by giving them a run into the country along with
some one to explain, it would conduce a great deal
more to their general health and happiness. Country
Museums want illustrating and simplifying as much as
possible. Call a spade a spade, *i.e.*, give the local name
as well as the scientific one. This education would be
another great saving to the nation if it were universal.

Half the things that are dug up now are only saved by the merest chance, because the men digging do not care what they are striking their pick through. This would be altered altogether if they had been taught in early youth to take notice of the value and interest there is attaching, often, to things dug up from the earth.

Thirty-five years ago Professor Forbes said : " I cannot help hoping that the time will come when every British town even of moderate size will be able to boast of possessing public institutions for the education and instruction of its adults as well as its youthful and childish population ; when it shall have a well-organised Museum wherein collections of natural bodies shall be displayed, not with regard to show or curiosity, but according to their illustration of the analogies and affinities of organised and unorganised objects, so that the visitor may at a glance learn something of the laws of nature ; wherein the products of the surrounding district, animate and inanimate, shall be scientifically marshalled, and their industrial applications carefully and suggestively illustrated ; wherein the memorials of the neighbouring province, and the races that have peopled it, shall be reverently assembled, and learnedly yet popularly explained ; when each town shall have a library, the property of the public, and freely opened to the well-conducted reader of every class ; when its public walks and parks (too many as yet existing only in prospect) shall be made instructors in botany and agriculture ; when it shall have a gallery of its own, possibly not boasting of the most famous pictures or statues, but nevertheless showing good examples of sound art : examples of the history and purpose of design, and, above all, the best specimens to be procured of works of genius by its own natives who have deservedly risen to fame. When that good time comes true-hearted citizens will decorate their streets and

D

squares with statues and memorials of the wise and worthy men and women who have adorned their province—not merely of kings, statesmen, or warriors, but of philosophers, poets, men of science, philanthropists, and great workmen."

How far are we from yet realising this ideal, and how slowly we seem to progress in so desirable a direction! Still there are many signs that the conscience of the nation is at last awakened, and if we see to it that all the discussions at present filling the air do not end simply in talk, but that practical good shall be the outcome, then our progress during the coming twenty-five years will not be so discouraging. In no better way can this ideal be realised than by an acute recognition of the place Museums should occupy in our national system of education.

CHAPTER IV.

EARLY ENGLISH MUSEUMS.

T is somewhat strange that we have no reliable record of any Museums existing in England prior to 1600. It would be rather gratifying to have some proof that during the reign of that enlightened King Alfred, there was in the ninth century, some attempt made to get together in one of his many residences, to which we can scarcely apply the designation of palace, some of the curiosities picked up by the foreign travellers who always found in him a friend, and in his court a

home. It is not improbable, indeed, that these homes
were full of specimens of foreign wares, and the miscellaneous articles which thoughtful men, with an eye to
what would please the Saxon King, would be sure to
bring, but the only relic of a personal character is King
Alfred's Jewel, now in the Ashmolean Museum. Alfred's
association with the foundation of schools in Oxford
which developed into colleges seems to be accepted by
that careful and accurate historian Professor Freeman.

THE ASHMOLEAN MUSEUM.

The first who formed a cabinet of natural and
artificial curiosities in England was Sir John Trades-
cant, in the reign of Charles I. He possessed large
gardens in Lambeth, and travelled over a considerable
portion of the globe with the distinct view of improving himself in natural science, and procuring specimens
of whatever appeared rare and curious. The son,
having imbibed the spirit of his father, followed his
example ; and by their joint exertions a very valuable
collection was formed, which afterwards became the
property of Elias Ashmole, and was comprised in
his noble donation to the University of Oxford.
The Museum thus formed at Oxford, called the
Ashmolean Museum, was erected at the expense of the University. It was begun in 1679 and
finished in 1683, at which time the valuable collection
of curiosities presented to the University by Ashmole
were there reposited, and afterwards put in order
by Dr. Plott, who was constituted first keeper of
the Museum. Considerable accessions have since
been made; as of hieroglyphics and other Egyptian
antiquities, by Dr. Huntingdon ; of an entire mummy,
by Mr. Goodyear; of a cabinet of natural curiosities, by Dr. Lister ; also of Roman antiquities, such
as altars, medals, lamps, &c.

The Ashmolean Museum has of late undergone considerable change. The Arundel Marbles have been removed to the British Museum, the specimens of Natural History to the New Museum, the printed books and manuscripts which belonged to Ashmole to the Bodleian Library, and the portraits, which formerly hung on the walls, to the University Galleries. The ethnological collection brought home by Captain Cook, containing many native implements of warfare and agriculture, has also been removed to the New Museum. This has consequently left the Ashmolean somewhat naked, but there are very many objects of interest left, and it is especially rich in several priceless antiquities. What is wanted is a little handy guide to the Museum. Now that it has probably been denuded of those treasures for the enriching of other Museums, the Ashmolean will perhaps be left alone for a fairly long season of usefulness.

The collections of Roman, Etruscan, Greek, and Egyptian antiquities are especially rich in gems, and Mr. C. D. E. Fortnum, F.S.A., of Stanmore Hill, Middlesex, sent in 1885, on loan, a splendid collection of antique bronzes, bronze implements, Greek and Etruscan figures in bronze, and other antiquities. These have been admirably classified and arranged in new cases, and have excited considerable interest. A descriptive catalogue of them would be helpful. The relics of the stone age are numerous, as also the specimens of Egyptian and Etruscan pottery. These specimens are used frequently for teaching purposes.

The six special antiquities to which the general visitor will devote his attention are Cromwell's watch, Queen Elizabeth's watch, Henry VIII.'s sword, given to him by the then ruling Pope as Defender of the Faith, the steel band which confined Cranmer to the stake in 1556, when he suffered with Latimer in the street close

THE ASHMOLEAN MUSEUM.

by; Guy Fawkes' lantern, rescued from the cellars of the Bodleian Library, where, for generations, it had been doing no good. One would like to know if there are any other valuables hid down in those cellars in a

similar way. The gem of all, however, is King Alfred's Jewel. This is a beautiful specimen of gold enamelled work, and an inscription affords unmistakable proof of the fact that Alfred gave every encouragement to artificers in gold and silver. The inscription is in old Saxon, " Aelfred mee heht gevvycan," which, reduced to modern English, means, Alfred ordered me to be made or worked. It was found in 1693, in the immediate neighbourhood of his retreat, in the Isle of Athelney, at the junction of the Rivers Parrot and Thone, in Somersetshire. The jewel was bequeathed to the Museum by Colonel Nathaniel

KING ALFRED'S JEWEL.

Palmer, of Fairfield, and was presented by his son in 1718.

The Ashmolean Museum building is still in a capital state of preservation. A charge of threepence is made to each visitor, unless accompanied by a student in canonicals, when he will then be admitted free. The engraving is from a drawing in the possession of Mr. Dunbar.

THE LEVERIAN MUSEUM.

About 1775 Sir Ashton Lever opened his magnificent Museum, which had cost him about £30,000 in collecting, to the public, in Leicester Square. This Museum was for a considerable time one of the most fashionable places of resort in London; and when disposed of by lottery, became the property of Mr. Parkinson, who erected a building for it on the Surrey side of the River Thames, near Blackfriars Bridge. The situation, however, was injudiciously chosen, being at too great a distance from the homes of that class of people most likely to support such an institution. As a consequence, the proprietor, not meeting with the encouragement he anticipated, was induced to dispose of the whole by auction, in several thousand lots, in the spring of 1806. Judging from a quaint old print of the interior of the Museum, it must have been a singularly interesting collection of objects of Natural History and antiquities.

It is worthy of note that in *Hone's Every-day Book* the statement is made that the whole collection was offered to the authorities of the British Museum and refused. In 1784 Sir Ashton Lever presented a petition to the House of Commons, praying to be allowed to dispose of his Museum by a lottery, as Alderman Boydell had done with his Gallery. On this occasion it was stated that it had been brought to London in the year 1775, and that it had occupied twelve years in forming, and contained upwards of 26,000 articles. It was further stated that the money taken for admission amounted, from February, 1775, to February, 1784, to about £13,000, out of which had to be paid £660 for house rent and taxes. Sir Ashton proposed that the entire Museum should go together, and that there should be 40,000 tickets at a guinea each. Some old writers have stated that only about 8,000 tickets were sold, and that although the proprietor held 28,000, he lost his Museum, which was won by a Mr. Parkinson, who held only two. There is good proof that this was not the case, for the Catalogue of the Leverian Museum filled an octavo volume of 410 pages, and the sale by auction took place in King Street, Covent Garden. In all there were 7,879 lots, and the sale occupied sixty-five days. Sir William Hamilton, an old English traveller, in speaking of this collection, said that he had seen the cabinets of curiosities at Moscow and St. Petersburg, and also those at Paris and Dresden, which were esteemed very curious and valuable, but none of them were in any way to be compared to the Leverian Museum.

THE PORTLAND MUSEUM.

The Museum of the Duchess of Portland was collected at an incredible expense to herself, and increased by some valuable presents from her friends, to which were added various curiosities inherited from her family. It comprised everything rich and rare in the vegetable, animal, and fossil kingdoms. The articles classed under the head of Conchology were so numerous and rare that even Linnæus had not seen a great number of them. Most unfortunately this splendid collection was scattered at her Grace's decease, whose acting executrix ordered it to be sold. It was accordingly submitted to public auction on April 24th, 1786, at her house in Priory Gardens, and the sale occupied thirty-seven days.

BULLOCK'S MUSEUM.

On the site of what is now the Egyptian Hall, in Piccadilly, there stood, in 1811, a building known as Bullock's Museum, containing one of the most complete collections of natural subjects and works of art at that time existing. The building was erected by William Bullock, as an establishment for the advancement of the science of Natural History. In magnitude and expense it was claimed to be unparalleled as the work of an individual. The specimens it contained were arranged according to the Linnæan system ; and consisted of upwards of 15,000 species of quadrupeds, birds, reptiles, fishes, insects, shells, corals, &c. These had been collected at an expense exceeding, it was said, £30,000.

Bullock's reason for parting with it was that he desired to retire to Mexico to form a Museum in that country for the instruction of its native population. The premises were purchased in order to let such portions as might be required for purposes of exhibition or as rooms for the display and sale of works in the fine arts. Here were exhibited the cast from Michael Angelo's Moses of the Vatican Galleries and other works.

The Museum was divided into two parts. The large room, with galleries round it, contained the birds, beasts, fishes, amphibia, insects, &c., besides many works of art, particularly various specimens of ancient and modern armour, and curiosities from America, Africa, and Asia. This was called the London Museum —a rather unappropriate name. This could be viewed separately, the price of admission being one shilling, and the number of visitors was considerable. The other part contained the quadrupeds, and according to the taste at that time for Greek names, was called the Pantherion. The arrangement of this place was on a novel plan, intended to display the whole of the known quadrupeds in such a manner as would convey a more perfect idea of their haunts and mode of life than had hitherto been done, keeping them at the same time in their classical arrangement, and preserving them from the injury of dust and air. It occupied a spacious apartment, nearly forty feet high, erected for the purpose. The arrangement of the objects was rather unique. The visitor was introduced through a basaltic cavern, similar in style to the Giant's Causeway or Fingal's Cave, into an Indian hut, situated in a tropical forest, in which were displayed most of the quadrupeds described by naturalists. In addition to these there were correct models from nature, or from the best authorities, of the trees and other vegetable productions of the torrid climes. The whole was assisted by an appropriate panoramic effect of distance, which made the illusion produced so strong that the surprised visitor found himself suddenly transported from a crowded metropolis to the depth of an Indian forest, every part of which was occupied by its various savage inhabitants. A similar plan might now with advantage be adopted. There are other old collections which might be named, but it is scarcely necessary to do so.

CHAPTER V.

RATE SUPPORTED MUSEUMS AND ART GALLERIES.

OR vigour and usefulness there are no Museums throughout the entire country which compare at all favourably with those which are the property of the citizens, and under the control of their duly elected representatives. This is a matter of vital importance to the whole subject. Many of the general Museums scattered about the country will continue to be restricted in their work and in perpetual need of financial help, until they form one in a link of educational institutions administered for the benefit of the district. In the statistics to be found at the end of the book these have been tabulated separately from the other Museums. Under this chapter it has been impossible to mention all, but those have been selected which are fairly characteristic of the rest. Friends of this movement, and those who do not at present look upon it favourably, may be urged to take the earliest opportunity of visiting, if they have not already done so, some of the institutions under this heading. On behalf of the Curators a courteous reception can be promised, and a willingness to give them all the information which the visitors may desire to know. Ocular demonstration has won many friends to this movement, and will win many more as it progresses. When opponents say that Museums and Art Galleries are simply places for lounging, and used chiefly by idlers, they make a statement so exaggerated and absurd that it might be passed by in silence.

In the large towns the evening is of course the best time for a visit, or on a Saturday afternoon. There will then be ample proof of the assertion that these institutions are used by all classes, from the retired professional man to the humble working man who has come to forget for a time his tools and the noise of the factory, in the beauty and instruction he sees in the objects around him, in the pictures of the Art Gallery or the objects in the Museum.

BIRMINGHAM.

The capital of the Midlands has the proud boast that it possesses the finest Art Gallery out of London, and the claim is well sustained by the actual state of things. Birmingham, in its Free Libraries, Art Gallery, Science Classes, and kindred work, sets an example to the rest of the country, and I am not acquainted with any American or Continental town where the institutions of a similar character are under better administration and doing a work of more far-reaching usefulness than is the case at Birmingham. It is very gratifying to know that the palm, in every respect in which these institutions can be viewed, comes to England, and is divided equally between Birmingham, Leeds, Liverpool, and Manchester. Each institution in the places named has some distinctive feature and merit, which causes it to stand out conspicuously from the rest.

The new Birmingham Art Gallery is less than three years old. In *Free Public Libraries* some general features of the building were named, so that it will not be necessary to repeat them here. It was intended from the first by the promoters of the movement that there should be a Gallery and Museum in connection with the Library, but from several causes it was found impracticable that the two should be started together. The actual beginning of the Art Gallery was in 1864, when a well-known local artist, Mr. Edward Coleman, presented a picture, but it was not until 1867 that pictures and other objects were got together in a room of the Free Library building, and there they remained until the opening of the new home, a capital view of which is given in the engraving.

The collection of Industrial Art objects comprises—

(*a*) Jewellery, gold and silversmith's work; enamels—Limoges and Oriental—ivory carvings; Oriental porcelain, bronzes and lacquer; European porcelain and earthenware; glass, decorative ironwork, steel-work; carvings in wood, marble, and stone; textile fabrics; electrotypes.

(*b*) A very fine and complete collection of specimens of Italian art, principally of the Renaissance period, comprising sculpture, woodwork, decorative ironwork, bronzes, majolica, metal work, glass, &c.

(*c*) A very valuable and unique collection of arms and armour, consisting of over 1,000 speci-

THE BIRMINGHAM ART GALLERY.

mens of all ages and countries, illustrating the origin and development of fire-arms, together with cross-bows, swords, rapiers, and other weapons of defence and attack.

(*d*) A large representative collection of Wedgwood and Wedgwood ware.

(*e*) The collection of pictures, containing typical examples of Sir Frederick Leighton, Bart., P.R.A., Frank Holl, R.A., Henry Moore, A.R.A., Albert Moore, C. Napier Henry, R.I., W. B. Richmond, A.R.A., John Brett, A.R.A., J. S. Noble, H. Stacy Marks, R.A., W. Holman Hunt, A. W. Hunt, Walter Langley, R.I., T. Phillips, R.A., W. Collins, R.A., George Morland, &c., and a very valuable and complete collection of works in oil by David Cox.

There are in the Museum six cases, besides numerous frames, which are kept constantly filled with objects on loan from South Kensington, and which objects are exchanged for others every twelve months. Loans are also obtained from private collectors.

The collections of metal work, glass, lacquer, &c., are formed with special reference to the industries of the town and district.

The general arrangement of the rooms will be seen from the sectional drawing here given.

The total value of the gifts up to the present cannot be less than £45,000 to £50,000, so that the Birmingham manufacturers know how to give money as well as how to make it. The list of gifts, in fact, is sufficiently comprehensive and valuable to make the mouth water of every Curator in the country. Up to the end of 1886 the list of such gifts extends to no less than eight closely printed pages, and the list of gifts for 1887 fills several pages. Would that every Museum

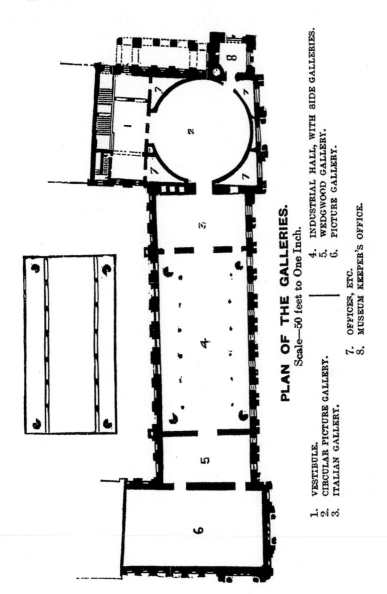

PLAN OF THE GALLERIES.

Scale—50 feet to One Inch.

1. VESTIBULE.
2. CIRCULAR PICTURE GALLERY.
3. ITALIAN GALLERY.
4. INDUSTRIAL HALL, WITH SIDE GALLERIES.
5. WEDGWOOD GALLERY.
6. PICTURE GALLERY.
7. OFFICES, ETC.
8. MUSEUM KEEPER'S OFFICE.

and Art Gallery in the country had as many friends ?
The Tangye collection alone would have richly
endowed any Museum. This consists of Wedgwood
medallions, cameos, portraits of "Illustrious Moderns,"
busts, figures, vases, lamps and candelabra of various
colours, in jasper and basalt; also cabinet and déjeûner
services, cups and saucers, specimens of "Queen's
ware," &c. In all 184 pieces, and the gross value
cannot be less than £10,000.

Next perhaps in value to this comes the John Feeney
collection, consisting of Japanese cloisonné enamels on
copper and porcelain, sixty-eight pieces; Chinese
bronzes, seventy-three pieces; Japanese porcelain,
ninety-eight pieces; Chinese and Japanese lacquer, 100
pieces; Japanese armour—four helmets, breast-plate,
&c., and a small collection of swords; Chinese and
Indian silver, 208 pieces. A later collection comprises
Persian, Turkish, and Damascus metal and woodwork,
twenty pieces; Indian metal-work, sixty-two pieces;
Indian gold and silversmith's work and jewellery,
twenty-three pieces. The Nettlefold bequest of pictures,
again, is one of the most valuable series of pictures
which has ever been presented to any public institution. The bequest consisted of some thirty-four
pictures by David Cox, and connoisseurs know the value
attaching to the pictures of this Birmingham artist,
born there in 1793. It is most appropriate that his
native town should possess so excellent a collection of
his works.

The question may naturally be asked, Are these
objects of art appreciated, and is the work extending? The answer is, Yes, decidedly so. This
is proved by the increased interest which many of the
Birmingham artisans take in the collections, requests
for permission to study and draw in the Museum, the
constant inquiries made as to collections, objects, &c.,

and finally the various objects which persons offer to present to the Gallery, many possibly useless and incongruous when considering the other collections. But still the fact of their being offered evinces a desire to help the Gallery, and so enable others to see those objects which would otherwise be hidden away, and seen only by themselves and their immediate friends. Several objects so presented—the result of the lectures—were of artistic merit and most acceptable, notably some old English enamels, embroidery, needlework, glass, arms, &c.

Up to the present no lectures have been organised by the Committee, but the Director of the Museum, Mr. Whitworth Wallis, F.R.G.S., has prepared a popular lecture on " The Art Gallery and how to see it," which he has frequently delivered in the Town Hall and various parts of the town and immediate district with great success, and which has created an appreciably greater interest in the Museum amongst the artisan classes. The lectures in the two seasons have been attended by between ten and eleven thousand people.

During last year the Museum and Art Gallery was visited by 998,321 persons, and the total visitors to the Art Gallery since the opening on December 1st, 1885, to March 31st, 1888, reached no less than 2,262,709. This can be accurately told, as there are registering turnstiles with which there can be no tampering. The hours of opening are :—Monday, Tuesday, Thursday, and Saturday, throughout the year, ten till nine ; Wednesday and Friday, Winter Season (October 1st to March 15th), ten till four; Summer Season (March 16th to September 30th), ten till six ; Sunday, throughout the year, two till five. And on all occasions admission is free. The aim all through of the Committee, and especially of the Art Director, is that the Museum shall be a model Museum of Industrial and Decorative Art,

E

which shall teach the visitors that art is something more than sculptures and pictures.

Since the opening of the Gallery 33,000 catalogues have been sold, and at the present time a cheap guide to the collections is in course of preparation. The better lighting of the Galleries is engaging the attention of the Museum and School of Art Committee, who have the control of the building, and with this object in view some negotiations have been going on with the Corporation Gas Department. A more enthusiastic and capable public servant than Mr. Wallis could not have been appointed. His past record in London was the best possible training he could have had for the work at Birmingham. He is clear-headed and practical, with a deep interest in the Museum movement. The past three years are full of satisfactory work, and the future prospects are pregnant with hopefulness. Mr. Wallis has a firm conviction that one main thing which will go far towards extending the utility of a Museum is to have every object labelled, not only with a label descriptive of the object, but also longer descriptive labels explaining such terms as "majolica," "Renaissance," "cloisonné enamel," or whatever it may be, and, if possible, the process of production should be added. These descriptions are the greatest incentives to visitors to further pursue the subject. The explanatory notes should be embodied in the catalogues issued, which should be as cheap as possible, and all pictures, to which a short descriptive note would be of service, should have the same inserted in the catalogue.

Then, again, he would urge that printed lists of the best books, bearing upon the various industries and objects in the Museum, especially those procurable in the Free Library, should be hung in the Galleries amid the collections, so that the artisan may refer to them and see at once the best books, elementary and advanced, he can consult with advantage. Mr. Wallis referred to this matter fully in a paper read before the Conference of Librarians in the autumn of last year, on "The Connection between Free Libraries, Art Galleries, and Museums." In speaking of the technical value of Museums, he said that the aims "of the Museum and Art Gallery, and its sister institution, the Free Library, were identical, for they had in view the one end, the culture of the people. They appealed to the same mental faculties, with which all men were endowed in a greater or less degree, and to a very great extent the Museum was dependent upon the Free Library. It looked to the Free Library to minister to the Museum visitors that knowledge and information which the most comprehensive catalogues and labels in the world would fail to supply. In a place like Birmingham that was particularly the case, for the books on art and art workmanship were as a rule beyond the reach of the ordinary workman, and his appetite having been whetted by a slight description of some object or process in the Museum, he must of necessity have recourse to the Library to acquire further knowledge. That had been brought home to him several times since he had been in Birmingham by the numerous inquiries made by visitors, mostly of the artisan and poorer class, as to the best books to be read on such and such a subject. With that end in view labels or lists had been prepared which hung in the various Galleries, containing the titles of the best works, elementary ones and others more advanced, which might be consulted with advantage. Such terms as majolica, hispano-moresque, Gothic, Renaissance, cloisonné enamel, and countless others were caviare to the multitude of visitors. It was therefore necessary that, apart from short descriptive labels attached to the objects—and above all things every object should be

E 2

so labelled—longer descriptions of the origin of the ware, or whatever it might be, and, if possible, various processes should be added. Such descriptions were the greatest possible incentives to visitors to further pursue the subject, and if their inclinations tended that way, they did so by taking themselves to the Free Library."

In the early part of his paper he said " that the intimate connection of Free Libraries and Museums in their aims and the uses they performed in the education and culture of the people must be apparent to all who took the trouble to consider their functions from the standpoint of a general principle in relation to the elevation of the masses. In the case of the Free Library, the mind, in its wider functions, was appealed to, and in the case of the Museum the eye was the organ through which the perception of beauty and of proportion and, one might almost say, the fitness of things were conveyed to the mind. The unity of the purpose of the two appeared to be essential to the perfection of each, and one might almost be tempted to say that the one without the other was only half complete. The Free Library aimed more particularly at the education of the mind, whereas it was to the eye that the Museum more forcibly appealed, and to the education of the eye, the cultivation of the powers of observation, it was of all things necessary that earnest attention be paid, more especially in the great manufacturing centres, where it was desirable that the eyes of designers and workmen, and, indeed, of the masters themselves, should be refreshed by the study and contemplation of the best and finest specimens of the arts and industries, which should be studied as guiding posts for the future, as they formed the landmarks of the past."

Aston Hall, a fine old Elizabethan building, situated about two and a-half miles from the centre of Bir-

mingham, now the property of the Corporation of
Birmingham, is also under the control of the Museum
and School of Art Committee. Some of the rooms are
arranged as Galleries, and contain collections of pottery
and porcelain, arms, glass, &c., whilst the Long Gallery,
one of the finest in the kingdom, is arranged as a ban-
queting hall, with old family portraits, furniture, &c.
The hall is also used for exhibiting collections not
required in the Art Gallery during special exhibitions
there. The hall is under the direction of Mr. Whitworth
Wallis, on behalf of the Museum Committee, and the
resident Curator is Mr. A. J. Rodway.

BOOTLE-CUM-LINACRE.

The Free Library and Museum at Bootle, near
Liverpool, would be a credit to any town in the
United Kingdom, and the citizens may well be proud
of so noble an institution. The engraving of the
building is reproduced from a photograph which was
specially taken for this book by Dr. Bark, the Chairman
of the Committee. This gentleman takes a warm and
active interest in the work of the Museum and
Library. The exterior is particularly imposing, as will
be seen, and the interior arrangements are so admirable that there need be no hesitation in recommending
the building as a model of its kind. An admirable light
is obtained in all the rooms, and every detail appears
to have been carefully seen to by the architect, with the
help of the Committee.

The exterior designs are made to correspond with
the Town Hall, and the two buildings, as they at
present stand, have a fine artistic effect. The front is
composed of Yorkshire parpoint with cevin dressings,
four long panels being reserved for special carving.
There is a pediment to the tower over the doorway
consisting of two carved figures, representing Art and

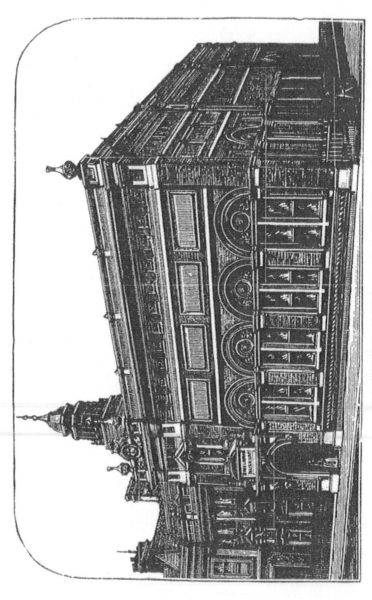

THE BOOTLE MUSEUM AND FREE LIBRARY.

Science reclining on a shield, and underneath are carved the borough arms. On the west front is a Reading Room forty-four feet long by twenty-six feet wide, and adjoining on the south side is a Lending Library thirty-three feet long by thirty-three feet wide. The Geological Museum is sixty-four feet six inches long by twenty-six feet wide. On the left-hand side are the Librarian's Room and a strong-room. Sectional drawings are shown

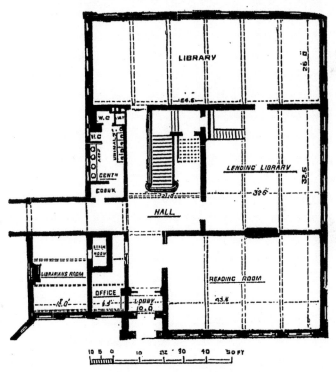

GROUND FLOOR OF THE BOOTLE MUSEUM.

of the ground and first floors, engraved from tracings, supplied by Mr. W. N. Blair, the Borough Surveyor. The Town Hall corridor is continued to the

Library entrance hall, so that when required the buildings may be used *en suite,* a capital feature deserving of being kept in mind when other buildings are being designed. The principal stairs, of stone, are immediately opposite the entrance, and lead

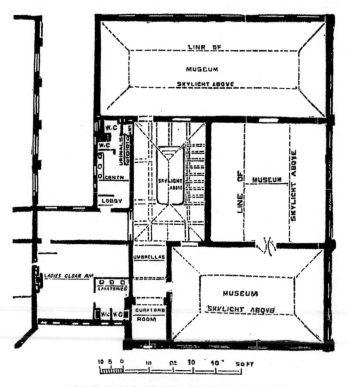

FIRST FLOOR OF THE BOOTLE MUSEUM.

to a very spacious landing on the first floor, the whole of the floor area, lighted by skylights, being arranged for Museum purposes. A Curator's Room is provided near the staircase. The rooms above correspond with those below. Improvements of the Town Hall were carried out during the erection of the Library buildings, the Council Chamber being lengthened nearly twenty feet on the ground floor, and a large room formed above on the first floor fifty-four feet long by twenty-six feet wide, available for lectures. Bookbinding rooms, store-rooms, and laboratories for attendants are most conveniently arranged on the mezzoline floor. The basement is approached by a cartway of easy gradient, so that all heavy cases can be unpacked and carried by the lift. The basement is twelve feet high, and well lighted by external open areas, the space left being available for stores, and a portion is reserved for a heating chamber, coals, &c. This basement might easily be formed into an excellent aquarium, and this is contemplated. The Library Committee have devoted much time in order to have the building erected with all possible arrangements for the convenience and comfort of the visitors. The total cost of the work is £8,450. The architect is Mr. John Johnson, of Queen Victoria Street, London, who designed the Town Hall.

Here is a record of work which shows thoroughly how Lancashire people know how to do these things. Some of the Metropolitan parishes, which have adopted the Acts during very recent years, might, with advantage to themselves and their constituents, take a copy from this provincial town in the despatch with which it placed those Acts in operation. The annals of the Library and Museum up to date are as follows :—

Mar. 19, 1884.	The Public Libraries' Act is adopted.
July 11, 1884.	Dr. Tudor notifies the gift of his Library of about 1,500 volumes.
Nov. 4, 1885.	The Mayor (Ald. J. Leslie, J.P.) lays the foundation-stone of the building.
Dec. 7, 1886.	The Trustees of the Danson Bequest apportion £400 to the Free Public Library and Museum.

Jan. 12, 1887.	Lord Derby promises £250 towards the purchase of the Royal Institution Collection.
Feb. 9, 1887.	The Council resolves to acquire the Collection of Minerals, Fossils, Insects, Shells, and Birds from the Liverpool Royal Institution.
Feb. 9, 1887.	The first Free Library and Museum Committee appointed.
June 15, 1887.	The first Librarian and Curator enters upon his duties.
June 22, 1887.	The Mayor (Ald. W. Jones) formally opens the Reading Room, Museum, and Art Exhibition.
June 22—Aug. 2, 1887.	First Loan Exhibition of Pictures.
Oct. 15—Dec. 24, 1887.	Second (Artists') Loan Exhibition of Pictures.
Oct. 31, 1887.	Miss Gregson's offer of the "Gregson Collection" of Shells, Fossils, Minerals, Economic Products, &c., accepted for the Museum.
Nov. 7, 1887.	Books first issued for Reference.
Jan. 1888.	Books first issued for Home Reading.

Evidently the Bootle friends have lost no time from the adoption of the Acts up to the present time. The acquisition of the collection from the Royal Institution of Liverpool has been a loss to Liverpool, but an enormous gain to Bootle. The sum of £500 paid for it represents merely a nominal value, for it is so complete and comprehensive that the Bootle Committee have been saved the work of years in being fortunate enough to secure this collection. The shells fossils, and insects are particularly full of good specimens. Mr. John J. Ogle, the Curator and Librarian, is hard at work classifying and arranging the specimens, and certainly he has his work before him to get the whole in order and properly labelled. To an enthusiast, however, such a task is not by any means unwelcome, and Mr. Ogle may be so designated.

The catalogues of the first and second loan collections held last year show that from South Kensington examples were lent of needle-point lace, embroidery and textile fabrics, fac-similes of illuminated MSS., etchings and coloured drawings of jewels, enamels, furniture, &c., and Gothic carving was particularly good. There were also four cases containing respectively examples of goldsmiths' and silversmiths' work, examples of ceramic art, Indian brocades and embroideries, Indian carving, lacquer and inlaid work.

In addition to these there were 122 water-colour drawings and about 150 oil paintings, all lent by local gentlemen or by the artists. A considerable number of miscellaneous objects added interest to the collection. The second exhibition, held last autumn, was equally successful with the first, both being visited by a very large number of persons. As one minor proof of the need of such a work as this giving particulars of Museums, it may be mentioned that many artists who sent pictures, when they saw the building and the admirable arrangements which had been made for exhibiting the pictures, expressed themselves surprised, and said that had they known it was to be so good a display they would have sent better pictures.

BRADFORD.

The Committee here report the continued popularity of the Art Museum and Libraries. The figures appended indicate as full a measure of success as can be obtained under the present conditions. This department of the Corporation work has developed so rapidly in recent years that the Committee have had great difficulty in keeping pace with the requirements of the public. Already the accommodation is very inadequate, and at no very distant time the question of extension will have to be seriously considered. The report makes special mention of last year's scheme for erecting a new

Art Gallery and Museum.   Mr. George Hodgson, who
has given on several occasions substantial help to the
institution, generously offered to give £3,000 towards
that object.   It is hoped that the project only remains
in abeyance for a short period.   The visits to all
departments, as compared with the previous year, have
been as follows :—

VISITS TO ALL DEPARTMENTS.

	1885-6.		1886-7.		Decrease.	Increase.
Museum	309,593	...	336,512	...	—	26,919
News Room	844,193	...	912,833	...	—	68,640
Great Horton	35,579	...	39,453	...	—	3,874
Girlington	30,410	...	36,512	...	—	6,102
Barkerend	14,952	...	13,841	...	1,111	—
Bowling	13,836	...	16,168	...	—	2,332
Manchester Rd.	—	...	24,880	...	—	24,880
Bradford Moor	45,210	...	53,889	...	—	8,679
Manningham	72,390	...	74,195	...	—	1,805
	1,366,163		1,508,283		1,111	143,231

To give more particularly the visits to the Art
Museum for 1887, it stands as follows :—

Open.	Hours Open Daily.	Number of Visits.	Daily Average of Visits.
311 Weekdays 33 Sundays	In Summer, from 10 a.m. until dusk. In Winter, on Mondays, Thursdays, and Saturdays, from 10 a.m. to 9 p.m. ; and on Tuesdays, Wednesdays, and Fridays, from 10 a.m. until dusk.	336512	Weekday, 1039·05 Sunday 405·00

The attendance during the last Christmas holidays was
phenomenal.   During the holiday week some 22,000
persons passed the turnstiles—a number exceeding that
of any week since the opening, and enormously in excess

of the proportionate attendance at the great national institutions of the Metropolis. It may be assumed that few of the visits were " repeats "—that holiday-makers were not likely, in any large percentage, to call twice in one week. It may fairly be said, then, that 20,000 individuals of the district, being a large fraction of the whole population, added this visit to the series of their holiday pleasures, few of which could be so innocent, and none more beneficial to them. How many pennies, out of the fifty pence in the pound which make the rates of the borough, are more wisely spent than the one to which the expenditure on the Library and Museum is limited ? In December, 1887, the Mayor, Mr. J. L. Morley, opened the fifth Winter Exhibition of Pictures and other artistic objects. The catalogue is issued at a penny, and it is a capital little publication. Amidst all the toadyism of the day, how cheering it is to meet with what is here given in a catalogue of a public exhibition. A small collection of portraits has been presented to the Museum by Mr. G. A. Gaskell, and the following extract is taken from Mr. Gaskell's letter to the Committee :—" I have observed with a feeling of dissatisfaction that while extravagant sums are readily subscribed for presentation portraits of rich men, memorial portraiture of poor men is almost entirely neglected. It occurred to me early this year that I might, if I were allowed, employ my art to rectify, in some degree, this injustice, and offer to the town some portraits of men who, without being wealthy, have won for themselves an honourable reputation in Bradford. My project met with encouragement, and, as a result of the facilities given me, I have pleasure now in handing over to your Committee, for the Free Public Art Gallery in perpetuity, the portraits of six eminent townsmen, in frames provided by friends." The portraits are of local men, unknown to fame perhaps, but remembered as worthy townsmen.

Mr. Butler Wood is the Curator and Librarian, and his views as to extending the work of Museums are worth noting. His idea of making a Museum successful is to constantly change the exhibits. They find at Bradford this plan to work remarkably well, as the public are always coming in to look at the fresh things. Another point upon which he feels strongly is the desirability of a plan for distributing the surplus pictures in the National Gallery and other Government institutions among the provincial Museums, either as gifts or loans. He is not far wrong when he says that, practically, many are debarred from using these institutions under the existing arrangements, whereas if some such circulating plan were adopted the result would be exceedingly beneficial to all concerned. The work at Bradford is worthy of high praise.

BRIGHTON.

The Brighton Museum and Library lack life and vitality. These institutions are supported from the rates, although not established under the Acts, and until they are Brighton must be content to see both the Museum and Library in a comatose condition. The annual expenses reach some £1,100, and the average number of visitors is about 1,000 per week. Brighton has a population of some 100,000, and to compare the work of the institution with that of Blackburn, with its population of over 104,000, is decidedly in favour of the latter. Considering that the Museum is composed entirely of objects which have been given, even on the ground of getting value for money we fail to see that Brighton is, for its annual outlay of £1,100, securing anything near the utility which should result from their Museum. The geology and archæology of the neighbourhood are well represented in the Museum. The copy of the twelfth annual report for the year 1885 which lies before me is, I presume, the last report issued up to this date, March, 1888. The meeting at which this report was presented was held on June 2nd, 1886. The report of the Museum and Library consists of eight pages, and the remarks about the Museum are confined to six short sentences occupying a page, and then another page given to the donations. There is not a word as to the practical work of the Museum, and how the Committee, who represent some of the best men in the Town Council, can be satisfied with such meagre results is a mystery. The entire record of work at Brighton is perhaps as unsatisfactory as any town in the country, when the size and importance of the district is taken into account, and until Brighton sets its house in order and adopts the Acts it must continue to remain in its present state. Some constructive alterations have been contemplated and discussed, but there is only one means by which the whole can be lifted out of the confusion worse confounded into which it has fallen. Surely Brighton is big enough for both a Picture Gallery and a large Lending Library, and it is little short of an insult to the intelligence of the most intelligent section of the citizens to allow this work to rest at its present low-water mark. Mr. Benjamin Lomax, the Curator, will in future confine his duties to the superintendence of the Museum and Picture Gallery, and this will no doubt tend to produce a better state of things.

CARDIFF.

This Museum has a good selection of local geological specimens, and offers, too, a good field for the palæontologist. Probably, however, its chief feature would be considered to consist of specimens of wood in a natural and fossil state. At the head of the former stands a piece of four-inch firwood planking from the side of a ship. This has been pierced by the horn of a narwhal ; the vessel was struck by one of these powerful chargers of the deep, at an angle of about 50deg., with such force that the plank was pierced as by a shot from a cannon, the horn passing through and its point projecting about six inches in the inside of the vessel. It may be mentioned that this fish retreated from the attack with a broken nose. Here is a copy of the label :—

"This specimen (of wood) was taken from a ship in a Cardiff graving dock, and was pierced at midnight while the vessel was in the Pacific. The blow was very severe, and was distinctly heard by the captain and mate on deck, who for the time supposed the vessel had struck a rock, or that an earthquake had occurred (these being frequent in the locality). The cause of the alarm was not known until the vessel was placed in dry dock, when it was taken out."

With a port like Cardiff, so closely associated by trade with tropical seas, the Museum is naturally rich in specimens of wood destroyed by the mechanical action of the *Teredo navalis.* Some specimens of pine and a slab of Havana cedar highly wrought or bored by these destructive animals are shown. A specimen of wood, showing the great durability of English oak, is found in a wooden spade labelled as follows :—" Oak spade found in a mine on the northern edge of the Dean Forest mineral field, probably Roman." This is probably the oldest wooden spade extant.

The specimens of fossil woods in the Museum are many and various. Competent experts say that these represent a flora anterior to the Creation. One specimen of petrified wood is looked upon as of considerable value, and its age is uncertain, but one geologist claims that it may be counted by millions of years. "Petrified wood" means wood turned into rock; but this is not explicit enough, for it may be petrified by being exposed to water containing a large admixture of carbonate of lime, and this in a comparatively short space of time, especially so if the operation is not extended beyond encrustation. The specimen just referred to is, more correctly speaking, "silicified" wood, that is, the carbon and other minor constituents, forming the infinitesimal fibres and cells of the wood, have slowly disappeared, and their place and form have been slowly occupied by silica, in the form of flint or opal. So elaborately has this process been carried out, that when plates one-hundredth part of an inch in thickness are cut for microscopical purposes, every detail, although changed from vegetable into mineral matter, is as distinct and perfect as in the living tree. Mr. Storrie, the Curator, has given considerable attention to this branch of study, and is the author of a work on *The Fossil Woods of the South Wales District*. His studies in this science incline him to the same opinion as other students of authority, that coniferous woods—that is, the wood of cone-bearing trees, such as is now represented by the fir, spruce, and larch —are traceable through the lignites of the miocene age down to the coal beds of the carboniferous age, beyond which no woods are found, as testified by the rocks, except a species of gigantic seaweed in the silurian strata. A recent present to this Museum has been from Mr. Lucas, a former student of the Cardiff Art Schools, now resident in Chili, who has given to the school various pieces of physical apparatus and three cases of Chilian minerals, including gold, silver, copper, and lead ores.

F

DUNDEE.

At this Museum, in connection with the Free Library, there is a unique collection of the Arctic fauna unequalled in any other part of the country. This is peculiarly appropriate to Dundee, seeing that the town is the chief seat in Britain of the whaling trade. They have also a good collection of fossils of the old red sandstone rock of Forfarshire, and a fairly complete representation of the ornithology of the basin of the River Tay. The last report of the Committee chronicles an increasing popularity of both the Museum and the Fine Art Gallery. The loan exhibitions of pictures and other Art objects have been most successful, and last year it was decided to add a new wing to the Albert Institute to be called the Victoria Galleries. The impetus for this came in the form of a gift of £10,500 from Mr. Keiller, who has been a warm friend of these institutions. The most recent gift of this local patriot is that of 572 volumes of works of the very highest literary and bibliographical value to the Reference Library. The extension in the buildings just referred to will give much needed room for the extension of the Museum, and allow its contents to be systematically classified, as well as provide space for additions being made to the other departments of the work in Dundee. The list of donors and lenders to the Museum for the past year occupies two pages of the report. The average number of visitors per week reaches no less than 4,000.

EXETER.

The Exeter Museum contains much to interest the general visitor, and several special features. The building is a handsome one in the Gothic style, and is situated in the best street of the city. A sketch of it is given on the opposite page.

ALBERT MEMORIAL MUSEUM, EXETER.

The institution, which comprises Museum, Free Library, and Schools of Science and Art, is the result of the patient efforts of a number of persons extending over a period of nearly twenty years.. There is a handsome frontage, and the entrance is by an arcade of three arches in the centre of the front. On the ground floor, a vaulted corridor on the right hand of the entrance leads to the Curator's Room, the Ethnological Room, and the Lower Museum, which last measures sixty-two by thirty feet, and is sixteen feet high. A corridor on the opposite side of the hall, and corresponding with the one before mentioned, gives access to the Reading Room and Library. An entrance on either side of the staircase opens into the Class Room of the Science School. The upper floor is very similar in arrangement to the one below. On the south side of the staircase is the Upper Museum, the larger room, sixty-two feet by thirty feet, and the Gallery of Engravings.

The whole of the upper floor on the north side of the staircase is given up to the School of Art. At the end of the corridor is the Elementary Class Room, thirty-eight and a-half feet by twenty-nine and a-half feet, lighted principally from the roof, which is constructed with curved wooden ribs and iron tie-rods. Beyond this, over the Library, is the Painting Room; and over the room for Science Classes are one for the Master of the School of Art, and one for casts. In addition to these there are the Class Rooms and the Chemical Laboratory. The staircase and all the principal rooms are supplied with fresh air drawn from the external atmosphere, and warmed by an apparatus in the basement; but each room also has a fireplace, which may be used if it should be found that the mode of heating is in any way objectionable or insufficient.

On the ground floor there are two rooms, termed respectively the Lower Museum and the Ethnological Room. The Lower Museum contains the Zoological Collections, so arranged as to be useful to students. At present, for want of space elsewhere, it also contains a collection illustrative of the Economic Geology of Devon and Cornwall, a small collection of British fossils, and specimens illustrative of Economic Botany. The Ethnological Room contains weapons and other objects, illustrative of the natural history of man, from all parts of the world, geographically arranged, and a small collection of Foreign Antiquities. Many of the specimens were derived from the Devon and Exeter Institution in the Cathedral Yard, where the first attempt at establishing a Museum in Exeter was made in 1813. In the Upper Museum, on the first floor, there is an ante-room containing collections of lace, coins, and a few antiquities, opening into a small Gallery of Engravings, in which are also shown illustrations of the processes used in manufactures. The principal room, termed the "D'Urban Gallery" in honour of the late Curator, sixty-two feet by thirty feet, is assigned to the local collections, and here is arranged the extensive collection of British birds, at present the principal feature of this department.

The bulk of the zoological specimens, both British and foreign, were derived from the collections of a townsman, the late Mr. Ross, but numerous additions have been made from time to time by other donors. The Museum was almost totally destitute of fittings when handed over to the Town Council. Efforts were then made to furnish cases for the specimens out of the annual income, and a portion of the money borrowed on the security of the rate. That the Museum has been, and continues to be, most attractive to the public is shown by the constant flow of visitors from the first time it was opened up to the

present date.   As far as can be ascertained without
machinery for recording the number, the annual
admissions are considerably over 100,000.   On one
occasion 5,000 persons entered on one day.

An interesting account of the origin and progress of
the Museum was issued in 1868 by Mr. G. T. Donisthorpe.
He expresses the opinion that " provincial Museums are
usually little else than collections of curiosities, falling far
short of the original signification of the name, originally
applied to that quarter of the magnificent palace at Alex-
andria which was set apart for the worship of the Muses
and the study of the Sciences, and which included
colleges with erudite professors and handsome revenues.
The Exeter and Devonshire Museum approaches, at
humble distance, the ancient model, for living agencies
as well as dead examples come within its scope, comprising as it will a School of Art, a School of Science,
a Free Library, and a Reading Room, in addition to a
Repository of Natural History and Antiquities.   Many
organisations of a useful character will cluster round
it ; and it is hoped that the Devonshire Association
for the Advancement of Science and Art, the Devonshire Archæological Society, the Exeter Naturalists'
Club, and the Devon and Exeter Graphic Society will
find a home within its walls, strengthened by their
connection with it, and imparting strength in return, by
assisting to make the Exeter Museum the grand county
centre of Art and Science."   After an interval of twenty
years, these expectations have been more than realised.

FOLKESTONE.

This pretty little watering-place has, as an additional
attraction, a new Library and Museum, opened in
1888.   The cost of the building has been about £5,000,
and it was well said at the opening ceremony that they
had bid good-bye to the crazy old building where the

Museum and Free Library had been housed for some years, and now entered a magnificent structure doing credit to the town. Mr. Ruskin purchased last year some water-colour drawings of Old Folkestone, and it was suggested that he should be asked to present them to the town Museum. In reply Mr. Ruskin wrote the following letter, which is so characteristic that it is given here:—" My attention has been directed to the letter headed 'A Peep at Old Folkestone,' to which I can only reply that as New Folkestone has sold all that was left of Old Folkestone to the service of Old Nick—in the multiform personality of the South Eastern Railway Company—charges me, through the said Company, a penny every time I want to look at the sea from the old pier, and allows itself to be blinded for a league along the beach by smoke more black than thunderclouds, I am not in the least minded to present New Folkestone with any peeps and memories of the shore it has destroyed, or the harbour it has filled and polluted, and the happy and simple human life it has rendered for ever in the dear old town impossible. The drawings were bought for better illustration of Turner's work and my own on the harbours of England, and will, I hope, therefore, be put to a wider service than they were likely to find in the Folkestone Museum."

HEREFORD.

The Museum and Free Library in this town was established in 1871. The present building was erected in 1872-4, at a cost of nearly £8,000. Of this sum upwards of £6,000 was contributed by Mr. James Rankin, of Bryngwyn, conditionally upon accommodation being provided in the institution for a Museum of Natural History, and also for the meetings of a local Naturalists' Field Club, when required. The building comprises within it a large room used as a Library and Reading Room ; a spacious Museum Room ; a room called "The Woolhope Club Room," at the service of the institution when not required by the Woolhope Club, and accommodation for a resident Librarian. The Museum, which cannot be said to be an extensive one, is formed principally of objects of local interest.

The institution thus affords great opportunities for the improvement and recreation of all classes of society in the city and its district ; and that these opportunities have been well appreciated is shown by the increasing numbers, who avail themselves of its advantages, in every branch ; and also by the success of the students in taking certificates and honours in the examinations of the Science and Art Classes.

The expense of carrying on such an institution in order to give full advantage to the public is necessarily great, whilst the income is limited. This is derived from the penny rate, and as this is made over so small an area, it is barely sufficient to cover the every-day working expenses of the institution, and is quite inadequate to provide the additional expenses so necessary for its complete efficiency, viz., the continual supply of fresh books—the requirements in the students' classes—and the many expensive wants of the Museum. The success of the institution demands increased means of supporting it, and its usefulness must of necessity be limited unless the income is considerably increased by assistance from other sources. Hereford Museum is clearly one of those cases which may reasonably look for Government aid.

IPSWICH.

A capital work is being done by the Ipswich Museum. The average number of visitors weekly is about 1,500. The building was opened in 1881, and cost £9,000. It claims to possess one of the finest local geological collections in Europe, and this claim is not by any means unfounded. The collection is, in fact, unique in

MUSEUM, LIBRARY, AND SCHOOL OF ART, IPSWICH.

English geology. It has also a fine herbarium, local Ornithology and Entomology. The collection of flint implements is particularly good. A course of twenty free lectures has been given every winter for some time past, and these are attended by an average of 500 people per night. Dr. J. E. Taylor, F.G.S., F.L.S., the editor of *Science Gossip*, is the Curator.

The sum of £10,723 was spent upon the purchase of the site and upon the buildings for the Museum, Free Library, and Schools of Science and Art; and of this sum only £5,100 is now a burden upon the penny rate, the remaining £5,623 having been provided by voluntary subscriptions of about £5,000 and about £600 granted by the Government for the Schools of Science and Art. And there is now added, from the Jubilee Fund, £1,280—viz., £880 in the erection of a Free Lending Library, and £400 to be applied in the purchase of books.

LEEDS.

The work of the Public Library here is deserving of great praise. The Art Gallery is making rapid progress as a building. The question how the walls are to be covered with pictures of permanent worth is now occupying the attention of the Committee as the opening has been fixed for the early part of October. The subscriptions amount up to the present to £6,000 for the purchase of pictures to become the property of the citizens. This is not a large sum for a town like Leeds, and it may very reasonably be asked shall Leeds be behind Sheffield in its Art Gallery? Last year £800 was set aside from the penny rate for the Art Gallery and Museum, and a similar sum will be set aside this year. Mr. James Yates, an earnest public servant, is the Librarian, and is acting as Curator.

LEICESTER.

In every aspect of the working of the Museum and Free Library they are well to the front in this town. The Museum is an imposing looking building. Two Russian cannon guard the front, which form excellent dummy horses for the rising generation to play upon, much to the amusement of onlookers. The original purpose of the building was a private school, but as this was not successful, the Corporation, in 1848, secured the building for a little over £3,000, and have made of it the very best use to which it could be adapted. To do this cost an additional £1,000, and in the year following the collection made by the Literary and Philosophical Society was transferred to the Town Council, and this collection formed an excellent nucleus for the present Museum. The expenses of maintaining it are defrayed by a rate of only a halfpenny in the pound, which, with the income derived from letting the School of Art, amounts to some £900 per annum.

Undoubtedly the chief feature of the Museum is the pictorial treatment of the mammals and birds in the general collection. The Zoological Room contains a magnificent range of thirty-nine oak cases, eight feet by five, glazed with plate glass, the finest yet erected in any provincial Museum. These are filled with carefully selected examples of the various orders of the Mammalia and birds, special attention being paid to the introduction of typical or well-known forms. Instead of the usual "peg and block" system, the specimens are arranged (in their zoological sequence) upon artistically-modelled rock work, which, with the surroundings and accessories, is planned to accord with the habitats of various species. The three "bays" devoted to fresh and salt water fish are also arranged in a very novel and striking manner. The aspects of a sea and river bottom respectively are reproduced with remarkable fidelity, the specimens, carefully modelled and coloured from nature, being thus presented as in their natural element.

The old unsightly method of labelling is entirely dispensed with, being replaced by a plan invented by the Curator, and already applied to several cases with perfect success. Miniature coloured drawings of the contents of each case are provided, in which each specimen is distinguished by a number, referring to printed lists placed close by, giving common and scientific name, range, &c., of the different species. The specimens are by this means referred to with the greatest facility, and the artistic effect is preserved from the ludicrousness that often attends the introduction of labels.

Another feature of this room is the nucleus of an Index Museum of Osteology which cannot fail, when complete, to prove of the greatest possible service to students of Comparative Anatomy, by the simple and effective manner in which the various points of structure are made plain. The method is one devised by the Curator, and consists essentially in showing, by means of colour on the actual bones, the homologues of the vertebrated skeleton ranging from man to fishes. Thus, any given bone in, say, the skull of man, may be traced with the greatest ease through the descending scale of life, and its various alterations and modifications in the different orders, and under various conditions, may be grasped almost at a glance, any bone distinguished by a special tint being coloured in an identical manner throughout the series. An Index collection showing the structure of birds, feathers, &c., is also in course of construction. The Museum also possesses a very fine collection of British birds, comprising many examples, bequeathed, some years ago, by Mr. H. Bickley, of Melton Mowbray, but these are not mounted pictorially, and the mistake had been made of only collecting most perfect examples of male birds, the female, young ;—change of plumage being unrepresented.

It is proposed to place on exhibition the pictorial representation of the life histories of the vertebrate animals of the county, and a number of cases have already been finished with marked success. In every instance where practicable, the male, female, and young, and, in the case of the birds, the nest and eggs, are exhibited in the group. The surrounding foliage, &c., is modelled with marvellous skill and exactitude by the Curator's own hands, so that this "local collection," when complete, will form one of the most interesting and beautiful features of the Museum collections. As might be expected from the important position occupied by Leicester in ancient times, the collections of local antiquities, more particularly the portion dealing with the time of the Roman occupation, are of great interest to archæologists. Many relics of great rarity procured in the vicinity are to be seen in the cases, whose contents will repay careful examination.

The Museum abounds with illustrations of mediæval life. The cucking stool, the branks, scold's bridle, and the scolding cart, illustrate the old methods of summary administration of judicial penalties. In the Geological Department are valuable typical collections of fossils and minerals. In the former division may be specially noted the famed Saurians of the Lias of Barrow-on-Soar in a good state of preservation, and other interesting forms. In the Annexe a number of fine palms, tree ferns, and other plants are placed, and by their luxuriant growth bear ample testimony to the suitability of their situation.

The Curator, Mr. Montague Brown, F.Z.S., has answered so fully and practically the question as to the best means of extending the work of Museums that his remarks are given a place here. He leads off with a feature really essential for the success of any Museum, but not in all cases looked upon as of special necessity. His suggestion will commend itself to those who would like to excommunicate brushes and dusters.

"1. Museums should certainly be kept clean, abundance of light admitted, and adequate arrangements made for securing thorough ventilation, and the various fittings, &c., should be solid and handsome in appearance, well made, and carefully planned to ensure the ends for which they' are intended in the best possible manner. 2. Taking an intelligent interest in the public—who in Museums such as ours supply the funds—and letting them see that you are always willing to provide for their wants, and will spare no pains to give them accurate information well up to date. 3. There should certainly be a 'General Zoological Collection' of vertebrates, which should contain representatives—one or two of each family—of the most striking species known from all parts of the world, and these should be carefully and artistically mounted and arranged in a pictorial manner for the use and interest of the general public. The general collections of invertebrates should also be rendered as complete as possible, and where space is limited, the more striking species should be selected for exhibition. 4. An important point would be the preparation of special groups illustrating the fauna of the county, and kept entirely separate from the general collections. These should be mounted in the highest style of art, the foliage and surroundings to be accurately copied from nature, and no pains or money spared in making the collection as complete as possible. In the local collections of invertebrates let the life histories of the various species be worked out as fully as possible, and coloured drawings illustrating their habits, anatomical distinctions, &c., be placed in close proximity. Where space will allow, this last suggestion may be applied to the general collection. 5. Let a series of cases be devoted to Index Collections of Anatomy and Physiology arranged with an eye to teaching purposes. Well prepared specimens, drawings, diagrams, and explanatory charts should be liberally provided. 6. General collections of fossils and minerals, in which type specimens are predominant, together with drawings and diagrams of places of geological interest, sections and phenomena of geological importance, &c. 7. Special local collections arranged on similar lines, illustrating *fully* the geology and palæontology of the district. This latter—palæontological—to be if possible arranged or referred to, as throwing light upon the existing local fauna. 8. Archæological collections illustrating fully the archæology of the district, and 9. Small ethnological collections of selected examples illustrative of the arts and industries of the various races, arranged with a view to throw as much light as possible on the strictly archæological portion of the Museum collections. 10. Let every object displayed be well and sufficiently described, and all objects devoid of a history be carefully excluded. 11. No collections of any kind whatever to be accepted with restrictions, such as that they must be kept separate. 12. A system of duplicates to be arranged between Museums. At the present time few institutions exchange with one another, and as some are very rich in one class of objects, and *vice versâ*, a definite scheme of some kind would be of the utmost utility to all concerned." Mr. Brown has hit the right nail on the head in many of these suggestions.

NEWPORT.

The Committee of the Newport Free Library and Science and Art Classes has at length arranged for the opening of a Museum on the site of the old Reading

Room. An exhibition of loans and purchases has been held very recently. South Kensington sent down exhibits more than sufficient to fill four cases. These comprised china, porcelain, Persian objects, electrotypes of the possessions of the London City Companies, and some magnificent specimens of Indian embroideries. The walls were decorated with painted and coloured photographs, and oil paintings, the bequests of Messrs. Jones and Sheepshanks, and Sir Richard Wallace, Bart., M.P., together with oil paintings of leading masters. The Museum thus begins in a very hopeful way, and bids fair to take sound root.

NORTHAMPTON.

The chief addition to this Museum during the past year is a collection of antiquities obtained while excavating at Hunsbury Hill (Danes' Camp). It is hoped that Mr. Pickering Phipps, who has lent them, will add them permanently to the antiquarian treasures of the town. The public appreciation of the Museum has been shown by a large increase in the attendance.

On the recommendation of the Town Council, the Committee decided to open the Reading Room and Museum on Sunday afternoons and evenings, from 2.30 to nine p.m., for six months by way of an experiment, and on condition that voluntary caretakers could be obtained. The extent to which the public have availed themselves of the opportunity of visiting both— particularly the Museum—has been a surprise. The greatest interest has been evinced in the contents of the Museum by the great bulk of the visitors, whose numbers have constituted the chief embarrassment of the new arrangement. The Museum and Reading Room have been in charge of voluntary caretakers, to avoid the necessity of imposing extra duties on the staff. On the first Sunday visitors numbered 1,400 or 1,500, on the second Sunday about 2,000, and on the third and fourth Sundays the attendance was quite as numerous. In connection with the Museum, it was resolved last winter to begin a series of Saturday Evening Talks in the Old Upper Museum Room. While it is desired to make these talks in some measure illustrative of the contents of the Museum, it is hoped to comprehend within them other subjects touching the higher education. The President (Mr. Campion) made a start with " A Trip down the Nene Valley."

There is great need at Northampton for better and more convenient accommodation, both for Library and Museum. The building was originally the old Town Hall, and in adapting it for its present purposes the best has been made of it. The Museum consists of one large room, well lighted and lofty, and in arranging the cases there has been as much classification as was possible. The rather clumsy shape and character of some of the largest cases has, however, created a difficulty both in the way of good arrangement and classification. If an extension scheme, now under discussion, is carried out, the Museum will have a greatly enhanced value, and will do better justice to the town.

The iron implements from the Danes' Camp already referred to are the most valuable find which has for some time taken place in any part of the country, and Mr. Thomas J. George, F.G.S., the cultured Keeper of the Museum and Librarian, has acted wisely in making the most of these. In the autumn of last year before a local Literary Club, he read a paper headed, " Notes on Pre-historic Man in Northamptonshire," which is a valuable addition to the archæological literature of that county. He traces the history through the Stone and Bronze Ages to the Iron Age. Of the place and relics

G

just referred to he gives some particulars well worth quoting :—

"Danes' Camp," he says, "is situated nearly two miles south-west of Northampton ; it occupies a strong position, command-ing extensive views of the country on all sides of it. By the side of the camp runs an ancient trackway connecting it with the camp at Arberry Hill, in Thenford parish, and perhaps joining the trackways on the other side of Banbury, which com-municate with Hook Norton, Tadmarten, and Mad-Marston Camps, all of which are British. Over the whole camp the navvies found, in what they term the 'on-bearing,' that is, the surface soil above the ironstone, numbers of pits sunk in many cases to the ironstone ; a few of these pits were walled round with flattish limestones ; the general run of these pits were from five feet to six feet in diameter, and about six feet deep ; they were full of black mould, and in them were found the numerous articles which now comprise one of the finest collections of, I believe, Pre-historic Antiquities in England. No such thorough excavation of any camp has been undertaken before, or is likely to again, except for a similar purpose, that is, commercial enter-prise. The cost of removing the soil in order to get out the ironstone amounted to several thousand pounds, a sum which would effectually bar any private digging operations. It is deeply to be regretted that the excavation did not receive that close supervision so important a place demanded. The collec-tion consists of numerous iron weapons and implements, bronze ornaments, bone articles, pots of rough hand-made pottery, remains of more than 400 vessels of different form and size, portions of about 150 querns for grinding corn, some of the corn they ground, spindle whorls, coombs used for weaving purposes, some peculiar triangular-shaped bricks perforated with holes at the corners, remains of the red-deer, roe-deer, goat, horse, short-horned ox, and domestic pig. The iron articles comprise twenty spear heads, several of which correspond in make and shape with those found at Marin, which belong to the Iron Age ; they are very unlike to the Anglo-Saxon spear heads, a characteristic feature of which is a longitudinal slit in the socket which receives the shaft ; numerous knives, a long sword, identified by Mr. Franks as British, remains of two other swords, apparently in an unfinished state—these resemble some found at Hod Hill, which are figured in Warne's *Ancient Dorset*, Plate II. ; five daggers, a dagger in its iron sheath, portions of three sword sheaths, five saws—one remains in a portion of its deer-horn handle ; these saws have the same shape as a bronze saw which is figured on Plate LV. of Keller's *Swiss Lake Dwellings ;* the teeth are equilateral ; nails, adzes, picks, a chisel, spuds, axes, a key, rings, pot hooks, some articles like large flat spoons, with long handles, and a peculiar object having a late Celtic pattern—the use of this is unknown, but Sir Henry Dryden suggests it might have been a brand for branding cattle ; a horse-bit, with bronze centre piece—this bit resembles those which have been found with interments of the late Celtic period ; portions of wheel tires like those which have been found at Polden Hill, and at Arras and Stanwick in Yorkshire ; three shield bosses—two are of the form usually attributed to the Anglo-Saxons, and are, I believe, the only objects which can be classed so by their form ; these were found outside the camp."

He goes much more fully into the matter, but sufficient has been quoted to show the interest and value attaching to these iron implements. An illustrated hand-book of them would be useful. One object in the Museum is unique in its way, namely, a large piece of work in wood, carved by a Bedfordshire working man named George Rawlins. It is sexagonal in shape, and occupied him 5,941 hours, says an inscription upon it. The working people take great interest in this piece of carving, and there is about it some very careful and excellent work worthy of high praise. The work is an example of marvellous patience, but it does not teach much to those who crowd around it, and that means everyone who visits the Museum. Had there been in the design a copy of some building, or a little more originality it would have been worthy of more admiration. It is a little too much like a wedding cake in wood, and, as a product of 5,941 hours of leisure, for the sake of the working men and the boys who look at it with pleasure and interest one would like to have seen a work doing greater credit to the man's patience and skill in carving. A higher aim and a guiding hand would have done this, but he has shown what a village workman can do and is capable of doing. A considerable number of other objects have been presented to the Museum, and among the most important are a number of natural history specimens, some books on natural science, and a collection of shells by the Curator, Mr. George.

NOTTINGHAM.

Nottingham is distinctly to the front with its Museum and Library work, and sets a worthy example to the rest of the country in extracting the fullest value from these educational institutions. In 1886 Mr. J. W. Carr, B.A., F.G.S., of Emmanuel College, and Assistant Curator of the Woodwardian Museum, Cambridge, was appointed Keeper, and has given a new impetus to the Museum work. The special features rest in two rooms of equal size, one above the other, the Lower Room being devoted to the vertebrate collection, and the upper to the invertebrata. The fittings in the Lower Room comprise a narrow table-case running along both sides of the room beneath the windows; tall wall-cases occupying the two ends of the room and the sides of the window recesses; fifteen large upright cases with plate glass on all sides, occupying the floor space. In the Upper Room a window table-case runs along the sides and wall-cases occupy the ends and window recesses. The floor space is occupied by fifteen table-cases.

The floor-cases in the Lower Room are filled with mammals and birds, mostly pictorially mounted; the fishes, reptilia, &c., occupy the wall-cases, while the window table-cases are filled with vertebrate fossils. In the Upper Room the fifteen table-cases are filled with a fine and well arranged series of invertebrata— all the divisions being more or less well represented.

The arrangement is almost identical with that described in the Rev. H. H. Higgins' paper on "Museums of Natural History," referred to in another chapter. The wall-cases contain minerals and rocks, &c., and the window table-cases hold the invertebrate fossil collection. A small room opening out of the Invertebrate Room contains the extensive Continental and British Herbaria.

The series of invertebrata includes a large and choice selection of marine forms from the zoological station at Naples, and the series of models (in plaster and other preparations) of Protozoa. The coloured drawings of these and other invertebrates are particularly striking. Blaschka's glass models of invertebrata greatly attract visitors, as do the "Marshale," a fine and complete collection of British mollusca. A good series of silk-producing moths in all stages of metamorphosis, together with their economical products in the various stages of manufacture, is deserving of mention. Also insect vivaria, in which the above were and are being bred. A fine group likewise of anthropoid apes includes skeleton and stuffed skin of probably the largest gorilla in any Museum in Britain.

Popular lectures and demonstrations are given by the Curator, illustrated by specimens from the Museum, and these are well attended.

The total number of visitors from 1st August, 1881, to 31st March, 1886, was 1,198,442, giving a daily average of over 1,100. The greatest number on any one day (Whit-Monday, 1883) was 10,646, and the least number 221. From 1st April, 1886, to 31st March, 1887, the daily average fell to 675, owing chiefly to the necessity of closing the Invertebrate Museum on public holidays, on account of the unsafe condition of the floor.

The tabular statement below of the attendance of visitors to the Natural History Museum, from 1st April, 1886, to 31st March, 1887, is very instructive, showing how popular are these citizens' institutions.

Year.	Months.	Number of days open each month	Number of Visitors each month	Greatest number of Visitors in any one day	Least number of Visitors in any one day	Average per day in each month.
1886	April	21	16888	3539a	433	804
,,	May.........	22	12600	928	270	573
,,	June	22	22700	5681b	360	1032
,,	July.........	22	11589	1486	307	527
,,	August ...	22	19290	2365c	488	877
,,	September	22	15725	986	522	715
,,	October ...	22	19767	3840d	384	898
,,	November	22	12481	858	415	567
,,	December	21	12358	2316e	268	588
1887	January ...	22	11039	1027	283	502
,,	February	20	10599	846	351	530
,,	March	23	11199	815	340	487
	12 months	261	176235	5681	268	675

(a) Easter Monday.   (b) Whit Monday.   (c) Bank Holiday.

(d) Fair Day.   (e) Christmas (Bank Holiday).

During the last Museum year the chief objects added by purchase to the Museum were :—Dissected skull of African elephant; stuffed specimens of weasel and stoat; seven South African bird skins; forty-five bird skins from New Guinea (purchased); Greenland shark (*Dalatias microcep-*

halus) caught off Scarborough, August 17th, 1886; twenty-two exotic Lepidoptera and Coleoptera; an extensive collection of insects, chiefly from Derbyshire; and other specimens. Among other objects presented during the same year we may mention the following :— *Cassis tuberosa*, cut for cameo; Echinoderms, sponges (one new species), and a *Gorgonia*, from the Bahamas (by Mr. G. B. Rothera); *Aceras anthropophora*, from Box Hill, Surrey (by Mr. W. Whitwell); a large series of fossils from the Lias and Neocomian formations of Lincolnshire (by the Curator, Mr. J. W. Carr); about seventy specimens of mollusca, &c., chiefly from the Tertiary formations of Hampshire (by Mr. H. Keeping, Cambridge); a few chalk fossils from Margate.

The penny descriptive guides are excellent models for terseness.

OLDHAM.

The Oldham Library and Museum was opened in 1883, and although not established under the Public Libraries or Museums Acts is a rate-supported institution, being under a special Act promoted by the Corporation. The Library and Reading Rooms stand in the same relation to each other as the nave and aisles of a church. The arched openings between each and to the staircase landings are filled in with ornamental lead-light glass, so as to secure quietude to readers and efficient oversight by the Librarian and his assistants. The front of the building consists of Ladies' Reading Room, Special Reference Room, and Committee Room. Ascending the principal staircase is the Statuary Hall on the level of the first floor, and thus access is obtained to the Museum and Art Gallery on the right or left. By following the main lines of the ground floor the architect has been able to get a Museum and

Art Gallery, each eighty-six feet by twenty-five feet, with a connecting corridor thirty - three feet by twenty feet, forming a hollow square, each end being connected with the principal staircase. The exterior of the building is a free and simple treatment of Gothic. The cost of the Central Library was £25,000, and of the Branch Library £4,000.

The complaint has several times been made that this Art Gallery and Museum is not so popular as it ought to be because there is rarely anything fresh to be seen; that it is impossible to maintain one's interest if only the same pictures, and art exhibits, and curiosities are to be seen. This complaint is not ill-founded, but the exhibit from the South Kensington Museum was changed last December. The cases, four in number, are full of valuable specimens of Oriental and English art work. One interesting object is a silk cover, embroidered with geometrical and floral designs, presented by the Shah of Persia to this nation. Near it is a Persian carpet, and pretty specimens of needlework. Another case is full of bronzes, notable amongst which is an imitation of the roots and stem of a tree. Near to the bronzes is a collection, in a separate case, of Indian pottery. The fourth case contains electrotypes, and is also interesting. In addition to these attractions, a fresh supply of pictures arrived from the same source. These oil paintings are not modern works. They are chiefly interesting as illustrating the difference between the old and new schools. The Curator and Librarian is Mr. Hand.

SALFORD.

A visit to the Peel Park Museum, Library and Park for the first time could not fail to be a revelation to anyone who takes an interest in the recreations of the people. The Museum and Library were initiated in May, 1849, by the then Mayor and the late Joseph Brotherton, M.P. The first room of the Museum was opened in 1850, and other parts and wings have been added at various times. The building now contains six Library Rooms, a Reading Room, eighty feet by thirty feet, three Natural History Rooms, sixty feet by twenty feet, three corridors about the same length, and two Galleries, eighty feet by thirty feet, occupied with paintings and the Museum collections. In 1879 the value was assessed at the following figures : — Buildings, £14,000 ; furniture, £3,000 ; paintings and works of fine art, £12,000 ; antiquities and general curiosities, £2,000 ; manufactures and products, £800 ; natural history and geology, £3,000 ; reference books, £7,000. The present value of the property is from £60,000 to £70,000.

In 1849 Major John Plant, F.G.S., was appointed Curator and Librarian, and still holds the post. In a handsome book giving photographs of the statues in the Peel Park, and the letterpress by Mr. Plant, there appears an interesting sketch of the Langworthy Wing. The view on page 91 is taken from the photo. in this book, which bears the name of Mr. A. Brothers, Manchester.

From the report of last year's work it appears that the number of visitors to the Museum was 304,270, and the total of persons attending both Museum and News Rooms was 921,689. Whit week is the busiest time in the year. There were 30,300 visitors during the Whit week of 1887. On Monday and Saturday the number reached 9,000 each day.

The following table is very instructive :—
STATISTICAL TABLES AND RETURNS FOR THE
YEARS 1850-87, OF THE MUSEUM AND
PICTURE GALLERIES.

Year.	Total number of visitors.	No. of Days opened	Daily average of visitors	REMARKS.
1850	16000	129	1240	Museum opened in April.
1851	276500	188	1465	Museum enlarged.
1852	303140	200	1515	Museum collections increased.
1853	67225	66	1018	Museum closed nine months.
1854	330274	217	1520	North Wing and Gallery opened.
1855	448220	260	1720	Museum enlarged.
1856	580069	241	2408	South Wing and Gallery opened.
1857	888830	279	3508	Local Artists' First Exhibition.
1858	538444	265	2032	Exhibition in summer.
1859	683575	268	2550	Exhibition of Paintings.
1860	588770	264	2230	Exhibition of Paintings.
1861	600120	277	2166	Travelling Museum of S. K. M.
1862	767700	260	2568	Exhibition of Paintings.
1863	454400	214	2123	Exhibition of Paintings.
1864	620370	262	2370	Summer Exhibition.
1865	600620	259	2315	Summer Exhibition.
1866	527400	261	2021	No Exhibition.
1867	566520	261	2170	Local Artists' Second Exhibition.
1868	544550	264	2063	Exhibition of Paintings.
1869	604900	261	2317	No Exhibition of special kind.
1870	438850	267	1643	,, ,,
1871	443170	268	1656	,, ,,
1872	583000	264	2208	,, ,,
1873	422920	263	1608	Venezuela Drawings Exhibition.
1874	527500	234	2200	Exhibition of Scientific Industry.
1875	553280	261	2120	Musical Promenades in Peel Park.
1876	425500	261	1614	Loan Exhibition. Mus. Promenades
1877	407600	266	1532	Musical Promenades in Peel Park.
1878	436450	283	1725	{ Local Artists' Third Exhibition. Langworthy Gallery opened.
1879	381000	260	1465	No Exhibition of special kind.
1880	527600	261	2000	Loans,& Miss Thompson's Balaclava
1881	431300	263	1633	Loan Exhibition of Paintings.
1882	528940	263	1213	No special attraction.
1883	540506	261	2071	Loans, Galleries Decorated.
1884	475450	261	1775	Loan from S. Kensington, &c.
1885	435000	257	1696	No Exhibition of a special kind.
1886	376776	265	1421	Loan of S. K. Museum objects.
1887	304270	256	1150	Loans of Paintings, &c.
38 Years	18,247,412	9232	2000	

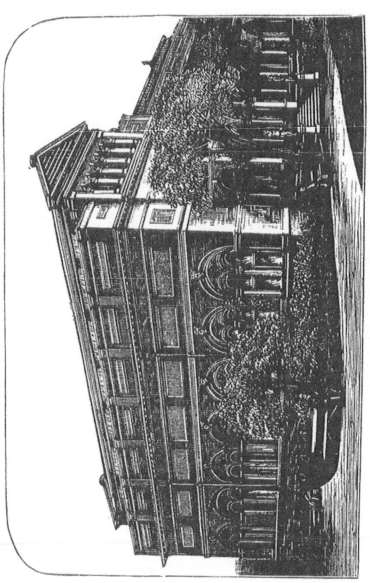

SALFORD MUSEUM.

The Salford Museum is an excellent institution, well managed, and deservedly popular throughout the district.

SHEFFIELD.

For many years the charge against Sheffield was a lack of public spirit and of public buildings, by no means creditable to the cutlery and steel metropolis. This stigma will in course of a few years be forgotten, for with its Firth College, Montgomery Hall, the Mappin Art Gallery, the Public Museum, and a new building to be by-and-bye erected for the Public Library, and the attractive buildings for branch Libraries, Sheffield will very soon be able to compare with almost any town of its size in the country, and indeed has now outstripped in educational progress many towns which started in the race before her.

The Sheffield Public Museum was established in 1875, in Weston Park. This park, purchased by the Corporation, contained a large house which was adapted to the uses of a Museum, by certain alterations and additions, and was opened to the public on September 6th, 1875. The building consists on the ground floor of one room fifty-five feet by eighteen feet, two rooms twenty feet by eighteen feet, and two galleries seventy-five feet by twenty-five feet; on the upper floor there are two rooms twenty feet by eighteen feet, and one room fifty-five feet by eighteen feet, besides passages and entrance. The collections comprise a technological series of objects illustrative of local industries, a natural history collection, including recent natural history, geology, mineralogy, and British botany; an archæological collection; and an historical collection of cutlery and art metal work of various countries.

On the establishment of the Museum, the Literary and Philosophical Society, possessing a good collection of invertebrates, fossils, and minerals, handed these over to the town, and they formed the nucleus of the Museum collection. To these have since been added several collections of considerable importance, including European birds and eggs, presented by Mr. H. Seebohm ; invertebrates and fossils, presented by Mr. H. C. Sorby, LL.D., F.R.S. ; an extensive collection of Australian shells, by Mr. J. Harris ; local collections of British Lepidoptera, Yorkshire and Derbyshire fossils have been added by purchase. There is also a collection of local plants made nearly a century ago, and presented by the Literary and Philosophical Society. This contains many species of plants that have long since been exterminated by the growth of the town, and it has grown until it now embraces nearly all the plants belonging to the British Flora. In addition to stuffed skins, the natural history collection contains skeletons, dissections, and anatomical preparations.

In 1876 the collection of British antiquities known as the Bateman Collection was placed in the Museum. With the exception of the Mayer Collection, in the Liverpool Museum, the Bateman Collection is probably the finest array of British antiquities in the provinces. A catalogue of 305 pages was published by Mr. Thomas Bateman in 1855, and many of the objects are described in the same author's *Vestiges of the Antiquities of Yorkshire* and *Ten Years' Grave Diggings*. Many other objects have been added to the various collections since the Museum was established, and the building is becoming greatly overcrowded. The front of the building is of two storeys, the upper floor being equal in size to the lower ; the two Galleries, seventy-five feet by twenty-five, are on the ground floor, lighted from the top, and without any storey above.

The Visitors' Guide to the Museum is excellent. For twopence the visitor can buy sixty-six pages of closely-printed matter, giving in a pithy manner an outline at once descriptive and special of the exhibits. It was written by Mr. Elijah Howarth, F.R.A.S., the Curator, and reflects the highest credit upon him.

The question of destructive distillation is little understood by the public, and it would be well if in other Museums there were specimens of the products of coal tar distillation, similar to those shown here. These not only contain lessons in themselves but are illustrative of what is being done in the utilisation of waste. The whole English nation would be the better for a few lessons in this subject, seeing that our national waste in all directions is disgraceful. No better means of conveying these lessons could possibly be adopted than through Museums.

The various stages in the manufacture of files, cutlery, and electro-plated goods are shown in most interesting cases. There are also specimens of old Sheffield silver plate. Long before the discovery of the process of electro-plating, silver-plated ware was manufactured in Sheffield and Birmingham. It consisted of a thin sheet of silver and a thick one of copper bound together with wire, then heated in a furnace, and afterwards rolled into a sheet, which was moulded into the article required, the silver forming a thin layer covering the copper. How suggestive it must be to an intelligent lad engaged in any of the electro-plate manufactories of the town to see the old and the new methods illustrated in this way. There are also objects illustrative of the various processes in the manufacture of local and other products, comprising spectacles, telescopes, glass etching, cotton and linen threads, vegetable ivory buttons, corn flour, destructive distillation for gas, paraffin, oils, &c., iron and steel, wire, saws, planes, cutlery, files, indiarubber, gutta-percha, and tobacco. This represents a fairly long list of Sheffield industries. The Natural History Gallery contains much to interest the visitor and the student, and the arrangement in this section is all that could be desired.

The case illustrated, and which might form a capital guide for other Museums, is fourteen feet long, slopes on either side like a desk, and has a flat centre twelve inches wide, upon which has been placed an upright case fourteen feet long and two feet three inches high. Under the case there are six tiers of drawers on each side, each tier containing six drawers in height, and as all these drawers can be opened and inspected by visitors, the exhibition space of the table-case is thus increased six-fold.

The upright central part of the case is intended for the exhibition of the more striking specimens, also for descriptive labels and drawings, the table-case itself being for specimens useful for the general student and ordinary visitor. The drawers underneath contain an extension of the specimens in the case, interesting to the student and specialist, and in this way the ordinary visitor is not confused with too extensive a display of specimens. These drawers are covered with glass lids, and while the student can pull them out so as to see the whole of their contents, he is prevented by a stop at the back of the drawer from pulling it right out of the cabinet, or taking off the glass lid, which is fastened at the back. This arrangement will serve admirably for minerals, fossils, and invertebrates, though not, of course, for the larger animals, and in this way space, which is always so scarce and valuable in a Museum, can be fully utilised. There are similar cabinets for insects and birds' eggs, the object being to protect them from the light, which causes the colour to fade. By this arrangement they are only exposed to light while a person is actually studying them; at other times the drawers, being closed, are protected from the light. Thus visitors can inspect the contents of the drawers without hindrance, but they are unable to injure their contents. In other Museums, cabinets under the table-cases are closed in with locked doors, and the student has to trouble the Curator to unlock them before he can inspect them.

The last report published gives the statistics from September 1st, 1886, to August 31st, 1887, as follows :—

Total number of visitors 146,405
Weekly average (fifty-three weeks) 2,762
Daily average (263 days) 557
Greatest number of visitors in one day 7,177

The total number of visitors last year was greater than it has been since 1880, and shows an increase of 40,941 as compared with the previous year, and an increase of 148 in the daily average. These numbers do not include the visitors to the Mappin Art Gallery, the communication between which place and the Museum was not opened till September 3rd, 1887. In future reports the statistics will include visitors both to the Art Gallery and Museum, without distinction, and it may, therefore, not be without interest to give here the total number of visitors to the Museum since its inauguration. The Museum was first opened on September 6th, 1875, and has now been open twelve years, the visitors in that period numbering 2,080,134, or a yearly average of 173,344. This is equal to about two-thirds of the average total population of Sheffield for the twelve years, and is clear evidence that the establishment of the Museum has met with popular favour.

The Committee also report that the interest taken in the collections by students has also steadily increased, due no doubt to the important additions made to the collections, and to the valuable loans received from the South Kensington Museum. Eighteen students have availed themselves during the past year of the privilege of studying in the Museum on Fridays, when it is closed to the public, but these represent but a small number of the visitors who may be seen daily with note-book or sketch-book in hand taking notes or sketches of objects.

The Museum is open to the public, free of charge, from ten in the morning to nine in the evening, on Monday, Tuesday, and Saturday; and from ten in the morning until dusk on Wednesday and Thursday. On Friday the Museum is closed to the public, but open to students by permission of the Curator.

There is one other branch of the work at Sheffield

H

to which it is a pleasure to call attention. That is the
Observatory. The Curator being a Fellow of the
Royal Astronomical Society, and the study being a
special one with him, he is able to throw an interest
into this work. From October to April the Observatory
was open thirty-four nights, and the number of students
was 283.

STOCKPORT.

The Museum in this busy town is perhaps as beautifully situated as any Museum throughout the country.
Vernon Park is known to everyone within a half-
dozen miles around it, and from several parts of it
views of some of the finest scenery in the country are
to be obtained. Here there stands on the highest part
of the park, the Museum, surrounded by a panorama of
hill and dale of great beauty. The first feature noticeable within is the cleanliness of the rooms and the
neatness and order of the contents, a feature creditable alike to the Committee and the Curator, Mr.
Tym. In May, 1888, some new exhibits arrived from
South Kensington. These include four pieces of Old
English furniture—viz., a small cabinet, a chess table,
a chess board, and a pedestal, the last named of these
articles having cost £100. Each of these exhibits is
inlaid with different kinds of wood, and has a most
handsome appearance. These occupy one of the large
glass stands. A second case contains specimens of
European pottery, including exhibits from Switzerland,
France, Germany, Russia, and England, the one from
Russia being a large glazed earthenware vase ornament
which occupies the principal position in the case.
Another exhibit is a handsome vase from the Royal
Porcelain Works at Worcester. The third case contains a number of electrotype reproductions of works
of art of exquisite design. There are also two large
shields. These are placed back to back, and the

embossing on one side represents scenes from Milton's *Paradise Lost*, and is known as the Milton shield ; the other is an embossing of scenes in *Pilgrim's Progress.* On either side of these exhibits are two large copies of cups and covers, the originals of which are in the Kremlin in Moscow. One stands three feet six inches high, and is a splendid piece of workmanship. In the fourth case are placed specimens of Indian and Japanese embroidery. These are silken cloths woven with gold and silver threads. In the upright stands to the left of the stairs leading into the Museum are a number of coloured photographs of crystals in the Louvre, or in the Madrid and other Museums.

SWANSEA.

Who has not heard of the Swansea Museum and Free Library ? There was, in the summer of 1887, the visit of Mr. Gladstone to open the Library. The ex-Premier then said, in the course of his speech, that "the opening of such a Library and Museum is itself a great event in the history of even such a town as Swansea. It recalls to me the early days of my political life, and the name of one whom I knew well from my boyhood upwards, namely, Mr. William Ewart, who passed the Public Libraries Act, and on whose memory and whose services I look back with the greatest respect and regard. There is no doubt that Mr. Ewart, by his efforts in this cause, entitled himself to be enrolled upon the list of England's benefactors. He was in point of fact not only a patriot, but a prophet in this case. He took up the question of Public Libraries at a very early date, and he reminds us of the phrase which is applied in a higher and holier sphere to a character familiar to us all—he was for the time the ' voice of one crying in the wilderness.' But by degrees there became apparent solidity and reality of the public interest which was involved in this question, and which was perceived by him in the far distance, long before others were aware of its existence, while the majority were perhaps inclined to treat it as a crotchet of a benevolent mind, and the product of his fancy rather than of his judgment. Notwithstanding such discouragements, Mr. Ewart laboured steadily in the cause, and could he now be amongst us how he would rejoice to think of the acceptance which his great purpose has obtained. And this foundation of a Library is a purpose impossible to recognise as a solitary object gained. It is one of a great group of objects which mark the character of the age. It is associated with the work of national education, and it is most interesting to reflect upon the history of that work of national education in this respect, that its growth, as a public purpose, was entirely after the true English manner. It began seventy or eighty years ago; it began in private and voluntary exertions. In the year 1833 it had attained a magnitude which caused it to be recognised as a legitimate subject of assistance from the public treasury. From that time was a continued course of growth in public acknowledgment and public importance, until the Act of 1880, in one sense, may have said to have crowned the work—that is to say, in so far as that Act was founded upon the principle that the whole of the country had a title to education. Happily that has not been a merely theoretical admission, but we have approached, with a rapidity beyond that which the most sanguine would have dared to anticipate, to the full application of that principle in practice; and yet, as I have said, as Libraries do not constitute an isolated object of regard and consideration, neither does the work of primary and of popular education. It has been accompanied with, and it has tended to engender other desires—the desire for the

extension of that primary education upwards, the
desire for a large application of approved means
for technical education for the labouring classes of
the country, and especially in those branches of industry where industry and art happily join hands,
a great department, and a department in which un-
questionably our country has, until recently, been less
forward than could have been desired, and less
forward than many other nations with whom we have
entered into the race of an honourable and a friendly
competition."

The Library and Museum, of which a view is given, is
a fine building, erected at a cost of £20,000 in a central
part of the town, from the designs of Mr. Holtom, of
Dewsbury. The style of architecture is Italian classic.
The front portion is four storeys high, and the back
portion three storeys, the circular Reading Room excepted, which is one storey only. Before many months
had elapsed from Mr. Gladstone's visit, it was stated
that the Library was in financial difficulty, and unless
someone came to the rescue or some practical method
was adopted the doors of this handsome building
would have to be closed. This paragraph went the
round of the entire Press of the country, and great was
the joy of those who in their pristine innocence asserted
that Museums and Free Libraries are costly luxuries
which ought not to be paid for out of the people's
money. The plain and simple truth of the whole
matter lay in the fact that the Committee had greatly
overbuilt themselves, bringing a burden on the penny
rate of some hundreds a year as interest, and so leaving
only a limited sum with which to work the Museum
and Library, and it was here that the shoe pinched. The
penny rate produces £1,060 a year. In April, 1888,
there was an important meeting of the Committee, and
several plans were suggested. The Library and Art School

are doing too good a work, and the Welsh people are too enthusiastic in educational matters for the Swansea people to be long content with the congested state of

SWANSEA PUBLIC LIBRARY AND SCHOOL OF ART.

things, out of which they have not extricated themselves. The Art Gallery and the School of Art are the most prominent features of the work at Swansea, next to the Library, and the Museum is only in a state so far of embryo.

WOLVERHAMPTON.

This important centre of the lock and other hardware industries was last year very much exercised over several schemes which had to do with the Museum, Art Gallery and Free Library. A municipal event of considerable importance occurred in February, 1887, when the burgesses rejected what is now well-known as Corporation Bill No. 1. The object for which it was promoted in Parliament is now a matter of history ; it contained many clauses to which the citizens objected, and when polled they vetoed it by an overwhelming majority. In May another measure was brought forward by the Corporation, relating solely to the maintenance of the Art Gallery, School of Art, and Free Library. This the ratepayers accepted, and it has now become law. The Free Library was established out of the rates, but the Art Gallery was given to the town by Mr. Philip Horsman, and the School of Art was erected by several other generous donors. It is estimated that £20,000 has been presented to the town in these two buildings alone. The prime object of the Bill, which was rejected by the ratepayers, was to obtain further powers to maintain these valuable institutions in an efficient condition, and the promoters announced that without these powers both the Art Gallery and School of Art would have to be closed. About £450 a-year was the further sum required to keep them open, which meant an additional halfpenny rate.

Ultimately a compromise was effected, and in course of a few years we may hope for a very considerable extension of the Museum and Library work of this busy town. Mr. W. J. Wheddon, the Curator of the

Municipal Art Gallery and Museum, has compiled penny and sixpenny catalogues of the paintings and water-colour drawings in the Galleries. The explanatory notes about the artist and the individual picture are very pertinent, and the first place is appropriately given to a local artist, E. Bird, R.A. Mr. Wheddon says that he "was born at Wolverhampton, on the 12th April, 1772, the son of a carpenter. While very young he began to sketch on the furniture and walls of the house with chalk. His first picture of merit, a scene from Sir Walter Scott, seems to have been painted in his fourteenth year. He was about that time apprenticed to a maker of japan ware at 'The Hall,' Wolverhampton. At the end of his apprenticeship he removed to Bristol, residing at Kingsdown, a pleasant suburb of that city. Here he taught drawing and painted many pictures. At this time Bird earned fair sums by his portrait painting, at which work he was very rapid—one instance being noted of his commencing and finishing a small portrait in oil in fifteen minutes. In 1807, by the advice of an artist friend, he contributed to an exhibition at Bath two pictures, which he sold for thirty guineas each. This was the commencement of Bird's prosperity. He shortly after painted a picture called 'Good News.' The applause which greeted this work, followed by its immediate sale, brought him many commissions at good prices, and his rise to fame was rapid. His 'Choristers Rehearsing' was bought by the King, and his next picture, 'The Will,' was secured by the Marquis of Hastings." It is not necessary to quote further, but this will suffice to show how interesting these notes can be made.

It would have been easy to have extended the number of Museums and Galleries in this chapter. The Museum at Southampton is deserving of an extended notice, but the town having adopted the Public Libraries Acts in June, 1887, the institution has been undergoing some reorganisation.   For some years it has been open free during five days of the week, and about 500 persons have, as a weekly average, passed through its doors.   It is particularly good in the botanical and geological sections.

CHAPTER VI.

GENERAL MUSEUMS SUPPORTED BY SUBSCRIPTIONS, DONATIONS, AND ENTRANCE FEES.

WITHIN the limits of this volume there is not space to describe all the Museums which fall under this head.   With one or two notable exceptions the record is one of noble and worthy aims cramped and hindered on all sides by scarcity of funds. Some of the collections are admirable, and of a thoroughly comprehensive nature.   It is a great pity that of these exhibits many of them so interesting should be reserved for the inspection and pleasure of a limited few.   Take the example of the Liverpool Royal Institution.   Here was one of the most magnificent collections in the entire country, yet it fell into almost entire disuse.   The old generation appreciated it, but the new generation, if one may judge by the result, were not interested in it, and it was allowed to go. Fortunately the collection has not gone far away from its original home. There is, again, a paucity of published reports of the general Museums. A large number have replied to the request for copies of reports, &c., with the statement, "no funds to publish reports," or "no report yet issued." The following are selected on account of their being fairly representative of the whole of the general Museums. The statistics in the Appendix give particulars of others where they have been obtainable, but in some cases there has been a difficulty in eliciting replies. What an excellent nucleus some of these Museums would form for a transfer into rate-supported institutions! The process is exceedingly simple, and would be a good incentive for the adoption of the Acts. It would give to many of these Museums a new lease of life and usefulness.

BATH.

Bath has not yet adopted the Act, although it has made several attempts to do so. In its Royal Literary and Scientific Institution, Bath has an institution sixty-two years old, and yet after an experience so lengthened, the Committee in their last report announce that in one particular there is always a struggle—that of finance. The confession is evidently not a palatable one to them. They have managed to keep out of debt simply by starving every department, and yet they say that "the diminution of subscribers has been caused by deaths and removals without a sufficient reinforcement. It might have been hoped that the advantages of the institution would have brought a constant accession of new members. The excellent Reading Room, the constantly increasing Library, the well-chosen modern books in circulation, and the facilities for scientific culture in the Museum are surely inducements not surpassed in many provincial cities. It would be supposed that with many residents there would be a wish that such efforts for aiding intellectual life should be well supported." It is the old, old story with regard to subscription Museums. Their day is over. The cliques and the coteries for which they have existed for so many years will not support them, and the larger public who would appreciate them cannot afford the subscription. This institute at Bath is an excellent nucleus, and the present subscribers would confer a lasting benefit upon their city by handing it over if the city adopts the Public Libraries Acts. They would not, by so doing, close it to themselves, but would give to it a larger and newer life. The admission fees for the year were less than £7, the donations to the Museum £1, and the "contributions in boxes" £2 4s. 2d. Among the receipts is an item of £21, "grant from the Corporation." Is this legal? Can a Town Council vote away citizens' money to a proprietary institution such as this? If so, every church and chapel may come upon them with equal claims. The grounds upon which this £21 were granted should be inquired into. The Queen is a patroness, the Earl of Cork is a vice-patron, the president is Viscount Portman, and the vice-presidents and Committee include many high sounding names.

BRISTOL.

The Bristol Library Society, of which the Museum now forms part, was founded in 1772. The double title which it now bears of Museum and Library originated from the fact that the present Association was formed in 1867, by the amalgamation of two independent Societies, the Bristol Institution for the Advancement of Science, Literature, and the Fine Arts, and the Bristol Library Society.

The terms of subscription are as follows :—

	One Year. £ s. d.	6 Mths. £ s. d.	3 Mths. £ s. d.
SHAREHOLDERS.			
Class 1—Subscription to the whole Institution	2 12 6		
NON-SHAREHOLDERS.			
Class 2—Subscription to the whole Institution	3 3 0	1 15 0	1 0 0
SHAREHOLDERS AND NON-SHAREHOLDERS.			
Class 3—Subscription to Library and News Room...	2 12 6	1 10 0	0 17 6
,, 4 - ,, Library and Museum	2 2 0	1 5 0	0 15 0
,, 5— ,, Museum and News Room	2 2 0	1 5 0	0 15 0
,, 6— ,, Library	1 11 6	1 0 0	0 12 6
,, 6a— ,, To read in Library but not take out books	0 10 6		
,, 7— ,, Museum	1 1 0	0 12 6	0 7 6
., 8— ,, "Member of the Family" of Subscribers to Library or Museum ...	0 2 6		
,, 9 - ,, News Room ...	1 1 0	0 12 6	0 7 6

It will be seen from this that Bristol affords an example of what can be done by a high class and select subscription Museum and Library. As the annual meeting was held on February 16th, 1888, the latest statistics of its work are accessible. The Council acknowledge that, in presenting to the subscribing shareholders the seventeenth annual report, they have not a very eventful history to recount. Although the Library and Museum and News Room have been fairly maintained, various much-needed repairs and embellishments of the Association's building have had, through straitened means, to be postponed. They can, however, this year report a slight improvement in their financial condition, owing to a reduction of the expenditure.

The income received in the year 1887 amounted to £969 18s. 7d., and it fell short of the income of 1886 by the sum of £45 13s. But the expenditure was less in 1887 than in 1886 by £110 1s. 8d., and the income of 1887 proved a little more than sufficient to meet the expenditure. Hence the debt to the bank, which at the end of 1886 stood at £1,093 13s. 3d., was slightly reduced at the end of 1887, when it stood at £1,073 1s. 8d. The subscriptions were less by £109 16s. 8d. than in 1886, but this is the only important decrease, while an increase took place in the amounts respectively received for admissions to the Museum and for the use of the Lecture Room, in one case of £18 1s. 10d., and in the other of £41 15s. The average number of visitors appears to be about 240 per week—a small number for a city of considerably over 200,000 people.

Looking more particularly at the work of the Museum, it appears that this department has received much attention, and has undergone considerable improvement. The Council, owing to the necessity they felt for retrenchment, had decided to deprive the Museum of the advantage of a paid Curator, but they agreed, at Mr. Wilson's request, to allow him for the present still to occupy the post, and he has accordingly continued his valuable but ill-requited services. During the summer the large glass case in the lower Museum, for the past two years occupied by the loan collection of Japanese china and bronzes belonging to Mr. J. E. Coates, having, by his resumption of them, become vacant, the Curator has provisionally arranged in it the collection of curious and interesting antiquities lately presented to the Association by the Egypt Exploration Fund. The Trustees of the British Museum some time ago announced their readiness to supply certain provincial Museums with an assortment of their duplicate zoological and mineralogical specimens, and the Curator on two occasions proceeded to London for the purpose of making a selection from the specimens so offered.   The collection has in consequence been enriched by a number of objects, comprising fifteen skins of mammals, 115 stuffed birds or skins suitable for stuffing, seventy-seven reptiles and amphibia, twenty-four fishes, seventeen crustaceans, fourteen corals, and 434 coleoptera; as well as some shells, 150 specimens of minerals, and a number of miscellaneous objects.   Over sixty of the bird skins have since been stuffed by the Museum assistant; and these and others of the above have been mounted, named, and catalogued.   About 100 of the Indian shells recently presented by Mr. A. Newnham, of Clifton, have been incorporated in the conchological collection. Various interesting donations have also been received from other Bristolians.

With a diminishing exchequer, and the Curator giving his services because the funds will not permit of his being paid, may it not be very respectfully suggested that the time has come when the Bristol Museum and Library should form a link in the chain of admirable work which is being done by the Bristol Free Public Libraries, established under the Acts?   No other place could be named which better presents side by side an example of what can be done by a citizens' institution, as free as the highways, and a select institution existing upon subscriptions.   Bristol has such a worthy past and a vigorous present in its Library work, that all friends of the capital of the West of England will be delighted to see the work extended.

The guide to the Museum is a handy little book, but to the ordinary visitor not very clear.   To take, for instance, a sentence at random, on page 47 the reader of the guide is informed that "the Lamellibranchiata, the next great group of the Mollusca, includes those numerous animals ordinarily termed 'bivalves,' from the possession of two more or less flattened shells, between which the living animal is contained. The Lamellibranchs are divided into two sections : in the first, the Siphonida, the mantle is furnished with two apertures, the one for the admission, the other for the expulsion of water."

CHESTER.

The Grosvenor Museum in Chester is housed in a very handsome building, as will be gathered from the sketch on next page.

This Museum was erected to meet the requirements of the Chester Archæological and Historical Society, the Chester Society of Natural Science, and the Schools of Science and Art, the work of which societies and schools had hitherto been carried on under serious disadvantages on account of inadequate accommodation. After much thought and deliberation the present site was chosen. The Duke of Westminster presented the Committee with such portions of the ground as belonged to him, the remainder being purchased from the county and others to whom the respective areas belonged.

The cost of the Museum, when suitably furnished and made complete, will be about £11,000.

The exhibitive portions of the building, including the Museums of the Archæological and Natural Science Societies and the Art Gallery, are open to the public, from ten a.m. daily, Sundays excepted. Admission sixpence each person. On Mondays the building is open to the public free of charge. Free admission to the building is granted to students, subscribers to the schools, and members of either of the societies.

THE GROSVENOR MUSEUM, CHESTER.

The management of the institution is entrusted to a Committee elected annually from the societies and schools before named, and meetings of the Management Committee are held monthly.

The leading objects of the Society are—(1) The preservation in a permanent Museum of the Remains of Antiquity and other objects of interest in the City and

County of Chester and North Wales. (2) The collection and publication of Archæological and Historic information. The Society consists of Life, Ordinary, and Honorary Members.

By the trust deed the Committee of the Chester Society of Natural Science are empowered to administer the fund in the manner they deem most desirable for the encouragement of scientific pursuits in the Society's district. This they do by the offer of prizes and by the award, annually or otherwise, of a bronze medal to some resident who has "materially promoted some branch or department of Natural Science."

The meetings of the following societies take place under this roof:—The Grosvenor Museum Club, Archæological Society, Chester Society of Natural Science, School of Science, School of Art, Chester Art Club; and lectures are given in connection with the University Extension Scheme.

There was a Grand Fête, at Eaton Hall, Chester, on Whit Monday, May 21st, 1888, in aid of the fund for the extinction of the debt on the Museum.

CHICHESTER.

The Museum is open from eleven a.m. to four p.m., and is free to members. To non-members the charge is threepence each. During the past year it has been visited by 732 persons, seventy-four of whom were members. In addition to this number, nearly 1,000 availed themselves of the opportunity of a free inspection when that privilege was granted, the occasion being an Industrial and Loan Exhibition. A clergyman has looked carefully through the entomological specimens of butterflies and moths in eighteen cases, and, after arranging them, he has supplied what was wanting as far as he has been able to do so from the duplicates in his own collection. He suggests that, as

I

there are still many vacancies, it might afford both pleasing and instructive occupation to younger members of the Society to endeavour to secure such specimens as are yet wanting. This should be a good incentive to some local Natural Science Association. The institution is supported by subscriptions and donations. Here is another excellent example of a capital work which would be trebled and quadrupled were it a rate-supported institution.

The Museum is a plain but substantial building, as will be seen from the cut below.

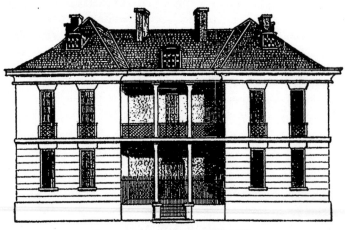

THE CHICHESTER MUSEUM.

DORCHESTER.

The Dorset County Museum and Library is a useful little institution of its kind. From the report for 1887 the Council have to lament, as they did in the report for the previous year, that want of funds has again caused want of progress. This is the complaint which might be placed in prominent letters outside nineteen out of every twenty Museums dependent, as this is, on subscriptions and entrance fees. The building is freehold, subject to a ground-rent of £6, the total annual expenses amounting to about £200, and last year there was a balance in hand of £23, but as the Curator's salary stands at £50, and no item appears for new specimens, the grounds for the lament of the Council are patent. Local specimens naturally occupy the chief place in the Museum. Of the eight bays in the room five are given up to Dorset specimens. These specimens comprise fossils, Dorset building stones, birds, Dorset shells, antiquities, and loan collections from two local gentlemen—Mr. Cunnington and Mr. Hogg.

KESWICK.

This town has a very useful Museum founded in 1873, in connection with the Literary and Scientific Society. The model of the English Lake district over twelve feet by nine feet is admirable and may well claim to be superior to the Ordnance models. It was the work of nearly seventeen years and cost the Museum £160. The cases of birds and birds' eggs are very interesting, and the insects are, for a small Museum, very comprehensive and contain specimens not found in some of the larger Museums. The plants and minerals are even more complete. This applies especially to the specimens of local minerals and of Cumberland iron ores, and ores from the lead and copper mines. The specimens illustrating rocks and minerals of the district used in the manufacture of jewellery, such as Shap and Skiddaw granite, quartz, felsite, jasper, calamine, garnet, and numerous others, possess considerable scientific as well as commercial interest. Among the miscellaneous exhibits are a set of musical stones, two and a-half octaves, from Skiddaw, the clogs worn by the poet Southey and a specimen of Keswick house plastering during the fifteenth or sixteenth century.

KING'S LYNN.

It is proposed to establish a new Museum in this town. A deputation of some of the leading inhabitants, headed by Mr. Beloe, the archæologist, waited upon the Town Council on January 9th, 1888, to induce them to lend a sum of money and give a site towards the building of a new Museum from plans prepared by Mr. W. Adams, architect, King's Lynn. Some opposition was shown against lending any money for the purpose, but it was ultimately agreed to give the site. The old Museum, in the Athenæum building, has had gifts to it amounting in the aggregate to from £4,000 to £5,000. The special feature is a large Ornithological collection presented by Mr. J. H. Gurney, in 1849, and known as the Gurney Collection. Mr. Gurney was one of the most enthusiastic ornithologists in the country. He went here, there, and everywhere in search of new specimens, travelling largely abroad.

The rental of the present rooms is £60 per annum, raised in 1879 from £30 to the present rental of £60, hence there is much difficulty in keeping up the institution in a satisfactory manner. The Committee are endeavouring to obtain from the Corporation a public building, for which an interest rent of 4 per cent. on outlay is offered. Their income for managing the Museum has been, during the last few years, about £90—a sum totally inadequate for its requirements. A building for which they have been negotiating with the Corporation would entail a payment of about £40 or £45 per annum as rent, which would be a great improvement upon present circumstances. There is no paid Curator.

LEWES.

The great feature is the building in which it is contained, which is a picturesque Norman Castle. From the top of the tower of the remaining keep (there were formerly two keeps) an extensive and beautiful view is obtained. In fine weather, numbers go to see the Castle and the view, and to inspect, as a secondary matter, the curios and tapestry, which, apart from the building, are of a comparatively unattractive character, although comprising some objects of considerable value, as illustrating local history. The Sussex Archæological Society hires the Castle, and uses part of it as a Library, Reading Room, Committee Room, &c., the members being admitted to the Castle free. The remains of the great Priory of St. Pancras, the cists containing the bones of the founders of the Priory and builders of the Castle, combine to make Lewes a place of antiquarian interest. Some efforts are now being made to improve both Museum and Library, but much remains to be done before either can claim a very prominent place.

LUDLOW.

The Ludlow Natural History Society has a small Museum consisting of one room sixty feet by thirty feet, with wall-cases on three sides containing a fine collection of British birds, &c. The chief feature of the Museum is the collection of Silurian fossils, which are purely local.

Among other items in the report it is noticed that steady progress continues to be made in filling up the various branches of the natural history and other collections. The Committee record a growing interest in natural history pursuits in some of the younger members of the community, who have contributed many interesting specimens of fossils, shells, seeds, &c., to the Museum. Among recent gifts to the Society is a quaint wooden money box, formerly belonging to the ancient Company of Stitchmen, which was incorporated in the town of Ludlow, in the sixth year of the reign of Queen Elizabeth. The box, together with the deed of incorporation, and the books and papers of the Company, have been presented to the Society. Several interesting coins have been added to the collection. A curious stone drinking cup found in a gravel pit at Wistanstow, and the top stone of a quern, or hand mill for grinding corn, found at the foot of the Long Mynd, near Wentnor, have been lent to the Museum.

NEWCASTLE-UPON-TYNE.

This is a very handsome building, as will be seen from the sketch on another page. The project of erecting a new building for the large collections of the Natural History Society of Northumberland, Durham, and Newcastle-upon-Tyne, originated with Mr. John Hancock, and has been carried out under his direction. The Society is also indebted to him for the splendid collection of British and other birds formed by himself, and presented by him to the Museum. The Society has received, from time to time, various important gifts which render its collections in other branches of natural history exceedingly complete. The Geological Department is remarkably rich in the fossils of the coal-measures, and of the adjacent formations, and it is especially distinguished by an unique collection of coal-measure fishes and amphibia, worked out of the black shale of the Low Main seam of the district.

The Society has also been presented with a valuable collection of original drawings by Thomas Bewick, the celebrated wood engraver, who was a native of the district; also, of original portraits of this artist, and a fine series of early impressions from his blocks. These Bewick relics are arranged in the Gallery of the first room. The new building has cost about £42,000. Of this sum about £37,000 has been raised by public subscription, the greater part of which has been contributed by the personal friends of Mr. Hancock. Important and unique collections of minerals and fossils from the coal-measures and other formations have been contributed by Lord Armstrong, C.B., Lady Armstrong, Mr. Norman Cookson, and the Committee of the Mining Institute. Mr. James Kirby presented an extensive collection of fossils from the magnesian-limestone of the district, and of fossils from the carboniferous rocks of Fife. Fine collections of fossils have also been given to the Society from the secondary and tertiary formations.

The list of subscribers to the new building begins with £10,000 from Lord Armstrong, £2,500 from Lady Armstrong, the late Colonel John Joicey, M.P., £12,000, the late W. C. Hewitson £3,000, and a number of other splendid gifts of money. Hardly any other Museum in the provinces has been financially so widely supported as has this. The list of the amounts is unique in its representative character. There are nearly 200 contributors to the building fund, in amounts ranging from a guinea to £12,000. The Museum is situated at Barras Bridge, about a mile from the Central Station. The Society depends for support on the annual subscriptions of members, the donations of friends, and a small admission fee from non-members. The annual subscription for members is one guinea, which includes free admission to their families and a copy of the transactions. Non-members are charged threepence, and children one penny each. The Museum is open in summer from eleven to six o'clock; on Mondays and Saturdays till eight o'clock; and from eleven o'clock till dusk in the winter. The Society was founded in 1829, and has for its object

NATURAL HISTORY MUSEUM, NEWCASTLE-UPON-TYNE.

the promotion of the study of Natural History in all its branches; the formation of a Museum of Natural History, and the publication of transactions in connection with the Tyneside Naturalists' Field Club, which have special reference to the fauna, flora, and geology of these counties.

The general guide, published at twopence, is a useful book.   Other publications sold in the Museum are : Guide to the Hancock Bird Room, twopence ; Catalogue of Coleoptera, by James Hardy and T. J. Bold, five shillings ; Catalogue of Mollusca, by Joshua Alder, two shillings and sixpence ; Catalogue of Permian Fossils, by R. Howse, two shillings; Synopsis of Geology of Durham and Northumberland, by R. Howse and J. W. Kirkby, one shilling.   These can be obtained through Messrs. Lambert and Co., Newcastle.

The Central or Hancock Bird Room is devoted to the collection of British birds collected, prepared, and presented to the Society by Mr. John Hancock, and number about 1,300 specimens.   These are arranged in the wall-cases, and extend all round the room, and comprise the leading orders of English birds and families, beginning with the raptorial birds.   The Mollusca section is particularly good.

NORWICH.

The Norfolk and Norwich Museum was established in 1824.   The terms of admission and advantages are :—

Subscribers of one guinea a year have free access to the Museum, and the privilege of introducing non-subscribers (whether resident in Norwich or not) to view the Museum during the hours appointed for public inspection.   Subscribers of half-a-guinea a year have free access to the Museum, and the privilege of introducing their families and persons not resident in

Norwich, to view the Museum during the hours appointed for public inspection. Subscribers of five shillings a year have the right of personal admission to the Museum during the hours appointed for public inspection. For shareholders, the holder of one certificate shall have the right of personal admission to the Museum during the hours appointed for public inspection.

There is a most influential Committee and a strong list of honorary Curators. Mr. John Gurney made in the autumn of 1886 a most liberal offer with regard to this Museum. The old castle which has been used as a prison has been handed over to the city, and Mr. Gurney suggested that the prison should be converted into a Museum, and he offered to defray the cost, which would be about £5,000, out of his own pocket. Mr. Gurney, in the letter announcing his offer, said: "I believe the Museum Committee will be favourable to my scheme, and I think it better that the Museum should remain in the hands of the present Society rather than be a purely city business, inasmuch as we should thus retain the interest and support of the county; and I understand also that the city has no funds which could be applied to the maintenance of a Museum, as the whole of the rate legally available for such purposes is required by the Free Library." The matter is still pending between the Corporation and the Castle Museum Committee.

PETERBOROUGH.

The Museum of the Natural History, Scientific, and Archæological Society of this cathedral city does not appear to be in a particularly prosperous state, to judge from the fifteenth annual report issued in the middle of last year. The total number of members at that time was 134, and the receipts and expenditure will be seen from the figures below :—

RECEIPTS.

	£	s.	d.
Member's' Subscription	51	18	6
Profit on Gilchrist Lectures	15	8	4
Donation—Sir H. Dryden	0	10	0
Moneys taken at Museum	1	7	7
Balance due to Treasurer	13	10	11
	£82	**15**	**4**

EXPENDITURE.

General Account—	£	s.	d.
Balance due to Treasurer, last year's account ...	4	2	9
Rent of Old Premises	15	0	0
Rent of New Premises (nine months paid in advance, on behalf of alterations and repairs) ...	33	0	0
Subscription to the Palæontographical Society ...	1	1	0
,, to Midland Union of Natural History Societies	1	8	0
Fire Insurance	1	2	0
Solicitor's Fee and Stamp for Lease	1	5	0
Conversazione Expenses at Museum Opening ...	1	8	0
Printing, Stationery, Stamps, &c.	3	15	8
Museum Account—			
Silver and Bronze Coins	0	14	6
Mounts	2	2	4
Cases, Tables, and Furniture	9	1	8
Fuel £1, Caretaker £3 6s. 8d.	4	6	8
Engravings 4s. 7d., Bird Stuffing 5s. 4d.	0	9	11
Men for moving to Museum, Carriage and Sundries	2	0	4
	£80	**17**	**10**
Books and Binding	1	17	6
	£82	**15**	**4**

This balance-sheet shows how the majority of these small Museums have to struggle for life, and then even at the best have only a bare existence. The Museum is open daily (Sundays excepted) from ten a.m. to four p.m. from October to March, and from ten a.m. to six p.m. during the other months of the year, on Tuesday evenings from eight to half-past nine, also on Monday and Thursday evenings from seven until nine o'clock for members and their friends only. The report states that " several persons have visited the Museum during the seven months it has been open." Several persons out of a population of 27,000 ! Will the Bishop of Peterborough, who is a patron of the society, kindly explain how it is that the Society is so scantily patronised by so large a population ?

SAFFRON WALDEN.

There is a useful and instructive Museum here, and one well and increasingly appreciated by the citizens. The collection of British birds is especially good, and the geology of the British Islands is well represented. A good collection of antiquities is also worthy of note. The gross value of the gifts to the Museum has been £3,000. There is a fine catalogue of the specimens. One good feature of the Museum is that it is free to all desiring to see it on application to the Trustees, or their Curator, Mr. Maynard. This gentleman believes that the success of Museums depends upon the educational use made of their contents, but the difficulty in the way of accomplishing this object arises in a great measure upon the value which those who have the management place upon the element of instruction as opposed to mere gratification of curiosity. Some mutual co-operation is needed to make them more attractive and instructive.

STRATFORD-ON-AVON.

No book of this description would be complete without some particulars of the Shakespeare Museum at Stratford-upon-Avon. The Amalgamated Trusts of Shakespeare's Birthplace, Museum, and New Place are doing, by means of this exhibition, a useful work not only for Shakespeare's birthplace, but for the nation, in thus preserving old documents and other relics associated with our greatest bard.   Mr. Ignatius Donnelly has probably not disturbed the appetite of a single Englishman with his marvellous cryptogram.   The collections comprise books, MSS., documents, and relics illustrative of his life and estates and the history of branches of his family ; editions of his works and books and MSS. devoted to their illustration ; printed books dated in or before the year 1700 in which the name of Shakespeare occurs ; antiquities and relics illustrative of passages in his works ; portraits of Shakespeare, real and supposititious ; works of art illustrative of his life, and scenes and passages in his writings ; portraits of actors and actresses in his plays and persons intimately connected with the history of Shakespearean representations ; books, records, MSS., antiquities and relics illustrative of the history of Stratford-upon-Avon and immediate neighbourhood.   A fee of sixpence is charged to view the birthplace, and another fee of sixpence for admission to the Museum and Library. These fees more than support the Trust. There is a small Museum of relics of New Place—where Shakespeare died—in the Custodian's house adjoining, for which a fee of sixpence is charged. The receipts from that source are small. The number of visitors to the birthplace during the past year exceeded 15,000.

WELSHPOOL.

That for which this book pleads, namely, general Museums becoming in the fullest sense the property of the citizens, has happened with regard to Powys-land Museum and Library.   The extract below from the report of the Council to the twentieth annual meeting of the Powys-land Club, under date of November 6th, 1887, may well be commended to other governing bodies of general Museums. This extract states that the transfer of the Museum by the Trustees to the Corporation of Welshpool " will in no wise interfere with the literary and printing operations of the Powys-land Club, which will be carried on as heretofore. Nor will the interest of the Powys-land Club in the Museum, or the Club's efforts to promote its object, be in any degree abated. But the change will have the effect, whilst retaining all the advantages of the Museum, of placing it on a permanent basis, and, moreover, of adding to it the inestimable advantage of a Free Public Library—the first in this part of Wales."

Will the reader please note the expression " permanent basis"? Such a basis only is possible by the adoption of the Acts, an event which took place last October in Welshpool. The Powys-land Museum and Gallery of Art in connection with the Welshpool Free Public Library is now an accomplished fact. Mr. Morris C. Jones, F.S.A., Gunrog, Welshpool, the honorary Curator,who had much to do with the transfer of the Club as a private property to the Corporation, will, doubtless, give any further information. In a letter to the Town Clerk of Welshpool, Mr. Jones says that " with regard to the Museum, there was nothing of the kind, so far as he knew, in any other part of Wales, and, from his knowledge of the Principality, which extended over thirty years, he did not see much probability of the example being followed in the other counties. The Museum was not only for the benefit of the town, but also for the whole community. They had articles in their Museum which were perfectly unique, rare, and of inestimable value." These curios will have a vastly extended value now that they have become accessible to the inspection of the many instead of the few.

Probably the fact of the Free Library and Museum at Shrewsbury having received a great impetus by becoming a public institution, was an incentive to the proprietors of the club to aid in a similar movement.

This short record of what has been done in Montgomeryshire is purposely placed under General Museums as the latest example at the time of going to press of a private Museum becoming public property.

WINDSOR.

The Museum of the Albert Institute, Windsor, is well deserving of mention. The contents of this Museum are arranged under the following heads, and duly named:—Antiquities: Egyptian, Grecian, Roman, Celtic, Anglo-Roman, and Anglo-Saxon or Old English; Geology: Minerals, Rocks, Sedimentary Deposits, and Fossils ; Natural History, Manufactures and Art, and sundry articles of interest. The handbook to the Museum contains within the limit of twenty pages all that could possibly be said of the various specimens. Some excellent examples of ancient pottery collected during the travels of the late Dr. Burman, an antiquary, some forty years ago, have been presented. Ancient vases were used for various domestic purposes, the form nearly always indicating the use. The beautiful vases imported from Greece were employed by the Romans in religious rites and funeral ceremonies. After the performance of the libations, the vessels were usually thrown away, and left in the corners of the sepulchres : hence the numerous fragments of pottery so often found in the tombs of Italy. Vases were also attached to the walls of the sepulchres, many of which have been broken by the falling in of the tombs. There are several cases containing geological specimens, and the natural history objects are fairly complete.

WISBEACH.

Here the Museum is open every week-day from eleven a.m. to five p.m., from April to September, and from eleven a.m. to four p.m., from October to March inclusive : also on Thursday evenings from seven to nine.   The admission fee is to non-subscribers sixpence each, except on Thursday evenings, when any non-subscribers may be admitted on payment of one penny on the written order of a Director.   Every annual contributor of five shillings is entitled to admission to the Museum when open, for himself and one non-resident friend, with the privilege of consulting the books in the Library.   Every annual contributor of ten shillings is entitled to admission for himself and family and any non-resident friends, with the privilege of consulting the books in the Library.   Every annual contributor of one guinea becomes a Director and, besides the usual privileges, is entitled to take the books to his own home.

There are seventy-three annual subscribers of a guinea, and from various sources the annual income reaches about £200.   The building, the full title of which is the Wisbeach Museum and Literary Institute, is freehold, and there is an annuity from £771 2s. 10d. in the New Three per Cents., and £1,500 invested on mortgage.   The Directors are appealing for additional specimens of natural history and antiquities, especially such as are found in the Isle of Ely and its vicinity. They also solicit loans of valuable pictures and articles of *vertu*, or any objects of special interest, for exhibition in the Museum.

There are others to which attention could have been directed.   The one at Whitby dates back to 1823, and is in connection with the Literary and Philosophical Society.   It has an excellent selection of local geological and zoological specimens.

CHAPTER VII.

SCHOOL AND UNIVERSITY MUSEUMS.

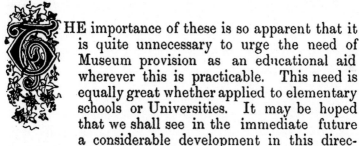HE importance of these is so apparent that it is quite unnecessary to urge the need of Museum provision as an educational aid wherever this is practicable. This need is equally great whether applied to elementary schools or Universities. It may be hoped that we shall see in the immediate future a considerable development in this direction, but this can only come about by a widespread awakening of the Museum spirit. When this happy time arrives every school will be looked upon as an auxiliary to a Museum, and even remote rural districts will not have to ask in vain for loans of cases of objects, with which to illustrate lessons. The Liverpool Museum has already done a most useful work in this respect, and other Museums are endeavouring to carry out a similar plan.

MANCHESTER.

It will be opportune to here call attention to a work which has been commenced in Manchester, and which has, so far, succeeded beyond the highest expectations of the founders and workers. Under the designation of the Manchester Art Museum, which has its home in the Ancoats Hall, situated in a thickly populated district of Cottonopolis, a work is going on of the highest import-

K

ance in the efforts being made to lift up the masses. In
this hall the promoters have a scheme which comprises
three co-ordinated parts, of which they have only been
able to do one with approximate completeness, while
another remains wholly undone. These departments,
as condensed from the statement of the Committee,
may be classed as follows:—

1. The Committee have formed a very comprehensive
collection of works of art of different kinds, and
by providing abundant teaching in the form of
written and oral explanations of the things shown,
by lectures on art and other subjects, by instruction in
drawing and wood-carving, and by giving entertain-
ments of an instructive kind, they seek to make the
Museum attractive and useful to persons of all classes,
but especially to working people, both old and young.

2. They desire to lend to every Elementary School in
Manchester and Salford a small collection of works of
art, consisting partly of historical portraits, pictures of
historical events, landscape, common wild and garden
flowers, common kinds of trees, birds, butterflies, &c.;
partly of a few textile fabrics and wall-papers of good
colour and design, a few good examples of pottery,
and one or two casts of sculpture—the collections to
be replaced by others once every six months.

Owing to want of money, the Committee have only
been able to lend collections to about twenty Elementary Schools ; but they have prepared part of the
material for several hundred school collections.

3. They would, if their funds allowed, offer to every
Elementary School, in which drawing is taught, and
the managers of which permitted the school children
to be taken occasionally to see the contents of the
public Art Galleries and public parks and gardens,
the services of a highly-trained supervisor of drawing
to improve the teaching of drawing in the school,

direct the attention of the children to the merits of the works of art in the school collection, and that of the teachers to the ways in which the pictures could be used in connection with lessons other than drawing lessons.

The Committee have been occupied for many years in developing their scheme, and in obtaining and classifying their possessions. They have now been actively at work for eighteen months in a Museum which has been most carefully arranged for the purpose of interesting the mass of the people, and which has been opened on the days and at the hours when work-people can most easily go to it, and their work has brought them into contact with a large number of persons of all classes and all ages. The experience gained by the Committee during the last eighteen months has strengthened the conviction with which they began, that while most people could by training in childhood be enabled to get in after-life much pleasure from the contents of Art Galleries, and would probably have the quality of their lives and of their work much improved thereby, without such early training not more than one person in a score is likely to get much good from Art Galleries. For it is obvious that if we are to care much for what is to be found in Art Galleries, we must (1) have the power to perceive beauty in form and in colour, and acquire the habit of finding pleasure in using that power ; (2) know a good deal about the subjects represented in pictures—it being certain, for instance, that no one will care very much for pictures of woodland scenery who does not know an oak from a hawthorn, or much for pictures of river scenery who knows no river but the Irwell; (3) know something about the ways in which works of art are made, and about what art can and cannot do ; (4) know something about the history of art. All the available evidence given in dress, choice of furniture, hangings, &c., tends to prove that the majority of the inhabitants of Manchester have no perception of the difference between good and bad colour or form.

The majority of the inhabitants of any large town do not know or care much about the constituent elements of even the most popular branch of art — landscape art. It would probably be an over estimate to say that so many as one in twenty know a Spanish chestnut from a sycamore, or can tell a beechwood at a distance of fifty yards, in summer or winter, from an oakwood. This kind of knowledge, too, it is not possible to induce men and women to acquire ; but, with the help of pictures and occasional visits to parks and gardens, all children can be made to gain it. Finally, most of the inhabitants of Manchester know nothing about the nature of art and of its history or about art processes, and cannot be induced to learn ; but our experience at the Art Museum proves that most children are delighted to learn a good deal about them.

As bearing upon this question one of the headmasters of a Manchester school, who has had great experience, says : "Upon the questions of cultivation of taste, and education in form, in colour, and in beauty, I am inclined to speak as decidedly, though I cannot support my position by actual examples. But nothing is stronger than my conviction that, as surely as the light and warmth of the sun breed the blossom, and perfect the fruit of the orchard, so surely the constant presence among children of what is truly tasteful, of what is correct in form and harmonious in colour, of what has been tenderly and lovingly fashioned in grace and beauty will generate and ripen a pure taste, a genuine refinement." The scheme of the Manchester Art Museum is so unique that all friends of education will watch with the deepest interest its growth.

The Committee is composed of men and women in earnest touch with the educational needs of the day. The Chairman is Mr. George Milner, and the Committee are Miss Jessy Fothergill, Mrs. T. C. Horsfall, Mrs. H. W. Reeves, Miss E. G. Thomson, Messrs. G. F. Armitage, W. E. A. Axon, C. Hardwick, Ward Heys, C. J. Heywood, H. H. Howorth, M.P., A. Hopkinson, M.A., Walter Hughes, B.A., Sir J. C. Lee, Messrs. J. D. Milne, Herbert Philips, C. J. Pooley, C. Rowley, jun., A. Samuelson, M.D., J. Slagg, M.P., Revs. S. A. Steinthal, W. A. O'Conor, B.A., A. G. Symonds, M.A., W. Walker, Owens College.

The Hon. Secretaries are Messrs. R. Newton, 24, York Place, Oxford Road, Manchester, and J. Ernest Phythian, 7, Chapel Walks, Manchester, from whom full particulars of the work can be obtained. The Hon. Treasurer is Mr. T. C. Horsfall, Bollin Tower, Alderley Edge, near Manchester, who has financially and by personal effort done much for the movement. The attempt means something more than the welfare of the immediate district in which Ancoats Hall is situated. It is an experiment in social work which, if successful, will cast its influence upon the entire country. Mr. T. C. Horsfall has written two papers, published in pamphlet form by Messrs. Macmillan and Co., price sixpence, one on *The Study of Beauty*, and the other on *Art in Large Towns*. Professor John Ruskin has written a preface to the papers, and both the preface and papers are well deserving of careful perusal.

How it makes one long to see other towns possess-ing similar popular resorts for the people. A new interest in life has been given to many of the people who are accustomed to frequent Ancoats Hall. In the Museum there are collections of pictures of common English trees, flowers, birds, and other animals, and there are also pictures and photographs of beautiful scenery in the immediate neighbourhood of Manchester, and these give a direct incentive to visit such places for Saturday afternoon outings. There are, further, pictures of architecture of all ages and lands, and of places of great interest in the physical geography of the world, such as Niagara Falls. There are two particularly interesting series of pictures. One of these illustrates the development of the graphic arts from prehistoric times down to the present time, and the other shows the growth of architecture and sculpture in Greece and Italy. Printed explanations accompany these, thus adding a double interest to them. One room is filled with beautiful Eastern designs for carpets, pottery, metal work, &c., and two model artisans' rooms show how pleasant a workman's house can be made at small cost. The Museum is the result of ten years of steady work. The willingness of the Committee to undertake that work has been due to two convictions—the first, that for the inhabitants of crowded towns certain kinds of knowledge of nature and art which cannot be gained in such towns except by the help of art are not mere luxuries, but are amongst the necessaries of healthy life ; and the second, that ordinary Picture Galleries and Museums, while of very great value to those who bring to them knowledge of nature and of art, are not well adapted for giving such knowledge to those who do not already possess it in some degree. It is evidence of its appearing to be well fitted for its purpose that, although it has been open so short a time, deputies from five other towns have already come to study it in the hope of setting on foot a similar system.

Several members of the Committee go to the Museum to explain the pictures, &c. ; a musical entertainment is given every Wednesday night; lectures on various subjects are given every Monday and Thursday night; a free wood-carving class is held twice a week; a free drawing class once; tales are read to children twice a week. Every week brings fresh offers of help in giving music, readings, lectures, and lessons: so that soon may be given some kind of wholesome teaching or recreation every evening. During the longer days physical training is given on ground behind the Museum to a large number of children and young people.

A handbook to the Manchester Art Museum, by Mr. Horsfall, has just been published. There are eighty-two pages of excellent matter for a penny. A copy of it ought to be in the hands of everyone interested in Museum and Art Gallery work. An extra penny must be sent for postage if applications for it are made through the post.

THE NEW MUSEUM, OXFORD.

This is one of the handsomest modern buildings in Oxford, and as a teaching school for natural science is probably unequalled by any other Museum. It had its origin in the movement which took place from 1840 to 1850 to promote a closer and more accurate acquaintance with scientific subjects. Many of the Oxford professors in the various sections of natural science had attained a world-wide eminence, but it was patent to all who had given thought and attention to the subject that much teaching power was lost for want of proper accommodation and specimens. Not that the Colleges were without specimens scattered among them, but the great need for these being properly classified and housed under one roof presented itself with great force to the professors and students. Hence the beautiful, artistic, and well-stocked building which Oxford now possesses. Sir John Acland, the Regius Professor of Medicine,

was one of the prime instigators, and the Universities
are proud of his long connection with Oxford. The
deepest sympathy has been expressed by the students
and professors in the affliction which has cost him the
sight of one eye.

THE NEW MUSEUM, OXFORD.

The style of architecture is that of the thirteenth
century. The frontage is somewhat plain and rather
lacking in ornamentation, as will be seen from the
sketch. The central court is covered in with a roof of
wood and glass resting on iron pillars. This method of
roof lighting gives the best effects, and for this the
chief court is admirably suited. In this large hall are
placed the principal collections, ranged partly on the
ground floor in the centre and partly in the corridors which surround the building. These are arranged
on the principle of a double cloister, one part being
over the other. These cloisters afford space for additions to the specimens and give access to the various
professors' lecture rooms. The largest of these rooms

is marked for its proportions and appointments. The shafts of the cloister as well as those of the windows are of different varieties of stone, illustrating the principal geological formations of the British Islands, ranging from granite up to the most recent formations. Between the arches there are corbels which support statues of the most eminent discoverers and promoters of natural science. These include Aristotle, the first classifier, Bacon, Galileo, Newton, Cuvier, and others. On the corbels, capitals, and bosses have been sculptured a series illustrative of various faunas and floras. The view is from the Guide to Oxford, published by Messrs. Parker and Co.

The most complete sections of the new Museum are the Geological and Mineralogical collections. It is of the Geological section only that at the present time an index guide has been published. This has been compiled by Mr. Joseph Prestwich, M.A., F.R.S., the Professor of Geology. It is an admirable index guide, and to the students must be invaluable.

On the northern side of the chief court there are cabinets of specimens illustrating Osteology and Physiology. The Zoological Department has been considerably added to of late, and the collections of birds and mollusca are fairly complete. The Entomological collection received a most valuable addition from the late Mr. Hope. A new wing has been added recently, containing a number of cases filled with objects from various parts of the world which are sure to interest the general visitor. There are numerous lecture and dissecting rooms.

THE INDIAN INSTITUTE.

This Institute in Oxford, of which Sir Monier Williams, the Sanscrit scholar, is Keeper, is in the Elizabethan style of architecture, with large octagon

tower at the north-west corner containing the staircase. A brass plate in the vestibule records the fact
that " This building, dedicated to Eastern sciences, was
founded for the use of Aryans (Indians and Englishmen)
by excellent and benevolent men desirous of encouraging knowledge. . . . . . By the favour of God
may the learning and literature of India be ever held
in honour; and may the mutual friendship of India
and England constantly increase." To that wish every
right-minded Englishman will say " Amen." There is
an excellent collection of objects and specimens from
India, and of photographs from India, perhaps the
largest to be found in the provinces.

CAMBRIDGE.

Many of the specimens in the Botanical section
of the Herbarium, under the charge of Professor
Babington, have undergone rearrangement and some
changes have been made in classification. The demon-
strators in this section look forward to making this
collection equal, if not superior, to any in Europe. They
will have much to do to accomplish such a purpose.

Professor J. W. Clark refers to the skeleton of an
African elephant which has been secured, and states
that only two other Museums, the British Museum
and the Saffron Walden Museum, contain skeletons
of this particular species.

In another section the whole collection of birds,
stuffed and in skins, consists now of 19,500 specimens,
representing about 5,000 species. The Cambridge
authorities are to be congratulated on this number, for
it is nearly one-half of all the species of birds known
to science.

Of the Anatomical section it will be scarcely necessary
to say anything. The additions to this Museum during
the year 1887 have been very numerous.

The Woodwardian Museum of Geology is one of the finest and most complete of all the Museums in connection with Cambridge University. The Mineralogical Museum has been exchanging specimens with Harvard University Museum.

The principal specimens added to the collection during the year were some of microlite, hornblende, zircon, chalybite, mispickel, anglesite, tourmaline, pyroxene, danburite, sapphire, idocrase, des-Cloizite, wernerite, mica, rutile, apatite, apophyllite, onofrite cookeite, thomsenolite, cryolite, delessite, willemite, fowlerite, ulexite, wavellite, and some pseudomorphs and fragments of meteorites.

MUSEUM AT RUGBY SCHOOL.

Art teaching has at this public school received considerable attention during recent years. Mr. T. M. Lindsay, the Art teacher at Rugby School, says: "In dealing with the subject of art education of boys in the great public schools, there are certain conditions to be noted which do not exist elsewhere. As a rule, we cannot expect boys to take up the study of art in the way they are obliged to pursue their regular school course. Usually the study is voluntary—at Rugby it is entirely so—and the problem to be solved is how to make the education as complete as practicable, considering that boys are at school, as well as the portion of time which can be devoted to it. Drawbacks are numerous; 'form' work naturally engages the chief time and attention; cricket, and the hundred tasks, attractions, and excitements of public school life—not to mention indolence—cause art to be heavily handicapped."

Notwithstanding these drawbacks the art classes have been well attended. The students begin at once to draw from the model, and not from flat copies. The

Art Museum in connection with the school is full of a choice collection of art objects, and thus here a new interest has been created which was not thought of

EXTERIOR OF THE RUGBY ART MUSEUM.

when "Tom Brown" played football and occasionally used his fists in the quadrangle.

There is an aptness and a readiness on the part of boys and girls in middle-class schools for such instruction, and teachers would not only bestow by such lessons a larger expansion of mind, but would quicken faculties which in many cases would give a greater inceptiveness for other subjects.

In adult education there is greater difficulty in suggesting means by which more attention could be given to art subjects. The presence of art as an element in life has only become universally recognised during recent years, but there is much need for definiteness and thoroughness in the information which people have on these subjects.

This Art Museum is a brick structure with light stone dressings, an engraving of the façade of which is given. It stands within its own grounds, not far from the larger building known as the Great School. The lower storey contains the Temple Library, and the Art Museum, a sketch of the interior of which is also given, occupies the upper floor. Fortunately the office of Curator of the Art Museum is united with that of Drawing-master, so that he can utilise the collection for the benefit of his classes. Though the Art Museum was only built in 1879 its treasures of art have gone on increasing by gifts and purchases, so that it is now a very efficient collection, comprising statues in plaster and marble, bronzes, pottery, pictures, great numbers of photographs of works of ancient and Renaissance Art, autotypes, coins, engravings, etchings, &c.

Some curious and interesting examples of the way in which some of the boys utilise their ability to draw have come to the knowledge of the teacher. There is a Natural History Society, in which boys have not only read papers, but have illustrated them by diagrams of their own production : among the papers so illustrated have been some of an archæological type.

In another direction this talent has been employed to make drawings for the illustration of a monthly publication issued at the school.

INTERIOR OF THE RUGBY ART MUSEUM.

The cost of the building was £9,000, and the art treasures already in the Museum amount to considerably over £6,000, and every year adds to the wealth of the collection.

HARROW.

Harrow School has long been in possession of a valuable collection of antiquities presented by Sir John Gardner Wilkinson, partly during his lifetime and partly by bequest on his death.   These antiquities consisted of Egyptian antiquities, classical antiquities, coins and medals, and fossils and stones from Derbyshire.   When some years back a visit was paid to the collection, specially with a view to the inspection of the Greek vases, the objects of research were found covered with dust and dirt, muddled up with fossils and odds and ends of every description, in an out-of-the-way place. A boy must, indeed, have had a keen archæological "flaire" to discover their merit.   But as regards the classical antiquities, Mr. Cecil Torr has changed all that.   With no small difficulty he got permission to attack the collection, mount, set up, and arrange the specimens, and have them transferred to the Museum of the School, where they are now duly exhibited.   The catalogue of the Egyptian antiquities is by Mr. Budge, of the British Museum : that of the classical antiquities by Mr. Torr himself.   Mr. Torr's catalogue is, of course, mainly in use by visitors to the Harrow Museum.   It should be widely known that the book is much more than a catalogue.   To begin with, there is a pertinent preface, dealing with that now momentous question, the claims of archæology in classical education.   In the plainest fashion he gives a boy or a beginner of any sort directions how to set about classical archæology, what books to read, and what to expect to get out of them.   Further, each department of antiquities is preceded by a few introductory remarks, just enough to set the student looking aright ; so that in vases, bronzes, terra-cottas, gems, there is, at least, a solid foundation laid, and in the matter, *e.g.*, of Etruscan moulded vases and Samian red ware, just the information is given which the student often looks for in vain.

ABERYSTWYTH.

A short handbook of the Museum of the University College of Wales, Aberystwyth, consists of sixteen pages, small octavo, and is published at threepence. The Museum was founded to supply two wants. Firstly, to furnish general elementary collections for the educational purposes of the College, and secondly, to present to the visitor as good a collection of local objects of interest as possible. The Museum was established in 1877. The Anatomical section appears to us to be very poor, judging from the handbook already referred to. The fossils and pottery are also not very special.

There is a magnificent new Museum completed and opened very recently in connection with the Victoria University (Owens College), Manchester.

There is a small Museum at Haileybury College, Hertford, used solely for teaching purposes, but it has no formal organisation.

CHAPTER VIII.

PRIVATE MUSEUMS.

N order to do full justice to this branch of the subject, an entire book would be necessary. There is not a county in the country which has not within it mansions or houses containing a profusion of art treasures and curios. It is not a little to the credit of the owners of these residences that they permit their treasures to be seen by the public when the family is away, or on two or three days weekly. Some counties are particularly rich in this respect, and it is to be hoped that someone will take in hand a book treating on the private Museums scattered throughout the country. The art treasures of the Dukeries would alone provide material for a most interesting book. Chatsworth is full of gems. Belvoir Castle, near Grantham, the seat of the Duke of Rutland, is the home of much art beauty. The ducal mansions of Trentham, Blenheim, and Eaton Hall are perfect storehouses of art, and Hatfield House, Hawarden, and other houses which could be named, are scarcely less so. Sussex is peculiarly rich as a county in historical residences full of relics of the past, and treasures from all parts of the world. Normanhurst, the residence of Lord Brassey, and Hurstmontceux, the home of the genial Hares, afford attractions for visitors to Hastings. No watering-place round the coast, or inland, but has

L

such old Museums full of curios and pictures open for a day's trip to health-seekers. Cheshire is another county especially rich in these home treasures. Lyme Hall, the seat of the Leghs; Bramhall Hall, Marple Hall, and numerous other mansions. Devonshire has an even greater number, and in Hertfordshire there are several. Were the whole number given it would total up to more than all the public and subscription Museums added together.

The two or three private Museums mentioned in this chapter, although coming under that head, are private Museums of a special character. The first place is given by right of merit to the Ruskin Museum at Walkley, Sheffield. Many of the people in that town who took an interest in the subject expressed themselves as disappointed that the founder of the St. George's Guild should have carried out his intention to establish it in what they described as a place outside the world. As some of our newspapers continue to refer to the Museum as if it was most inaccessible, it will not be irrelevant to give the founder's reasons for placing it where he did.

In *Fors Clavigera*, Vol. V., there is an account of what took place. On Mr. Ruskin stating that the first Museum of the St. George's Company was to be located at Sheffield, he received a letter from a Sheffield gentleman offering him space in the public Museum. Mr. Ruskin replied in what he meant to be a private letter. The letter was, however, read at a public dinner, and comment was made upon it. Mr. Ruskin was naturally hurt at the Sheffield Press characterising his efforts as "setting up an opposition Museum at Walkley," and went on to say, "I am glad to find the Sheffield branch of English journalism reprobating, in one instance at least, the—I had imagined now by all acclamation, divine—principle of

competition. But surely the very retirement to the
solitude of Walkley might have vindicated St. George's
first quiet effort in his own work from this unexpected
accusation—especially since, in so far as I can assert or
understand the objects of either of the supposedly
antagonistic showmen, neither the Sheffield Museum
nor St. George intend taking shillings at the doors."
And so " the Museum has been sent there, not by me, but
by the second Fors (Lochesis), on the top of a high and
steep hill,—with only my most admiring concurrence
in her apparent intention that the approach to it may
be at once symbolically instructive, and practically
sanitary."

On that hill the Museum stands, and plans have
been prepared by Professor Ruskin and Mr. Robson,
architect, of London, for the erection of a suitable
building for the Museum, and funds are now being collected for that object. The building is to be vested in
Trustees, to be used for the purposes of the St. George's
Museum exclusively, and its management is to be in
the hands of the St. George's Guild, by whom the cost
of such management is to be defrayed. All objects
placed in the Museum are to become, with certain
restrictions, irremovable.

Mr. Howard Swan, son of the Curator, has prepared a
preliminary catalogue. The preface states that it " contains a complete list of the objects, with the exception of
the library of books, the coins and seals, the paintings and
engravings of birds, fishes, insects, &c. (of which there
is a vast number awaiting mounting and arrangement),
and the minerals and precious stones. It cannot
be too clearly stated that visitors cannot possibly
see all with understanding on one visit. Weeks might
easily be spent in going through the objects carefully
with their descriptions. Each object has been selected
by Mr. Ruskin specially for its teaching, and the student

will find in this Museum specimens of what Mr. Ruskin considers the finest work in art hitherto done, with reasons explanatory of why they are the best—an example and a teaching to guide him in his future work. It is hoped that the publication of this catalogue will give the public a more clear idea of what Mr. Ruskin's aims have been in establishing the St. George's Museum for their use."

The Museum contains originals and copies of the old masters, casts of sculpture, and specimens of modern art, " in illustration of the finest art hitherto produced, selected from the countries and times of their highest development—in painting, drawing, engraving, illumination, architecture, sculpture, or other arts ; and arranged so as to show the influence of the character of the workman upon the arts, and to indicate the circumstances and surroundings which produce the finest art, and thus the finest men and women." It also contains a very valuable collection of minerals and precious stones, arranged to show the various orderly and beautiful shapes of natural formation : works on natural history (including the Eyton Ornithological Collection) for illustration of the appearance, life, habits, characteristics, instincts of animals, birds, fishes, and insects ; and in botany,—of the development, surroundings, habits, uses and beauties of flowers and plants ; and also a Library of the best standard literature, with ancient manuscripts ; a collection of Greek and English coins, &c. The Museum is open free on all days except Thursdays. The classification of birds, flowers, and minerals is special—aiming to interest students in their *life* and beauty, not in their anatomy and death in birds and flowers ; and their crystallisation in minerals.

It is almost impossible within the narrow limits of a section of a chapter to do justice either to Mr. Ruskin's aims or to what is really to be seen in the Museum. Those who go to his works and his life in a merely superficial way see naught but a cultured dreamer, but those who have not been content with merely skimming the surface have, years ago, discovered a man whose life is one long living example of his own teaching : who has helped them to see beauty everywhere, and who has given them a new inner life, with higher aims and more noble purposes than they before had. He believes that when those in other towns see how easily such a thing can be done they will have their Museums of the same kind as the one at Walkley, as being institutions no less useful to them than their churches, gasometers, or circulating libraries.

SURREY HOUSE MUSEUM.

Among the private Museums of the country there is scarcely one more complete and better arranged than that of Mr. F. J. Horniman at Forest Hill, London, S.E.

The house and grounds are situated on a beautiful hill within sight of the Crystal Palace. So large has the collection grown that the owner was gradually cornered out of his house, and has built a dwelling in another part of the grounds. The original mansion is devoted to the Museum, and every corner of it is packed with specimens from every quarter of the globe. The Museum is not open to the public, but Mr. Horniman permits Natural Science classes, or parties interested in the works of nature and art, to go over it under the charge of the Curator, Mr. C. D. Watkins. It is, however, necessary to arrange beforehand in order that a convenient time may be appointed for the visit. At Easter or Whitsuntide, Mr. Horniman has thrown open his Museum for ten hours during the day, and schools, societies, clubs, and other organisations have in large numbers availed themselves of the opportunity to see so excellent a collection. In 1888, on Whit Monday and Tuesday 5,207 passed through the Museum. The visitors are received in a hall lined with splendid specimens of Japanese work, and the signing of the visitors' book, in which are some celebrated names, occupies some little time. In this reception room are shown albums of autograph letters, carved ivories, ancient and modern coins, and specimens of fine Sèvres china. If the company is numerous they are divided into two or three parties, each taking a different route.

The second section contains ancient manuscripts, illuminated parchments and books, a Biblical library, with a collection of ancient and curious Bibles. Here is the Bible used by Martin Luther, a New Testament which belonged to Ridley the martyr, and one translated and used by Tyndall. In an adjoining room are antiquities from Egypt, Greece, Cyprus, Troy, and Rome; urns containing the calcined bones of some ancient Greeks; an assemblage of the idols of all nations; specimens of the Egyptian mode of embalming, two interesting specimens in this section being a young lady's right hand and the hand of an Egyptian task-master, besides embalmed pet crocodiles.

In what may be termed Section IV. are numerous specimens of Japanese curios, needlework, bronzes, china, &c., and then begins the Museum proper. At the entrance stand men armed *cap-à-pie*, and in the corridor there is a fine collection of ancient and modern armour.

This leads on to the most interesting section of the Museum, at least to many, for in this and the adjoining room are numerous cases of corals, stuffed humming and other birds, and a splendid collection of shells. Mr. Horniman has probably the finest private collection of insects not only in this but in any country. In 500 drawers there are arranged, classified, and labelled considerably over 12,000 specimens of Coleoptera and Lepidoptera. The beautiful Goliath beetles in their varied shades of green, the tiger moths, the West African hawk moth, and the Indian Great Atlas moth, which extends eleven inches across the wings, are specimens over which the entomologist would .linger. Some of these specimens have been named by the various societies after Mr. Horniman, in virtue of their rarity and first capture by the founder of Surrey House Museum and his daughter. It is especially rich in tropical, African, and South American specimens, and the collection of British butterflies, moths, and beetles is as comprehensive as time and money have made it possible to get together.

Other rooms contain a great variety of artistic and interesting objects, collected from all parts of the world. Skin coats of the Esquimaux and the war dress of the Red Indians are here side by side, and in the same room there is a very complete entomological reference library, including books of travel. A lower room is devoted exclusively to ancient and modern china, Old English porcelain, Venetian and other glass. One large casket contains a magnificent Viennese tea service of eight pieces, each hand-painted with mythological subjects ; that of the tray representing "Psyche bringing gifts to her sisters" —most delicately treated by a master artist. A Sèvres service, designed for two only, contains the portrait of Louis XVI. and family ; while two other services of great value belonged originally to Napoleon III. and the Royal Family of France respectively. In the Elizabethan Chamber is the bed hard as a rock, a collection of Old English chairs of the period in oak, chests and drawers, and many other interesting objects.

HUDDERSFIELD.

The Natural History Museum, at Beaumont Park, of which Mr. S. L. Mosley is the proprietor, was " established to promote a love of nature and decrease of intemperance; every assistance will be given to students, who are permitted to see the private collections any Wednesday evening during the winter, or on Sunday mornings during the summer. The public collections consist of a rich collection of British birds, educational collections of insects as supplied to the Royal Gardens, Kew, Museums, and Schools, collections of insects injurious to farm and garden plants, with methods of prevention."

It has been a struggle with Mr. Mosley to keep going his little Museum, and the Huddersfield people, who have twice refused to adopt the Public Libraries Acts, will yet, it is hoped, adopt the Acts, and accept as a nucleus of their work this little Museum which has been offered to the town.

It is proposed to institute a Museum of Mineralogy at Redruth in connection with the Mining Association and Institute of Cornwall. The Museum is to bear the name of the late Mr. Robert Hunt, F.R.S., in recognition of his services to mineralogy.

Mr. L. F. Bingham has adopted a very commendable plan at Bakewell in throwing open to visitors free his Geological Museum. It is open from ten to four p.m. daily. This interesting collection, embracing upwards of 2,250 mounted specimens of fossils, minerals, lavas, zoophites, madrepores, corals, agates, gems, conchs, &c.; immense fossil horns of the red deer (*Cervus Elaphus*, found in the neighbourhood), inlaid tablets, plain and coloured surveys and maps of Derbyshire strata, lists, manuscripts, parchments, &c., having recently received valuable additions, is still open to the public as before; also works treating on its contents and a study thereof, particularly those relating to the county of Derby.

CHAPTER IX.

WHAT PRIVATE MUNIFICENCE HAS DONE FOR MUSEUMS.

PRIVATE munificence has done much for these institutions, but it may be doubted whether it has done as much as might have been reasonably expected. Some Museums and Art Galleries have fared exceedingly well. Gifts or bequests of collections or money have gone out towards them, with a liberality at once commendable and distinctive. Others have, however, been left stranded high and dry on the beach, and no private generosity has come their way. No benevolence can more fully and thoroughly secure the greatest good of the greatest number than gifts or bequests to Museums or Art Galleries. It is a species of charity which is more than twice blessed, it blesses him that gives, and the recipients continue years after the donor's death.

Scattered throughout the country in snug country houses, or in town residences, are collections representing every section of natural science, which have been gathered through years of patient, but loving labour, by some enthusiast. There are, again, crowds of good pictures hanging on walls or placed away in dark closets, which have given pleasure to their owners, but now, perhaps through removal into a smaller house, they are either less well placed or out of sight altogether. For gifts such as these I plead, and would earnestly place before the owners the pressing claims of Museums and the sister institutions. No better use could be made of these treasures than a transference to the nearest Museum of importance. By this means a new and useful life would be given to collections which, in some cases, represent the acquisitions of a lifetime.

If the collection is of an important character the name of the donor could be associated with it, and so handed down to posterity. The Harris gift to Preston, the Nettlefold bequest of pictures, and the Tangye gift of rare pottery to Birmingham, the Mappin Art Gallery at Sheffield, and others of a similar character in various parts of the country, and referred to in these pages, will always have associated with them the name of the donor. Could a perpetuity of pleasure and instruction be secured by any better means?

Hospitals and other excellent institutions for like purposes have received much attention during past years. Should not the sympathy of the wealthy now go out in these other directions? In the majority of cases the rate-supported institutions are the most suitable for such gifts, where they will be best looked after, and most useful.

It may be urged upon colonists, travellers, ships' captains, missionaries, and others who have occasion to spend their days in wanderings in other lands, that specimens of natural history, which lie frequently with such profuseness around them, would be most acceptable to Museums.

There are, of course, gifts and gifts. Museums are not

places where rubbish may be shot. Some most valuable gifts to Museums have been looked upon by the donors as unimportant, and gifts the most trumpery and insignificant have been extolled by the giver.

PRESTON.

This busy Lancashire town bids fair to possess, when completed, the finest Museum in the provinces. Mr. Edmund Harris, who died there ten years ago, left a fortune that was not to be realised in full until this period had expired, which was in May last. The whole sum is £285,300, and the last portion being utilised is £30,000 for the erection of a Victoria Jubilee Technical School; in order to carry on this building in a suitable manner, the Corporation of Preston has presented a site for it of the value of £10,000. The scheme of most importance in connection with the Harris gift is the erection of a Free Library and Museum, on which £100,000 is being expended, as well as another £5,000 for various requirements and the collecting of desirable curiosities and treasures. Here, again, the Corporation has come forward in a generous spirit, and presented a suitable site worth £30,000. The Avenham Institute receives a gift of £40,000 from the Trustees. There is also a " Harris Orphanage " nearly completed, on an estate of twenty-seven acres outside the town, which has been given by the public, and is to be conducted on the Cottage Home system; and in addition to all these benefactions scholarships are to be founded, and the Preston churches are to receive some £10,000 amongst them.

Mr. Harris was the son of a Rector of one of these churches, who held his living for sixty-four years, and at the time of preaching his last sermon had attained the ripe age of ninety-seven. The building operations are

HARRIS MUSEUM AND FREE LIBRARY.

now completed ; but it is not expected that the formal opening will take place until the end of this year or the beginning of 1889.   To this building will be removed the whole of the volumes now composing the Free Library, numbering about 15,000 ; Dr. Shepherd's Reference Library, 8,000 volumes; and 20,000 other volumes will be purchased.   Since the commencement of the building another wealthy Prestonian, the late Mr. R. Newsham, bequeathed to the town his fine collection of oil-paintings, water-colour drawings, and curios, valued at upwards of £30,000, and these will form part of the Picture Gallery in connection with the Free Library and Museum.

The pediment of the Free Library and Museum, Preston, is now practically completed.   It is a work of art which has been most favourably spoken of by the journals specially interested in architecture and the allied arts.   Its design, as indeed the design for the whole building, is the work of Alderman James Hibbert, of Preston.   The carving of the sculpture has been carried out by Mr. E. R. Mullins, of London.

The subject of the design is the " School of Athens ; Age of Pericles "; and represents the Athenian states-man with the most famous of his contemporaries in philosophy, poetry, literature, and art :—

> " The dead, but sceptered sovrans, who still rule
> Our spirits from their urns."

In the centre, Pericles, with his friend and adviser Anaxagoras, confers with Phidias and Ictinus respecting the Odeon and the Parthenon.   On his right, Par-menides, Zeno, and Socrates discuss philosophy ; and Thucydides meditates history.   On his left are Pindar, Æschylus, Sophocles, Euripides ; and Herodotus with his completed books.

The old Museum in this town is situated in Cross Street, and during the past year the number of visitors has been 17,801, or a daily average of fifty-nine, the Museum having been open 301 days. The donations for the year 1887 were as follow :—Mr. John Allsup, brass coins; the Rev. F. J. Dickson, first brass coin of the Roman Emperor Domitian, lately found at Ribchester; Mr. W. H. Heathcote, specimens of freshwater mussel found in the Lune; Mr. Hurry, of Glasgow, fossil fish; Messrs. Irvin and Sellers, beetles from Asia Minor and America; Mr. W. F. Moore, fossil corals; Mr. James Oddie, fossil plants from Australia; Mr. Herbert T. Parke, Whitnell Fold, large limestone striated boulder from near Chorley; Mrs. Perrin, various objects from New Zealand; the Rev. J. Shortt, various remains of fossil trees; Mr. T. M. Shuttleworth, impressions of the seals of the Duchy Palatine and of the County Palatine of Lancaster; Mr. Sutcliffe, stone axe from the Ribble Dock excavations, twenty-three pairs of antlers of red deer, twelve urus heads, four human skulls, pigmy urus horns, skull of pilot whale, skull of stag, ancient dug-out boat. There have also been the usual loans from South Kensington Museum, and a number of interesting drawings lent by Alderman Hibbert, illustrative chiefly of early English water-colour art in landscape.

LIVERPOOL.

This busy city presents an excellent example of what has been done for these institutions by private munificence. The Museum, Art Gallery, and Library have each been largely benefited by numerous gifts, and it may be doubted, with the exception of Preston, if as much has been done by local patriots for any other town in the United Kingdom. The gift of the building for the Free Library and Museum by Sir William Brown, and opened in 1860, was the beginning of a long series of gifts.

I commend to the Curators and managers of other Museums a method adopted at Liverpool with the best results.   In 1862 a pamphlet written by the able Curator, Mr. T. J. Moore, and entitled " Suggestions Offered on the Part of the Literary and Philosophical Society of Liverpool to Members of the Mercantile Marine who may be desirous of using the advantages they enjoy for the promotion of Science in furtherance of Zoology," was published in the Proceedings of the Liverpool Mercantile Marine Society.   Copies of this paper, together with dredges, nets, and other appliances, were supplied from time to time by the Museum Committee to captains and others willing to collect. Numerous and important additions resulted therefrom, both to. the preserved collections of vertebrates and invertebrates in the Museum, and to the living collections in the Aquaria. The collections were accompanied in many cases with valuable notes and observations on the specimens.   The Society in the year named instituted an order of associate members limited to the mercantile marine, and elected thereto those who thus distinguished themselves ; and the Society from year to year have published in their Proceedings many of their notes and observations.

The contributors to this section are so numerous that it is impossible to give a list of them, but the particulars serve to show how widespread is the interest which can be aroused.   Among other gifts may be mentioned the collection of minerals made by the late William Phillips, F.L.S., the father of modern mineralogy, with his original drawings, illustrations, and measurements of crystals, as given in the third edition of his book on mineralogy.   These have been arranged by Mr. F. P. Marrat, the mineralogist, conchologist, &c., of the Museum, and are displayed in open table-cases in the Reptile Room.   At the decease of Mr. Phillips, the collection was purchased by Dr. Rutter, formerly an eminent physician in Liverpool. It was bequeathed by him to the Medical Institution under certain trusts, which, by the consent of the Trustees, have been superseded, and the collection has been unconditionally handed over to the Museum. Its value is estimated at about £1,300.

The Austin Collection of Fossils forms also a special feature of the Museum. It consists of the well-known collection of carboniferous and other crinoids, to the study of which the late Major Austin, long resident in Ireland, and subsequently at Bristol, devoted so many years of his life. Also his collection of fossils from the millstone grit discovered by him in England. In mollusca a large and important collection of shells, rich in rare and valuable specimens, was presented by Mr. Samuel Smith in 1870.

In the Marrat Collection of Shells of the genus *Oliva*, are included the specimens figured in the *Monograph* of the genus published in Sowerby's *Thesaurus Conchyliorium*. There is also the Marrat Collection of Shells of the genus *Nassa*, comprising more than a thousand varieties recorded by him in his paper on this genus in the Proceedings of the Literary and Philosophical Society of Liverpool for 1879-80.

Important collections of butterflies and moths, and their transformations, from Santo Paulo, Brazil, were presented by Mr. E. Dukinfield Jones, C.E. The Cooke Collections of British and European Lepidoptera, in two large cabinets, were bequeathed in 1885 by the late Mr. Nicholas Cooke, of Liscard.

The Committee have very recently received a valuable presentation from .Mr. Frederick Taylor, of Rainhill, and a collection of humming birds, with handsome case and accessories, as a Jubilee gift. A collection of skins from Palestine,

India, &c., formed by the late Mr. Hugh Heywood Jones, has been presented by his family. A collection of skins and horns of large game animals from the Caucasus, has been specially collected and presented by Mr. St. George Littledale.

THE "ARGO" COLLECTION.—In 1876 Mr. Reginald Cholmondeley, of Condover Hall, Salop, chartered the large steam yacht *Argo* for a scientific collecting expedition to the West Indies, and offered to take any deputation the Museum Committee might send. This generous offer was gladly accepted, and the Rev. H. H. Higgins, with two assistants, Messrs. Chard and Wood (the former the Museum draughtsman and assistant in the Invertebrate Department, and the latter the experienced attendant in the Aquarium), accompanied the expedition. The yacht was absent about four months, and visited the Canary Islands, several of the West India Islands, and the Spanish Main, taking Philadelphia on the homeward voyage. The collections made, particularly of fishes, insects, crustacea, shells, corals, sponges, &c., were extensive, and form a very valuable addition to the Museum. The Natural History section is particularly strong.

In Vertebrates there is the Derby Collection of mammals and birds, 20,000 in number, with very numerous additions thereto in all the classes of vertebrates. The mammals occupy the whole of five rooms, measuring 250 feet in total length, on the principal floor, and lighted by side windows. The birds occupy the wall-cases of corresponding rooms above, and lighted from the roof. Reptiles and fish fill the wall-cases of two similar rooms, measuring respectively fifty feet and forty feet in length. Pictorial groups, osteological specimens, and a few fossil remains are exhibited in due order among the whole of the vertebrates.

In Invertebrates, the "animals without bones," in the

M

Liverpool Museum, occupy twenty table-cases, ten feet in length by five feet in breadth, thus affording 1,000 area feet of horizontal exhibition space. These cases accommodate 240 trays or drawers, each holding a group, and capable of being removed for lecture purposes, or of being used as a drawer in the cabinet portion of the table-case.

These twenty table-cases occupy the central floor space of the five Bird Rooms, and have been arranged under the direction of the Rev. H. H. Higgins, M.A., who has given full information concerning them in the following publications relating to, and purchasable in, the Museum :—

Synopsis of an Arrangement of Invertebrate Animals. Second edition, 1880. One shilling.

Museum Talk about Animals which have no Bones. Fifth edition, 1885. One penny.

Museum Memorandum Book, containing plans showing the main features in the Natural History Department. 1887. One penny.

Museums of Natural History. Illustrated by plates of fittings, appliances, &c. 1884. One shilling.

It would be impossible to speak too highly of these publications. In Museum work they are simply invaluable, and they might well be adopted as a standard by the Museums throughout the country. With a little local adaptation one or two of them might, with Mr. Higgins' permission, be reprinted and used throughout the country. The name of the author should, on all occasions when this is done, be used.

The Gallery of the large Central Hall is occupied by geological and palæontological specimens, arranged stratigraphically, the larger in wall-cases, the smaller in table-cases, resting on the balustrade. Among the latter are the two following inportant local collections : An extensive series of fossils, including plant, insect, testacean, and fish remains, from a recent railway cutting through the coal measures at Raven-head, near St. Helens, collected by the Rev. H. H. Higgins ; and illustrations of the post-glacial geology of Lancashire and Cheshire, by Mr. T. Mellard Reade.

The circulating Museum collections, for educational purposes in schools, introduced by the Rev. H. H. Higgins, have been attended with great success. They are small and limited in number, but specially selected and arranged, and are lent in certain order, and usually for a month at a time, to elementary schools within the boundaries of the city. Duplicate specimens are also lent from time to time on application, for special object lessons by teachers, and for other educational purposes. An increase in the number of children and young persons, evidently resulting from the use of the circulating collections, has long been noticed, especially on Saturdays.

Wherever there is an available basement to a building it cannot be turned to a better use than to make an aquarium of it as they have done at Liverpool. A basement room fifty feet by twenty-seven feet is devoted to aquaria and vivaria for reptiles, amphibia, fish, and invertebrates. It contains seven large tanks, sixteen of medium size, and over twenty smaller vessels. The vessels containing them are of various forms and material.

The collection of Historical Art Treasures, given to Liverpool in 1866 by Mr. Joseph Mayer, F.S.A., is the finest collection of the kind ever yet presented to the public. In some of its departments—those of Wedg-wood ware and ivory carvings—it is unique. It contains the best collection extant of illustrations of Liver-pool pottery ware, a manufacture for which the town was once celebrated, but which has been long extinct. In Egyptian and Assyrian antiquities it is very rich.

M 2

The Fausset Collection of Anglo-Saxon remains, the finest extant, forms a portion of it, together with a large number of ancient manuscripts and illuminations. The Town Council suitably recognised its appreciation of this noble gift by erecting a marble statue of the donor in St. George's Hall. Numerous additions to this department have been made from time to time by donation and purchase, especially of ethnographical specimens. Mr. Charles T. Gatty, F.S.A., is the Curator of this section.

A ground plan of the building is given below :—

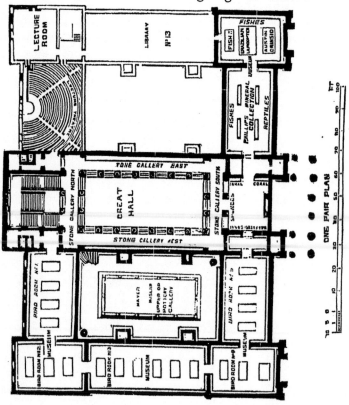

The Museum is open on Monday, Wednesday, Thursday and Saturday from ten to early dusk (*i.e.*, varying from ten to eight at midsummer, and ten to four in mid-winter). On Tuesday and Friday the Museum is closed for cleaning, arranging, &c., and admission is restricted to students, artists, and persons presenting written orders from members of the Town Council.

The visitors to the Museum during the year 1887 have been as follows:—Total visitors in the year (215 days) 255,616, against 357,916 in 1886 (212 days); weekly average 4,915, against 6,883; daily average 1,118, against 1,688.

The Walker Art Gallery owes its existence to Sir A. B. Walker, Bart. Prior to its erection the Corporation possessed a comparatively small collection of . works of art, acquired from time to time by presentation and purchase, and for the time deposited in the Library and Museum Buildings. In 1871 an Annual Exhibition of Pictures by modern artists was inaugurated, and was largely instrumental in creating and promoting a taste for art in this locality. This influence soon became so manifest that the pressing necessity for the erection of a Gallery of Art, which should be worthy of a town so important as Liverpool, presented itself very forcibly to the Committee, and to others interested in the subject, the result being that in 1873 a report was presented to the Town Council recommending the erection of a Gallery of Art as an addition to the Library, Museum, and Art Department.

In November Mr. A. B. Walker, Mayor, announced his intention of erecting the building at his own cost, and presenting it to the town. The foundation stone was laid on September 28th, 1874, by the Duke of Edinburgh. The building was completed in 1877, and opened to the public on September 7th of the same year by the Earl of Derby. In 1882 the permanent collection had so increased that additional space became necessary, and an extension, at an estimated cost of £11,500, was sanctioned by the City Council. On its completion, Sir A. B. Walker gave an additional proof of his generosity and public spirit by defraying the entire cost.   Mr. Charles Dyall is the Curator, and has written a descriptive catalogue of the permanent collection of pictures.

During the year 1887 the Gallery has been open on 292 days, and closed for cleaning and other purposes on twenty-one days.   The total number of visitors was 416,820, or a daily average attendance of 1,427. Included in the above total are 55,428 visitors to the Autumn Exhibition, and 9,693 scholars admitted free. The Autumn Exhibition resulted in receipts to the amount of £2,329 14s. 6d., exclusive of £4,791 19s. realised by sales.   The sales in the previous year realised £8,576 18s., and the other receipts amounted to £2,189 3s. 7d.   During the seventeen years these exhibitions have taken place 4,503 of the pictures exhibited have been sold for £151,075 11s. 6d.   Of these sixty-six were purchased by the Corporation for their permanent gallery, the catalogued prices of which added up to £23,968 10s.

DERBY

possesses a handsome, well-appointed Museum and Library under capital management.   That the twin institutions are appreciated by the townspeople is evidenced by the returns.   Derby has much reason to be grateful to the late Mr. T. Bass, who represented the town in Parliament for a considerable time.   He gave the building which provides the home of these institutions, and the gift is one worthy of the man and the town.   In the report for 1887 the Curator, Mr.

W. Crowther, states that his work during the Library year has consisted largely in the completion of the re-arrangement of the shells, and a commencement of the fossils.

DERBY MUSEUM AND FREE LIBRARY.

The Art Gallery has been open 264 days, of which forty-three have been free. The attendance on the free days has been 14,673, or a daily average of 341 ; by payment 15,477 ; average, seventy daily, making a total of 30,150 visitors against 28,326 in 1886. The Autumn Exhibition extended from November 6th to February 19th, and was attended by 10,160 visitors.

The Spring Exhibition consisted of pictures by local artists, and a loan collection, and was open from March 5th to June 4th.

THE MAPPIN ART GALLERY, SHEFFIELD.

In 1883 Mr. John Newton Mappin, of Sheffield, bequeathed the sum of £15,000 for an Art Gallery to contain his collection of pictures (which he also bequeathed) and other works of art that might afterwards be acquired by the town. It was erected on land adjoining the Museum and was opened to the public on July 27th, 1887. Mr. Mappin's collection comprised 153 modern paintings, and a bronze group, and to these have since been added forty-eight modern oil paintings, given by Sir Frederick T. Mappin, Bart., M.P. Four rooms in the Art Gallery not occupied by the permanent collection are used for loan exhibitions of pictures.

It was a red-letter day in the history of Sheffield when this beautiful building was opened. Sir Frederick Mappin, M.P., presented to the Mayor, Sir Henry Stephenson, £15,000, the cost of the building, and the trust deeds. In speaking of his uncle, the donor, he said that "his objects were varied. He desired to promote a taste for art, and for the love of the beautiful; for I know his opinion of his townsmen was that they did not possess too many opportunities of indulging in and obtaining that education which is such an advantage to all of us. He also thought that by providing a home for his own pictures, he would set an example which might be followed by those who came after him. Not only that, but he hoped that men during their lifetime would assist in filling these handsome Galleries with works of art, and I have no doubt that his example will be a successful one, and be productive of much good to this great town.

MAPPIN ART GALLERY, SHEFFIELD.

The Trustees built these Galleries with the same object that he had."

Mr. A. J. Mundella, M.P., in presenting the gold key to Sir Frederick Mappin, said : " I know nearly all the Galleries in Europe, and most of the provincial Galleries in Europe, and I do not think that I can recall to mind at this moment a single Gallery which for its dimensions is more beautiful in its construction, better adapted for the purposes of a Gallery. . . . . We have in the adjoining Gallery forty-eight pictures of the highest merit—some of them the very noblest specimens of modern British art—which Sir Frederick Mappin has commissioned me to present in his name to the town." The possession of such a building and its contents by the people of Sheffield must exercise profound influence on both the commercial and the moral future of the town. It cannot fail to be humanising and elevating on all who resort to the Gallery, while its effects on the artistic products of the town will be shown not so much directly in the production of designers as in a cultivation of the public taste demanding high artistic excellence.

The engraving on page 169 gives a capital sketch of the interior of the central Gallery containing pictures. No public room for the exhibition of pictures is designed in quite the same way as this Gallery, the object being by means of a series of recesses to allow an artistic grouping of the pictures, and to prevent the distraction to the eye which arises from a long unbroken line of pictures. The treatment of the light is the special feature of the Gallery, the counter lights being so placed that the light comes from above and behind the spectator, and is thus thrown on the pictures without any glare, the spectator being in the shade.

The public appreciation of this Gallery will be seen from the fact that from July 27th until the end of August, 1887, the visitors numbered 108,450, being a daily average of 3,498. The Gallery was open on every weekday but Friday, and on Sundays from one to five, the average number of visitors each Sunday being 4,236. On Bank Holiday, August 1st, there were 14,062 visitors. The catalogue of the permanent collection is just what such a catalogue should be. It has been compiled by Mr. E. Howarth, the Curator.

A view of the elevation of the Art Gallery is given. It is built of stone ; all the Galleries are lighted from the

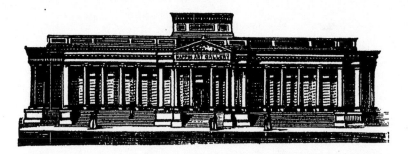

roof, and at night by Siemen's regenerative gas burners enclosed in glass globes, with a ventilator to each burner passing out through the roof, and thus carrying away all deleterious products of combustion.

EASTBOURNE.

The origin of the Caldecott Museum in Eastbourne is this: The gentleman after whom it is named resided for many years at Meads, and during his life accumulated a large collection of specimens, chiefly geological, which he was desirous in his latter days of making over to the town for the benefit of its inhabitants. He died suddenly in 1870, without having made any provision for the disposal of his collection ; but his sister, knowing his intentions, transferred it to Trustees for the benefit of the town. No pecuniary endowment accom-

panied it.   The Trustees endeavoured by a public
meeting, and otherwise, to induce the authorities to take
over the collection and provide accommodation for it.
To facilitate matters a short Act of Parliament was
obtained (Public Libraries Act, 1855, Amendment Act,
1871) extending the Act to Eastbourne.   The ratepayers would not, however, assent to the adoption of
the Free Libraries Act, and thus the Trustees were left
to their own resources.   In this dilemma two liberal
gentlemen offered at a nominal rent a room as a
temporary habitation for the collection.   In 1872 it
was opened to the public for three days in the week,
from July to October, at a charge to each visitor of
threepence, and this was continued down to 1886.
Recently an improvement has been made; and the
Trustees threw the Museum open to the public during
the season free of charge.   The visitors then rose in
number to an average of 143 per week.   Good
service to the cause of education would be
rendered by the Corporation of Eastbourne if they
recognised the value of a collection such as this, which
is capable of being easily formed into a complete
Museum of objects of geology and natural history.
The catalogue is incomplete.   There are about 5,000
fossils, including a good collection from the chalk,
about 600 specimens of minerals, a fine collection
of agates from India and other parts, a small collection
of lepidoptera, a collection of crustacea found at Eastbourne, about 100 birds found in the neighbourhood,
and a fine collection of eggs from all parts, a collection of
mollusca, fresh water and marine, found at Eastbourne,
mounted and named, a few pre-historic remains.
Specimens of rocks of all ages, unarranged and undis-
played for want of room.

Lord Brassey has recently given a School of Art to
Hastings, the erection of which cost about £15,000.

CHAPTER X.

POPULARISING MUSEUMS, AND THE IDEAL IN MUSEUM WORK.

T is always a good thing to aim at the ideal even although that may appear unattainable. This applies both to the individual and to institutions, or even nations, governed as these are by individual units making one concrete force. There is no more consoling fact to thoughtful humanity than that there is no limit to human progress. Taking 1682, the date of the founding of the Ashmolean Museum, as the first existing collection of any importance in this country, we may ask, What is 200 years in a nation's life or in the history of Museums? Unmistakably useful as are a large number of Museums and Art Galleries, we have, as yet, only touched the fringe of their possible usefulness. As we come universally to more and more recognise the softening and refining influences of art and beautiful objects with their concomitants drawn from nature's immense storehouse, so will efforts towards enlarging the scope of these institutions be certain to develop. I have watched minutely the faces of visitors at many an Art Gallery and Museum, especially in the evening, and the faces of the working-class visitors have provided a study in physiognomy so gratifying that I never now enter a Museum without giving some attention to the faces of the visitors as well as to the objects in the Museum. How the eyes light up at some picture, where the " one touch of nature makes the whole world kin," and I have more than once seen a wife with a pale careworn face cling more closely to the arm of her husband as some picture of child life was being looked at, or something else suggestive to them, perhaps, of little fingers lying cold in mother earth. Let any opponent of these institutions open to conviction go some weekday evening or Sunday to the Birmingham Museum and study for himself the faces of those who come to see perhaps for the twentieth time the pictures and other art objects, and he will be convinced. He might notice the weary listlessness of some, but if he observed faithfully he could scarcely fail to notice the deep interest of others.

The chief element in the increasing popularity of Museums lies in an ever widening range of knowledge. The gifts of knowledge enable a man to enjoy all he sees. Even a little elementary instruction in botany gives quite a new interest to a country walk. Not a few view with dismay the higher curriculum of Board School education now being given. They see at every turn the increasing difficulty of obtaining good domestics, and a deteriorating British workman, and are not slow to attribute it all to the masses being educated, as they say, above their station. They appear to overlook the fact that the intelligence the people have gained is a new power with them, and a proper use of that intelligence will most surely follow in course of time. When this period arrives, and there are signs of it even now, there will be no boy or girl, however humble their station in life, who will be educated above his or her position. The truism that all labour is honourable will, as it goes hand in hand with education, rectify the apparent defects at present disturbing the minds of many.

The next step in the educational ladder is Free Education, and this will bring a further impetus in the popularity of Museums. This is not the place to discuss the *pros* and *cons* of this large question, but there are many indications that what was looked upon with horror a few years ago is now being calmly thought over by thousands. The subject will stand in a very different position shortly when it comes within the range of practical politics.

The "little knowledge" theory even with regard to Museums, is becoming an exploded fallacy. Each stage of knowledge is "superficial" to a man who knows more, but even a little knowledge may be thorough as far as it goes. It is not given to everyone for years to minutely study, say, the woodlouse, as has been the case, but it is wise not to sneer at the man who does so, for he can by means of his close study tell all people more than they would ever find out for themselves. Where would our knowledge of earthworms stand had it not been for Darwin's careful study of these creatures? The public smile at the reply of the old domestic in the Darwin household, who, in reply to an inquiry as to how her master was, said, "Ah! poor man, he would be better if he had only something to do, but there he is, day after day, doing nothing but looking at those nasty worms."

That every one should be the friend of art and Museums is an ideal which under our fickle sky and the varying conditions of life is almost beyond hope. Still it may be safely asserted that there are nowhere more true friends of art than the multitude who visit Art Galleries and Museums. They come not to criticise but to enjoy, and they like a good story on canvas or

Bristol board well told. Their hearts and their interests
are excited by the man who draws what he knows and
not what he dreams. The " Village Wedding " of Luke
Fildes, is worth more to them than all the works of
Rubens in the National Gallery. It must then be right
to do all we can to spread a familiarity with art
through all classes, and in all places, in order that
Englishmen and Englishwomen may, as a people,
appreciate what their countrymen have produced. Mr.
Frederic Harrison closed his lecture on " The Future of
Great Cities," delivered in the early part of 1888, at the
Toynbee Hall, in describing his ideal of what London
should be, with a sentence which may be immortal. He
said : " It must be a city where our noble river will
flow so bright and clear that the young people can swim
in it with pleasure; where we shall again see the
blessed sun and clear blue sky, and the towers and
steeples rising aloft in the bright air—a city which at
night will be made as light as day with electric lamps,
and in whose midst fountains will pour forth water
from the hills of Snowdon or Helvellyn; a city where
noxious refuse will be unknown, and where no deadly
exhalations will be pumped into homes; a city where
typhus and typhoid and small-pox and fevers will be as
rare as the plague, and as much a matter of history as
the leprosy ; a city where the dead shall no longer be a
terror to the living, where preventable disease will be
a crime chargeable to some one and an opprobrium to
the district in which it breaks out; a city where no
child shall go untaught because it has no suitable
school at hand; a city where no man shall go without
recreation, or society, or religion, because there are no
Libraries or Museums near his abode, no Galleries of
pictures to visit on Sunday, no Parks within easy reach,
and no free seats in the church which he cares to enter."
There is room for gratitude to teachers who hold before

us high ideals and urge us to steadily aim towards reaching them.

The popular and ideal Museum and Art Gallery of the future shall be in the fullest sense a continuation school where old and young shall come for instruction in those measureless departments of nature which lie at our feet, and a knowledge of which should give an infinitely higher and more deeply reverential feeling of the Almighty. In this ideal Museum the Curator and his assistants will be men thoroughly sensible of the capabilities of the specimens under their charge for conveying high moral, intellectual and often physical lessons.

The ideal building will be well lighted and well ventilated, and present throughout a cheerful aspect. With these and other characteristics it will aid largely in the conquest of the craving for strong intoxicants, on the part of many at least, often at present resorted to because the mind has no other resource to draw it away from the care and canker of daily worry.

The evenings of the future in the ideal Museum will be occasionally occupied by pleasant and informal gatherings, open to all, and at these students and the more advanced give information to those less informed. New interests in life will be created all along the line. Such instructors will remember that as they have themselves freely received, so it is a privilege to freely give. The object of all education should be to make the most of life, not the attainment of merely worldly success, but an esteem for what is really good, true, and noble, accompanied by an earnest desire to benefit their fellow men. Can this be better accomplished than in the utilising of Museums for cheerful and instructive conversaziones, such as that indicated, where the invitations are not reserved for the favoured few, but thrown open to the many.

N

The sovereign people are becoming keenly sensible that there is something more to be got out of life than mere existence. As reading increases and Museums and Art Galleries multiply, crime decreases, so that these ideal institutions of the future will play, as they now do, an important economical part in the nation's life.

Foremost among the means of popularising Museums and Art Galleries are meetings of Curators annually in conference to discuss the many matters of interest and importance connected with these institutions. This is vital to the development of their work, and no time should be lost in formulating some plan in this direction. Librarians have quite enough to do in their Conferences exclusive of matters relating to Museums.

The rapidly-advancing tide of scientific thought is making continual change in the method of classification and in all the details of Museum work, so that Curators, more than any other class of men, require to be brought into contact with each other at frequent intervals. This has been recognised for a long time, and has been agitated at intervals, but in vain, until the Yorkshire Philosophical Society took it up. A meeting was called at York last May, and provincial Curators from every part of the country were invited to take part in the formation of an Association.

The circulars were issued by Mr. H. M. Platnauer, the Curator of the admirable Museum at York. The first was issued on February 29th, 1888, and stated the object of the proposed meeting to be to consider the advisability of establishing a Museum Association for mutual help, and more especially to discuss the possibility of obtaining the following objects:—

1. A compendious index of the contents of all provincial Museums and collections.

2. Some method of facilitating the interchange of specimens and books between various Museums.

3. The full discussion of the best plans for arranging Museums and classifying their contents.

4. The organisation of some concerted action for the obtaining of such Government publications as are interesting or important from a scientific point of view.

The meeting was held at York on May 3rd, 1888, Mr. S.W. North (a Vice-President of the Yorkshire Philosophical Society) in the chair.

Finally it was unanimously resolved that the provincial Museums of England should be approached, and the following suggestions offered for their consideration :—

1. That a Museum Association be formed.

2. That this Association consist of Curators and those engaged in the active work of Museums, and also of representatives of the Committees or Councils of Management of such Museums.

3. That the Association publish—either (*a*) an annual volume of original scientific papers, or (*b*) a periodical more frequently published, giving both practical and original scientific papers.

An Art Congress Association, on the lines of the British Association, and to hold meetings at the various chief provincial towns successively, which was initiated a little while ago by the Municipality of Liverpool, has recently taken active development. The Duke of Westminster took the chair at a meeting at Grosvenor House on June 8th, 1888, for the formal establishment of the Association, and Sir F. Leighton, Mr. Alma Tadema, Mr. A. Gilbert, A.R.A., Mr. Aitchison, A.R.A., Mr. P. Rathbone, and Mr. Colvin have agreed to preside over various sections at the first annual meeting, which it is intended to hold at Liverpool.

A paper read before the Literary and Philosophical Society of Liverpool on March 21st, 1887, by Mr. W. A. Herdman, D.Sc., F.L.S., F.R.S.E., Professor of

Natural History in University College, Liverpool, on
" An Ideal Natural History Museum," would, had there
been an Association of Curators with their journal, have
found a resting place, and with its practical suggestions
would have become the property of Curators at large.
So important is this contribution to Museum literature,
at present so scanty, that Professor Herdman's permission has been obtained to quote from it freely, and I avail
myself to the full of this permission, as the principles
and methods laid down are the best which have up to
this time been put forward.

AN IDEAL NATURAL HISTORY MUSEUM.

It is a remarkable circumstance that the Darwinian theory of
Evolution, which has exercised such a profound influence during
the last quarter of a century upon almost all departments of
thought, has apparently had little or no effect as yet upon the
structure and the arrangement of Museums of Natural History.
The Descent theory, which has now become the central idea
of modern biology, and which has given an entirely new and
more scientific aspect both to original investigation and to the
teaching of the subject, seems to be utterly ignored by those
institutions which are intended to give to the general public a
correct representation of our present knowledge in regard to the
various groups of animals and plants and their relations to one
another.

In what respect is a Museum better or higher than a mere
collection of curiosities made by an amateur, or than the confused assemblage of heterogeneous objects seen on the shelves
of the bird-fancier's shop, if it is not that in the Museum the
specimens are supposed to be arranged and labelled in a natural
(that is, a scientific) manner ? Now it is generally admitted
amongst biologists that the only natural arrangement of animals
or plants is according to their genetic affinities, and this when
carried out gives rise to a branched or tree-like form,* which
represents graphically at one and the same time the blood-
relationships of the different groups, and also their phylogenetic
or ancestral history. Why is it then that Museums do not
follow this, the only correct method of classifying and

---

* For example, see Herdman, "A Phylogenetic Classification of
Animals." Macmillan, 1885.

arranging organic objects ?   I believe the reason is simply that Museums are costly institutions, most of which were already established before the Darwinian epoch. They are placed in buildings which it would be a serious matter to rebuild or to adapt, and which are for the most part quite unsuitable for the new genealogical arrangement, being generally in the form of a series of corridors and galleries, in which the specimens are arranged in linear series—a method known to all biologists as an absurd one, giving a totally erroneous idea of nature. The great objection to a linear classification is not felt so strongly by those who have no special knowledge of biology ; and I shall, therefore, make use of an illustration which may seem at first somewhat childish, but which will, I think, demonstrate clearly the unnatural character of a linear arrangement. Let us imagine that some intelligent animals, in some future geological period, found the fossil remains of the long extinct race of man, of whose structure and appearance all knowledge had been lost ; and let us further suppose that all the fossil men found were in fragments, the head, body, arms and legs being separated from one another. Now, how would the scientific Museum Curator amongst those intelligent animals arrange the fossil fragments so as to give a correct impression of the shape of extinct man?

Of course the proper way would be to arrange them as shown in Fig. 1, when the form produced is a branched one, resembling a phylogenetic arrangement of animals ; but if he was bound down by tradition, or by the shape of his Museum cases, to a linear arrangement of the fragments of man, he would produce the very unnatural forms shown in Figs. 2 and 3. If the Curator in question knew absolutely nothing of the relations of the fragments he was dealing with, then he might turn out some such absurd arrangement as Fig. 3 ; but, if he discovered the true positions of the various pieces, then the very best arrangement he could make in a linear series would be that shown in Fig. 2, which everyone will admit gives a totally erroneous idea of the human figure. It is, however, no more unnatural than the best possible linear arrangement of plants and animals seems to the scientific biologist, and the order of the groups shown in some Natural History Museums is almost as absurd as the positions of the man's limbs in Fig. 3.   It is no argument in favour of the existing state of affairs, and no excuse for delaying the necessary changes in Museums to point out the fact that in modern text books of biology the linear classification is still adopted.   That cannot be avoided.   Books, unlike natural groups and Museum cases, cannot spread in a dendritic manner. Their pages and chapters *must* follow one another in a continuous series.

Then, again, the linear arrangement seen in Museums is usually not even the best possible.   The exigencies of space, and the size and nature of the specimens exhibited, seem to necessitate the placing together of groups of animals which are not at all closely related.   In the Liverpool Free Public Museum,* the collection of invertebrate animals is placed in table-cases, in a series of rooms, the walls of which are occupied by the collection of birds, and the reptiles are associated with the fishes, in a distinct part of the building from their relations—the birds.   And I understand that in the Otago Museum, New Zealand, the birds and the mammals (the two highest groups of the vertebrata) are separated by a Gallery containing the lower vertebrata, while the invertebrata are placed in the same Galleries as the lower vertebrates and with the birds.   Some such unnatural arrangements as these—caused more or less by the shape of the building and by the fact that the wall-cases are more suitable for the display of certain specimens, such as stuffed birds and jars of snakes, while table or desk cases do better for dried shells and insects—are to be found in nearly all Museums of Natural History, and are greatly to be deplored as leading to confusion and mystification in the mind of the non-scientific observer.

It should always be remembered that public Museums are intended for the use and instruction of the general public, who have no special knowledge of biology, and not of the scientific man or the student, and on that account alone the attempt should at least be made to give a correct representation of nature.   For the student, and still more for the professed biologist, it is a matter of comparatively little moment how the specimens he is examining are arranged.   The student has his previous knowledge, his books, and his professor's lectures to guide him, and to prevent him from being misled by an

---

* This excellent Museum is taken as the first example simply because it is probably the Museum with which the members of the Liverpool Literary and Philosophical Society are most familiar.

erroneous arrangement ; but the ordinary Museum visitor—for whose benefit the institution is chiefly intended—is entirely at the mercy of what he sees before him in the cases, and usually, I am afraid, leaves the building in greater ignorance as to the order of nature than when he entered it. It is no wonder, indeed, that Museums are regarded by most ordinarily intelligent non-scientific people as very dreary and unprofitable places. Can nothing be done to remedy this unfortunate state of affairs, and to render Museums of Natural History what they ought to be—correct representations of nature, demonstrating better than could be done by any books or lectures the great doctrine of organic evolution ? I believe a great deal can be done. Something can be done even with existing Museums, and still more could, and doubtless will be done, with those of the future. Small beginnings are being made here and there by some scientific Museum Curators. Professor Haddon, Dublin, has constructed a model out of differently coloured and labelled blocks of wood, connected by wires, and arranged on successive horizontal plates of glass, so as to show in three dimensions the evolution of the various groups of animals. Professor Parker, of the Otago Museum, has placed in his Museum a model genealogical tree of the animal kingdom, near the bottom of the stem of which is a model of *Amœba*, while the various branches and twigs above are occupied by specimens or models of typical representatives of the various groups of animals. The specimens are carefully chosen and labelled, and there are references to the particular part of the Museum where the remaining specimens of the group are to be found.

Such models illustrating the evolution of animals in public Museums are steps in the right direction, but they do not go nearly far enough. They can only be regarded as explanatory notices correcting and apologising for the linear classification which follows them, and they will probably produce little or no impression on the non-scientific observer. In order to have a proper effect the whole Museum must be in accordance with the order of nature. Any part arranged otherwise is so much space and material wasted, or worse than wasted, so far as the instruction of the general public is concerned. Natural History Museums are still in what may be called their Pre-Darwinian condition, and must undergo great changes before they can be regarded as abreast of modern science. I have no doubt that as a result of the rapid advances which are being made in biology, the Museum will, in the near future, become evolved into a much

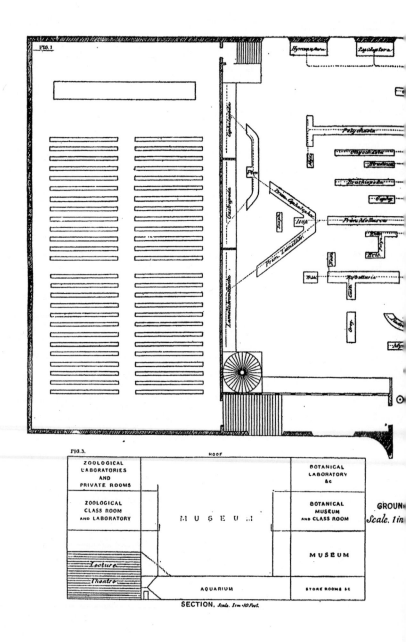

FIG. 1

FIG. 3.

ZOOLOGICAL LABORATORIES AND PRIVATE ROOMS	ROOF		BOTANICAL LABORATORY &c
ZOOLOGICAL CLASS ROOM AND LABORATORY	MUSEUM		BOTANICAL MUSEUM AND CLASS ROOM
			MUSEUM
Lecture Theatre		AQUARIUM	STORE ROOMS &c

SECTION. Scale. 1in. 10 Feet.

GROUN
Scale. 1in

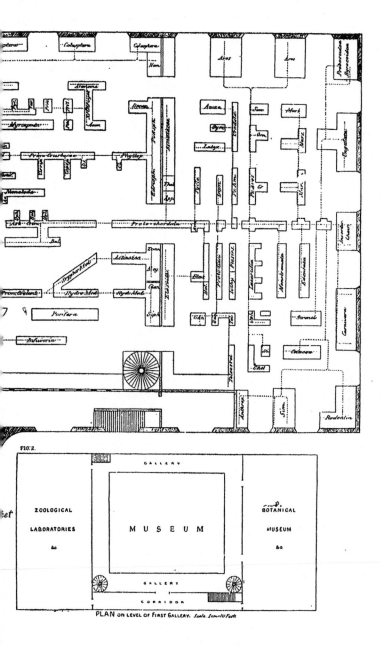

FIG. 2.

GALLERY

ZOOLOGICAL

LABORATORIES

&c

MUSEUM

BOTANICAL

MUSEUM

&c

GALLERY

CORRIDOR

PLAN ON LEVEL OF FIRST GALLERY. *Scale. 1cm=10 Feet*

more perfect instrument for teaching natural science to the masses than we can even imagine just now ; but still it may be of some use to the founders and Curators of future Museums if I make the attempt to show what I think should be the constitution and arrangement of a Museum such as would adequately represent the state of our knowledge of organic nature at the present date.

MUSEUM LABORATORY AND LECTURE HALL.—The first point I would insist upon in the constitution of my ideal Museum is that it should have connected with it a teaching and an investigating department. A large lecture hall, and a laboratory in which work is constantly being carried on should form an essential part of the institution. It is impossible otherwise, I believe, for the Museum to keep up with the advances made daily in natural science. Nothing is easier now-a-days than to fall behind the time, and even a teacher, if he is not also an investigator, is very liable to find that the wave of discovery has passed on and left him hopelessly stranded. Biology is an eminently practical science. It is no longer possible to acquire a knowledge of natural history by reading books or by attending lectures. Direct contact with the animals and plants, and the actual investigation of their structure and life history is necessary for anyone who wishes to know and to teach natural science, and it is doubly necessary in a Museum which should reflect the latest knowledge and the best theories as to the nature and affinities of every animal or plant exhibited. A laboratory in which original research is constantly being carried on would be, I hold, one of the most important adjuncts of the Museum, and would exercise a vitalising influence, enabling that part of the institution open to the public to undergo a constant development, growing and changing so as to keep pace with the progress of discovery instead of being, as is frequently the case now, a quarter or even half a century behind the condition of science.

AQUARIUM.—Another valuable department which I would like to see connected with every Museum is an aquarium. Not merely a few small globes and vessels containing sea-anemones and other attractive objects, but a series of large well-lit tanks in which the natural conditions surrounding the animals are, as far as possible, reproduced, so that observations may be made upon their habits and life histories. In inland Museums the tanks should be laid out so as to resemble ponds, ditches, and running streams, and should be kept well stocked with the appropriate plants and animals. In Museums near the coast

marine tanks should be added, illustrating various kinds of
shore pools, with sandy and rocky bottoms.

In all cases the animals should not be for show only, but for
study. They should be taken advantage of by the Curators and
the students in the laboratory for the purpose of observing
carefully and systematically the habits of the various animals
under various conditions, and also for studying their embry-
ology and life history. Comparative Physiology—that very
important science of the future—might also be greatly edvanced
by experiments and observations made in such aquaria. I
believe there is a great future before aquaria and vivaria of
all kinds—but, they must be purely scientific, they must be
under the control of a scientific man, and they must be
arranged primarily for the purpose of conducting scientific experiments and observations. They will be none the less interesting to the general public on that account.

CLASSIFICATION OF COLLECTIONS.—Now, passing on to the
collections exhibited in the Museum, I would divide them
into :—1st, and most important, a large type (or phylogenetic,)
collection, occupying the great hall or ground floor of the
Museum, and arranged so as to illustrate the evolution of plants
and animals. 2nd. A local collection, which should aim at being
a complete one. 3rd. Special collections, illustrating geographical distribution, variation of species in the natural condition,
variation in domesticated animals and plants (races of dogs,
pigeons, &c.), parasitism and commensalism, &c., &c.

PHYLOGENETIC COLLECTION.—In the diagram (Plate I., Fig. 1)
the arrangement of cases which I would adopt in the chief or
"phylogenetic" collection is shown. The Museum is supposed
to occupy an area 200 feet in length and 100 feet in breadth,
and it is divided into a central part 100 feet square, and two
lateral parts each 100 feet by fifty feet (see ground plan, Plate I.,
Fig. 1). The right wing is occupied, on the ground floor, by the
large lecture hall, while the left wing contains the vertebrate
part of the collection. Each of the wings is three storeys in
height, the two upper storeys being occupied by the zoological
and botanical laboratories and private work-rooms, while the
central part of the Museum is open to the roof, from which
it is lit, and has two galleries surrounding it (see section,
Plate I., Fig. 3). The main entrance is in the middle of one
of the sides and leads into a wide corridor running to the
right and left and ending each way in a flight of steps. That
on the left hand leads to the back of the lecture hall, while
the stairs on the right give access to the laboratories above.

The wall separating the corridor from the central part of the Museum might be a glass partition, so as to admit more light. Through the middle of this partition a wide door-way leads to the central part of the Museum, a great hall 100 feet wide by ninety feet long and say eighty feet high, lit from the roof and by a row of windows along the end opposite the entrance, and having two galleries (an upper and a lower) running round its four sides and approached by spiral stairs at the corners nearest to the entrance. The cases are arranged round the walls and in lines and groups on the floor, so as to indicate the lines of development of the leading groups of animals. The connection between the various groups, and the directions of evolution are shown by a stout brass bar, branching where necessary, which runs over the centres of the table-cases about seven feet from the ground, and has the names of the larger groups and other explanatory labels suspended from it. This bar would take its origin from the first case encountered by the visitor entering the Museum—a table-case containing one or more models of *Protamœba*, and, possibly, a series of specimens and models showing the chemical elements present in protoplasm. In front of this first case might be placed an upright tree-like model of the animal kingdom. From the models of *Protamœba* a line of cases would lead in each direction, to the left through the Mycetozoa and the earliest plants, and then on to the various existing groups of Protophyta, which might be arranged (illustrated fully by models and drawings) in desk-cases placed against the glass partition to the left of the entrance. The line from *Protamœba* to the right would lead through the Monads to the Infusoria—the various stages in the evolution of that group being shown by carefully constructed models fully explained.

Next to *Protamœba* in the middle line of the hall would be a case containing models of *Amœba*, and showing how that form became differentiated into primitive Foraminifera and primitive Radiolaria. The further evolution of these two groups would be shown in cases diverging to the right and left. The Gregarinida and other Sporozoa should, on account of their uncertain affinities, be placed in an independent case standing by itself, and not receiving a branch from the brass bar; but at any future time when their exact history became known they could readily be attached in their proper place. Beyond *Amœba*, in the middle of the hall, would be placed a series of models representing compound Amœba-like Protozoa leading up to Gastræa, the beginning of the Metazoa, and the point of origin of the primitive Cœlenterata. Beyond Gastræa would come the earliest Vermes, the first of that series of ancestral worms from which all the other groups of animals have arisen. Consequently the central line of cases in this room would represent *Protamœba*, *Amœba*, Compound Amœbœ, Gastræa, and a gradually advancing series of worms. The sponges might occupy an independent case, like the Gregarinida, to show that it is doubtful where they arose from the main stem. The Cœlenterata would extend outwards from Gastræa, branch into the two main divisions, and reach the side wall where the corals, the Alcyonarians, the Ctenophora, and the Siphonophora would be shown in wall-cases. The various groups of lower worms would naturally form an off-shoot a little above the Cœlenterata. Degeneration would be shown, for example, in the Cestoda, by the case containing that group being directed backwards towards the Protozoa. Further on in the hall the cases containing the groups of Polyzoa, Nematelmia, Brachiopoda, Gephyrea, Hirudinea, Earth-worms, &c., would be found all diverging independently from the ancestral worms. The points of origin of the remaining great groups of animals—the Mollusca, the Crustacea, the Insecta, the Echinodermata, and the Vertebrata—would also be found in the central series of worms. I need not go over the detailed arrangement of all the groups, but shall take one of them as an example of how I would arrange some of the specimens in the cases. The Mollusca (shell-fish) will serve for this purpose.

The Mollusca arose from some group of the lower worms (Plate I, Fig. 1), and we can reconstruct in a good many of its details the ancestral form which first diverged and became the ancestor of all existing molluscs. This form I would represent by a model, or possibly more than one model, showing not only the external form but also the internal structure. Then I would have a series of models showing how this ancestral worm-like form became gradually modified into something more like the typical mollusc as we know it now. These models would show the gradual formation of the "foot" for creeping on, of the "mantle" for covering the dorsal surface of the body, of the "shell-gland" with its small median shell, of the heart and gills, and of all the other characteristic organs of the body. These models, along with their explanations, would enable any intelligent observer, even if he knew nothing of the subject before, to follow the gradual transformation of a worm into a mollusc. And he would also learn from them what the essential characters of the Mollusca are, and how they have been acquired. This is shown in no existing Museum so far as I am aware.

Having arrived now in our series of models at a form which is recognisable as a mollusc we would represent, by a forking of the case and the brass rod, a divergence of two lines of Mollusca. In the one of these the animals became burrowers in mud and sand banks on the shore and in shallow water, and so gave rise to the existing Lamellibranchiata with their bivalve shells. The body in these forms became flattened laterally and tapering towards the ends, the foot became pointed in front and adapted for boring through the sand ; while, on account of the changed habit of life, food could only be obtained by drawing in constant currents of water containing microscopic plants and animals, and so the large plate-like hills covered with cilia become developed at the sides of the body for the purpose of causing and directing these currents of water. I would illustrate by dissections, by drawings and by models the more important arrangements of gills found in the existing Lamellibranchs, and show how they fulfil more or less perfectly their important functions. For example, a large model of *Mya arenaria* would show how the water is drawn into a long tube, the inhalent siphon, at the posterior end of the body, passes forwards along the mantle cavity until it comes under the influence of the labial palps where it is strained, all the food-particles being collected in the grooves which cover the surface of these organs and then transferred to the mouth, while the water passes onwards through the walls of the gills and so reaches passages by which it is conveyed to the exhalent siphon leading to the exterior. The current of water entering the body contains food and oxygen. When it leaves the body it has lost a great part of that food and oxygen, and it carries with it various waste materials from the body of the mollusc.

There are a number of other important points like this in connection with the physiology, the habits, and the life history of our common shell-fish which I would illustrate freely by dissections and models. I would show how the clam shuts and opens its shell, how the oyster has two muscles running across its body like those of most other Lamellibranchs when it is young, and how it loses one of them when it grows older, thus showing that the oyster is degenerated from a more ordinary mollusc. I would show the remarkable life history of the fresh-water mussel—how it undergoes its early development inside the cavity of the external gill of the parent, how it is hatched as a "Glochidium," quite unlike its parent, and how it undergoes its further development after it has attached itself by its sharp serrated spines to the fins or tail of some passing fish, and so on. All these are matters which could be shown by dissections and models, and which would, I am convinced, not only educate the Museum visitors, but prove deeply interesting to them. And yet none of them are to be seen in our Museums of the present day. When we go to the cases of Lamelli-branchiate Mollusca we find nothing but row after row of dead dried shells all looking very like one another, teaching nothing whatever to the non-scientific observer, and devoid of all human interest. What would we think of a library in which the books on the shelves were nothing but the boards and the backs, with the names printed thereon but with all the pages and illustrations carefully removed? That is what the collections of shell-fish in our Museums are like. They show merely the boards and backs—the important part, the animal itself which formed the shell, and which we may compare to the pages of the book, has been removed. It may be said: "But the shells show modification, and are different from one another." Well, so do the backs of the books in a library, and a person who could not read and knew nothing about books might think that the boards were the most interesting part, and that the pages ought to be cut out and thrown away. No doubt the collection of dried shells has a certain value and interest just as a collection of book-bindings has, but in both cases they can only be appreciated by the specialist. To the ordinary Museum visitor it would be much more instructive and much more interesting to be shown by dissections and models the more important points in the animal's structure, and the uses of the various parts. Ask an intelligent non-scientific person who has just inspected the collection of Mollusca in a Museum of the present day what he has learnt as to their structure. Ask him if he knows whether molluscs have a heart, blood, a nervous system, or even a stomach, and he will probably answer, "I suppose they have none of these. All I have learned is that they have shells, and I fancied there was nothing but a soft pulp inside the shell."

The second group which diverged from the ancestral molluscs took to crawling over rocks and sea-weeds. They developed strong shells on their backs instead of on their sides, as the bivalves did. The foot became large and flat, and was used for walking on. Their heads became large, and acquired eyes and feelers, so that they could go in pursuit of prey and avoid enemies. As their food was not brought to them by currents of water it did not always consist of small particles, and, therefore, it required to be torn to pieces and chewed. This resulted in the formation of a complicated rasping or chewing organ on the floor of the mouth. These animals became the Gastropoda and the Cephalopoda of the present day, some of which have again changed their habits, and have had their structure greatly modified. Here, again, as in the case of the Lamellibranchiata, I would illustrate freely by dissections and models the physiology, the habits, and the life-history of the animals, and I believe this method of exposition of the structure would go far towards supplying that feeling of life and motion which seems to be so much wanted in our Museums. All unnecessary repetition of similar forms should be avoided. The rows upon rows of specimens all more or less alike which we see in the collection of corals, molluscs, and insects in most Museums are very objectionable. They teach nothing beyond what could be taught by a few well-chosen types, and they are usually very uninteresting. To the Museum visitor who is not a specialist, they are no better than so many hundreds or thousands of crystals, or of variously shaped and coloured beads. It has been urged in justification of the great series of very similar species exhibited in some groups that they illustrate at least the numerical side of nature—the relative numbers in the groups ; but, on the same principle, a large (that is, a common) species ought to be illustrated in the Museum cases by large numbers of individuals—a course which no one would think of adopting. All that I have said with regard to Mollusca applies in principle with equal force to the remaining large groups of animals, such as the Crustacea and the Insecta. The treatment of the Crustacea in even our best Museums is very unequal. The lower groups are almost wholly ignored, with the exception perhaps of the Cirripedia. Why is this ? Merely because the specimens are of small size, some of them microscopic. That is no sufficient reason. Microscopic animals should not be left out of the Museum. They should be represented by models, and by specimens placed under fixed magnifying glasses and microscopes. The large, important, and very interesting group of the copepoda, which swarms on the surface of the sea in Liverpool Bay and round other parts of the coast, and which forms a great part of the food of many fishes, and, even in higher latitudes, of the whale, is not represented in most Museums, and is in consequence almost wholly unknown to the general public. Yet the group contains a large number of species and genera, and shows many interesting modifications of structure. It could be satisfactorily represented in our phylogenetic Museum by a few specimens (mounted on glass slides) of one of the larger and one of the smallest species, to show the range in size and general appearance, and then a few enlarged models illustrating the more important points in their structure and life-history.

The arrangement of the remaining invertebrate groups in the proposed Museum may be seen from the diagram. Those that are extinct would be represented by their fossil remains, and by models showing restorations ; and throughout all the groups the more important fossil forms would of course be placed in their natural position along with their living relations.

The origin of the vertebrata is taken as being, along with the Echinodermata and *Balanoglossus*, from the lower worms, and the early Proto-Chordata would be represented by a series of models placed in a long narrow case which passes through the middle of the archway leading into the Vertebrate Room. Thus the connection between the vertebrated and invertebrated animals is pointed out, and the models of the Proto-Chordata would show the gradual evolution of the backbone and other characteristic vertebrate features.

The first groups of existing vertebrate animals we come to are the Tunicata and *Amphioxus*. The latter is one of the most interesting and important of animals to the biologist, and yet in many Museums it is looked for in vain. The Tunicata are generally placed in our Museums in some absurd position amongst the invertebrata ; often along with the Polyzoa or the Brachiopoda, to which they are not at all closely related ; sometimes they are placed amongst the Mollusca, with which they have no direct affinities. Occasionally they are placed in the Vermes, and that is not such a bad mistake as the former ones. If the Tunicata must be put in the invertebrata, then place them along with the worms, because the vertebrata, as we have seen, are derived from the worms ; but the true position of the Tunicata is at the beginning of the vertebrata, below the fishes. The Vertebrate Room shows a central row of cases containing models of ancestral forms from which the various groups of fishes, amphibians, reptiles, birds, and mammals have been successively evolved. I shall not follow the detailed arrangement of these groups, but merely lay down the general principle that the Museum must show, not merely the outside shape of the animals, and not merely the internal skeleton, but must illustrate all the more important points in structure, physiology, life history, and habits, and must point out as far as possible how these have been brought about. This brings us to the end of the phylogenetic or chief collection.

LOCAL COLLECTION.—The next most important part of the

Museum is the local collection. This should be made as complete as possible. In the case of the British Museum the aim should be to have a complete collection of all groups of British animals. In provincial Museums the local collection should embrace the animals found in the county or district, or the neighbouring parts of the sea. This collection is not intended, like the phylogenetic collection, for the general public. It is for the local naturalist. It will be a great help to him, and he will be a great help to it. It will show him what species have been found in the neighbourhood, and will stimulate him to explore and investigate. It will raise up and foster a body of local naturalists, who will in time help to complete the collection by their discoveries and donations. The local collection will also be of great interest to scientific men and students from other parts of the country visiting the Museum. What a scientific visitor wishes chiefly to see, and hopes to see, in local Museums is a collection illustrating the local Fauna and Flora.

SPECIAL COLLECTIONS.—Turning now to my third and last head, the special collections, we come to a part of the Museum which is of subordinate importance, and which might be made of large or small extent, according to the space available. Here I would place the general collection of the larger groups of animals, such as the corals, the shells, the insects, the fishes, the snakes, the birds, and the mammals, including all those genera and species which were not used in the phylogenetic collection. These series might be placed in the desk-cases and wall-cases of the upper Galleries and corridors of the Museum. Then I would advocate the formation of special collections, illustrating such subjects as parasitism and commensalism, and the variation of species, both in the wild condition and also under domestication.

Lastly, if there was space sufficient, it would be a magnificent addition to have a part of the Museum devoted to the subject of geographical distribution. This should be divided into six sections, showing the characteristic Fauna and Flora of the six regions—Palæarctic, Ethiopian, Oriental, Australian, Neotropical and Nearctic—as laid down by Wallace in his *Geographical Distribution of Animals.* This part of the collection would, without any loss of scientific value, be capable of picturesque treatment—the animals of the various regions being arranged with the appropriate surroundings of plant-life and scenery, so as to illustrate their habits and actions, somewhat in the manner suggested in the *Nineteenth Century* for March, 1887, by the Rev. J. G. Wood. It would be a mistake, I consider, to arrange the whole

Museum or even the chief part of it in this somewhat confused, though no doubt interesting, pictorial manner ; but, after the phylogenetic collection and the local collection have been provided for, the remaining specimens and space might well be devoted to such a purpose as a series of popular illustrations of the geographical distribution of plants and animals, and as far as possible of their habits and mode of life.

Such then is the Public Museum of Natural History as I would like to see it, and as I believe it will be seen in the future. The best wish that I can express in regard to this paper I have just laid before you is that it may have some slight effect in exciting public discussion in regard to Museums, and in bringing the future within measurable distance of the present. In conclusion, the chief advantages which I claim for the phylogenetic arrangement described in this paper over the linear arrangement now employed in our Museums, are as follows :—1st. It would give a much more accurate representation of nature. 2nd. While being more intelligible and instructive to the general public, it would also be more in accord with the present state of biological knowledge, and could very readily be slightly altered from time to time so as to keep abreast with the progress of science. 3rd. It would be a perpetual illustrated lecture of the best kind, demonstrating to every one with ordinary intelligence the great doctrine of Organic Evolution.

EXPLANATION OF THE PLATE.—Fig. 1. Ground plan of the proposed Phylogenetic Museum, showing the arrangement of the cases. The dotted line represents the brass bar which shows the connection between the various groups. P.A. Position of *Protamœba;* A. Position of *Amœba ;* G. Position of *Gastrœa ;* N. Position of *Nauplius;* T. Position of *Model Tree of the Animal Kingdom.* The positions of the more important groups of animals are indicated on the cases in the figure. Fig. 2. Plan of the First Floor of the Museum, showing the first Gallery and the positions of the Zoological and Botanical Laboratories, &c. Fig. 3. Vertical Section of the Museum, showing the positions of the Galleries, the Laboratories, the Lecture Hall, the Aquarium, &c.

CHAPTER XI.

THE SUNDAY OPENING OF MUSEUMS.

HIS is rapidly becoming one of the pressing questions of the day. Many prominent men who have hitherto hesitated about expressing an opinion on the subject no longer find themselves able to maintain a neutral position. It is well that this should be the case, for the matter is of too great importance for anyone who really takes an interest in national progress to stand aloof and allow things to take their course. It is undeniable that many earnest Christian men have been compelled—reluctantly, perhaps, in some cases — to come to the conclusion that it is both wise and politic to give non-church goers a choice between the street or public-house, and Museums and Art Galleries on the Sunday. I shall endeavour to discuss the question impartially, and will give the views *pro* and *con* upon the matter of a few well-known people.

The opening of Art Galleries and Museums on the Sunday is resisted in this country rather from tradition than on principle. Nobody can point to any moral deterioration likely to arise from such a conces- sion. Most of the experiments yet made in the direc- tion of bringing the treasures of art and antiquity within reach of the people on the day when they have most time available have been crowned with success. Many who resist such a step in modern progress derive their impulse rather from the past than the present. Their ideas are a survival of Puritanism, or so much as is left of it. However, the hands of the clock cannot stand still, and it is impossible to scotch the march of progress.

It may, no doubt, be taken as an axiom that the alienation of the sympathies of the working classes from places of worship is one of the most deplorable signs of the times. Very many Nonconformist ministers and clergymen of all sections recognise this fact as acutely as do any sections of society. Further, they have strained every nerve and adopted every means to stem this tide of abstention from churches and chapels, but without any appreciable success. Many of those who come in close contact with the working classes, and have thus had opportunities of learning some of the causes of this state of things, have come to the conclusion that the abstention from religious services on the part of the working classes does not arise from any antipathy against the Church or yet any anti-religious feeling they may hold. The two primary causes are, first, the need of physical rest after the work and worry of the week is over, and, secondly, the deeply-rooted feeling that the occupants of high-backed and cushioned pews look so much askance at the presence of the sons of toil worshipping side by side with them. It is a pleasant fiction to say that all stand equal in the Church as worshippers of the Almighty so far, at least, as the estimation of men is concerned. How much irreligion pews, pulpits, gowns, and "man millinery" *en bloc* have caused it is impossible to conceive. It may reasonably be asked, Why is there such an enormous waste of force in the churches ? Surely there

is a terrible anomaly in the fact that churches and
chapels should be open, say, six hours in the week and
public-houses open something like 156 hours. The
waste, again, of force in not utilising an intelligent
laity to a far greater extent is most lamentable. The
evils arising from a one-man ministry, whether
applied to the Establishment or Nonconformity,
are considerable. It is very certain that matters
must continue to remain very much out of joint until
we readjust these and other anomalies with regard to
Church life. In the meantime the appearance of
dismally-empty churches must continue to present
itself to our gaze to the sincere regret of all who have
the true welfare of the nation at heart.

The position of the nominal Christians on the
subject has to be largely taken into account. We are,
as a nation, perpetually prating about our Christianity,
and there is much in our national life which is as far
removed from the true spirit of the Teacher of
Nazareth as light from darkness. It may reasonably
be asked, By what right do Christians indulge in their
own pleasure and deny those same pleasures to others ?
They have only the right of might, and surely Christians
should be the last to exercise such a right ! The
musical have the melodious songs of the church, the
peals of the organ and the harmony of the string
instruments in which to indulge themselves on the
Sunday; the literary man has the use of books
belonging either to himself or to some of the libraries
to which he is able to subscribe, through which to
commune with the great of the past and the present;
those who love a good dinner on Sunday as well as on
the other days of the week do not feel it necessary to
give their domestics instructions not to stay at home on
that day to cook it while they go to church. The man
who loves to commune with nature has the green fields

and pleasant woods in which he can take refuge and study on the Sunday. To sketch a flower or tree on Sunday is counted by many a crime ; yet those same censors will sometimes pass hours in the criticism of their neighbour's bonnet, or in the circulation of silly and mischievous scandal, or in the verbal planning of a dress, or the arrangement of balls and parties for the ensuing week. There seems to be no clear or definite idea where the sanctity of the Sunday begins or ends among many people; but on one point they all seem firmly agreed, and that is that the opening of a Library, a Picture Gallery, or a Museum is an offence against the law of the good old English Sunday.

According to the views of many of these good people the admirer of paintings, and natural science, is not to cast his eye upon these beautiful objects because, through no fault of his own, he is not able to go where they are on any day but the first day of the week. Museums and Picture Galleries belong to the nation, and not to only a portion of it. Consequently the convenience of the people as to when their institutions shall be open should be taken into account. Sunday must ever be mainly a day of repose to those who undergo hard intellectual, or manual labour. It is obviously a sin against himself, and ultimately against the community, if a man goes on with his work on a Sunday. He utterly ruins his higher powers, and brings himself down as nearly as possible to the level of the brutes. It is the duty of everyone to try and bring his fellow-creatures into such a position that they could have the advantage of studying nature in some way or other, and we have now reached in education a point at which something more on the Sunday than the teaching of churches, chapels, and Sunday-schools has become absolutely necessary. People must be brought under the influence of pictures and other beautiful objects and books. It is not creditable to our boasted civilisation that in this time of the life of the world we should calmly allow so many of our fellow-creatures to live so little above the level of savages, when there are so many things in our civilisation which, if only used aright, would tend to raise them high above their present condition. How can all the instruments of civilisation be used if they are not to be used on the Sunday as well as on other days? To the mass of people Sunday is the only day of leisure, and every opportunity should be given for their getting on that day the best kinds of mental and intellectual recreation. If people are to get the full benefits from the study of books, pictures, and the contents of Museums, such places ought to be opened for certain hours on the Sunday.

The one main reason why many are so much opposed to the Sunday opening of Museums is that it may be the getting in of the end of the wedge to continentalise our Sunday. The statement is very frequently made that if we open Museums, Picture Galleries, and Free Libraries on the Sunday, as a logical sequence theatres must be opened too. But it does not at all follow that we must fall into the groove which unfortunately characterises the Continent in the method of spending the Sabbath. The reverential feeling is far more deeply rooted in the minds of the English-speaking peoples than of any other nation on the face of the earth. This is sufficient safeguard for the proper and reasonable extension of the opportunities for a rational spending of Sunday. Again, what Museums, Picture Galleries, and Free Libraries give us are absolute necessaries of mental and moral life. This cannot be said of the theatre. Museums, with other kindred institutions, are national property, and there is no money-making element in the question, but with theatres the question is different. Consequently the opening of these two descriptions of institutions stands on a totally dissimilar footing.

It will be opportune to call attention to the general position of the question, and to the expressions of opinion of some public men. A few years ago, when the matter was before the House of Lords, the Bishops were conspicuous either by their absence or silence. Out of twenty-six, seven only were present, and these do not seem to have made any exertion to express their opinion upon the matter.

Following this, a Royal Commission declared that the Sunday opening of Museums and Art Galleries has exerted a salutary influence on the moral and intellectual condition of the people. Immediately after the report of this Commission was published Sir Henry Roscoe asked the House of Commons to recognise " the justice and expediency of opening the Natural History Museum at South Kensington and the Bethnal Green Museum in East London on Sundays without further delay, thus extending to London the advantages already provided at Kew, Hampton Court, Greenwich, Dublin, Birmingham, Manchester, and ten other provincial towns." Sir Henry Roscoe, M.P., mentioned these places where Sunday opening has been in practice for some time with excellent results. Dublin holds a foremost place for liberality in this respect. The collection in that city, of painting, sculpture, archæology, and zoology, is free of access on the Sunday, and a fine Sunday attracts a larger number of people than all the other days of the week combined. If it be objected that Dublin, being in another country, is not a convincing example for England to follow, we have the home illustrations of Manchester, Birmingham, New-

castle-on-Tyne, London (partially), and several other
places, and not a single evidence that anything but
advantage has resulted.

The long discussion which took place during the latter
part of 1887 and the early part of this year as to the
opening of the Salford Museum and Free Library on
Sundays has given the question a great impetus.
Mr. B. Armitage was the prime mover throughout, and
championed the question, notwithstanding much
obloquy, in a manner highly creditable to him.

The Right Hon. John Bright, M.P., writing in March,
1888, to Mr. Armitage, said: "I have noticed the discussion on the question of opening the Free Libraries
in your borough on Sunday afternoons and evenings. If
I were a dweller in your town, and one of your Town
Council, I should be one of your supporters on the
question in which you have taken so much interest. I
hope you may succeed, and that the results of your
success may convert many who are now your opponents."

Mr. Thomas Burt, the miners' representative, wrote:
"I entirely approve of your action in trying to have
the Reading Rooms of the Free Libraries at Salford
open on Sunday afternoons and evenings, and I wish
you every success."

Dean Oakley, referring particularly to the labour side
of the question, says: "I am for the fullest protection
of liberty to serve or not on Sunday, and for the good
Manchester rule of permitting an alternative day's or
half day's holiday to the Sunday workers.   .   .   .
My notion of the Christian Socialist's attitude in
this case is to share the means of Sunday rest
and recreation with as many of our less fortunate
fellow-citizens as possible, and not to bar their access
to books and comfort on that day which are, after all,
their own." The Dean on another occasion wrote: "We
can treat imputations of Secularism and irreligion, and

of robbing the poor of their weekly rest, with the
silence of indignant scorn for the charges, and of
sorrow for the good men whose conscientious opposition
is discredited by such language and tactics. Personally
I welcome your action, and wish it success, for a further
reason.   It has happily shown that there are principles
of faith and morals and points of Christian conduct on
which Bishops and other ministers, as well as earnest
laymen of the English Church, of the Roman Catholic
Church, and of the churches of Protestant Nonconformity can agree entirely, and can adopt a common
policy in furtherance of what they alike believe to be
the will of God and the welfare of their fellow-men.
May it lead to further like co-operation."

The Mayor of Manchester, Alderman Harwood, of
high standing as a Methodist, and of unimpeachable
orthodoxy, says: " Why should the people be compelled
to read in dark, dingy dwellings, when they paid for
commodious halls that stood empty?   To enlarge the
idea of Sunday, to embrace healthy relaxation and
intellectual exercise, was to help to make a happier,
more sober and contented people, and to strengthen the
fibre and raise the tone of this great nation."

Dr. Fraser, the late Bishop of Manchester, whilst he
never " publicly and formally " (the phrase is his own)
advocated Sunday opening, never opposed it; he did
justice to the motives of those who desired it, and
preserved all along an attitude of " benevolent neu-
trality."   Thus in his address as President of the
Social Science Congress, he gave the statistics of the
first year of Sunday opening at the Manchester
Libraries.   He did so without one word of disapproval.
" We must be taught by experience," said Bishop
Fraser; and, taught by experience, the present Bishop
of Manchester adds the weight of his ecclesiastical
status, his intellectual power, his high character and

practical philanthropy in favour of Sunday opening. This is what he said : " I heartily support your effort to secure the opening of the Public Library at convenient hours on Sunday.   No one more prizes than I do the rest of the Sunday, and no one would oppose more strenuously any effort to deprive the working classes of that advantage.   It is for this reason that I have always opposed all attempts to organise amusements or to call into action any large amount of labour on the Lord's Day.   But when I was a layman I always found that quiet reading added to the profit and pleasure of my Sundays.   Now, I know that there are hundreds and thousands of young men in Manchester who, living in lodgings or in narrow and populous homes, have neither the books to read nor opportunities for reading.   To these the opening of the Public Libraries would be a priceless boon, and it would be easy to prevent any too great infringement of the rest of the ordinary employés of the Library."

Mr. H. H. Howorth, M.P. for Salford, has strong views on the subject, as will be seen from his words : " I have always held the same view on this question, and took an active part in opening the Manchester Libraries on Sunday, and have never regretted the step I took.   There are a great many people who do not go to church or chapel ; there are many others who go only once.   Many of these are young men in lodgings. It seems to me that to compel them to find their only Sunday occupation in the public-house or the club is neither Christianity nor is it even rational.   On the other hand, there are classes, like the railway servants and cabmen, who can only read, if they read at all, on Sunday.   The argument about employing people in Libraries on Sunday is to me a very hollow one.   The very men who raise it employ postmen and railway guards in large numbers, and read their Monday's paper (the result of Sunday labour) quite comfortably. When men like the Bishop of Manchester, Mr. Oliver Heywood, and others strongly support the movement, the outcry about desecrating the Sabbath becomes ridiculous. Of course I am aware that a large number of men still hold, in spite of very serious testimony, that man was made for the Sabbath and not the Sabbath for man. With such theologians argument is useless."

The experience of the Rev. S. A. Barnett in his work in the East End in the Sunday opening of his annual picture exhibition, has more than confirmed him in the wisdom of the step.

The Rev. Bernard J. Snell, a Nonconformist minister in Salford, in preaching from the texts, " The Sabbath is made for man," and " It is lawful to do good on the Sabbath Day," said " the value of Sunday in giving opportunity for the development of those faculties which lie dormant under life's drudgery was too keenly appreciated for practical men to throw it away ; but Sunday was not kept holy by being kept empty and dull. The dismalness of Sunday was the great cause of Sunday intemperance ; men were fatigued with too much idleness, and in sheer despair of anything better to hand, soaked themselves in liquor. On the Continent public Galleries, for which the admission charge on week-days was a franc, were free as air on Sundays, and thronged with working folk. Our Museums and Free Libraries were among the finest results of civilisation, and it was remarkably thriftless that in a free nation like ours these places were not accessible at the most convenient times. The only plea worth consideration was the fear lest the liberty of employés should be curtailed, but the number of workers in Libraries was very small compared with the number of visitors. Rotation could be readily arranged without any unreasonable burden, or one-seventh more

workers could be employed without appreciable cost.
The caretakers and pew-openers of one Salford church
would keep going all the Salford Libraries.   A public
Library was a temple where men studied the wisdom
and greatness of the dead and living.   What if some
few did serve on Sundays; their service was no less
sacred than that of ministers. In 1887 nearly 300,000
readers went to the Manchester Libraries on Sundays,
and read books above the standard of those ordinarily
perused."

The Roman Catholic Bishop of Salford says: " In
a quiet way I went round myself to several of the
city Libraries on Sunday evening some two years ago,
or thereabouts, for the purpose of seeing how much
they were used, and was very favourably impressed with
what I witnessed. I was more struck by the number
of boys I found in the reading-rooms than with anything else, and with their quiet demeanour.   I asked
myself—Is it better that they should be here than in
the streets ?   Is it reasonable to expect them to spend
the whole evening in church ?   Is there any positive
obligation that they should spend even one hour of the
evening in the church ?   How many of those persons
seated quietly in the reading-rooms would go to the
church to say prayers were the reading-rooms closed ?
The answers to these questions are obvious.   What do
they want who desire to close the reading-rooms on
Sunday evening ?   Surely not to compel everyone to
go to church willy-nilly twice a day ; and, if not, why
not encourage the quiet and improving occupation of
reading ?   Suggest to the young what they should read
as much as you please.   Encourage the reading of
religious books if you please.   But do not say you may
hang about the streets, you may go to the public-house,
you may invent your own way of whiling away the
Sunday evening, but you shall not spend the time in

reading your own books in your own Library, because both the books and the Library are not private but public property."

Some opinions against Sunday opening are here given.

The Right Rev. John Charles Ryle, Bishop of Liverpool, says: " I heartily wish success to the movement for opposing the opening of Museums, &c., on Sunday. I am fighting the same battle here in Liverpool to the best of my ability. The advocates of the unhappy movement which we oppose mean well, I believe, and think they are doing God's service and benefiting the working classes. In my opinion they are totally mistaken. Our old English Sunday is one of the greatest blessings which God has given to this country, and if the working classes of Great Britain allowed themselves to be deprived of it they would soon find to their cost that they had made an enormous mistake."

Canon Stowell, of Manchester, says: " The advocates of Sunday opening lay great stress on the importance of providing a counter-attraction to the public-house and plead for it in the interests of temperance. I would suggest that a more excellent way of promoting those interests would be to close the public-houses on Sundays. If the gentlemen who so earnestly advocate the adoption of this remedy would take half as much pains to secure the removal of the evil as they are doing to counteract its effects, it would soon cease to exist." Canon Stowell made much of these failures.

In September, 1884, the Town Council of Chester resolved to open their Public Library on Sundays. After three months' experience the Town Council resolved to close it again on Sundays, with only three dissentients out of twenty-eight members present.

The Town Council of Maidstone, after an experiment of three years of Sunday opening, decided in February, 1881, by sixteen votes against three, to close their Museum and Library on Sundays. The results of Sunday opening were strongly condemned by the Mayor.

After four years' experience in Stoke-on-Trent, the Librarian wrote to the Mayor, in November, 1885, a letter, in which the following statements were made : " 1. The persons the opening was intended to benefit are conspicuous by their absence. 2. The thing has degenerated into a promenade and conversazione for children on their dismissal from school, about 3.30 or four o'clock. These children, besides running about and making a noise, do more damage to the books, periodicals, &c., than would be done in a year by the ordinary visitors. 4. There are several members of the Council who are prepared to confirm these statements." In December, 1886, the Public Library was finally closed on Sundays.

In May, 1884, the Town Council of Worcester resolved by eight votes against four to open their Museum on Sundays. At the meeting of the Council, in June, after a month's experience of Sunday opening, it was resolved by sixteen votes against fourteen to close the Museum on Sundays.

The City Fathers rejected in January, 1888, by a small majority, a proposal to open the Guildhall Library on Sundays for the benefit of the warehouse clerks and others who are compelled to stay in the City on that day. The motion was lost by fifty-four votes to fifty, three of the four aldermen present voting with the majority.

A memorial from the Liverpool Sunday Society, for the opening of the Museum and Gallery of Art on Sunday afternoons, from two o'clock to six, was under

the consideration of the City Council on the 7th of
March, and was negatived by twenty-six votes to
seventeen.

The Trustees of the British Museum, it is anticipated,
will, this year, allow the Museum to be open during
certain hours on Sundays.

Museums, Art Galleries, and Free Libraries should
be opened whenever and wherever this is necessary
to meet the needs of the badly housed, the
homeless, and the working classes in large towns
and cities. Whether observed ecclesiastically or
otherwise, the Sunday is too valuable a boon to
be wasted in low self-indulgence. When we consider
the incessant toil and sacrifice that are ever necessary
to counteract the tendencies and temptations to careless
living, the Sabbath ought to be jealously guarded and
respected as a day consecrated to social, moral, and
religious culture, when the great verities of life, truth,
beauty, love, justice, goodness are made present and
impressive to men.

It is difficult to think that one single person who has
hitherto been accustomed to attend a place of worship
would be drawn away from church to visit a Museum
or Picture Gallery. The great success which has
attended Sunday opening in Birmingham, Manchester,
and other places should give the greatest encouragement to other places to adopt a similar plan. When
ever possible a *plébiscite* of the citizens should be taken
so that the matter may come fairly and fully before
those who own these institutions, and who naturally
do not all think alike upon the question.

CHAPTER XII.

MUSEUM LECTURES.

WHEREVER possible there should be in connection with all Museums and Art Galleries, at stated times, lectures on the objects in the Museum or on subjects incidental to the work of these institutions. Curators have already done much in this direction.

The Oxford University Extension Lectures have given an impetus to this method of oral teaching the good effects of which it is impossible to estimate. The chief aim of University Extension Teaching is to form and encourage permanent habits of continuous and systematic reading and study, and if the increasing popularity of these lectures is any gauge, there can be no doubt about that point. Those who have promoted the scheme and who have the extension of the work under their care have been the means of giving a stimulus to thought and the study of special subjects. The purpose of all education should be to encourage continuous study, to infuse in the mind the principle that there is no limit to either human intelligence or progress.

The subjects of the various courses of lectures

adapted specially to Museums and Free Libraries, are divided into the following classes :—

I.—LITERATURE.

II.—HISTORY.

III.—ART.

1. English Painters (illustrated).
2. The Great Schools of Art (illustrated).

IV.—SCIENCE.

1. The Life Work of great English Scientific Men.
2. The Darwinian Advancement of Knowledge.
3. Life on the Surface of the Earth.
4. Physical and Political Geography.
5. Physiography.
6. Germs and their Relations to Disease.

V.—POLITICAL ECONOMY AND INDUSTRIAL HISTORY.

Each course is delivered by an experienced lecturer, and each course consists of from six to twelve lecture classes.

Each lecture is followed by a class with whom the Lecturer discusses any difficulties which may have arisen during the lecture. Between each lecture the students are invited to write short essays which are corrected by the Lecturer. At the end of the course there is held an examination, entrance to which is optional and open to all students, men and women, who have attended two-thirds of the weekly classes. According to the result of the examination, University certificates and a prize are awarded to successful students.

Mr. Sadler, University Extension Department, Oxford, who has done much to develope this scheme, will gladly give any further information which may be required, and Governing Bodies of Museums should consider the advisability of placing themselves in communication with him.

It is impossible to overestimate the value which attaches to the lectures given at the British Museum. The course by Mr. W. St. Chad Boscawen has been particularly instructive. The subject was the "History and Civilisation of the later Babylonian Empire"— that is, the period from the fall of the Assyrian Empire and the capture of Babylon. A further series was on "The Middle Babylonian Empire."

Two lectures by Mr. T. Tyler given in the Assyrian Galleries of the Museum on the additional light thrown on the Hittites by the Yuzgat and Tarsus seals, which have been recently discovered, were also well attended. The lecture was devoted chiefly to a historical sketch of the Hittite people and their relations with surrounding Powers.

Up to the present time it is chiefly in the Geological Section that lectures have been given at the Natural History Museum. Lectures on "Plants" have recently been delivered.

May it not be reasonably urged that the lecturing element at the British Museum, South Kensington, and the National Gallery might with advantage be considerably enlarged? The reason given why this is not done is the lack of funds for the purpose. Until some wealthy donor comes forward and endows a few lecturers' chairs, could not voluntary work be encouraged? There are many University men and scientists who would readily place at the disposal of the authorities and the public, their knowledge of special subjects. This is one of the avenues where the endowment of research would, if the funds were properly administered, be useful; for those benefiting from such a fund could place their knowledge at the disposal of audiences at one of these national institutions.

At the Harborne and Edgbaston Institute during the past winter, a lecture on "Natural History for Busy Workers" was delivered. The reverend gentleman who gave the lecture referred, at the outset, to the strong recommendations for the study of nature, and then gave an interesting account of the "Busy Bees," enlarging upon the various lessons taught mankind by them. A lengthened allusion to plants, animals, and fossils, and the lessons taught by them to lovers of natural history, concluded the lecture.

At Liverpool a winter course of evening lectures of a popular character was instituted by the Committee in 1865, and in 1866 was increased to forty in number. In the autumn of 1879 courses of evening lectures of an advanced character were also instituted; and both series are continued with increasing success to the present time. The earlier courses of autumn lectures were delivered in connection with the Cambridge University Extension Scheme until the establishment of the University College of Liverpool. Eminent literary and scientific men take part in these lectures, including the Principal and Professors of the University College.

The Rotunda Hall, under the Picton Reading Room, capable of accommodating over 1,500 hearers, is usually densely crowded by audiences of all classes, and often hundreds cannot obtain admission.

The last of the twenty-third course of winter lectures took place on March 15th, 1888, before a crowded audience, the Chairman of the Lectures Committee (Mr. W. J. Lunt) presiding. The subject of the lecture was "Eloquence of Music," by Mr. W. H. Jude, Principal of the Liverpool Organ School. The Chairman, in his closing remarks, referred to the large and constant attendance of the public throughout the series of lectures which had been given under the auspices of the Library and Museum Committee.

At Leeds they have had several successful series of Museum lectures. One of these, delivered this last winter by Professor Ransome, of the Yorkshire College, in the Philosophical Hall, was on " The Battle of Leeds." He alluded to the outbreak of the Civil War in 1642, saying that Yorkshire soon found itself divided into two hostile camps—Royalists and Parliamentarians. He noticed the efforts of the Royalists to get possession of the clothing towns, so that they might levy contributions upon them, and the defence made by Bradford against their attacks. He pointed out that Leeds, which had then 7,000 inhabitants, and was about the size of the town of Otley at the present time, was held by the Royalists under Sir William Savile. By means of a plan of the town, shown on the screen by the aid of a lantern, he described the position of the entrenchments thrown up by the defenders, and the attack made upon them by the Parliamentarians under Sir Thomas Fairfax on January 23rd, 1643, the result being the defeat and flight of the Royalists with very little bloodshed. Personally, the lecturer remarked, the battle of Leeds was interesting, because it was the first success of Sir Thomas Fairfax, and it was the forerunner of the great success at Marston Moor and the crowning victory of Naseby. Several cannon balls picked up in the neighbourhood were shown. Both at this and the other lectures of the course there was a good attendance.

All technicalities should in these lectures be avoided, and all terms with which artisans might be unacquainted should be explained, and an object should be shown which will impress the fact on the minds of one half of them.

The use of the lantern is most advisable, as, by means of the excellent views which can now be obtained, so much enhanced interest is given to the lectures. As in all other departments of life, there have been improvements, and the magic lantern, with its crude pictures, is a thing of the past. Now we have excellent effects by means of photography and the lime-light, which make it comparatively easy to bring a lecture on the most abstruse scientific subject within the comprehension of all.

Much information may be conveyed and actual teaching done by the informal lectures, or chats, on the specimens in the Museum to small groups of visitors. An example of one of such lectures is given after the statistics at the end of the volume.

There are many other lectures in connection with Museum and Art Gallery work to which attention could be called, but sufficient has been said to show the increasing interest there is in this part of the work of these institutions. Chats on pictures are none the less necessary than in other branches. A greatly enhanced interest is given to any picture by a few words from one who has grasped the artist's idea, or knows the subject upon which the picture is founded.

CHAPTER XIII.

THE BRITISH MUSEUM AND ITS PLACE IN THE NATION.

HIS is our national institution *par excellence,* and we need not yield the palm to any country for having a finer and better Museum than we have at Bloomsbury. America may possibly have at Washington, when completed, a more imposing structure, but there are treasures in the British Museum of unique and intrinsic value such as no other country can boast. After visiting the national Museums in Rome, Berlin, Naples, Paris, New York, and other cities, I have always come away feeling the prouder of our own pile of buildings, with their well-kept departments, each so complete and so accessible to the public free of any charge. In this respect it differs from some of the institutions just named.

So many people have visited the British Museum that it is not necessary to give more than a few brief particulars of its general characteristics.

An Act of Parliament was passed in 1753, "for the purchase of the Museum or collection of Sir Hans Sloane, and of the Harleian collection of manuscripts, and for providing one general repository for the better reception and more convenient use of the said collections; and of the Cottonian Library, and of the additions thereto." This was the year of its foundation, and we will forgive the legislators of 135 years ago the clumsy wording of the Act. What Parliament then did has been one of the most useful Statutes which has ever been passed. The real germ, however, of the British Museum dates back to the end of the sixteenth and beginning of the seventeenth centuries, when Sir Robert Cotton was gathering his noted collection of manuscripts. These were eventually presented to the nation in 1700 by his grandson.

The three collections specially named in the Act of Incorporation were brought together in Montagu House, Bloomsbury, the site of which is occupied by the present buildings. Many additions have from time to time been built, necessitated by the extending work of the British Museum. The last of these—the "White Wing"—was opened to the public in March, 1888. The extension takes its name from the original donor or founder of the fund which pays for it. William White, who has so benefited the Museum, and through it the nation, was a resident in Bloomsbury, and died as far back as 1823. By his Will, made only five months before his death, he enjoined upon his executors, in the event of his widow marrying again or at her death, to transfer and pay over the residue of his property to the Trustees of the British Museum. He gives his reason for this in a sentence worth repeating. "*From the nation my property came,* and when I leave my son enough to be a farmer, he has that which may make him as happy and respectable as he can be in any station, and it is my charge that he be so brought up." Would that there were more good sense of this nature to be found in wills. This son died in infancy, and in 1826 the Court of Chancery disallowed the claim of the Museum Trustees to the landed estates, which were situated in Hampshire and the Isle of Wight. The widow died in 1879, and there then came into the possession of the Museum Trustees a total sum, less legacy duty, of £65,411.

The style of architecture of the White Wing is similar to the main structure. In accordance with directions in the will the gift is commemorated by an inscription bearing the donor's name. He was evidently a very modest man, for he says, " This is a little vanity of no harm, and may tempt others to follow my example in thinking more of the nation and less of themselves.'

One Gallery is filled with a splendid collection of Chinese and Japanese paintings. Most of these are dated and classified according to their various schools. Another long Gallery contains a very fine collection of Greek, Roman, Venetian, German and French glass. In addition to this glass there is a splendid collection of German pottery and Italian majolica ware. There are also some cases of Rhodian, Sicilian, Spanish and Persian ware. Palissy and other French ware occupy one case.

A third and smaller room is devoted to English pottery, and one would be glad for the sake of the reputation attaching to English ware if some of the specimens in this room were conspicuous by their absence. A case of English slip-ware, and a case of Staffordshire ware are well worth noticing. These cases of glass and pottery afford considerable scope for study and enjoyment. The classification is excellent, and by means of the penny guide even the casual visitor cannot fail to find much to interest.

So much space would be required for even the most cursory glance at the history of the various sections that we pass them over, and proceed to note the work accomplished by the Museum as recorded in the last report issued in the Return for the House of Commons, and published in July, 1887.

The Return exhibits excellent housekeeping in every department. The management of the different trust funds shows a judicious outlay with wise thrift for that rainy day when great treasures come into the market, and the Museum has to hold its own in the bidding against the collectors of the world.

Within a compass of seventy-nine pages there is a capital epitome of the work of this institution. The total number of visitors during the last official year was 1,165,350. The cry is still for more space, and hints are thrown out in the Report that there are some good things in sepulchral monuments hid away in the cellars which should see the daylight if there were only courts and space in which to place them. The arranging of the Ethnological collection bequeathed by the late Henry Christy occupies, and deservedly so, the first mention in the Report. A large portion of the Return is occupied with a list of the additions to the departments of charts, manuscripts, prints, drawings, &c.

The department of Egyptian and Assyrian Antiquities is constantly receiving additions, and those made during the last Museum year are of a very valuable character. This department is of infinite importance, and reflects the greatest credit upon the antiquarian research and skill which has brought so many objects of this nature under one roof. It is very interesting to turn after this to the department of British and Mediæval Antiquities and Ethnography. The list of acquisitions and presentations in this section is very numerous, and illustrates very clearly how keenly alive the authorities are to what is worth procuring, and

LYCIAN ROOM, BRITISH MUSEUM.

[Drawn by J. W. Benn.

what ultimately the British Museum might become if the Government were not so parsimonious in its Grant for the Museum and so lavish when it is a question of powder, shot, pensions, and Royal yachts.

Mr. Augustus W. Franks, the Keeper of the British and Mediæval Antiquities, has contributed most of the gifts already mentioned. It is only right that the public should know that it is to his generosity as Keeper of the section to which reference has just been made that the Museum is indebted for treasures of great value. These comprise British and Anglo-Roman antiquities, coins and medals, topographical and other drawings. Of even still greater value was a large collection of Chinese and Japanese pottery and porcelain worth not less than £10,000. These contained some very rare specimens, and also a number of specimens of Italian majolica, Palissy and sgraffiato ware, plaques, &c. It is estimated that the gross value of these collections presented by Mr. Franks exceeds £20,000, and that of the collections which have been presented to the Museum through his influence reaches £60,000. The collections which have thus come to the public have been formed with all the advantages of knowledge and experience acquired by Mr. Franks. With his known taste and skill in making the most of the objects under his care, he has arranged them in a way which has added greatly to their value. Mr. Franks has displayed a most commendable public spirit, and within the last few months he has been made a C.B. Had he shot, from behind a trench, a handful of defenceless Soudanese, he would probably have received a higher honour.

The British Museum is exceptionally fortunate in its chief officials, in whom the public have the fullest confidence. With a knowledge of this fact it was not surprising that the resignation of Dr. Bond, in the middle of June, should have come upon the literary and scientific community with considerable abruptness, and many eager inquiries were made as to what could have been the undercurrent which was the cause of it. He has held the post of Principal Librarian and Secretary for so many years, and with so much honour and distinction to himself and the profession, of which he has held the blue ribbon. This makes it all the more difficult to understand that he should, without a word of warning, or the least symptom of failing health or waning powers, suddenly abdicate on the ground that it is his duty to make way for younger men. A knighthood and pension will scarcely content the public if there is not some valid reason behind. The question is not settled at the time of closing this part of the book for press.

There is one department which many would like to see mentioned which does not at present find a place in the Museum. That is a section for Christian Archæology for Great Britain. The Christian religion as shown by its monuments is not taken into account by the authorities of the British Museum and South Kensington. Anyone visiting either of these places might infer that this country had been pagan throughout the greater part of its history. No other nation in Europe possesses so splendid a series of early Christian monuments illustrating our national art in its most interesting phases and supplementing the knowledge derived from the Celtic and Saxon MSS. Certainly not less than 500 such monuments remain, rude pillars with ogham inscriptions and elaborate crosses covered with a profusion of those forms of ornament so highly developed in Ireland in the eighth and ninth centuries; yet no attempt has hitherto been made to preserve any record of their existence in our public Museums by means of casts or photographs of typical examples.

According to the system at present adopted the objects

in the British Museum are arranged partly chronologicall
and partly according to material, and thus in the Mediæval
Room a crosier of the early Irish Church is placed side
by side with an Arabic candlestick because both are of
bronze and both mediæval. At South Kensington
matters are worse, and the cast of the Anglian cross
from Gosforth, in Cumberland, is associated with reproductions of Trajan's Column and of Scandinavian forts.
This is a matter demanding the consideration of the
authorities.

There has probably never been in the entire history
of the British Museum a more earnest desire on the
part of those in charge to aid provincial Museums, and
thus to realise its legitimate place as the head of these
institutions. By supplying duplicate printed books and
engravings, electrotypes of ancient coins, and casts of
gems, the Museum may become a most powerful aid to
provincial institutions, and in this direction there has
been no niggardliness save through want of funds.
A further departure has been adopted, namely, the
first part of a series of *fac-simile* reproductions
by photography and other methods of some of the best
drawings by old masters in the collection. These reproductions are intended in the first instance for free distribution to provincial Art Museums and Public Libraries, and their cost is defrayed out of a special grant
allowed by the Treasury for that purpose. The selection
will include all the studies preserved in the Department
of Prints and Drawings for pictures, as well as other
miscellaneous examples, chiefly taken from recent
acquisitions of the department, and will be accompanied
by a critical text by the Keeper, Professor Colvin. By
efforts such as this the British Museum will, in the
near future, far more usefully fulfil its place in the nation
than it has been able to do in the past.

The annual allowance from Government. for the

maintenance of this and our other similar national
institutions is practically the most important point.
The last discussion in the House of Commons on the
annual grant to South Kensington and the British
Museum took place in May, 1888. Only a night or two in-
tervened between the discussion respecting the many
thousands of pounds voted year after year for the maintenance of Royal palaces, and the suggestion that the British Museum should be lighted throughout with the electric
light, in order to give the middle and working classes
some opportunity of seeing its treasures in the evenings.
The leader of the House said that he could not possibly
see his way to expend any more of the public money
on such an unimportant matter. " It would cost too
much, and he was not justified in asking the House of
Commons to incur such an outlay and annual charge."
It is precisely the same whichever party is in power,
and John Bull grumbles and pays the bill. A Government which would reform and readjust our national
expenditure would confer a permanent benefit upon the
nation. Thus far, sad to say, it would appear that the
economy plank in political life is worked by both sides
in turn merely to catch votes. As Ruskin has said,
" We are obliged to know what o'clock it is, for the
safety of our ships, and therefore we pay for an observatory ; and we allow ourselves, in the person of our
Parliament, to be annually tormented into doing something, in a slovenly way, for the British Museum ;
sullenly apprehending that to be a place for keeping
stuffed birds in to amuse our children." The English
people would do well to take an active interest in
finance, and adopt means to set our national Treasury
House in order.

The grant on this last occasion for the Museum
buildings was £10,940. The *Financial Reform
Almanack* for the current year gives the statistics

below of Class IV. of our national bill for Education, Science and Art.

ENGLAND.	1887-88 £	1886-87 (Grants in Session of 1886.) £	Compared with Grants for 1886-87. Inc. £	Dec. £
Public Education	3,458,807	3,402,989	55,818	..
Science and Art Department	438,558	420,043	18,515	..
British Museum	147,385	162,285	..	14,900
National Gallery	8,908	8,607	301	..
National Portrait Gallery	1,916	2,361	..	445
Learned Societies, &c.	23,900	24,400	..	500
London University	13,321	13,152	169	..
University Colleges, Wales	12,000	12,000	..	..
Deep Sea Exploring Expedition(Report)	2,987	4,337	..	1,350
SCOTLAND.				
Public Education	553,392	524,263	29,129	..
Universities, &c.	19,018	19,508	..	490
National Gallery	2,100	2,100	..	..
IRELAND.				
Public Education	874,051	828,073	45,978	..
Teachers' Pension Office	2,015	2,145	..	130
Endowed Schools Commissioners	720	670	50	..
National Gallery	2,501	2,501	..	..
Queen's Colleges	10,028	11,028	..	1,000
Royal Irish Academy	2,259	2,520	..	261
Royal University of Ireland	..	5,000	..	5,000
Total....	£5,573,866	5,447,982	149,960	24,076

NET INCREASE......£125,884

It would be useful if the Annual Return of the British Museum presented to the House of Commons showed exactly how this money was spent. An account of the various funds and bequests is given, but not an income and expenditure account, and it is very essential that a detailed account of both should be given.

The British Museum has, since 1753, been under the government of a Board of Trustees. This body includes certain family Trustees, representing some of the legatees to the Museum, and insisted on by the terms of the bequest. The number of Trustees who must thus share in the deliberations of the governing body is nine, and it may very seriously be doubted whether this irresponsible and irremovable element is a source of strength. Surely the administrators of the Museum may be trusted by intending legatees to faithfully carry out their wishes with regard to contemplated bequests, without such an appointment as this being insisted upon. The remaining Trustees are composed chiefly of the great officers and dignitaries of the State. Among these are the Archbishop of Canterbury, the Lord Chancellor, the Speaker, the Secretaries of State, and one nominated by the Queen. Fifteen others are co-optated by the rest, and it is in these fifteen that the real life and vitality of the Museum work is represented. In this practical age this elected section should be largely composed of experienced men of business, the Presidents of the learned Societies or other representatives who would bring force to the work. The Secretaries of State and the Archbishop have their hands so fully occupied that they cannot give the time and attention to the work of the Museum which is absolutely necessary. The same may be said of others among the co-optated section. The matter is of great importance in the future of the Museum.

The following are the Trustees who have been elected by the official and family Trustees :—

Date of Election	
27 Feb. 1857.	The Right Hon. Spencer Horatio Walpole.
16 March 1858.	Charles, Viscount Eversley, G.C.B.
1 June 1864.	Robert, Viscount Sherbrooke, G.C.B.
10 May 1865.	George Douglas, Duke of Argyll, K.G., K.T.
26 July 1871.	John Dalberg, Lord Acton.
29 March 1876.	Thomas, Lord Walsingham.
13 March 1878.	Major-General Sir Henry Creswicke Rawlinson, K.C.B., LL.D.
13 March 1878.	Sir John Lubbock, Bart., M.P., D.C.L., LL.D.
6 May 1881.	His Royal Highness Albert Edward, Prince of Wales, K.G.
6 May 1881.	The Very Rev. Henry George Liddell, Dean of Christchurch, Oxford.
25 April 1883.	Archibald Philip, Earl of Rosebery.
9 Nov. 1883.	John Alexander, Marquis of Bath.
16 May 1885.	The Right Hon. Sir George Otto Trevelyan, Bart., M.P.
10 Nov. 1885.	James Ludovic, Earl of Crawford.
29 Feb. 1888.	Professor Thomas Henry Huxley, LL.D.

Much has been said and written from time to time about treasures hid away in the cellars of the British Museum, where there are supposed to be duplicates or other valuable objects stowed away. The late Mr. W. Stanley Jevons, LL.D., in a very pertinent paper on *The Use and Abuse of Museums*, says upon this matter : "I cannot profess to say from my own knowledge what there may or may not be in these cellars, but I have no hesitation in asserting that a great national Museum of research like that at Bloomsbury ought to have great cellars or other store rooms filled with articles which, though unfitted for public exhibition, may be invaluable evidence in putting together the history of the world both social and physical." He then goes on to say that "it injures the effect, for popular educational purposes, of fine specimens of art and science to crowd them up with an infinite number of inferior or less interesting objects ; accordingly a great number of imperfect remains, fragments of statues and monuments, inferior copies or approximate duplicates, should be stowed away. This both saves expense, prevents weariness and confusion of ideas to the public, and facilitates the studies of the scholar." Mr. Jevons doubtless is right, but the disposition to stow away should not be carried too far, as it easily may be, and thus become a leading virtue. In support of his argument he quotes a remark of Dr. Gunther, in which he shows that "by far the largest part of the biological collections should be packed in drawers and only the more distinct and typical specimens exposed to view." Mr. Jevons recognises that there may reasonably be two opinions about this, for he says : "But then come a number of zealous, well-meaning men who urge that these drawers and cellars full of expensive articles ought to be offered to the provinces, so that fifty Museums might be filled out of what is unseen in one."

This is exactly the point, and a governing body of Trustees, having in it a larger element of scientific and business men, could best judge what out of the thousands of objects stored away ought to remain in their present home and what could be distributed among the provincial Museums.

Considering the magnitude of the work of the British Museum, the number of collections which have been given to this national institution during the lifetime of the donor, or the number of bequests made by will, does not by any means make an imposing list. Taking the 144 years intervening between 1753 and 1887, the total number only reaches 174 individual gifts or bequests of an important nature, and some of these even are not of an extravagant character, which would leave the donor seriously impoverished. Some of the collections which have thus come to the British Museum are of a most valuable and useful character. We cannot, however, be expected to become enthusiastic over the bequest of Dr. Matthew Maty in 1762 and 1776, of "various busts and a portrait of himself." Taken seriously, if this list of gifts and bequests, occupying only sixteen octavo pages for 144 years, represented our national giving, it would be a sorry record. What surprises us most is the marvellous absence of the names of the titled families of the United Kingdom. These have, in very many instances, collections of a most valuable character, so valuable, indeed, that they go down from generation to generation as heirlooms, but are altogether too precious for the nation to share. This matter may be commended very seriously to the attention of the rich and others possessing collections. After these collections have received the attention and care of a lifetime in some cases, the very best home which could be provided, and where the care will still be continued, is the British, or some other public Museum.

The publications of the British Museum are of such a character that the highest credit is reflected upon the compilers. Minute care and attention to detail have been manifest throughout their preparation, and some of the plates are perfect works of art. They should be widely distributed among the provincial Museums and Libraries.

The guide-books are models which any Museum in the world might follow. In price they are low, and within the reach of all. The guide to the Exhibition Galleries, containing some 220 pages, is sixpenny worth of excellent literature unequalled in value even in these days of low-priced publications. The catalogue of the Kouyunjik Gallery, to be had for fourpence, gives as much Assyrian and Babylonian history almost as an ordinary reader requires. Some are published at a penny, like the new guide to the English Ceramic Ante-room, and the Glass and Ceramic Gallery.

These guides and other publications aid most materially in constituting the British Museum a centre of culture not only for London but for the provinces, and this aspect of the work at Bloomsbury cannot be too closely scrutinised by the public, or too much kept in mind by the authorities. Still it is very patent, in order that the provinces share to the extent they can reasonably claim, that its treasures must be more liberally distributed throughout the country, and as the institution is maintained out of the general taxes this claim is both reasonable and just.

The British Museum is not exclusively for the student and the expert, but for the whole nation. This is its true place, and never in the entire history of the British Museum has there been a greater disposition to recognise this fact on the part of the authorities.

It is reasonable to say that loans and gifts from the British Museum ought not to be made to private and subscription Museums. These latter are proprietary institutions, and the taxpayers' money ought not to be used for the purposes of Museums which are only intended for the use of a select few. It is only rate-supported institutions which can legitimately claim these loans or gifts.

The principle of decentralisation is of pressing national importance, and with this desirable end in view, Museums and Libraries are destined to take a most important place. Mr. John Morley once said: "For my part I look with the utmost dismay at the concentration, not only of population, but of the treasures of instruction on the banks of the Thames." The note of alarm which is here rung is by no means unnecessary, as the extending latitudes and increasing population of the Metropolis make more and more manifest each year to all thoughtful minds.

THE NATURAL HISTORY MUSEUM.

This is a branch of the British Museum, and is, without exception, the finest Museum building in the entire United Kingdom. The style of architecture and decoration are so appropriate for the purpose for which the building is intended that, although there may reasonably be two opinions about the great amount of space allotted to the staircases, there can be only one opinion as to the practical utility of Mr. Waterhouse's design. Long prior to 1860, when it was moved in the House of Commons by the First Lord of the Treasury, and carried, "That it is expedient that the Natural History Collection be removed from the British Museum, inasmuch as such an arrangement will be attended with considerably less expense than will be incurred by providing a sufficient additional space in immediate contiguity to

PRINCIPAL ENTRANCE OF THE NEW NATURAL HISTORY
MUSEUM.

the present building of the British Museum," the need for enlarged space was felt. Governments move slowly, and it was not until twenty years after this that the new building in the Cromwell Road, South Kensington, was habitable.

In 1863 the site had been decided upon, and the estimated cost was £350,000—a sum far exceeded before the completion of the building. The death, in 1865, of Captain Fowke, whose design for the building had been selected, considerably delayed matters, and it was not until 1873 that the actual work of erection commenced. As already stated it was not until the middle of 1880 that the building was handed over to the Trustees of the British Museum by the Commissioners of Works.

Then came a busy time for the authorities at Blooms-bury, and the work of removal commenced as soon as the new building was sufficiently dry to receive the cases and specimens. In the course of the same year the departments of Geology, Mineralogy, and Botany were arranged in their respective sections, and other departments were completed at later dates.

It is recorded in the last report of the general progress of the Natural History Museum that the Gallery devoted to invertebrated animals was sufficiently advanced in its arrangements to be opened to the public in March of last year. The new Gallery, also, behind the grand staircase, containing a special collection of animals of all classes which are or have been in recent times found in the British Isles, either as permanent migrants or occasional visitors, will in time become very interesting. The lists of acquisitions in the Natural History Museum during the year fill some eight pages. The report closes with the department of Botany.

All who have seen the building know how largely terra-cotta has been employed. It is in fact

claimed that the Museum is the largest in which terra-
cotta has been exclusively used for external façades and
interior wall-surfaces. Anything better could not
possibly have been conceived for a Museum building.
These decorations comprise fishes, birds, reptiles, and
flowers modelled in raised terra-cotta tiles, and which
convey a sense of finish and completeness alike striking
and restful to the eye.

The entire space occupied by the buildings and
grounds is over twelve acres, which cost £10,000
an acre. The extreme length of the front is 675 feet,
and the height of the towers is 192 feet. The architect
is wise in announcing the fact that, "in judging the
appearance of the exterior of the building, it must
never be forgotten that these fronts are required to complete the design, as the externally unsightly brick
galleries which run back from the main front, and are now
conspicuous when the Museum is seen from either west
or east, are intended to be concealed by them." The
side galleries and towers contain several features which
may be told in the architect's own words :
" Branching out of the Central Hall," he says, " near its
southern extremity, are two long galleries, each 278
feet six inches long by fifty feet wide. These galleries
are repeated on the first floor, and in a modified form on
the second floor. They are divided into bays by coupled
piers arranged in two rows down the length of the
galleries, and planned in such a manner as to allow of
upright cases being placed back to back between the
piers and the outer walls, so as to get the best possible
light upon the objects displayed in the cases with the
least amount of reflection from the glass, and leaving
the central space free as a passage. Owing to the
nature of the specimens exhibited in one or two of
these galleries requiring for their exhibition rather
table-cases than wall-cases, advantage has only been

taken to a limited extent of this disposition of the plan.
These terra-cotta piers, however, are constructively
necessary, not only to conceal the iron supports for the
floor above, but to prevent these supports being affected
in case of fire. Behind these galleries on the ground
floor are a series of top-lighted galleries, devoted, on the
east side, to geology and palæontology, and on the
west to zoology. The towers on the north of the
building have each a central smoke-shaft from the heating apparatus, the boilers of which are placed in the
basement, immediately between the towers, while the
space surrounding the smoke-shafts is used for drawing
off the vitiated air from the various galleries contiguous
thereto. The front galleries are ventilated into the
front towers, which form the crowning feature of the
main front. These towers also contain, above the
second floor, various rooms for the work of the different
heads of departments, and on the topmost storey large
cisterns for the purpose of always having at hand a considerable storage of water in case of fire."

Thomas Hobbes, of Malmesbury, who lived and
wrote in the first half of the seventeenth century,
defines natural history as "the history of such facts or
effects of nature as have no dependence on man's will."
Nowhere have science, tact, and wide knowledge been
better displayed in the arrangement of these "effects of
nature," as quaint Hobbes says, than is evidenced at
Cromwell Road. Especially must mention be made of
those two veterans of Museum work, Dr. Albert Gunther,
F.R.S., and Dr. H. Woodward, F.R.S., the former the
Keeper of Zoology, and the latter the Keeper of
Geology, who not only have accomplished for the
Natural History Department of the British Museum
a work which will pass on down the ages, but to
Museums generally have given a practical aid
which will ever associate their names with these

institutions. Professor Flower, F.R.S., has also distinguished himself during his term of office as Director.

The guide books sold at the Museum, and also to be had through Messrs. Longmans, Green, and Co., 39, Paternoster Row, E.C., and Messrs. Trübner and Co., 57, Ludgate Hill, E.C., are so low in price, and so admirably cover the ground, that to attempt to improve upon them would be like gilding gold. Their names and prices are here given.

ZOOLOGICAL DEPARTMENT.

Guide to the Galleries of Mammalia. 8vo. pp. 125, with fifty-seven Woodcuts and two Plans. 4d.
———————— Gould Collection of Humming Birds. Illustrated. 8vo. 2d.
———————— Gallery of Reptilia. Illustrated. 8vo. Second Edition, 6d.
———————— Gallery of Shells. 4d.
———————— Gallery of Echinodermata. 4d.

GEOLOGICAL DEPARTMENT.

Guide to the Department of Geology and Palæontology. 8vo. 4d.
———————— Fossil Fishes. Illustrated. 8vo. 3d. Second Edition, 4d.
———————— Specimens of Native Silica, by Mr. John Ruskin. 1s.

MINERAL DEPARTMENT.

An Introduction to the Study of Minerals, with a Guide to the Mineral Gallery. 8vo. 3d.
An Introduction to the Study of Meteorites, with a list of the Meteorites represented in the collection. 8vo. 2d.
An Index to the Collection of Minerals. 8vo. 2d.
A General Guide to the *Whole* Museum (brief summary). 2d.

The last-named book is a really good twopennyworth of Museum literature, and makes it quite unnecessary to enter into an elaborate description of the building and its contents.

MAMMAL SECTION, NATURAL HISTORY MUSEUM.

Whit-week is usually a very busy time at Cromwell Road. A more interesting sight never presented itself than was seen on last Whit Tuesday in the groups which stood around the cases, representing every age from the child in arms to the infirm old man or woman. There were scores of young children apparently by themselves, and beyond the general supervision by the policemen, one of whom is in each room, no one was needed to prevent injury to the cases or to keep them from touching the exhibits. The day before being Bank Holiday the number of visitors was, of course, much larger. It stood at 4,567 against 6,067 for the previous Whit Monday, a change effected by the beautiful weather of this year's holiday and the wet day last year. Many of the visitors lingered in the unique Bird Gallery, and here might be noticed several touches of nature which illustrated very clearly the fact that the early country recollections of one's life are never effaced by the hue and cry for mere existence which is the lot of so many of the working classes in London.

The wall-cases in the long bird gallery contain mounted specimens of all the principal species arranged in systematic order, beginning with the vultures, and ending with the penguins. In the middle of the room and in the spaces between the wall-cases are placed various isolated groups of particular interest.

These are cases showing the nesting habits of our best-known British birds. The great value of these groups consists in their absolute truthfulness. The surroundings are not selected by chance or imagination, but in every case are carefully-executed reproductions of those that were present round the individual nest. When it has been possible, the actual rocks, trees, or grass have been preserved, or where these were of a perishable nature they were accurately modelled from nature. Far more care has also been taken in preserving the natural form and characteristic attitude of the birds than was formerly the case in Museums, as a large number of the old specimens in the wall-cases unhappily testify. The eyes of some of the working men glistened with pleasure as they called wife or children to come and look at birds and nest, while they had something to say about the habits of the bird, or perhaps bird-nesting, in bygone years.

This collection is simply excellent and most instructive, and the plan is well worth adoption by other Museums. Far-reaching good must accrue from visits to these national institutions of the working classes which will make itself apparent sooner or later. It is impossible to gauge results and there is no register of good impressions received from visits to Museums and Picture Galleries.

CHAPTER XIV.

THE NATIONAL GALLERY.

WE have been living of late in a surfeit of jubilees, and not the least important to the general public is that of the National Gallery. This institution was opened first to the public, in its present home, in April, 1838, although actually founded in 1824, by the purchase for £57,000 of a collection of thirty-eight pictures during the administration of Lord Liverpool. It is a significant fact that up to twenty-five years after its original foundation it only contained forty-one pictures of the British school. The turn in the tide of its affairs came in 1847 in the first bequest to its collection of 157 pictures, all but two being of the British school. The gift was from the late Robert Vernon, whose name well deserves being associated with the National Gallery. The original cost of the building was £100,000, and it has four times been enlarged, viz., in 1861, 1869, 1876, and 1885-87. On the last occasion a new staircase in the centre of the building was erected, adding much to the appearance and convenience of the various galleries and smaller rooms. At the present time the entire collection consists of about 1,250 pictures.

Probably no public institution has received so much public attention, and discussions respecting it, both in the House of Commons and in the Press. Its site has been frequently described as unsuitable, and its utility has been repeatedly questioned. It is unfortunately only too apparent that there has been unnecessary extravagance in the purchase of pictures, as instanced in the Paul Veronese pictures, which could at one time have been bought for £400, and were ultimately secured for the nation for £3,500; the £3,000 odd going for red tape, officialism, and want of despatch.

Forty years ago Mr. Ruskin termed the National Gallery a "European Jest," a term fully merited at that time and long afterwards, and no criticisms have done more to lift the National Gallery into its proper place in the nation than those of Mr. Ruskin. He has, by his ceaseless exertions in person and by pen, caused officials, combined with generous arrangements for the public, to awake to their responsibilities, and to the fact that they and the institution of which they have charge are public servants, of whom was reasonably expected economy in management and

fullest utility.   The story of his unearthing of
Turner's pictures from the dark underground rooms
is familiar to all.   What other discoveries of a similar
nature remain to be made the future will show.   This
much may be safely asserted — never in the fifty
years' history of the National Gallery did it stand
so high in public estimation as it does at the present
time, and never were its prospects brighter and more
hopeful.   Sir George Trevelyan, M.P., not long ago
gave it as his opinion that it was "the best selected and
best cared for collection (of pictures) in the world"; and
this eminent statesman has thus given us in a sentence
reason to be proud of this noble pile of buildings which
occupies " the finest site in Europe."

The weakest point in the entire administration is the
fewness of the loans to other departments and to provincial Museums.   These institutions, supported by
Government grants, are the property of the nation,
who contribute in taxes towards their maintenance
and extension.   This being so, the entire country has
a right to share in the benefit and pleasure accruing
out of them, by means of loans to provincial Museums;
and country Curators and Committees of Management
may reasonably claim greater liberality in this respect
than has hitherto been granted.

There are at the present time only about 180
pictures out on loan out of 1,250, and this can scarcely
be considered a fair proportion.   The point is vital, and
it is only by persistent advocacy that a readjustment
will be brought about.

Its annual cost in salaries is as low as an institution
of this kind could well be, and the admission fees on
students' days and the receipts for catalogues materially
help the charge upon the revenue for maintenance.
Greater and more uniform civility never characterised
the officials of any public institution than is shown

at the National Gallery, and the same may be said of the two departments of the British Museum and South Kensington, and in this respect a marked example is exhibited to the officials of all like institutions. In holiday time when temper is sometimes taxed, and when a country cousin is not quite clear why he should give up, for a time, his umbrella, a very commendable patience may be observed at these places. The fact of a million people or more passing through the turnstiles of the National Gallery during each year shows the extraordinary increase in the number of visitors during recent years. This increase is very important, as being an excellent barometer of public estimation, and none the less of the inherent love of art in the democracy.

The extension of time to seven p.m., to which the Gallery is kept open during the months of May to August inclusive, is a most important gain, and the admission of the public on Thursdays and Fridays, as well as students, on the payment of sixpence, is also an advantage.

The list of pecuniary bequests to the Gallery for the purchase of pictures is not large, and this is surprising, as is the paucity in the bequests to the British Museum. From 1864 to 1885 inclusive, it stands only at £45,716—about the market value of a successful racehorse. It is worthy of note that each of these four individual gifts, making up the total named, came from a plain "Mr." The largest gift was £23,104, and the smallest £2,612. We are a long way from reaching high water mark in generous giving to our national institutions.

A considerable delay has taken place in the publication of the larger edition of the catalogues, but the admirable abridged catalogues which can be had for sixpence each give all the information which the general visitor requires. These catalogues are two only in number, one of the British and Modern Schools and one of the Foreign Schools. Mr. Walter Armstrong has done for the National Gallery what Mr. Henry Blackburne has done for the Royal Academy, and the *brochure* of the former is a chatty guide to the pictures in the National Gallery. Mr. Armstrong writes: "The National Gallery is about half the size of the Museums of Dresden, Madrid, and Paris, the three largest in the world, and considerably less than those of Berlin, Munich, and St. Petersburg. But in quality it is surpassed by none of its rivals. Its standard has been set higher than that of any other collection, and in each of the great foreign Galleries there are scores, if not hundreds, of pictures which would not be received in Trafalgar Square." This is important testimony, and a general consensus of opinion amply supports the verdict.

Considering that it was only in July, 1887, that the new rooms were thrown open to the public, and that for the first time there was something like order and arrangement in displaying the pictures to the best advantage, the authorities may be congratulated on a most encouraging twelve months' result of their administration. The institution is now fully in touch with the needs of the day. Formerly they were cramped for space and harassed on all hands with confusion sometimes worse confounded. Now we have a Gallery worthy of the nation, and an enhanced value given to the whole collection. The new staircase, with its pillars of red African marble, has an imposing appearance, and turns what was an ill-constructed interior into handsome and spacious Galleries. The welding of the old part to the new has been admirably accomplished. The re-hanging and re-arranging of the pictures, never a light task, but surrounded with special difficulties in a building not designed, as was that at Berlin for scholastic division, has been successfully accomplished.

The classification into schools has produced order where before there was chaos. Rembrandts had been hung previously with some of the Italian masters, and French and Dutch works had, for years, been side by side on the same wall. The National Gallery is not now open to the charge of having no great masterpieces of the old artists within its precincts. The Raphael Madonna, from the Blenheim Collection, which cost the nation £72,000, has, with the Leonardo Virgin, removed this stigma. There may be two opinions about the price paid for the Madonna, and personally I have no sympathy with those art critics who have sneered at the outcry against what some of them were pleased to call the pretended waste of public money.

The writer of a very sensible article on the National Gallery in the April issue of the *Church Quarterly* is not far wrong when he says: "The growth of our national collection is the more remarkable when we reflect how modern its origin is compared with that of other great public Galleries. Only one of these belongs to the present century. This is the Berlin collection, which, founded in 1815 by the Prussian Government, has been gradually enriched with pictures of different schools from the first, selected and classified in the most admirable manner by a succession of Directors, which include names as famous in art history as Von Rumohr, Waagen, Meyer, and Bode. The Galleries of Florence, of the Louvre, of Dresden alike owe their existence to princely founders, who began these superb collections as early as the sixteenth century. The art treasures of the Uffizi and the Pitti were first brought together by the Grand Dukes of the illustrious House of Medici. The Elector Augustus III. and his favourite Count Brühl acquired the masterpieces of Correggio, Titian's 'Tribute Money,' and the Sistine Madonna for the Dresden Gallery; while the Louvre was founded by Francis I. in the best days of the Renaissance, and successively enriched in munificent gifts of the Grand Monarque and the spoils of Napoleon's conquests. Kings and emperors of another august line collected the precious works which to-day adorn the halls of the Prade and the Belvedere, and make these Museums the pride of Spain and Austria. . . . . Charles I. bought the famous collection of the Duke of Mantua, which included the cartoons of Raphael and Mantegna, the 'Holy Family,' known as the Pearl, and many of the finest Titians now at Madrid and in the Louvre, and selected forty-six masterpieces by Raphael, Titian, Correggio, and others, to adorn his own rooms at Whitehall. The dispersion of that magnificent collection by public auction was indeed a national calamity, and although Cromwell saved the cartoons of Raphael and Mantegna, most of the great prizes had already gone beyond seas, and were irrecoverably lost to England. It was left to our own generation to form a new Gallery which, if it could not equal its foreign rivals in antiquity, should at least be a worthy monument of the civilisation and culture of modern England." This sums up what the Trustees of the National Gallery have had to contend with in the past and what has been accomplished.

The number of Trustees is now six, and in Sir Frederick W. Burton as Director and Mr. Charles L. Eastlake as Keeper and Secretary, the Gallery and the public have two able and cultured servants.

The value of some of the collections has been greatly enhanced by the lapse of years. As recently as 1871 the Peel Collection was purchased for £75,000, and is now looked upon as worth at least £250,000. Some of the pictures which were bought at low prices could now be sold at many times the prices paid for them.   Competent authorities fix the present value of the entire collection at not less than £2,000,000 sterling. £400,000 of the people's money have been spent in acquiring the pictures. Fifty years ago there were four large Galleries and two small ones. Now there are twenty-two Galleries all well stocked with valuable pictures.

To sum up, the work of the past fifty years, when the conditions under which it has been carried on are taken into account, is satisfactory, but the new start for the next fifty places the National Gallery on a pedestal higher than ever and has given a new lease of life which will redound to the credit of the nation.

CHAPTER XV.

SOUTH KENSINGTON MUSEUM AND ITS WORK.

T is undeniable that the group of national buildings at South Kensington is in many respects a great credit to us, and any Englishman may look upon it with a pardonable pride. But are we getting the full value for money invested, and does it fully and comprehensively fulfil its true aim and object ? These are serious questions, and they deserve patient inquiry and careful consideration.

It is unnecessary here to enter into a history of the South Kensington Museum. The most important

concession yet granted is the Return promised
in the House of Commons on April 6th, 1888, during
the discussion of the Civil Service Estimates, when a
vote of £9,900 was under consideration. The Leader
of the House promised that this Return should be
made as complete as possible, so as to illustrate the
cost of South Kensington from its establishment to the
present day, and until this Return is before the public
it is impossible to do full justice to this branch of the
subject. During that debate there were three short
and good speeches made, and these epitomise so fully
the position of South Kensington that the pith of them
may be given.

Sir Henry Roscoe said that the accommodation at the only
Government school in this country for teaching science teachers
would be a disgrace to any third-rate German town. He had
that day visited the school at South Kensington, which was
under the control of Professor Rücker. A temporary building
which was put up for the International Exhibition had been
rented from the Exhibition Commissioners of 1851, and was
now used as a laboratory. This building was not only insufficient, but was about to be taken away from the Science
School because the ground was required by the authorities of
the Imperial Institute. The consequence would be that the
students who now worked in the building would be thrown out
of employment, and the school would actually have to reject
a very large number who wished to study there. This was not
a desirable condition of things, and he hoped that the First
Commissioner of Works would give his serious attention to the
question of providing accommodation of an efficient character
for this really great national institution. Even from an economic
point of view the matter required the attention of the Government, because if the students were turned away the fees, which
now amounted to £3,500 a year, would no longer be received
by the Exchequer, and the Government would suffer a loss.
There was a wider question still upon which he wished to say
a few words, and that was the housing of the National Science
Collection. This country possessed one of the most complete
collections of scientific instruments in Europe, and for the
housing of the collection the Government now paid a rental of
£2,000 a year. Some time ago the matter attracted the atten-

tion of the Government, and a Departmental Committee was appointed to consider how the collection should be housed. Evidence as to the importance of the collection was given by all the leading men of science, and the Committee reported most favourably as to the necessity of having a building in which the instruments could be arranged in proper form.   The question of cost was carefully gone into by the Committee, and it was shown that, as a very large rental was paid at the present time, £32,000 would be sufficient to defray the cost of what was required.   He hoped that the Government would look into the matter and put our science collections on a footing worthy of the nation.   A great deal had been said about protecting British industries, and one way of protecting them, and in this they could all assist, was to improve our scientific education. When other countries, such as Switzerland, spent £70,000 or £80,000 in erecting a single building, it was time to turn round and put our own house in order with regard to science collections.

Later on in the discussion Mr. Mundella said that

The hon. member for South Manchester did not use too strong language when he said that the condition of the department at South Kensington was a disgrace to the country and a public scandal.   If the public had any idea of the state of things they would not tolerate it a day longer.   Men were working in crowded passages, corridors, and cellars under conditions in which no public or private servant ought to be asked to work.   The accommodation for the Science School was very insufficient, and it had been found necessary to find room for part of the apparatus of the laboratory in the French annexe of the Museum.   That annexe would be required for the purposes of the Imperial Institute, and then he supposed that the Science and Art School would have to "clear out."   Sixty students would be displaced, and the consequent loss of fees would be considerable.   It would seem, in fact, that we were about to diminish our supply of science teachers in consequence of a lack of accommodation in our science training school. Another point inviting criticism was the housing of our science collections.   Stowed away in the Patent Museum and in other buildings we possessed many unique mechanical specimens, such as Arkwright's first loom and Stephenson's first steam-engine, of which it was very difficult to obtain a view.   The First Commissioner of Works had suggested that the residences of the Museum officials might be removed.   But surely the officers of an institution which contained so much that was of great value ought to reside on the spot in order to be at hand in case of fire or other disaster.   They knew where the most precious articles were placed, and could best direct the work of salvage.   The Treasury could not escape blame for the inadequacy of the existing arrangements.   Whenever that Department wanted to make a saving the word went forth to cut down science and art.   The noble lord opposite (Lord R. Churchill) had declared at Newcastle that if the subjects of science and art were left to local effort their advancement would be secured without any aid from the Government.   But when the noble lord was making that statement he was actually referring to a school which could not have continued to exist for a week without Government support.   In no other country in Europe was so little done as in England for the training of scientific men.   (Lord R. Churchill observed that £500,000 a year was spent in the cause of science and art.)   The sum named by the noble lord included all the science grants in the country, the whole amount spent on art teaching, the cost of South Kensington Museum, and the cost of the Circulation Department. It was rather less than was spent on science teaching alone in a single institution in Berlin.   In his opinion, the recommendations of the Departmental Committee that reported in July, 1885, pointed to a satisfactory way of settling the whole question which they were then discussing.

Whether this wretched accommodation accounts for the falling off in the number of visitors it is impossible to say. Some assert that South Kensington Museum and its branch at Bethnal Green are losing their popularity. The number of visitors at South Kensington last year was less than in any previous year since 1868. There has been a falling away for the last few years. In 1886 the number was 823,999, and in 1887, 788,412. In 1869 and 1870, and in several other years, the visitors numbered more than 1,000,000, and the average for the last twenty years was over 700,000. A similar diminution in numbers has occurred at Bethnal Green. This Museum was opened in 1872, when 901,464 persons visited it; in 1873 the number was 709,472; in 1874, 530,676, but last year only 446,722—the smallest for the last five years, and except on two occasions the smallest since the opening. This is significant, and it is a fact worthy of some attention.

It is a point open to serious doubt whether the number passing through the turnstiles is the best criterion from which to judge, although it is wise to take it into account. The value or degree of instruction derived from a visit to any Museum or Art Gallery is quite incapable of statistical calculation. There is great truth in the words of Mr. Jevons when he says that "at the South Kensington Art Museum they make a great point of setting up turnstiles to record the precise numbers of visitors, and they can tell you to a unit the exact amount of civilising effect produced in any day, week, month, or year. But these turnstiles hardly take account of the fact that the neighbouring wealthy residents are in the habit, on a wet day, of packing their children off in a cab to the so-called Brompton Boilers, in order that they may have a good run through the Galleries. To the far greater part of the people a large brilliantly lighted Museum is little more or nothing more than a promenade, a bright kind of lounge, not nearly so instructive as the shops of Regent Street." The contention with regard to South Kensington lies wrapped up here, that the whole of the South Kensington buildings are situated, and have been intentionally situated, among the aristocracy, who really do not value the Galleries except as fashionable lounges. It is one of the many, many side issues where the privileged classes, acting for the people at large, have taken good care that what they have had to do shall be on the side of the privileged classes.

The Department has never been looked upon with favour by those who decide the proportions in which Government funds shall be allocated to different branches of the public service. If a fair and reasonable view, to say nothing of a sympathetic one, had been taken of this matter, the buildings at South Kensington would long since have been completed, and a noble institution would have been provided with ample space for the storage of its collections, and with a decent entrance. At present the way of access to the Museum is a discredit to the nation, and although the Galleries themselves are admirable in construction and arrangement, and are priceless in their contents, they do not afford nearly room enough for the collections, and the parsimony shown in extending them forbids the hope of providing space for acquisitions alike desirable and available.

There is, again, far too much favouritism in the management. The " South Kensington clique " is, after all, not an inaccurate or uncalled-for designation. No charge is made against individuals, but it may unhesitatingly be asserted that the country never will get full value for its £400,000 a year until there is some radical change in the manner of administration.

The funds appropriated for the purchase of examples for Museums and schools throughout the country are being seriously reduced. So far as relates to the provinces, this branch of the work and the sending out of loan exhibits constitute the very life of the Department, and present the only ground fairly upon which the entire country can be taxed for its maintenance.

From the outset the circulation system has proved of value to provincial Museums and Art Galleries. It was instituted early in the history of Museums by the late Sir Henry Cole, aided by Sir Charles Robinson and Mr. George Wallis. During the year before last there were thirty-two provincial Museums, twenty-six temporary exhibitions, and 260 Science and Art Schools to which the Department lent examples of works of art, the number of specimens thus distributed through the country reaching the total number of 26,000.   All these were chosen from the stores of the Museum with special reference to the industries of the districts to which they were lent.   It is impossible to overestimate the benefits thus conferred upon the centres of trade and manufactures from one end of England to the other ; and it would be a blunder of the worst description to interfere with an arrangement so advantageous, and so economical, in the use of national collections by bringing selections from them, at no great cost to the State, under the continuous observation of the artisan classes.

The chief complaint made with regard to these loan exhibits is that they are sometimes made to exhibitions of a very private character, and this ought not to be the case.   Being public property the exhibits should only go to institutions of a distinctly public character, and this should be insisted upon by the public Press and in Parliament. Amongst the exhibits last year to private exhibitions we notice to the Bradford Church Institute fourteen pictures and sixteen objects on deposit loan.   To the Mechanics' Institute of the same town twelve pictures and fifteen other objects.   The St. Vincent's Convent Branch School in Cork, ten pictures.   A small private exhibition in North Islington, London, had 192 objects and thirty paintings.   Lincoln had 281 objects and ninety-six pictures.   Here the receipts were £1,412 in charging the public to see these and other exhibits, but of this last-named there need be no complaint.   The London Polytechnic and the Southampton Philharmonic Hall were the recipients of small favours in the way of loan objects.   There are others to which attention could be called.   Where is this to end ?   These objects are bought out of public money.   Public money pays the wages of

STAIRCASE TO CERAMIC GALLERY, SOUTH KENSINGTON.
[Drawn by J. W. Benn.]

the men who go with them to unpack and arrange these
particular exhibits, and they are lent to private individuals who happen to have influence with the South
Kensington coterie.   John Bull should look after his
property a little better.   Everybody's business in this
case happens to be nobody's.

The following provincial Museums received aid for
the purchase of objects in 1887 :—

Name of Museum.	No. of Objts.	Description of Objects.	Aid by the Dept.			Total Cost.		
			£	s.	d.	£	s.	d.
Birmingham Corporation Museum	30	Specimens of jewellery and plaster casts	35	10	0	71	0	0
Bradford, Public Art Museum	1	Plaster cast	8	12	0	17	4	0
Glasgow, Corporation Art Galleries & Kelvingrove Museum	46	Indian art objects ..	48	4	1	96	8	3
Manchester, Queen's Park Museum	591	Indian art objects, repro- ductions of armour, fictile ivories, photographs, and Departmental publica- tions	224	8	10	448	17	10
Nottingham, Midland Counties Museum ..	1	Indian carved window ..	15	0	0	30	0	0
Sheffield, Weston Park Museum	21	Indian art objects ..	23	13	6	47	7	0
Wolverhampton, Art Gal- lery and Museum ..	38	Indian art objects ..	137	1	9	274	3	6
Total	728	.. ..	492	10	2	985	0	7

With regard to the proposed reduction of science and
art grants, there was on May 10th, 1888, a deputation to the Vice-President of the Education Council.
Sir E. Reed, M.P., introduced the deputation, and
amongst those present were Dr. Taylor (Cardiff), Dr.
Rutherford (Newcastle), Mr. T. G. Ashton (Manchester),
Mr. J. Newton Coombes (Sheffield), Mr. Henry Laird
(Birkenhead), Mr. Burt, M.P., Mr. Craig, M.P., and
others.   Sir E. Reed, M.P., said the deputation was a
unique one, as he believed it was the first coming from
the Committees of the Science and Art Schools in the
country.   Their visit had arisen out of the minute
of the Department of February 10th, which had

created a great deal of alarm.   More than twenty towns
were represented.   Dr. Taylor (Cardiff) explained in
detail the action of the Education Department with
reference to Science and Art Schools, and said that the
proposals of the minute of February 10th would have
the effect of reducing the income of the schools, which
was now brought down to the lowest possible point for
the benefit of the poorer industrial students, and it was
essential that no source of income should be taken away.
By the alteration in the subjects and the grants dependent thereon the poorer student who was not able to
remain at school so long as his more fortunate fellows
would be placed at a great disadvantage.   Hitherto the
Department paid on successes in three subjects, exclusive of geometry and mathematics, but it now proposed
to reduce that to two.   This would greatly affect the
industrial classes and apprentices, who should be induced
to learn as many of the arts and sciences which might be
applicable to their trade as possible.   Again, the reduction of the grant would tend to raise the fees of the
scholars, which was very undesirable.

Mr. Ashton (Manchester) said that he had been in
communication with many schools, and he gathered
from them all that the effect of the proposed reduction would be to close several of the schools.

Mr. Lewis Williams (Cardiff) said that on the strength
of the recommendations of the Commission appointed to
consider the whole question of education, they had
erected a building which cost £10,000, and which
would accommodate 850 students. If the proposed reduction was made it was feared that and other schools in
Cardiff would no longer be self-supporting, and if that
went forth it would have a great check on the development of what was necessary in all large towns, viz., the
establishment of advanced elementary schools.   True
economy would be in developing the means of education.

Sir William Hart Dyke, in reply, said he was pleased to have been able to discuss these matters with men who had a practical knowledge of the subject, and secondly because they had been challenged and were threatened with opposition in the House of Commons to the votes for educational purposes. With regard to the subjects which it was proposed to amalgamate, the Department found that the two subjects had practically overlapped each other, and were practically one subject. That was a solid reason for the change they proposed. He contended that the poorer class of students in elementary schools would still be able to make eight pounds a year, which was a considerable encouragement to any student. It had been urged that the Department acted not quite fairly or justly in proposing the reduction of three subjects to two, but he did not think he could give any satisfactory reply to the gentlemen who urged that they should change back again to the old system. He thought they should give the change a fair trial; and as the restriction was only for one year students might take up other subjects in succeeding years. The appeals which had been made to him actually amounted to this, that the grant made for science and art teaching under this new minute was not, in the opinion of those present, so generous as the State might have allowed. He was between two fires, and perhaps if he had been Chancellor of the Exchequer as well as Vice-President of the Council he might have been able to deal more generously, but he was compelled to deal economically as well as efficiently with regard to these matters. The number of subjects was an educational question, but it struck one that it was better to learn one or two subjects well than to get a mere smattering of many subjects. He would give the points raised his consideration. He mentioned that the Government this year were determined to pass a Bill in support of technical instruction which would be most valuable to all engaged in that work.

These particulars are given in order to link up the history of the discussion at present going on.

The vigorous criticisms as to the South Kensington methods of teaching, which have been called forth from various quarters, have created much discussion. Mr. J. C. Horseley, R.A., led the way, and has done a good public service by so spiritedly taking up the matter as he did in the spring of last year. Following up the question at the close of 1887, he said, " that from the date of Redgrave's retirement the whole character of the school has become changed, and from being one in which the all-important work of design for manufactures is the chief consideration, it has drifted slowly but surely into a place of perfunctory art teaching for the delectation of shoals of female amateurs, and for the turning out of a cartload of most mediocre artists of both sexes, who flood the country and public exhibitions with worthless productions. It is doubtless owing to this action that in the Royal Academy, for instance, whereat some fifteen or twenty years since from 4,000 to 5,000 works were sent for annual exhibition, that number has of late years more than doubled. I cannot, however, do more now than hint at this large and important question, which calls for the most searching investigation, and especially at the hands of the British taxpayer, for whereas in 1837 the original grant to the School of Design was £1,500 per annum, the total cost of the present establishment in 1886-7 was £410,337."

Professor Hubert Herkomer, Slade Professor of Art at Oxford, made a vigorous attack on the system supported at South Kensington in a speech delivered to the students of the Salisbury School of Art. He remarked that, from experience, he was no friend of great systems of tuition in art. With science it was different, and those schools had helped the country by enabling workmen to do their work better than they formerly did it ; but they could not have a school for any kind of art tuition which did not in some way excite the ambition of mechanics to get away from their craft and become painters. That was a fatal feeling, because they had not always the faculty, and they lost the dignity of their craft.   How far did South Kensington permit the artistic ?   There was a sort of feeling there that tidiness, neatness, and an orderly look in a picture was a great thing, and that a little artistic work would revolutionise the place.   If a student did a very artistic piece of work and sent it away, what was the criticism ?   That it was rough, that it looked so unfinished. Now finish was a most difficult feature in art, and a student who attempted to make drawing look passable for competition was cramped, and he found he lost the little grip he had in the artistic way.   He found the greatest difficulty in getting students who had passed through Kensington to feel what was artistic, but if he had a student who had been nowhere, and who had the faculty, he very soon saw the artistic side of a thing.   In his youth he remembered the miserable agony of doing heads from the cast, and he could not believe that it was necessary to force a person into such monotonous work.   They were made to do outlines, but men who had practised all their lives could not do outlines unless there was one, and a distinct one.   Why should students try to do the most difficult things first ?   He maintained that such things, instead of developing the mind, blocked the way.   They did not educate the art faculty, but stopped its growth.   If they could work in the way he had suggested, and Kensington would accept it, they would find a different art spring up all over England.

Sir John E. Millais, Bart., R.A., writes as follows :   "You have the rich accumulation of centuries before you, casts from the ancient Greek and Renaissance sculpture, photographs, re-productions of the best ornamentation of all periods and nations, and, besides our National Gallery, private loan collections annually submitted to the public afford the student an oppor-tunity of seeing at his convenience the greatest works of the greatest masters in every department of art.   All these facilities must be included in the art education of our time, for do not forget that studying fine examples is the *best teaching* after you have learnt your alphabet.   Why, then, complain and question the existing order of things in your school, which has been handed down to us by our forefathers as an excellent method of instruction ?   When a man is continually dissatisfied with his

S

tools there is generally something else the matter. If some of the malcontents do not think much of Flaxman's outlines, I would refer them to Retz's 'Song of the Bell,' Hogarth's designs for escutcheons and engraving on silver plate, or to Tenniel's and Sambourne's drawings in *Punch*, which are almost entirely dependent on outline. In the delineation of form, features, and flowers, a faculty of outline is indispensable."

Mr. William Morris said : "I do not know what the South Kensington system of teaching is, except very vaguely, though I conclude it is not likely to be perfect. Common-sense would surely point out to people engaged in teaching drawing that the first thing to be done is to get the pupil into a habit of accuracy, to discourage anything like sloppiness or vagueness, while at the same time he has put before him the limits which the material he is working in puts to the representation of the object he is working from. It seems to me that the attempt to teach students ' style,' which some of the writers whose correspondence you enclosed to me appear to advocate, is a great mistake, a putting of the cart before the horse ; there is nothing gained in teaching a clever young man to pick up the more superficial part of the style of a master, though it is much easier to do so than to learn to draw clean and accurately what you have got before you."

Mr. Walter Crane writes : " I am glad to see such questions discussed. It is a wholesome thing for all of us to have to give reasons for the faith that is in us ; and, after all, methods of art training are very much matters of faith. Good results are reached by more than one road, and it is impossible to be absolute in questions of art. The controversy, like most controversies, has a main stem and many branches. In the main it seems to me to be a battle between two different conceptions of art or ways of regarding or representing nature, always more or less in opposition or, at least, quite distinct. No system that I am aware of will enable a student to dispense with the necessity of giving his own solution. Goethe's saying, ' Art is art precisely because it is not nature,' is a portable maxim which one can always carry with one, and its application will clear up many a doubt.

" The South Kensington system was devised to educate the artist in design, to give him definite knowledge of form and construction, rather than to cultivate dexterity in the rendering of effect, or phrase. Objects do not move about with thick *or* thin lines round them, and no one supposes they do ; but it is noticeable that directly a man wishes to convey a definite notion of the form of a thing, he uses an outline. In the sense of conveying facts, a good outline drawing may be considered as naturalistic as the most modern painter's rendering of the same thing. It all depends upon what you want to express. For my part, I consider outline the most terse and expressive method in design, and the most direct language, though the simplest, for the embodiment of one's thoughts. It is the alpha and omega of art. Children naturally take to it, and it is a characteristic of the art of the earliest periods ; yet it still remains a test of an artist's knowledge of form and power of draughtsmanship. Pen or brush, however, give better quality of line than lead pencil, and I should be glad to see their use adopted in the schools.

"I am not concerned to defend the South Kensington system in all its details. Every system has its weak places no doubt, and the fault of all systems is that enough account is not taken of individual predilections. If I were consulted and had to systematise my notions on the subject, I should probably devise a different course, grounded on a practice I have mostly worked out for myself, though I had the advantage of inheriting the traditions of a family of artists to begin with."

The discussion first commenced, and was most vigorously carried on in the columns of the *Manchester Guardian*. Summing up the discussion, this well-known paper remarked :—

"Can anyone tell us where the South Kensington system came from—who, so to speak, invented it ? Was it Owen Jones ? Was it Sir Henry Cole ? Who was it ? If it really represents the ripe convictions of our greatest artists—men like Sir John Millais himself, for instance —then the public ought to know it. Sir John Millais himself was taught in the first place by the portrait painter, Henry Sass, one of those second-rate artists who often make the best teachers, and afterwards at the Academy Schools. In any case, it does not much signify where or how a man of genius was taught the elements of his art. A genius teaches himself, and Sir John Millais appears to favour the view that the teaching of art in the ordinary sense is futile when he says that ' studying fine examples is the best teaching after you have learnt the alphabet.' The other point made by Sir John Millais, as to the high place held by ' the present British School' in Continental opinion, needs a certain amount of qualification. We have repeatedly shown of late, principally with reference to the Berlin Jubilee Exhibition, that a very high place in foreign opinion is now held by a few English artists of genius like Sir John Millais, Mr. Herkomer, Mr. Burne Jones, and Mr. Richmond. But that foreign opinion recognises a high standard of merit, particularly of technical merit, in English art in general is not the fact. The exact contrary is the fact. It may be that you can only teach what Sir John Millais calls 'the alphabet' and Mr. William Morris 'the elements or grammar of art,' leaving the rest to the student; but there may still be a fundamental difference of opinion as to the way in which the 'alphabet' can best be taught. Mr. Morris insists on the study of the human figure apparently from the first, and Mr. Walter Crane speaks of that study as 'the basis of all design.' The upshot of the letters may, in fact, be said to be that only the A B C of art can be taught at all, and that that A B C must consist to a very large extent in systematic drawing from the figure."

The real point of the whole matter lies in the question whether our Government scheme of Art Education is efficiently, and with due regard to the requirements of the time, doing the work for which it was designed, and for which the nation expends annually so large a sum. Broadly speaking, to enable British manufacturers to hold their own in foreign competition, and to develop the art resources of the nation to some degree of perfection, the Government organisation for the teaching of art should aim at the accomplishment of two great objects. First, to educate designers and art handicraftsmen, with a view to the production in their work of a maximum degree of artistic value, with a minimum degree of cost of production. Secondly, to educate the general taste so as to create and maintain an appreciation of beauty and artistic value. That the South Kensington system has aimed at the second object, and with a considerable degree of success, few who remember the deplorable condition of public taste at the time of the Great Exhibition of 1851, will be inclined to deny. But in regard to the first and the more important object, the Government Art Department of to-day is open to just and searching criticism. That the art masters are practically powerless in the matter is clear to anyone who has had experience of the schools. They are bound to rigidly follow the strictly-defined laws laid down for them by the Department of Science and Art. The sum annually spent is over £400,000, and is distributed under the surveillance of the Education Department of Her Majesty's Government. The chief officers of the Art section of this department are a Secretary, a Director, and an Assistant Director. The Secretary is a colonel of the Royal Engineers, the Director for Art is a painter of semi-classical and Italian easel pictures, and the Assistant Director for Art is a teacher of perspective drawing in the Schools of the Royal Academy. The general staff is made up of a number of inspectors, examiners, examination clerks, &c., &c.

The money voted annually by Parliament is expended under the following heads :—

(*a*) Medals and prizes.

(*b*) Grants on work done during each school year.

(*c*) Grants for work done at an examination in a given time.

(*d*) Scholarships.

(*e*) The training of teachers.

(*f*) Building grants.

(*g*) Grants for examples and fittings.

(*h*) The circulation of art examples and objects.

(*i*) The South Kensington and other Museums.

(*j*) Salaries, and expenses of administration.

THE BETHNAL GREEN MUSEUM.

This branch of the South Kensington Museum was opened in 1872 in response to a feeling and frequently expressed desire that the East should share some of the national treasures as well as the West—a perfectly natural desire. The building is pleasantly situated between Bethnal Green and Cambridge Heath Stations, and the sight of green grass plots from one side of the building harmonises well with the purpose and object of the Museum. The Museum building is a painfully plain structure, and the impression that one receives in looking at it is that it must have been designed with a feeling that anything would do for the East End. Were it not for the chaste and handsome fountain presented by Messrs. Minton and Co. in front of the building, the Museum might be taken for any kind of structure, from a fire station to a coach builder's factory. Why should the privileged West Enders possess the cream of the national buildings and the best be kept for them ? This is really an important question for the whole of London.

There are, again, some other drawbacks attaching to Bethnal Green Museum which should be at once removed. An elaborate display is made of South Kensington handbooks of the more expensive kind, but there is not a general guide to the objects in the Museum to be had. In fact, if the visitor wishes for any literature as to the special objects to be seen, beyond a penny guide to the National Portrait Gallery, he must make one for himself.

During a Whit week visit the question was asked why this was so, and the courteous matron in charge of the catalogue stall informed us that the cases were being so often changed that it made it impossible to publish a general guide. The force of the argument is not very clear, and if the authorities are not equal to the production of penny or twopenny guides to sections or the whole Museum the sooner they allow the enterprise of some private firm to provide the unmistakable need the better.

One large section was closed during Whit week for the arranging of the Hon. Massey Mainwaring's Collection. This surely was not a wise proceeding during a holiday

BANK HOLIDAY AT THE BETHNAL GREEN MUSEUM.

week. The general exhibits consist chiefly of objects of ornamental art in gold, silver, bronze, porcelain, sculpture, &c. The departmental collections comprise foods, animal products, waste products, and the Doubleday Collection of insects. The collections of foods and artificial models of fruits are arranged in a very interesting manner. The case illustrating beef, mutton, veal, pork, and poultry contains run-and-read lessons which cannot fail to be remembered. Here, side by side, are shown the models of a pound of beef, a bottle containing the water extracted from a pound of beef, the ossein-like substances and the fat in a pound of beef, and then on a plate there is the mineral matter (350 grains) in a pound of beef. The other articles are treated in a similar way.

The commercial products of bone, leather, ivory, and other substances are fully and instructively illustrated. In the lower part of the building there is, in a series of long wall-cases, a very comprehensive series of products illustrating the utilisation of waste. These might be most interesting and useful, but in a dark corridor, and without a scrap of printed matter respecting them for the visitor to carry away, either by purchase or otherwise, their utility is considerably lessened. And yet there is no part of the whole Museum so calculated to produce solid lessons on the mind of the visitor as this section. Here in proper form there are specimens of products, arranged by that veteran in the utilisation of waste products, Mr. P. L. Simmonds, of cotton, jute, nuts, straw, wood, barks, leaves, oil, silk, glass, metal and other substances.

In one of the upper Galleries there is a case containing an elaborate display of the diet for convicts. Pray, is this a joke? If so, who is responsible for it? Is it intended to convey a lesson to the East End people of what to expect if they are unfortunate enough to get incarcerated in what they delicately call the "stone jug"? If so, by all means let a like case go in the South Kensington Museum for the particular benefit of the Bromptonian Company promoters and adventurous stockbrokers, many of whom are not, but ought to be, living on the wholesome prison fare, models of which are to be seen within the before-mentioned case. At the best it is a piece of polished satire to place such a case in any Museum, but in the Bethnal Green Museum it is an insult. In a general exhibition such a case is not out of place, but surely it is interpreting the word Museum very widely to show specimens of prison skilly.

The birds shown in one division of the animal products collection are intended to illustrate the art of stuffing and mounting them, and the application of their feathers to various industrial purposes.

The resident officer in charge of the Museum is Mr. W. Matchwick, F.L.S.

The attendance at the Museum, which is open free on Mondays, Thursdays, and Saturdays from ten a.m. to ten p.m., Tuesdays and Fridays from ten a.m. to six p.m., Wednesdays, on payment of sixpence, up to six p.m., is shown by the following table :—

1888.	FREE DAYS.		Students' days.	TOTALS.	Corresponding Nos. in		
	Morning.	Evening.			1887	1886	1885
JANUARY ..	100,466	71,738	4,555	176,759	38,175	36,487	32,759
FEBRUARY .	90,393	53,294	9,326	153,013	33,862	30,661	29,191
MARCH......	97,424	52,342	5,378	155,144	35,831	36,527	32,549
APRIL	84,426	30,591	189	115,206	48,098	47,915	50,782
MAY					40,937	35,907	47,184
JUNE					27,664	41,765	31,744
JULY					23,837	28,202	27,530
AUGUST					38,777	48,352	47,565
SEPTEMBER					30,606	33,017	32,711
OCTOBER ..					28,607	31,713	33,104
NOVEMBER.					26,768	38,104	41,506
DECEMBER..					36,767	38,072	43,814
Totals	372,709	207,965	19,448	600,122	409,929	446,722	450,439

COMPARISON OF THE YEARLY NUMBER OF VISITORS.

Years	Number of Visitors.			Years	Number of Visitors.		
	Morning.	Evening.	Total.		Morning.	Evening.	Total.
1872	532,358	369,106	901,464	1880	214,335	210,074	424,409
1873	405,120	304,352	709,472	1881	250,783	200,404	451,187
1874	253,873	276,803	530,676	1882	237,199	206,493	443,692
1875	234,940	287,158	522,098	1883	239,838	207,914	447,752
1876	441,634	497,160	938,794	1884	231,330	216,000	447,330
1877	334,007	336,207	670,214	1885	241,614	208,825	450;489
1878	236,142	263,239	499,381	1886	232,179	214,543	446,722
1879	219,198	224,823	444,021	1887	226,148	183,781	409,929

That the Museum is greatly appreciated is patent, but its work is capable of useful extension, especially in pithy and interesting chats on the contents of the various cases to be given at stated intervals.

CHAPTER XVI.

OTHER MUSEUMS AND ART GALLERIES IN LONDON.

FOR a city so large and wealthy as the Metropolis it is not by any means rich in Museums and Art Galleries, if we exclude the British Museum and South Kensington. There is, however, gradually coming a new life of London pregnant with hope, and the rise of Museums and Free Public Libraries is only one of a number of co-ordinate social growths which may not seem particularly imposing if taken individually, but which are very significant if considered collectively. The two most vital facts with regard to London life are these—the awakening of a united civic consciousness, and, perhaps what is still more important, a civic conscience. There is, too, something more than a merely rudimentary movement for attaining through combined effort to what Mr. Frederic Harrison calls "more civilisation." What is most remarkable is that it is precisely in the localities in the Metropolis where the conditions of life are hardest and most grinding that the new intellectual movement is most eagerly appreciated. The large crowds that listen to the University Extension lectures on Science and Literature in the East End are an entirely new feature in London life. The People's Palace will not be long before it has counterparts in South and North London, and altogether the outlook for the future, of corporate life in the great city, is full of hope to those who look below the surface. It should never be forgotten that the People's Palace is the creation of a distinguished man of letters. This true Palace of Delight will ever be associated with the name of Mr. Walter Besant, and had he been offered some tinsel reward on the day of opening in company with the two nobodies who were knighted, it could never have made his name more of a household word than it already has become. Few but those who have visited it can realise what a boon the People's Palace is to the inhabitants of the East End. The conditions and surroundings of life of the dense population of the East End have for generations been so sad and distressing that all with an atom of thought in them for others must feel the utter helplessness of lifting them out of their present misery so long as they were fettered by the mass of ugliness and moral and mental unwholesomeness which environs them. Now there are rays of hope. The People's Palace as a building does not attract the attention of the passer-by. As seen outside, it is a huge, unadorned structure, looking very much like many

of the large and smoky buildings around it. The transformation is wonderful indeed when one enters it. It
is seen best at night, for though there is no electric
light, no cooling fountain spray, the hum of conversation
that is kept up by the thousands that are to be met in
the various rooms, the excellent music, the perform-
ances in the gymnasium and in the swimming bath,
give to the place an air of sprightliness and excitement
only to be seen at public exhibitions. The institution
was opened in October, 1887 ; its membership now numbers between four and five thousand persons.

The subscription for the men is two shillings and
sixpence annually, and that for women one shilling and
sixpence, the ages of admission being from fifteen to
twenty-five. Every member for the sum stated has
free access to the gymnasium, the billiard rooms, the
concerts, the exhibitions, and the shows. For the sum
of twopence admission is obtained to the magnificent
swimming bath. The members have their own clubs
—cricket, football, sketching, dramatic, amateur boxing,
rambling, literary, shorthand, and art. There is also a
debating society, and the members have brought out a
journal of their own to record their doings. The
founders of the Palace evidently believe that development of the muscle is as necessary as that of the
intellect, and that expansion of the chest is not less
desirable than expansion of ideas. There was a Workmen's Exhibition a short time ago which was remarkably
well attended. The experiment of Sunday opening is
thus far succeeding well.

A most important movement is likely to grow
out of the People's Palace. Almost immediately
following the opening of this building in the East
End, South London bestirred itself and rightly thought
that the time had arrived when something should
be done for the south side of the Thames. The Charity

Commissioners were visited in the early part of the present year by a deputation, and gave a most favourable reception to the memorial presented to them. It is no secret that the Charity Commissioners are earnestly in touch with the great need that exists for an extension of Free Libraries and Museums in all parts of the Metropolis. Mr. James Anstie, Q.C., one of the Commissioners, has, in particular, displayed in his speeches to the various deputations which have waited upon him an earnest sympathy with the movement. The Commissioners have promised to give one pound for every pound subscribed up to £150,000 for South London, and the same offer holds good for other parts of London. The great ground landlords of London have now an opportunity for distinguishing themselves, which, it is to be hoped, they will not allow to pass. It is only by the promise of many thousands from them that there is the prospect of the success of the efforts. In the early part of this last June a very influential meeting was held in the Mansion House in furtherance of this movement. The Premier and Lord Rosebery were the chief speakers. The Marquis of Salisbury spoke well and powerfully. It may very reasonably be asked, What limits are there to the possible benefits from a network of such institutions over London and other large cities?

THE CITY MUSEUM.

This Museum has its home under the Dick Whittington Library in the Guildhall. But it really does the City fathers little credit, and, in fact, for the annual outlay of some £5,000 to £6,000 for the Library and Museum, the Metropolis gets an exceedingly poor return. The most important features of the Museum are the relics showing the occupation of Londinium by the Romans. There are amongst the

antiquities collected by the Corporation a perfect
Roman tessellated pavement found in Bucklersbury,
interesting fragments of buildings of the Roman era,
consisting of sculptured stones, cornices, friezes,
spandrils, capitals of columns with Corinthian mould-
ings, a life-size figure of a Roman warrior in military
costume, with the toga and characteristic legionary
sword, &c., a lion overpowering another animal,
personal ornaments such as fibulæ, armlets, rings,
chains, &c., also locks and keys, tablets for writing,
and pens in iron, bronze and bone, whorls for spinning
and bobbins for weaving, spear heads, swords, &c.,
specimens of glass vessels, Samian ware of all descriptions, bowls, vases, &c., lamps, spoons, pins, needles.
The Early English collection contains many objects of
great interest, such as signs of Old London.

These are now better arranged than they have ever
been, and the late Mr. Overall, who acted as Curator, is
to be congratulated upon having accomplished a difficult
task. Conspicuous among the curiosities in the Museum
is the collection of clocks and timepieces. One of
Harrison's wooden clocks is well worth inspection.
Horologists record that Harrison's first clock was made
as large as a room, and when he had got it right he
gradually reduced his sizes until he got the works into
something like reasonable compass. There is a
hydrogen gas clock and some curious watches, but they
are only of general interest. On the staircase is a
quaint old panorama of the Thames showing the
gentlemen's houses along the banks. Some files of old
newspapers, a model of Holborn Viaduct, and drawings
of Old London Bridge will interest a few visitors, and
among a number of antiquities are some old bone
skates with which the apprentice boys of London used
to skate on places now covered with buildings.
Unfortunately, the whole of these exhibits being in the

basements, there is a great want of light, and some of
the cases are placed away in dismal corners where the
gas has always to be lighted.

The latest City Corporation child is the Art Gallery,
and if the City fathers were not such experts in advertising, there would have been less heard about this
Gallery at the time of the opening in the early part
of 1887. Here there are a number of City
pictures, interesting in themselves, but scarcely worth a
second visit. On a Saturday afternoon in June I had
the entire Gallery to myself with the exception of the
attendant. There is one good-sized Gallery, and a very
small room in which are hung chiefly framed engravings of the large pictures. Several of the pictures are of
an enormous size, and the walls are covered with these.
Certainly we have bulk if not quality, but while the
Corporation may well be pardoned for preserving such
pictures as the " Death of Wat Tyler" and other pictures
of like a character, we scarcely need a surfeit of art of
this kind. War and murder form so large a portion
of the pictures that it was refreshing to turn to
" The Stream in Summer," a little gem by Mr. B. W.
Leader, A.R.A., of last year's Royal Academy, which
was placed on an easel. It is a gift from the Drapers'
Company. What a good thing it would be if the
wealthy City Livery Companies would do something to
place antidotes in the Gallery of such a character as the
little sketch just mentioned. It is well that visitors to
the Gallery should be reminded of the history of
London through pictures such as there are in this City
Gallery. But the lurid gleam of dagger, sword, and
gun requires toning down. Busts of leading statesmen
are placed around the room, but the Library and Art
Gallery Committee may be asked to spare us from placing
alongside them the busts of deceased aldermen. There
is already one such bust there, but surely its proper

place is in the new Council Chamber, where it may be gazed at by the wearers of the mazzarine gowns and new cocked hats. The average daily attendance at this Gallery is given at between 300 and 400.

The expenses of conducting the Library, Museum, and Art Gallery are, as already stated, nearly £6,000 a year, and mark! ye critics! there is out of this huge sum scarcely an item for books, new specimens for the Museum, or pictures for the Gallery. Since the cost is so large, the public should enjoy its benefits.

ST. JUDE'S, WHITECHAPEL.

It would be almost impossible to name a more earnest attempt to brighten the lives of the poor and the horny-handed sons of toil than that made each year at St. Jude's, Whitechapel. This is a church situated in one of the most densely-populated parts of London. The name of the Rev. Samuel A. Barnett is a household word in the East End of London, and most deservedly so, for none have recognised more acutely the joyless lives of thousands who have daily to struggle for a mere existence than has he. Further, not only has he recognised it, but in a most practical way sought to bring some rays of light each year into their midst.

The eighth annual Whitechapel Fine Art Loan Exhibition was opened in St. Jude's school-house on March 20th and closed on April 8th, 1888. No fewer than 55,000 persons visited the Exhibition last year, giving an average of 3,000 per day, including Sundays. Mr. Barnett says about opening it on Sunday that people are "beginning to see that Sunday could only be preserved as a day of rest by making it a day of recreation." Mr. Holman Hunt, who has shown himself a true friend of this annual exhibition, gave the inaugural address, and took as his subject the present position of English

Art. It is worth noting in passing here that he did not take a favourable, or even hopeful, view of his subject, but pointed to our coins, our costumes, and our ornamentation, architectural and otherwise, to indicate the low standard of English art. Of course, happy features might be met with. There was Mr. Morris's shop in Oxford-street, for instance. Ornamentation was neglected, and painting and sculpture held to exclusively represent art. The tendency in the Government Art Schools was for the pupils to abandon design, and go to swell the already overcrowded ranks of the artists and sculptors. To cure this the co-operation of the working classes—of whose appreciation of art he was persuaded—would be needed ; and hence the importance of such exhibitions as the one they were opening.

One useful outcome from these exhibitions is the starting of a workshop in Whitechapel for producing artistic manufactures, and there is, in fact, a carrying out of the old mediæval custom of artist and artificer working hand-in-hand together. As the new schools for art products are working for artists and not for the public, there is every reason to hope for a large measure of success in this worthy attempt.

Those who desire to ascertain particulars of this effort to bring art and the workman in closer unison should write to Mr. C. R. Ashbee, Toynbee Hall, London, E. The objects of the Guild are to train men and boys in the higher sides of technical education, that is to say, where the workman is engaged in making beautiful things. There is a large workshop with the appliances necessary for the classes, and the workshop contains lockers at the disposal of workmen who desire to do art work in their leisure hours. No fees are charged for attendance at the classes. The classes already commenced are for lessons in decoration, art metal working, and wood working.

T

Anyone visiting the St. Jude's Exhibition when its popularity might be fairly tested, could not fail to come away with a profoundly deep conviction that its educational and softening influence could not be too highly appreciated. Here may be seen young and old go from picture to picture with deep interest depicted in their faces. The sailor lad has been there fresh from his ship, and by his side the sweetheart about whom he no doubt dreamed when on his midnight watch far away on the ocean wave. Boys and girls fresh from school, tripping from room to room, and passing some of the most quaint remarks about the pictures which made one smile and laugh alternately. Working men and working women were there in strong force, and many a wearied mother, as she carried her baby, brightened up as she gazed on some picture, say of a young, fresh face, with blooming youth and merry eyes.

No student of human nature could visit St. Jude's Exhibition without being greatly amused at some of the remarks at the pictures. Two little girls standing gazing earnestly at Josef Israel's picture "Silent Conversation." One asks the other, "What can that mean? People aren't silent when they talk." The other explains, very seriously, "Oh, but don't you see it's the dog that's talking to his master."

The little catalogue sold for a penny is capital value, and Mr. Barnett is even so modest that nowhere in it does his name appear. There is on its cover the pertinent saying of Ruskin that "life without industry is guilt, and industry without art is brutality," and the other pages of the cover are occupied with appropriate quotations. This catalogue, with its pithy notes about the pictures, is the work of Mrs. Barnett, and last year some 20,000 copies of the catalogue were sold.

It is quite safe to assert that there are between 300

and 400 schools in London where a small collection of pictures might with great advantage be exhibited during such holidays as Easter or Whitsuntide, and at a small outlay. If this were done the gain in momentarily brightened lives, quickened aspirations and awakened new emotions would be incalculable. But alas! that there should be so few Samuel Barnetts.

MUSEUM OF PRACTICAL GEOLOGY.

This Museum has been justly spoken of as one of the best models, combining strictly scientific purposes and classification with good popular effect. It is not generally known that it receives Government aid, and that it is open free daily except on Fridays. On Mondays and Saturdays it remains open from ten a.m. to ten p.m., and in the evening is illuminated with the electric light. The expenses for this financial year paid by State aid are as follows :—Salaries and wages, £2,135 ; purchases, £450 ; police, heating and lighting, £981 ; furniture, travelling, &c., £260, making a total of £3,826. The building, which is the headquarters of the Geological Society, is situated near the Regent Street end. The number of visitors during the last year was 43,115. Of these 26,085 visited the Museum in the morning and 17,030 in the evening. The Museums and rooms are the headquarters of the Geological Society.

It is a common remark among geologists that if you want to identify a fossil take it to the Museum of Practical Geology in Jermyn Street. In no other part of the world is there so good and comprehensive a selection of fossils and rock specimens.

THE SOANE MUSEUM.

The Soane Museum, on the north side of Lincoln's Inn Fields, might become a very attractive little

Museum if there was less caprice in the times of throwing it open to the public. It is only open on certain days of the week, and then only at certain hours, so that a visitor might make several attempts to see it without success unless he had informed himself beforehand of the hours at which it was opened. The most interesting feature of the Museum, of a general character, is Hogarth's Election series hinged on doors in such a way that they have to be folded in and out to each other.

The Royal Architectural Museum in Tufton Street, Westminster, is situated not far from Westminster School. It is open free on all days from ten to four. It is full of casts of portions of Gothic architecture, and here bosses, gargoyles, and other architectural anatomical specimens reign supreme, and to the untechnical mind in a conglomeration which may be described as confusion worse confounded. To the young student articled to an architect this Museum cannot fail to be of practical service, and not the least interesting of its collection will be the plaster casts from Venice.

The Parkes Museum of Hygiene in Margaret Street is an excellent institution for plumbers and sanitary inspectors, where they can see old and obsolete traps, siphons, and the rest, but to the general public it can scarcely be interesting. The authorities know how to get hold of subscriptions and donations, for each week, or at stated intervals, a paragraph is duly sent round to the Press announcing gifts from Lord this and Sir somebody else with the Livery Companies figuring with their £25 by way of make weight.

The Museum in Kew Gardens is most interesting. Here the collection is botanical in the widest sense, and fruits, plants, or seeds can be identified at

Kew if they can anywhere. The Museum is free every day from noon.

Efforts are being made in South Lambeth and other parts of London to secure parks as open spaces for the people. In several of these parks are large residences, and it is intended to try and get these for Museum purposes by the adoption of the Acts. Two or three of such schemes are maturing.

CHAPTER XVII.

THE SCIENCE AND ART MUSEUMS IN DUBLIN AND EDINBURGH.

HERE are annually published of these national institutions full and exhaustive reports. The Dublin people have, for some time, been concerned respecting the new buildings for the twin institutions which are being erected in Dublin. The time is not now far distant when the National Library of Ireland will be housed in its new home in Kildare Street. It will be similar to the noble building standing opposite to it in the historic courtyard, and when it has been completed by the stonemasons and carpenters there will occur no delay in furnishing it with its vast literary treasures. The people of Dublin—and not the artisans alone—await with impatience the consummation of this work. When it is completed the National Library will become a great popular club, accessible to all, and for which there will be no subscription. Everybody will find a welcome within its spacious halls. Everybody will be served with what he chooses to call for with equal attention and respect, and the benefit will be such as the people of Dublin have never heretofore enjoyed.

In the last votes in the House of Commons for Civil Service expenditure, there was one of £42,500 for these Science and Art buildings in Dublin. The question was asked whether this was the end of the vote, and the Secretary to the Treasury said that he could not promise that this was the end of the expenditure. There might be alterations required from time to time, but there was no reason to suppose that there would be excess expenditure over the contract. There would, of course, be additional expenditure for furnishing and fittings.

The buildings will, when finished, be among the handsomest and most satisfactory public buildings which have been erected for many years, but it is undeniable that the jumble at the Treasury is a serious matter for the country. The estimates as given to the House were fictitious and worthless. There is scarcely one which is at all near the estimate published. £60,000 here and there in excess, as admitted by the Secretary to the Treasury, are serious items. An extra £45,000 has already been expended over the £100,000 estimate for this Museum of Science and Art in Dublin.

Professor Ball and his colleagues have begun to map out the allotment of the rooms of the new building. In his scheme for this purpose full consideration has been given to the relative importance of the several collections which have to be provided for. It is not yet possible to say when they are likely to receive over the completed building, and as the date of the opening to the public will depend on the completion of the internal fittings and the subsequent arrangement of the specimens, it would be premature to attempt to fix it at present.

The report of the Natural History department is very interesting, and there is in it a brief reference to the dredging expedition on the south-west coast of Ireland, which has been productive of so many valuable specimens for the Museum. The rearrangement of the collections is progressing. The Director notes that the provision made in the vote for this year has enabled them to begin to rectify the disadvantageous and defective means of exhibition of the Mammal Collection in the gloomy cases under the galleries. It was not until all suggested modifications, by means of which light might be admitted into them, had been experimentally tried that it was decided that the best course to adopt would be to construct an entirely new set of cases which would occupy the centre of the floor, and in which the contained specimens, well lit from above, could be seen from both sides. In the cases which are being made in the Museum workshops, the old sashes are being worked up for the purpose, and thus the Museum will be supplied with a practically new range of cases in which special attention has been paid both to rendering all parts readily accessible and guarding against the possibility of dust obtaining access.

The success of the groups of birds illustrative of their building habits at the Natural History Museum, referred to on another page, has induced the officials in Dublin to prepare similar groups. Small maps, showing the geographical distribution of particular genera and species are also being prepared. There is one exceptionally important paragraph in the report to which attention should be called. Dr. Ball is of opinion that they are right in their endeavour "to make this Metropolitan Museum something more than a provincial or purely educational Museum, neither of which could attempt successfully to deal with large systematic series of specimens. Over and above," he says, "the geographical argument of our situation in favour of this view, there is the very important fact that, not only do we possess both admirable typical series of all groups generally, and special collections illustrative of the zoology of Ireland, but we also have considerable numbers of specimens which have accumulated during a long series of years from all parts of the world. I therefore hold it to be our duty to arrange these for reference, and as far as possible to fill up *lacunæ* rather than neglect them in order to concentrate all our available force on the two first classes of specimens alone. Were we to adopt such a course, the question would arise whether we should accept donations which contained neither typical specimens not already in the collection, nor Irish specimens which were among our desiderata. Further, the question would have to be decided whether we should even retain collections already acquired, no matter how valuable they might be, supposing we resolved not to spend time on them in order to have them available for ready reference." Friends of Museum work will watch with interest how this problem is solved.

In the Royal Botanic Gardens it is noticed that the number of visitors during the year exceeds a daily average of 1,000 persons, which, considering the distance from town, affords ample testimony, not only of their well sustained but also of their

growing popularity.   The total of the Sunday is to
that of the weekday visitors very nearly as three to one,
and the largest number which passed through the gate
on a single Sunday (June 20th) was 9,810.   How gratifying it is to know that the conduct of these large numbers
of people has been most satisfactory, and, with one
exception, no injury has resulted from the perfect free-
dom with which all who visit the gardens are allowed
to circulate throughout all parts, including the green-
houses.

In the Metropolitan School of Art the number of
students was 503.   The head master's report for last
year states that the teachers have discovered " that
students very generally are unable to continue at their
studies as long as in past years, or for periods sufficiently
long to enable them to pass through a full course of
instruction with a view to a more or less complete education in art, and it is to be regretted that many
possessing special aptitude for art pursuits are, owing
to ill-health, home-requirements, and the distractions
of a great city, prevented from attending the school
with regularity, or during the full number of hours that
it is open for study.   I beg to remark that a system by
which small weekly allowances could be made to some
of the more advanced students of the school, on condition of regular and full attendance, and the following
of a prescribed course of study, might probably be
attended with satisfactory results."

This is certainly a novel suggestion and would
be quite a new departure in art instruction to
poor students.   Usually the most promising students
are those who are too poor to give themselves
wholly up to study, and were such a plan
as this in operation it might, if very judiciously
exercised, be the means of rearing some students to
produce work far beyond the range of mediocrity.

With the present grants, however, it will be at once said by the authorities that this is impracticable. There are any number of fat pensions for Government officials, who are supposed to work from eleven to four o'clock, and during this limited number of hours perform as much work as would be comfortably done by a business man of good despatch in about an hour. But when it comes to giving a lift to honest effort on the part of poor students in the Art schools, it is not likely that officialism will be quick to take up the suggestion. In saying this reference is made to the headquarters and not to the teachers in Dublin from whom the suggestion comes.

Ireland is not particularly rich in Museums. The Royal Dublin Society, founded in 1749, had for years the chief Museum in Dublin. The Royal Irish Academy has a Museum specially rich in Irish antiquities. For educational purposes the Museum of Trinity College, the Museum of the Royal College of Surgeons in Dublin, and one at Armagh, may be mentioned. Belfast hopes to have its Free Library open to the public this year, and when in full operation it may, perhaps, prepare the way for a Museum also supported out of the rates. It is difficult to understand the lukewarmness in the Belfast Town Council respecting the Library building. Several years have been absorbed in its erection.

EDINBURGH.

The Industrial Museum of Scotland had its origin in 1854. By a good deal of pressure brought to bear upon Parliament at the time, the House of Commons granted £7,000 for the purchase of a site upon which the Museum should be built, and a further sum was voted for expenditure in the acquisition of specimens and the salaries of the officials. Among the reports sent is the one for 1858, a little pamphlet of fifteen pages. From this it appears that the Natural History Museum of Edinburgh has been in existence since the year 1812, when it was established in connection with the University, receiving at the same time for its maintenance a Government grant of £100 a year. In 1819 Mr. Bullock's Museum and the very extensive collection belonging to M. Dufresne, of Paris, were for sale, and £3,000 was voted by the Senatus Academicus from the funds of the College for the purchase of a selection from Bullock's Museum and of the entire of the collection belonging to M. Dufresne. From the manuscript catalogue which accompanied M. Dufresne's collection it appears that this collection contained 1,600 birds, 2,600 shells, 12,000 insects, 600 eggs of birds, 200 fossils, with a considerable number of radiata and a few mammals.

In 1820 the Museum was opened to the public at an admission charge of two shillings and sixpence, which was subsequently reduced to one shilling, and in 1831 the Government grant was increased to £200 a year, the sum at which it has since remained. In 1855, by a vote of the Town Council, the Museum was handed over to the Department of Science and Art, then under the Board of Trade; and in 1857 the Department of Science and Art, having been transferred from the Board of Trade to the Privy Council Committee on Education, the Museum passed under the control of the last-mentioned body.

The last report, issued in February, 1888, records that the interest taken by the public in the Museum as indicated by the number of visitors has been fully maintained. The number of visitors during the year was 316,704, and of these during the year 9,359 were students who entered on the free days. As a guide to the work of the Museum the following figures are very instructive :—

Months.	Free.		Pay Days.		Total.	Amount of Admission Fees.
	Days.	Evenings	At 6d. each.	Free Students		
						£ s. d.
January...	18,177	13,919	285	519	32,900	7 2 6
February.	10,562	13,440	228	1,173	25,403	5 14 0
March ...	9,947	11,926	255	1,571	23,699	6 7 6
April	10,468	13,760	565	375	25,168	14 2 6
May	8,429	8,024	494	918	17,865	12 7 0
June	10,579	8,102	572	1,371	20,624	14 6 0
July	15,874	9,530	1,175	1,772	28,351	29 7 6
August ...	14,757	12,331	1,174	306	28,568	29 7 0
September	12,246	16,185	745	112	29,288	18 12 6
October ...	11,506	16,431	648	290	28,875	16 4 0
November	10,599	15,154	344	520	26,617	8 12 0
December.	14,266	14,530	118	432	29,346	2 19 0
Total...	147,410	153,332	6,603	9,359	316,704	165 1 6

Average annual attendance for last five years ... 340,299.

Average daily attendance in 1887 ... ... $\begin{cases} \text{pay days} & 108. \\ \text{free days} & 1,856. \end{cases}$

The list of donations to the Museum of Science and Art, and to the Natural History Department, covers a considerable space. Colonel Sir Murdoch Smith is the Director. The list of objects acquired during 1886 is particularly interesting, and comprises a multiplicity of curios and specimens for the Industrial Section.

CHAPTER XVIII.

THE SCOTCH MUSEUMS.

HE cast of the Scotch mind is essentially philosophic and scientific, and the hard matter-of-fact sciences like geology and kindred subjects especially have received an impetus from the attention which Scotchmen have devoted to these questions. There are probably among the sons of Scotia more collections of geological, mineralogical, and ethnological specimens than would be found among a corresponding number of any other nationality. This is highly creditable to them, and has tended to produce a type of working naturalist such as would be an invaluable acquisition in any large Museum. Of this type of man was the late Thomas Edward, the Banff naturalist, who was nearly starved till Dr. Smiles wrote his life. He henceforth became "passing rich on fifty pounds a year"—for he was put on the Civil List, and richly he deserved it. He was an old correspondent of mine. If rich men would but distribute their abundant coin as zealously as rich intellectual men do their mental accumulations there would be less misery in the world. Dean Swift said of the mere money-grubbers that "you could see what the Almighty thought about money by the people He gave it to." Science is engaged in redistributing knowledge. Nowadays it is no man's monopoly—three centuries ago it was the rich man's perquisite. Science is the most democratic element in modern society. These remarks are suggested by the announcement that poor Edward's natural history collection (to which he devoted his life) has been " graciously accepted" by the Town Council of Aberdeen. It contains about 2,000 specimens, which, it is to be hoped, will not be transferred to some dark room, with the spiders for curators.

Thomas Edward was a born naturalist, and his passion clung to him up to the last. In " Eminent Naturalists," by the same author as the present book, there is a sketch of him. In that short series of sketches there is a description of how in 1846 Thomas Edward exhibited in Aberdeen a former collection. Six large carriers' carts were required to convey the cases from Banff to Aberdeen. He took a shop in Union Street, the finest thoroughfare in the granite city, and forthwith sent out his handbills, which announced that " Thomas Edward takes the liberty of stating that the collection is allowed by eminent naturalists to be one of the greatest curiosities ever offered for public inspection in this quarter, amounting, as it does, to about 2,000 objects; and being the work of one individual, who had to labour under every disadvantage, having none to tell how or where to find the different objects; none to teach him how to preserve these objects when found; no sound of promised reward ringing in his ears to urge him on his singular course; no friend to accompany him in his nightly wanderings; help from none, but solely dependent on his own humble abilities and limited resources." Such was the appeal made to the Aberdeen public; helped on by kindly notices in the local papers. The prices of admission were low enough for all, being, " Ladies and gentlemen, sixpence; tradespeople, threepence; children, half-price." After all was ready for the crowd, which he fondly thought would gather at the door, he looked around his eight years' collection with a pardonable pride. He thought he had reached the Rubicon and was just on the threshold of better and more prosperous days. The Aberdeen public little thought of how their "saxpences" would have helped to cheer that worthy soul, but they were very chary of parting with them.

Sad to say, there were very few who came to see his little show. Some of Edward's chief visitors were those who had stuffed birds and animals to sell, or others who mistook him for a dog doctor and wanted cures for pets of the canine tribe. He was told by several professors of the Aberdeen College that his collection was very fine ; but, Job's comforters as they were, they generously informed him that "he was several centuries too soon, as the people of Aberdeen were not yet prepared for such an exhibition, especially as it had been the work of a poor man." Poor Edward, his heart and his all were in that collection, and the attempt was a failure through no fault of his own. After a tragic incident, too long to recount here, he sold his collection for £20 10s. With this sum he paid the rent of the shop and his bill for printing, and returned again to his cobbler's last, but only to make another collection, which has again gone to Aberdeen. It is to be hoped that the Aberdonians have been less stingy about this than they were about the last.

This has been mentioned somewhat fully as a not by any means exceptional case. Scattered all over the country, not only in Scotland but England, there are working men naturalists who spend their leisure in searching for specimens, and whose specimens would often be a perfect windfall for local Museums. It is to be hoped that more attention will be given to these plodding naturalists in the future than has been the case in the past.

"Let Glasgow flourish" is the proud motto of Scot-

land's commercial capital, but the majority of the
Glasgow citizens think that their city can flourish
without the adoption of the Public Libraries Acts, for
they have again, by a considerable majority, refused to
adopt them. By so doing they again say " no " to the
offer of most valuable and immense collections of books
which would come to the citizens for the fullest use for
home reading, instead of as at present ·for reference
only. Glasgow has yet to place itself in line with other
large cities in this matter of Public Libraries before
the city motto can receive full force.

Many of the citizens have been so much engaged in
the gathering of bawbees that they have scarcely had
time or inclination to acquaint themselves with the
work being done by the Art Galleries and Museum. In
order to remove this ignorance, a very interesting paper
was read before the Scotch Philosophical Society in
1886, by ex-Bailie Dickson and Mr. James Paton, superintendent of the Museum and Art Galleries, on " The
Present Position of the Museum and Art Galleries of
Glasgow." The beginning and progress of the Museum
and Art Gallery is sketched in this paper. Their
origin dates back to 1856, when the Town Council
purchased the M'Lellan collection of pictures. It was
the intention of the late Mr. Archibald M'Lellan, a
prominent Glasgow citizen, to devote this collection
to the public, but although this was expressed in a
Deed of Bequest, the testator's affairs were so involved
at the time of his death that it could not be carried
out. The collection was ultimately purchased by the
Town Council for £15,000, and the heritable property in which Mr. M'Lellan had erected a suite
of Galleries for £29,500, the two sums together making
£44,500. This heritable property and other adjoining
buildings required some structural alterations, and
portions of the building then became the headquarters

of the Glasgow School of Art, the Philosophical Society, and the Institution of Engineers and Shipbuilders. Each of these Associations paid a rental. It may also be noted that the Galleries had a further tenant, from 1862 onwards, in the Glasgow Institute of Fine Arts, and its yearly exhibitions were for a time the only real artistic use to which the Galleries were devoted. This exhibition seems to have been a pecuniary failure, and on Mr. Wilson resigning the Curatorship of the Galleries a decreasing interest was manifested in the institution, and it gradually fell into the most regrettable and detrimental condition of public neglect.

The authors of the paper say that "the landlord attitude of the Town Council came indeed to over-shadow and crush out all other relations and responsi-bilities, and the M'Lellan pictures, and other art pro-perty which had been added by gift and bequest, were regarded as mere ornamental adjuncts to balls, concerts, bazaars, and dinners, for which the halls were hired. It can scarcely be wondered that, under such a course of treatment, the pictures fell into disrepute, people began to doubt whether they were even ornamental, and their presence was regarded as a hindrance to the free use of the halls for miscellaneous purposes." This is a rather serious charge against the members of the Town Council who from year to year permitted such a state of things to exist. By-and-bye there came other bequests from Mr. Ewing and Mr. John Graham-Gilbert, and it was immediately after the receipt of this latter bequest that a serious effort was again made to rehabi-litate the Galleries and to bring them back to their original object and purpose.

With the relinquishing of their rooms in the Galleries by three of the Associations already named, in 1880 the authorities decided upon a series of temporary exhibitions in order to advertise the existence of the

Galleries to the great mass of the population of Glasgow,
who seemed unaware that they had such an institution in their city.   These exhibitions fulfilled their
educational purpose very satisfactorily.   The intrinsic
value of some of these collections was enormous, but
fire having broken out no less than four times in as
many years, these loan exhibitions were discontinued.
And now comes a sentence which is simply amazing in
its meaning when it is taken into account that it refers
to the Art Gallery of one of the leading cities in the entire
United Kingdom.   The authors state that the " exposure
to the chance of conflagration has not yet been lessened,
and although the responsibility of the Parks Trust to
private owners is decreased, the great Glasgow art collections—in which are included some of the works
which rank among the treasures of the world—and
which embrace donations and bequests from among
many of the most esteemed citizens of recent times, are
still daily exposed to the tender mercies of careless and
irresponsible outsiders, who deal in the most inflamma-
ble commodities."   Surely this is a stigma which the
city ought at once to see is removed. ·

So much for the Art Galleries, and it is to be feared
the Museum is not in a very much better condition.   In
1869 the Town Council resolved to convert the mansion
house of Kelvingrove into a temporary Museum, and in
the year following the City Industrial Museum saw life.
Some four years afterwards appeals were made for
money to extend these premises, and the response produced £7,500.   This extension was opened in 1876, but
sad to relate, this addition to the former buildings did
not materially relieve the difficulties of their position.
Let Glasgow men tell their own tale of the indifference
and lukewarmness of their fellow citizens.

" Principally by gifts from private persons, and from
public institutions, a large accumulation of useful and

instructive Museum specimens have been made, much of which cannot at present be exhibited. A certain amount of relief has been obtained by transferring to the Corporation Galleries those portions of the Museum collections which have an artistic bearing—the art pottery, glass, metal work, &c., but that relief has been obtained by impoverishing the Museum, and by breaking up continuous series of specimens, and, to some extent, it has consequently resulted in decreasing the educational value and significance of the objects themselves. The Museum has hitherto depended for its growth almost exclusively on contributions obtained either by begging or by voluntary contribution. No donation or bequest has been received of such outstanding prominence as to give a distinctive character to the collections, and additions which accrue from miscellaneous benevolence are apt to be miscellaneous in their character." To sum up, Glasgow has an excellent collection of pictures, some of them of considerable reputation. These are disposed of in a straggling, ill-lighted building which, according to the best authorities, can never be rendered bright and cheerful. At any time there is a lively prospect of the whole being destroyed by fire. Gas burners, coal-fire dust and dirt, and other atmospheric influences, are rapidly accomplishing destruction. The Museum is situated in an inconvenient and unsuitable position, and neither care nor money has been lavished on the collections.

May not the members of the Town Council and the leading citizens be asked whether such a state of things shall continue? The words with which Messrs. Dickson and Paton close their paper are very appro priate to the situation :—" We are now," say they, " on the threshold of other important changes in connection with scientific and secondary education; and in the efficiency of all these educational movements the Museum of the city ought to be an important factor. It ought to be the centre around which educational institutions should cluster, the store-house whence they could draw the material examples and illustrations required on the lecture-table and in the class-room. Such an influential position, however, cannot be obtained without earnest labour and sacrifice; but a city like Glasgow cannot afford to do its work on a mean scale. It is open for the Municipality to elect whether a Museum shall be established or not; but having made the choice, it has no right to found such an institution on an insufficient basis, nor to maintain it on a scale which deprives it of its most important and useful function." It is only natural to look for an example of vigorous civic life from Glasgow instead of an example to the contrary which it has been necessary to chronicle.

The Exhibition of this year will, it is to be hoped, be a great financial success and produce a large surplus which shall form the nucleus of better and worthier institutions in this northern city.

The Hawick Museum has been in a transition state for some time back. The old building having become very unsuitable it was sold, and with the proceeds accommodation was purchased in a new building erected for Science and Art Schools and Museum. They have only recently begun to arrange the collection in its new home and things are still unsettled. The Trustees of the British Museum have placed them in the list of institutions to receive duplicate specimens from time to time, and they are promised by a private donor a collection of geological specimens which will, he estimates, number about 12,000, but this will not be completed for some time. Monthly meetings, at which papers are read on kindred subjects, and these papers are reprinted for the members, take place during the winter months.

There is given below a sketch of the Elgin Museum.

ELGIN MUSEUM.

This was first instituted in 1836, and the purpose of the Association was for the study of literature, ancient history, antiquities, archæology, geology, botany, and natural history. The report and full list of members published in 1882 consists of just eight very small pages. Ordinary members pay a subscription of five shillings a year, and life membership may be purchased by a donation of not less than £2 2s. The names of eight life members only are given.

It is to be feared that not only this Museum at Elgin but many others in Scotland are in a very bad way. It is necessary to again repeat the statement that both in Glasgow, Elgin, and other places in Scotland, as well as in other parts of the United Kingdom, the only practical refuge is the adoption of the Public Libraries Acts for infusing new life in these institutions.

CHAPTER XIX.

THE CLASSIFICATION AND ARRANGEMENT OF OBJECTS IN MUSEUMS.

HIS is a subject upon which Curators themselves differ widely. So multifarious are the objects, and so vast the varieties, that it would be impossible to lay down fixed rules for guidance in all cases. Even if it were possible the author makes no claim, as stated in the preface, to speak authoritatively on this important department of Museum work. This is peculiarly a subject on which only a ripe experience inside a Museum can qualify to give advice of a practical nature. The daily handling of specimens is the best education, and it is wise to look to those who stand high in the profession, and are thus able to give authoritative opinions. The British Museum and its branch, the Natural History Museum, are the models upon which most Museums classify and arrange, and by common consent they are the best. Reference has already been made to the Guides of the British Museum, and these in the hands of Curators would be sufficient to direct if a visit to London is not practicable. Dr. Woodward's Guide to the Department of Geology and Palæontology is so clear and comprehensive, and moreover so well illustrated that in these sections it may be taken as the safest guide-book.

One of the general guides to the Natural History Museum puts the case very clearly :—

"Although the validity of the old division of all natural objects into *inorganic* and *organic* or *living* has been the subject of some discussion, and although the separation of the latter into *vegetable* and *animal* is perhaps less absolute than was once supposed, yet for practical purposes, mineral, vegetable, and animal still remain the three great divisions or 'kingdoms' into which natural bodies are grouped, and this classification has formed the basis of the arrangement of the collections in the Museum.

"1. Inorganic substances occur in nature in a gaseous, liquid, or solid form. With very few exceptions, it is only in the latter state that they can be conveniently preserved and exhibited in a Museum, and it is to such that the term 'mineral' is commonly limited. The collection, classification and exhibition of specimens of this kind is the office of the Mineralogical Department of the Museum.

"2. The study of the vegetable kingdom, as far as it can be illustrated by preserved specimens, is the province of the Department of Botany.

"3. In the same way the animal kingdom belongs to the department of Zoology.

"It will thus be seen that a department of the Museum corresponds with each of the great divisions of natural objects ; there is, however, a fourth department, which owes its separate existence to a period of scientific culture in which the terms Zoology and Botany were limited to the study of the existing forms of animal and plant life, and the extinct or fossil forms were associated with the minerals, rather than with their living representatives. This arrangement prevailed in the British Museum until the year 1857. The fossils were then severed from this incongruous connection, and placed in a separate department for which the name of 'Geology' was reserved."

Any reference to classification would be very incomplete without mention of *An Introduction to the Study of Minerals,* by Mr. L. Fletcher, with a Guide to the Mineral Gallery of the Natural History Museum. He lays down the law that "a mineral collection, in order to be complete, must aim at presenting all the definite varieties of chemical composition of the distinct mineral substances which occur in the earth's crust, and at the same time must illustrate the often very extensive varieties of crystalline form assumed by the minerals of a species or group. But besides these chemical and morphological features other important characters have to be illustrated, among which are the various modes of occurrence of each particular mineral, including its associations with other minerals ; and in a great national collection that is to illustrate the mineralogy of the world, it is important that there be specimens from all localities where a mineral occurs under special and noteworthy circumstances; and it must be a special object that examples of each mineral species should show its most complete development, whether in magnitude or perfection of crystals, in the colour and limpid purity, or in any other important quality which may belong to it in its more exceptional occurrence."

The handbooks published in connection with the Liverpool Museum are simply indispensable in the scientific and popular classification of the specimens of which they treat, and rank, in fact, among the most useful of all Museum literature. One of these is *A Synopsis of an Arrangement of Invertebrate Animals in the Free Public Museum of Liverpool*. It is by the Rev. H. H. Higgins, M.A., and bears the date of 1880. Both Mr. Higgins and Professor Herdman offer to communicate details to inquirers connected with Museums. They have come to the conclusion that few collections exhibited to the public will bear comparison with corresponding series contained in private cabinets. They naturally ask, Why should this be so any longer ?

Mr. Higgins dwells on the anomaly that the public should be encouraged to esteem art treasures as so much more valuable than the choicest productions of Nature. " One hears," he says, " of a pair of vases being sold for

£2,000, a sum which would provide twenty first-rate table-cases, and stock them with very fair illustrations of the whole of the invertebrate groups. . . . It is a happy circumstance that a Museum of common objects may at a trifling cost be established in almost any village, and, with a judicious local influence brought to bear upon it, may prove both useful and creditable."

The engraving below is reduced from the frontispiece to this pamphlet.

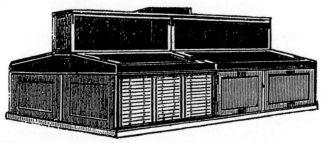

This case has been constructed to admit as much light and to obstruct the view of the specimens as little as possible. The upper wooden frames of the table-cases are reduced to the narrowest limits consistent with firmness and security. In the upright compartment, the top, bottom, and ends, as well as the sides, are of plate glass, and if a shelf is required it is made of the same material. To give readier access to the specimens, both sides of the upper compartment fall. To exclude the dust pianoforte hinges are used; each frame closes on double strips of velvet; zinc gutters underlie every crevice; in addition to the locks bolt screws are used, which by a half-turn bind the frames closely down in every part.

The other contribution to Museum literature is a pamphlet on *Museums of Natural History*, also by Mr. Higgins, at the end of which is a phylogenetic scheme of the pedigree of animals and vegetables by Professor Herdman, of the University College, Liverpool. This deals in a most practical way with Museum arrangements and Museum appliances. These books should be in the hands of all interested in Museum work. They can be obtained from Messrs. D. Marples and Co., Printers, Lord Street, Liverpool.

The following is a brief outline of the methods of classification and arrangement at present adopted in various parts of the country.

BATH.—Geological specimens are arranged in stratigraphical and zoological groups.

BIRMINGHAM.—All objects are numbered and registered with a consecutive number, and the year of acquisition, No. 841 '87 meaning object No. 841 received during 1887 ; No. 23 '88, the twenty-second object received during 1888, and so on.

BOLTON.—In Geology the palæontological specimens are arranged in stratigraphical order, and in each strata the organic remains classed according to their natural order. Minerals grouped. Zoological objects classed in natural order from Protozoa to Mammalia. Objects all labelled popular and scientific name.

CAMBRIDGE.—At the Woodwardian Museum the palæontological collections are arranged stratigraphically, and, subordinate to that, geographically ; and, subordinate to that, zoologically and botanically.

IPSWICH.—The text-books of each division of natural science are followed. Every species of cray shell is arranged according to Wood's *Monograph of Cray Mollusca.*

LEICESTER.—The classification of the most modern authorities is adopted, viz.: Professor Flower and others for the mammals, Mr. P. L. Sclater and others for the birds, and Dr. A. C. Günther and others for the fishes, and these again are corrected from time to time as the labours of specialists prove it necessary.

NORTHAMPTON.—The geological collection is arranged both zoologically and stratigraphically. The antiquities, except special collections, will, it is hoped, some time be arranged chronologically. The wall-case which we are filling with birds of the county, will eventually be arranged in their natural order and families.

READING.—Here they have no catalogue ; but everything is labelled. They classify as well as their series will permit, so that neolithic shall follow palæolithic, and bronze follow both; after these come the Roman and Saxon.

SCARBOROUGH.—Geology is minutely classified in the respective orders of rock formations.

SHEFFIELD.—In order to utilise all the available space for exhibition of objects, special cabinets have been made to fit under the table-cases. These cabinets contain six drawers in height; the drawers are glazed and can be opened by the visitors, but are so made that visitors cannot draw them entirely out of the cabinets, though far enough to see all that is in them. By this means the space of the table-cases is increased six-fold. This, of course, applies only to invertebrates, eggs, and such like, having the further advantage of a minimum exposure to light of such objects as lepidoptera, eggs, &c., which fade upon exposure to light.

SOUTHAMPTON.—The Hartley Institution here is admirable in every way. Now that the Public Libraries Acts have been adopted there will be a new lease of life for this institution. With regard to classification many examples of each geological specimen are preserved, with a view of showing the gradual change in form of different species. A large collection of recent mollusca exhibited close by a large collection of tertiary mollusca.

STAFFORD.—In the Zoological Department the arrangements of Cuvier are adopted.

WARWICK.—According to the plan adopted in the national collection at South Kensington; fossils lately arranged and named by Mr. Newton from South Kensington; minerals by Mr. Mallet, head of Indian Survey. Few country Museums are so good as is to be found here.

CHAPTER XX.

COMMERCIAL MUSEUMS.

NE of the important requirements of the times is the establishing of Commercial Museums, particularly in the manufacturing districts. The special scope of these should be to collect specimens of manufactures in use in foreign countries, such as are made in that locality, so that manufacturers and work people may have an opportunity of seeing the particular kind of goods which are in use in various parts of the world. There is serious ground for the belief that the cause which, more than any other, has helped to prolong commercial depression, and especially to make loopholes for foreign competition to make itself felt, is, that English manufacturers have not, as a body, been sufficiently desirous of adapting their products to the particular needs of each market. There has frequently been too much independence on the part of the English maker, and he has only of late discovered that the class of goods which he has shipped to India have not been suited for the South American markets, and so on all along the line of our export trade. While the English commercial public are displaying an acute sense of the absolute necessity for adapting goods to the needs of a particular market, those at home are unable to see for themselves samples of goods in use in foreign countries. The Continental manufacturer has a decided advantage over his British competitor in this respect. Not only is he more disposed to meet the requirements of his customer, but he has at hand in a very large number of instances, a Commercial Museum, to which he can go for the purpose of inspecting the patterns of various goods.

The establishing of Commercial Museums would, at first glance, be looked upon as a matter merely of interest and importance to the trading classes and work people, who should provide themselves with whatever in this way is thought to be necessary and likely to be useful. There is, however, a wider use than this, and whatever can benefit a district or interest a class, should receive attention at the hands of Museum authorities. It is only in such a city as Manchester, or a town like Leeds, that a separate Museum for commercial purposes could be required, so that there is the greatest need for assimilating such a work with existing Museums, or extending the work of general Museums to embrace this department.

The London Chamber of Commerce have done for Commercial Museums what no other organisation could have so well and fully accomplished. Two years ago they sent out Mr. K. B. Murray to visit the leading Commercial Museums of the Continent, and to report to them the result of his observations. This he did in the autumn of 1886. His report is very suggestive throughout. He points out that a radical difference exists, and is intended by their founders to exist, between Commercial Museums and the export pattern depôts. He explains how the former were instituted chiefly for historical and technical objects. The export pattern collections were devised solely for the transaction of business, and not as Museums at all. Most of the Commercial Museums of the Continent were established by State aid. As to the merits of the question whether we should look to the State to do everything as they do on the Continent, particularly in Germany, it is not necessary to enter, but it would appear to have many disadvantages when applied to the establishing of these institutions.

Mr. Murray says very pertinently that "it certainly must appear astonishing to an outsider that Great Britain has not already a Commercial Museum on a large scale. Which nation, other than the British, is so peculiarly fitted and so largely interested in possessing such a Museum? It is true that the large firms, which have been, in the aggregate, the creators of our trade, hold, each of them, in their offices or warehouses the records of past years' transactions; it is equally correct that those firms note from day to day, week to week, and month to month, the alterations in the requirements of the world. But as year after year passes, and especially as generation follows generation, those records are lost and history knows them not. Should there not be a method in business as there is in the sciences? Will it not be as interesting, and as valuable to business men a hundred or a thousand years hence, to scan, examine and recognise the productions of to-day, as it is interesting and useful to the artist, the littérateur or the scientist to consult the collections made and existing in connection with each of their professions for past times? Have the industrial productions of the world no value but to disappear as soon as consumed?"

The difference in the need which presents itself for

Museums of this nature on the Continent, and in this country is considerable. Our export trade is established, and is represented by a round total of £270,000,000 a year. This is a considerably larger value than several of the leading countries of the world put together. So that whilst our export trade already exists, the foreign trade of some of our competitors has still to be made. The need, however, for these Museums is vital to the interests of English commerce. The landmarks of foreign trade do not by any means stand where they did, and, if we are to maintain our own ground, we shall find it necessary to adopt many new departures, for which our rather stereotyped method in many respects hardly fits us.

The subject of technical instruction, so closely allied with Commercial Museums, is one to which considerable attention has been drawn. Magazines and newspapers of every shade of opinion and value have advocated such instruction, and the quantity of literature which has thus been created on this question is already assuming important proportions. Without Commercial Museums there cannot be practical and useful technical education, so that development in one direction means development also in the other.

The Technical Education Bill of 1887 proved abortive. Whatever may be the fate of the present Bill the friends of that movement should see to it that the discussions which have taken place, the speeches, magazine articles, and editorials upon the subject do not remain unproductive. This is the danger, and against it all true friends of progress will guard. The abstract of the Government Technical Education Bill has appeared, and this the Government express their determination to pass. It defines technical instruction as instruction in the principles of science and art applicable to industries, and in the application of special branches of science and art to specific industries or employments. It does not include teaching any trade.

The chief features of a Commercial Museum should be, as sketched in the report to which reference has already been made, as follows :—

Raw produce of all kinds and every origin, classed by articles, and not by place of production.

Semi-raw produce, same classification.

Manufactured articles, similar articles of home and foreign production juxtaposed. A second department to be created on a geographical basis—viz., articles of local consumption compared with the supplied articles of British and foreign manufacture.

Information, prices of all samples, discount, credit, &c., duties to which each article is liable under tariffs of various States.

Railway and freight charges on various goods to and from various markets.

Style of packing, and making up goods for various markets.

Laboratory for analysis, testing of samples, new fibres, pigments, &c.

Commercial library, books, newspapers, trade journals, price lists, &c.

The specimens of raw produce, clearly labelled, could not fail to be of interest to the general public as well as to commercial men.

The Commercial Museum of Brussels is a veritable storehouse of knowledge. Merchants and manufacturers find there all kinds of information which may be useful to them. It occupies a large building, almost in the centre of the town, and its organisation testifies to a thorough knowledge of the needs of industry and commerce. It contains patterns of goods manufactured in foreign countries, which have been sent by the Belgian Consuls from the various countries where they have met with them. To each of these patterns, which are exhibited under a glass case, is attached a ticket, which indicates the place where it was obtained, its selling price, and its origin. Special care is taken not to divulge the name of the manufactory whence the pattern has come. The patterns of manufactured products are shown in great numbers; they are met with in all kinds, and from every country. If a merchant needs a more detailed explanation than that afforded by the label, he applies to the Curator. The Museum contains samples of raw material in just as large numbers as those of manufactured goods, the former also having tickets attached to them, showing the name of the country and of the particular town from which they have been exported. One of the most useful features of the institution is an office where every information is given to Belgian producers, who wish to export their goods. Thus, if a Belgian manufacturer wished to send some goods to France, he would, if left to his own resources, very soon be lost in the labyrinth of railway companies' tariffs. The office in the Museum will save him all this trouble; he will be told the charges on the different routes, and be shown the shortest way by which the goods will reach their destination. Everything in the catalogue has been arranged in order to facilitate reference. Anyone desirous of studying the goods imported and exported by a given country will, in the alphabetical index, find a list of the goods sent by diplomatic and consular agents, with the number of the page corresponding to each article. This Museum is remarkable as being a Government creation carried out in 1881. It is under the management of the Minister of Foreign Affairs, but the Ministry of Posts and Telegraphs has charge of some of the

x

services and contributes a portion of the expenses. The staff rank as Government clerks and receive their pay and promotion on the same basis as in the Government offices. This would not be desirable in this country.

The Antwerp Institute, founded in 1852, appears to have been the first establishment which really corresponds to the idea of a Commercial University. The instruction extends over two years. Practical lectures are given on trade and commerce in general, mercantile transactions of every kind, and the building and fitting out of merchant ships. These lectures are delivered by the professors attached to the mercantile office, or by any other well-qualified persons selected and approved by the managing committee. Some experienced brokers also on the Antwerp Exchange occasionally give lectures on the most important articles of Colonial produce. The lectures are given in the morning and afternoon, before and after the hours of the mercantile office, which correspond with those of the merchants' counting houses in the city, and thus the students occupied in business can attend.

In 1887 a Commercial Museum was opened at Belem, a suburb of Lisbon. In 1885, circulars were sent to the Portuguese Consuls in this and other countries, requesting them to obtain for their respective consular districts samples of raw materials and finished products for exhibition in the Museum. Either the Consuls in England did not comply with their instructions, or they encountered obstacles which they could not surmount, for when the Museum was opened Great Britain was practically unrepresented. It was different with the exhibits from Buda-Pesth, for its collection occupies nearly one-half of the space allotted to foreign exhibits, and illustrates with considerable fulness the natural products and manufactures of Hungary. The exhibits in the Lisbon Museum include silk, cotton, wool, flax, and hemp in every stage, from the growing plant or raw material to the most highly finished products of the loom. Excellent collections of grain, teas from China, and coffee from Brazil; honey, tobacco, sugar, chemicals, paints and colours, vegetable and mineral oils, marbles, minerals, including coal, leather, with the tools employed in working it, and specimens of the different varieties of bark used in tanning, carpenters' tools and specimens of various useful and ornamental woods, household furniture, sewing machines, agricultural implements, bricks, terra-cotta, glass, porcelain, and pottery, in fact, most of the principal manufactures of the world are here represented.

A Museum for small industries has existed in Moscow for two years. Statistics given show that in the province of Moscow there are sixty-six different small industries and 62,000 industrial establishments of this kind, employing 111,000 hands and producing various products to the value of 37,500,000 roubles. The Museum has received all the collections exhibited in Moscow in 1885, and these collections have since then been gradually completed. It is intended to find outlets for the sale of the products in question, and for that purpose a depôt has been opened where the samples of all these products are represented.

The Export Society for the Kingdom of Saxony is able during its second year to chronicle a considerable increase of its activity. The number of its members, and of the visitors to the Export Sample Exhibition, has largely risen. For the opening and extending of commercial relations a catalogue in thirty languages has been sent out, a sample exhibition opened at Amsterdam and a branch established at Bagdad; at other important commercial centres representatives have been

x 2

appointed, and it is further intended to send out travellers.

With shrewdness—a faculty which appears to be highly developed throughout all ranks of the Japanese in commercial as in social and political matters—the Government Educational Department of Japan have added to a Commercial College which exists in Tokio a Commercial Museum. Thus, in two ways, this progressive people in the extreme East have shown greater adaptability to the needs of the times than we have in the West. The Commercial College will serve as a nursery to form a body of merchants for the future commerce of Japan, and since a great waste of time would necessarily result unless the education imparted were of a practical as well as a theoretical nature, the governing body have found the complement to the theoretical branch in a Museum conveying practical initiation into the articles of modern commerce, the varying conditions surrounding their sale, measurement, transport charges, and similar details.

It is interesting to notice what is said on the other side of the subject, and a series of articles on " Commercial Panaceas " has appeared in the *Bulletin* of the French Chamber, written by M. Giraud, and in the December number of 1887 he deals with the agitation in favour of establishing national Commercial Museums in foreign countries. He says the objects of such institutions are to place, for instance, the manufacturers of France under the eyes of native buyers ; that the buyer may find in the depôt articles of whose existence he was unaware ; goods of better quality than he supposed ; articles suitable to the country ; and that therefore, by a visit, French business will be increased. " That is the theoretical side—it is enticing. Pass to the practical. In the first place the point of

departure is wrong.   French products are known.   The
reports of French Chambers of Commerce abroad
prove that they are known.   If more are not bought
it is because they are *too dear*, or that their first cost is
too high, or that by reason of railway rates, their price
is higher than that of similar goods—or apparently so—
offered by our competitors."   On this ground it is contended that National Museums abroad are useless, but
it is admitted by M. Giraud that such Museums may
be useful for countries with new industries—such as
Germany and Italy—but not for England and France.

CHAPTER XXI.

MUSEUMS IN THE UNITED STATES.

THE American theory and practice of Sociology
is summed up in the dictum of Washington,
that the virtue and intelligence of the
people are the two indispensable securities
of republican institutions.   Upon this
principle the Government of the United
States act, and the general verdict of
opinion respecting American educational
matters is that they are considerably in advance of us.
It is significant to note that works of art were rarely
seen up to comparatively recent years in any part of
the United States, and the first picture gallery of any
consequence was that of the Pennsylvania Academy
in Philadelphia, opened in 1871.   Other cities remained

until a comparatively recent date without art collections worthy of the name. Libraries existed also in collections and public buildings of the State Capitol, but few collections of books were accessible to the people. Previous to 1830 only three or four cities had State libraries, and these were unimportant. Taking all these matters into consideration, the progress has been extraordinary. Mr. Andrew Carnegie, in *Triumphant Democracy*, is naturally eloquent over the change which has taken place in these matters in so short a time. It may further be said for Mr. Carnegie what he would not say for himself, that it is largely owing to men such as he that this change has come about. Men of sturdy will, downright common-sense and foresight, who, by personal influence and handsome gifts of money for the founding of these institutions, have furnished the educational impetus. Libraries, Museums, and Art Galleries are springing up in the United States with surprising rapidity, and there will soon be a network of these institutions all over the States. At the end of 1886 the total number of Public Libraries was 5,338. The number of Art Galleries and Museums is uncertain, but it must be proportionately large. Philadelphia, with Boston, better reflects the intellectual life of the country than New York, Washington, or Chicago.

The New Academy of Natural Sciences, of which an engraving is given, is situated at the corner of Nineteenth and Race Streets, Philadelphia. It is a very handsome structure, built of Serpentine stone trimmed with Ohio sandstone in the collegiate Gothic style. Its Library contains between 26,000 and 30,000 volumes, and there are very extensive collections in zoology, ornithology, geology, mineralogy, conchology, ethnology, archæology, and botany. The collection of birds is especially rich, as is also the cabinet of botany. The cabinets

of geology and mineralogy are also very complete. The
Museum contains upwards of 250,000 specimens in all.
Agassiz pronounced it one of the finest natural science

NEW ACADEMY OF NATURAL SCIENCE.

collections in the world. The Academy of Fine Arts,
now housed in a magnificent new building, in florid
Gothic style and richly ornamented, but in such a way
as not to be gaudy. The collection of paintings,

statuary, &c., is very fine and reflects the highest credit upon the generosity of the Philadelphians.

The Metropolitan Museum of Art in New York is the outcome of a public meeting held in 1869, when a Committee of fifty was appointed to draft a plan of organising an institution having for its object the art culture of the people of the city. This Committee, which was afterwards increased to twice its original strength, included the principal patrons of art among the wealthy classes, and also some of the leading artists belonging to the National Academy of Design. The Committee went to work with energy, and in the April following the Legislature granted a charter "for the purpose of establishing a Museum and Library of Art; of encouraging and developing the study of the fine arts; of the application of art to manufactures and to practical life; of advancing the general knowledge of kindred subjects, and to that end of furnishing popular instruction and recreation." By the constitution adopted in pursuance of the charter, the number of members of the Corporation is limited to 250. New members are elected by the Corporation only on the nomination of the Trustees. The members of the Corporation are such for life, and the Trustees—twenty-one in number—who are elected by it, are to hold office for seven years, the term of one-seventh expiring each year. The officers are elected annually by the Corporation, and are *ex-officio* members of the Board of Trustees. The contribution of £200 to the funds of the Museum confers the title of patron; of £100 that of Fellow *in perpetuo;* and of £40 that of Fellow for life. Contributions of works of art, or of books to the value of twice the amount may be accepted in lieu of the cash payment.

The Museum may be said to be still in its infancy, but it now rests on a firm basis, and in course of time it will be able to take rank with the older and more famous institutions of the same character in the leading European capitals. Indeed, in one department, that of ancient antiquities, it already occupies a prominent place. The first acquisition of any importance was the Blodgatt Collection of pictures; these consist mainly of examples of Flemish and Dutch masters, but also contain some good specimens of the French, Spanish, and English schools. To exhibit these, a large house was rented, and there the Museum was first introduced to the general public. The lease of these premises had, however, not expired when the remarkable archæological collection already alluded to was acquired. This collection, consisting of over 10,000 objects, gathered chiefly among the ruins of Cyprus, gave the Museum a standing among *savants* everywhere, which has been of value in many ways. To properly house it the Douglass Mansion—until very recently the finest private residence in New York, and still one of the most spacious—was leased, and the collection transferred and arranged for exhibition until better and more suitable quarters could be obtained. The Legislature, convinced that the success of the Museum was in a measure assured, authorised the Park Department to erect a suitable building for its use in Central Park, the cost not to exceed £100,000. The result of this is the present structure, which, however, is only a small portion of a proposed gigantic series of buildings for the use of the Museum. The various collections have all been removed to this building. Several wealthy Americans are making bequests, and some of these are of a special character. The late Mrs. Astor's laces, which form one of the finest collections in the world, are, in accordance with her wish, to be given to this Museum of Art. The future of the Museum is altogether very promising.

The Museum of Natural History in New York

dates from 1869, in the spring of which year it was incorporated by the Legislature. The governing body is a Board of Trustees of twenty-five members, who fill all vacancies occurring on the Board. The officers are chosen annually by the Trustees from among their own number. The privileges of the Museum can be purchased in the same manner as in the Museum of Art already named. The contribution of £500 at one time entitled the giver to be a patron, of £200 to be a Fellow in perpetuity, and of £100 to be a Fellow for life. Books and specimens to twice the above value may be accepted instead of money. Each patron or Fellow is furnished yearly with a number of tickets admitting to all the departments of the Museum at all times. By the payment of two pounds yearly a ticket can also be procured either for the purposes of study or to see the exhibits. The nucleus of the Museum was purchased in the autumn and winter of 1869, the necessary funds being subscribed mainly by the members of the Board of Trustees. The acquisitions obtained by purchase were exhibited in the old Arsenal buildings in Central Park until the completion of the present structure. The beginning of this building, like that of the Museum of Art, is only a single wing of an immense mass of buildings to be erected from time to time, as the requirements of the Museum demand and the liberality of the State will allow. The relations of the Museum to the city and State are, like those of the Art Museum, of a reciprocal character. The Trustees are to furnish all the exhibits, and to keep them accessible to the public, free of charge, on Wednesdays, Thursdays, Fridays, and Saturdays of each week. In return, the Park Department, as the representatives of the city and State, furnishes the grounds and buildings, equips the same, and keeps them in repair. As may be inferred from the building projects of the Museum, its aims are exceedingly ambitious, being avowedly the establishment of a post-graduate University of Natural Science at which students from all parts may find as full collections of specimens as are to be found in London or Berlin. In furtherance of this plan one story of the present building is divided into small rooms, fitted up especially for purposes of study. The present building of the Museum was formally opened in December, 1877. Its style is a modern Gothic, the material used externally being red brick for the walls, and yellow sandstone for the window trimmings, &c. The general interior arrangement is probably the best that has yet been devised in America for the purpose. The collections are arranged in large halls, or in balconies running round them. At each end of these halls is a large vestibule, containing stairways and offices for the Curator of the department to which the floor is devoted. Each hall is 170ft. long by sixty feet wide inside the walls. The lowest story is eighteen feet high ; the second or principal story, including the balcony or gallery, thirty feet ; the upper story twenty-two feet, and the story in the Mansard roof sixteen feet. On the lower story the desk-cases in the centre of the hall are filled with the Jay collection of shells, presented by Miss C. L. Walfe, as a memorial of her father, the first President of the Museum. The remainder of the hall, excepting several cases filled with building stones, marbles, woods, and wax fruits, is devoted to mounted specimens of mammalia. The floor of the second story hall contains specimens of birds arranged in geographical order. The Gallery is set apart for the Archæological Department and contains specimens of the implements of the Pacific Islanders, spears and lances of various peoples, carved war clubs, Indian dresses and weapons, stone axes, pottery, skulls, and skeletons. These are all placed in upright cases. In the railing-case is a collection of stone implements from the valley of the Somme, Northern France; the Bement specimens of the stone age of Denmark; specimens from the Swiss lake dwellings and other collections. The peculiarity of arrangement of the different wall-cases containing the collections is that they stand out at right angles to the windows, the end against the wall is but a small part of the whole, while the light, which, owing to the large window space gained by this arrangement, is exceedingly abundant, is permitted to travel to every nook and corner of the hall, so that there is not a spot anywhere in the exhibition rooms where a shadow is cast. During this last spring a Butterfly Exhibition took place in New York, at which there were 100,000 specimens shown.

The Peabody Museum, New Haven, is a beautiful building in this, the largest city of Connecticut. New Haven is also the seat of Yale College, one of the oldest and most important Universities in America. In the Peabody Museum, of which an engraving is given, are the collections of the University in geology, mineralogy and the natural sciences, including the famous collection of Professor Marsh.

The Harvard University is the oldest (1638) and most richly endowed institution of learning in America. It is situated at Cambridge, three miles from Boston. The Zoological Museum is a plain substantial structure, and is well used by the students. The collection of Agassiz, who was a Professor here, has been given to the Museum.

The useful character of the Government publications issued by the *Bureau* of Education, at Washington, is a conspicuous fact. These are not dry statistical volumes like so many Blue-books, but contain practical articles by practical men, written expressly for

these publications.   The two volumes describing the
history, condition, and management of the Libraries
consist of 1,200 pages.   Another volume bears the title
of *Art and Industry,* gives a report on American
education in fine and industrial art, and is devoted
more particularly to the subject of drawing in public
schools.   This was issued in 1885, and in its 800 pages
contains a mass of matter dealing with this question in
all its bearings. The compilers say that the "interest of
the multitude in the works of pure art, wholly removed

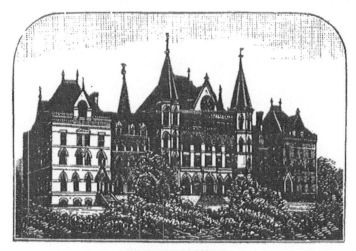

PEABODY MUSEUM.

from utility, was evinced by the thronging thousands
that, at the Centennial Exposition, crowded the
Galleries devoted to the fine arts. This popular interest
was a surprise to many, who had fancied a love for
beauty, and an appreciation of the works of the artists,
to be a result of education alone and confined to a
class."   The titles of some of the articles contributed
are as follows :—" The Democracy of Art "; "The
Church as a Patron of Art "; "The Term ' Art '

Considered " ; " Art in Political Economy " ; and others.
A large portion of the book is taken up with a
history of the Science and Art Department at
South Kensington, and other matters from a
variety of English sources, and these have un-
questionably added to the general utility and interest
attaching to the work.   These American volumes are
closed with a strengthened conviction that in the
matter of Public Libraries America is ahead of us, but in
Art Galleries, Museums, Schools of Art, and technical
education England is in advance of our enterprising
cousins.   There is, however, a further conviction, which
becomes deepened more and more each year, that in
commerce and education there will be a neck and neck
race between England and America.   But to what
departments of life could friendly rivalry be more
worthily exercised ?

CHAPTER XXII.

THE MUSEUMS OF GERMANY.

ERMANY will ever occupy a worthy place
in the record of Museums and Art Galleries.   Education in the Fatherland has
been so practical that it would be impossible
for these institutions not to have filled a
large place in Teutonic estimation.   In
peregrinations over those in Berlin, Dresden,
Hamburg, and other places, the Museum-hunter would,
however, come away with the conviction that England

had, as a nation, not a great deal to learn from Germany, either in the matter of classification, arrangement, cataloguing, or in the structural features of the buildings themselves. In point of number we are no doubt outdone. Still this is not an essential feature, and we are yet in a position to hold our own. In military pictures England is far in the rear when compared with Germany, and when North German art is mentioned this class of productions must necessarily be taken into account. The most raw student transplanted from anywhere and placed in a German Art Gallery or the Royal Palaces of Berlin, and the palaces of the petty Princes in the various provinces, if asked his impressions, would probably say that the glorification of powder and shot was the chief characteristic which the pictures of Germany presented.

It is almost impossible to come away from some of the North German Galleries save with sickened feelings. The truth

" Man's inhumanity to man makes countless thousands mourn,"

as pictured in much of the so-called North German Art, impresses itself on the mind. There is in it a surfeit of cannon balls, epaulettes, guns, and bloodshed portrayed in terribly realistic colours. Is it not a misnomer to dignify such works with the term Art ? It is in the very nature of Art to give repose and rest to the mind and to quicken the finer sensibilities, and it is beyond the possibility of pictures of battles to do this, any more than can a visit to the Arsenal or Military Museum in Berlin convince one that nations are yet within measurable distance of the pruning-hook and plough-share period of Scripture hope. Whatever plea may be urged for a strong military power in Northern Europe, it is undeniable that both the art and the commerce of the Fatherland have suffered a serious blight from the spirit of military despotism so rampant.

The Hall of Fame in the Military Museum fully supports its designation. Whether Carlyle conceived some of his ideas of hero-worship from this conglomeration of statues and military insignia is not certain. One of the guide-books remarks, with a humour more dry and caustic than perhaps the writer intended, that the "exterior of the building is richly adorned with fine sculptures of the heads of expiring warriors, especially remarkable for the vigour of their expression." Happily there is reason for thankfulness the number of Military Museums in the world is limited, although in some respects the Museums attached to Greenwich Hospital and the Tower of London might bear this designation. It is to be hoped that we are reaching a period in the history of civilisation when there will be less glorification of the science of killing men, and when the peaceful arts will sway the powers and dominate the aspirations of mankind.

The chief Museums of Berlin may be given as follows:—The Royal, the New Museum, the Old Museum, the National Gallery, the Industrial and the Ethnographical. Among special Museums may be mentioned the Post Office and the Christian Museums. The Old and the New Museums form one of the most striking groups of buildings in Berlin. The Old Museum, erected as recently as 1824-28, is in Greek style, with an Ionic portico of eighteen columns. The entire length is 284 feet, depth 175 feet, and height sixty-two feet. The frescoes designed by Schinkel in the upper vestibule and representing the struggle of civilised mankind against barbarians and the elements. The Gallery of Antiquities in the Old Museum owes its origin to Frederick the Great, who purchased in Rome the valuable collection of one of the Cardinals who had amassed treasures of almost priceless value. The location of what is termed the Hall of the Heroes will be seen from the sketch below, reproduced from the official catalogue by permisson of the publishers, Messrs. Spemann.

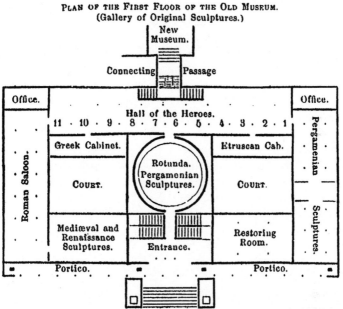

PLAN OF THE FIRST FLOOR OF THE OLD MUSEUM.
(Gallery of Original Sculptures.)

This is divided into eleven compartments, and chiefly contains marble statues. The Etruscan and Greek cabinets have, as the special objects of interest, several archaic reliefs and ancient sacrophagal urns and some figures dating from the fourth century B.C. The cabinet of coins is in a room of the Old Museum, opposite the entrance from the Rotunda. This contains no less than 200,000 specimens, of which about 55,000 are Greek and 35,000 are Roman. The purchase of two collections of Greek coins, each of which cost £15,000, has added greatly to the value of the Greek collection. The Oriental, mediæval, and modern coins are numerous and striking.

Y

The Mediæval and Renaissance Sculpture contains some fine masterpieces of Donatello, Michael Angelo, and Luca della Robbia. The Picture Galleries received their first important addition by the purchase in 1821 of the collection of Mr. Solly, an Englishman, for which the State paid £110,000. These largely consisted of Italian pictures of the fourteenth, fifteenth, and sixteenth centuries, and some works of the early Flemish and German schools, and a considerable number of later Dutch and Flemish artists. This is one of several instances where our Governments have allowed foreign Museums to secure the collections of our countrymen without making some attempt to keep them at home. The example of the early and later works of Hubert and Jan van Eyck, Holbein the elder and younger, Dürer, Rembrandt, the two Teniers, Van Dyck, Botticelli, Raphael, and other masters, are, perhaps, unequalled in intrinsic value, and as illustrative of the life's work of these artists as the collections in any other part of the world.

The new National Gallery, finished in 1876, is a handsome structure built in the form of a Corinthian temple 200 feet long and 105 feet wide, elevated on a basement of thirty-nine feet in height. The estimated number of pictures is 500, and they are frequently lent to provincial exhibitions and collections. The Ethnographical Museum, the newest Museum building in Berlin, contains many interesting and valuable pre-historic and anthropological collections. Dr. Schliemann has given some of his Trojan relics to this Museum. The Industrial Museum of Berlin, founded in 1867, is unique in many respects. The new building, opened in 1881, is a prominent edifice designed in the Hellenic Renaissance style. The exterior is decorated with mosaics executed by Salviati, representing the principal epochs in the history of civilisation. The

Museum is exactly what its name indicates, and is the best example of its kind. The ground floor is filled with objects in the making of which fire is not used. Domestic furniture in the Gothic styles, in cabinets and chests of simple construction, adorned with carvings and metal work, Gothic hangings and caskets, mediæval ivory carvings, objects in perforated leather, Spanish carvings, and numerous other specimens. The windows on the ground floor are filled with excellent specimens of stained glass of the thirteenth and sixteenth centuries. On the first floor are the objects in the manufacture of which fire is necessary. Specimens of pottery, glass, metal work are numerous, the fifteenth and seventeenth century specimens of majolica and pottery being particularly fine. A separate section contains stones, models of stones, Dutch tiles, door knockers, dinner plates, and silverware, gold work, and enamels ; precious stones, ancient Persian and Indian metal work are well represented. Chinese and Tibetan hangings and textile fabrics are as comprehensive as could well be. Other sections contain small articles of domestic use, such as knives, forks, spoons, combs, fans, many of them elaborately carved and ornamented. The collection of woven fabrics claims to be the largest in the world, and the rare textile productions of the Middle Ages can nowhere else be studied to so great advantage. Of needlework, carpets, and lace almost the same might be said. The Industrial Museum of Berlin is the most complete of its kind, and in the classification and general arrangement might well form an example for similar Museums.

DRESDEN.

The capital of Saxony is particularly rich in Museums and Art Galleries. It will long retain the designation of the Cradle of Rococo Art, and as a nursery of Art it must occupy a prominent place. The chief Galleries and Museums are the following : The Picture Gallery, Green Vault, Museum of Plaster Casts, Museum of Armoury, the Museums of Natural History, of Antiquities and of Porcelain.

The Green Vault, so called from the colour of its walls, forms part of the Palace buildings, and contains a valuable collection of curiosities. Here are jewels, trinkets, and other small works of art, such as bronzes, enamels, vessels of gold, silver, and crystal. The Museum, completed in 1854, is a good example of modern architecture. The original foundation dates back to 1711-22, but it was left unfinished for more than a century. The Museum proper forms the north-east wing of the Zwinger. The Picture Gallery, engravings, drawings, and one room of casts are situated in the Museum, and the Zoological, Mineralogical Museums, and the casts are in the Zwinger. The Picture Gallery ranks with the Louvre. Its masterpieces have been acquired at various dates, but few of great note since 1755. The golden period of Italian Art is, perhaps, the best represented, and the Venetian masters rank next. The collection of engravings, comprising some 350,000 plates, from the fifteenth century down to the present time, is probably the largest extant. Many of these are kept under glass, and others are in portfolios. Other entrances in the Zwinger lead to the Zoölogical and Ethnographical Museums. The Museum Johanneum, or Historical Museum, is well deserving of note. Here are weapons, armour, domestic chattels, costumes, and other objects of historical or artistic value.

Some other Museums in Germany are that in Brunswick, the Museum of Rhenish Antiquities at Bonn, and the Wallraff-Richartz Museum at Cologne. At Frankfort-on-the-Maine the Städel and Senckenberg Museums; in Hanover a celebrated Picture Gallery; in Leipsic the Städt Museum. Munich boasts of the National Museum, the Schwanthaler Museum, Ethnological Museum, and the Museum of Natural History.

There is an impression that we in England had completely exhausted human ingenuity in the way of limited joint stock companies. In Berlin, however, they take the palm from us, for, under the style of "Urania," a limited company for the advancement of natural science, especially astronomy, has been formed. Its promoters include a number of scientists, high functionaries, and bankers, and the share capital is fixed at £10,000. The Company purposes to popularise the science of physics by founding a public observatory, under the name of "Urania," where popular illustrated lectures will be given, by the publication of a monthly journal to be called *Heaven and Earth*, and by a permanent exhibition of instruments and apparatus used in the science of astronomy.

CHAPTER XXIII.

THE FRENCH MUSEUMS.

RANCE stands well in the way of Museums, and this holds good not only for Paris and the other large cities, but for many of the towns of average size. Paris possesses, in a Museum of Religions, an institution peculiar and unique. It is in the west end of Paris, a district already rich in Museums. In close company with each other are the Trocadéro, with its numerous Galleries of plaster casts illustrative of monumental art; a collection of anthropological materials, and an Astronomical Hall. There is, too, the

Galliera Museum, now in course of construction, and intended to be the headquarters of an art collection. This is being erected by a Duchess of this name. The Museum of Religions is being built by M. Emile Guimet, a native of Lyons, who for years has been collecting a curious mass of objects relating to the creeds of all peoples. He came to the conclusion that a provincial town like Lyons was not the place for a Museum of this nature, and so resolved to transfer his collection to Paris. The Municipality voted £40,000 for a site, and an arrangement was entered into between the State and the donor, whereby the Municipal Council were to defray half the cost of construction as well as bear the cost of maintenance when the building was completed. So miscellaneous is the collection of M. Guimet that its value is said to be £160,000. " My Museum," says the donor, " is not only a collection of curious objects ; it is, above all, a collection of ideas. Each glass-case represents a dogma, a creed, a sect. There are bronzes, sacred vases, rolls of papyrus, and piles of paper, on which are written some verses or formulas of invocation. When I could not procure originals, I had copies executed." Vedism, Bramahism, Buddhism and other religious systems are well represented.

All who know Paris know the Museum of Natural History. It suggests a discovery which M. Frémy, the chemist of that institution, claims to have made. He recently submitted to his colleagues a number of polyhedral crystals, demonstrating that the problem of the chemical production of the natural ruby is now practically solved. The Professor of Mineralogy at the Museum declares that he has made a most minute examination of the rubies engendered in M. Frémy's crucibles and discovered no fault in them. They were identical in chemical composition and in physical properties with the finest specimens of the natural product. They were of perfect crystalline form, of adamantine brilliancy, of absolute transparency, and without the slightest trace of borium. It is true they were of small size. This, however, was the utmost that could be managed at the laboratory of the Museum. But the experiment is judged to have been sufficient to show what might be done with a large apparatus affording a constant and easily regulated temperature. This is an important discovery, and it remains to be seen what will be the practical outcome of it. The fact has only just been given to the world, and it is said to have already been productive of a very uncomfortable feeling on the part of the ruby merchants. Artificial rubies as the product of a Natural Science Museum will be new in the annals of Museum work.

The Louvre is, as all know, the National Gallery of France. It was originally intended as a palace for Royalty, but it has not been the residence of a French monarch since the minority of Louis XV. During the latter years of Napoleon I. this Gallery was the richest and most magnificent that existed, having then to boast of the *chefs-d'œuvre* of Rome, Florence, and, in fact, of the greater part of Continental Europe, carried off by the conquering legions of France. But victory having deserted Napoleon, these treasures were restored to their former possessors, and the Louvre has no longer the Apollo Belvedere, the Venus de Medici, and other matchless productions. The collection is a very noble one, notwithstanding. There is considerable meaning in the fact that until 1802 the greater part of the Louvre remained without a roof, and the whole seemed to be destined to fall into ruin. Napoleon I., however, resumed the works, and under him the Louvre was finished, and the surrounding streets and places

cleared.   Charles IX. inhabited the old Louvre, and
is said to have fired from its windows on the victims
of the St. Bartholomew.   The space between the old
Louvre and the Tuileries had long been disfigured by
a number of old buildings.   In 1852, Napoleon III.
decreed that a million pounds sterling be spent in
clearing away these, and uniting the two palaces.   The
expenditure of so large a sum has given France the
finest Museum buildings probably in the world.   Almost
all the interior of this palace is devoted to the Museums
collectively known as the Musées du Louvre, for which
it is so celebrated.   The works in sculpture—statues,
busts, vases, and inscriptions—are distributed in five
collections.   The ancient Greek and Roman marbles
occupy the lower part of the south-west, a part of
the ground floor and two large halls.   They are of
little importance, being chiefly antique, but not of
the highest quality.   To the left on entering there
is a long hall, at the end of which is the Rotonde.
The five rooms of this suite are devoted to works of
Greek and Roman sculpture.   The celebrated Venus
of Milo is in the Salle de Diane.   Leading out of
the Hall of the Caryatides, so called from four colossal
caryatides by Goujon, a French sculptor, and to whom
this apartment may be considered a funeral monument,
since he was shot here while at work during the
massacre of the Huguenots, is the Long Hall, one
of a suite of apartments decorated for Catherine de
Medici.   A second long hall contains a colossal statue
of Melpomene, also the Borghese Gladiator, the Venus
of Arles, and the huntress Diana.   The rich Egyptian
collections of statues, sphinxes, sarcophagi, and the
larger and more cumbrous specimens of Egyptian art
are in two halls on the ground floor.   Here are fine
specimens of the ordinary class of Egyptian sculpture,
many the like of which are not to be found out of Egypt.

The Susa Gallery, which belongs to this section, is the latest addition to the Louvre. Mr. Henry Wallis, of, South Kensington, a well-known expert in antiquities contributed to the *Athenæum* of June 16th, 1888, an interesting article on this Gallery. In arranging the results of his excavations on the mounds of Susa, M. Dieulafoy was occupied two years. Mr. Wallis says that "in this instance the work of arrangement was necessarily more than ordinarily complicated. Where the objects are bas-reliefs, statues, or architectural remains, their display is comparatively simple; but here gigantic friezes and large specimens of wall decoration had to be built up with separate bricks, and this involved the preparation of a vast amount of inner brickwork, in fact demanding only less engineering talent than was called into play in unearthing the monuments. As far as the Gallery permitted it must be said that the arrangement is admirable. Like all the rooms in the Louvre, except those dedicated to the paintings, the light is from the sides, and this, it must be confessed, seriously militates against the due effect of works intended to be seen in the open air and in the full brilliance of an Eastern sky—of a sky that bathes every object in the purest light, and affords, at the same time, the requisite background of deep sapphire. The architect of the Louvre has selected red of a deep vermilion hue for the predominating colour of the walls. Admitting the extreme difficulty of exactly hitting the right tone and colour, we venture to think that the choice is scarcely happy." Later on Mr. Wallis states that "the Susa find will occupy two Galleries, the one now open being the larger; the smaller room will contain for its chief artistic attraction portions of a frieze of winged animals in unglazed terra-cotta. The monuments now on view, and which all interested in art and archæology will hasten to see, are the famous friezes of the

Archers of the Guard of Darius (the Immortals), that of the lions, some staircase panelling, and the colossal double-headed bull capital. It might be premature to discuss the relative position of these remarkable examples of ancient art as compared with the results of other excavations of the present century ; but certainly nothing which has been hitherto brought to Europe, since Sir Henry Layard enriched the British Museum with the Nineveh series possesses equal artistic attractions. We know that the decoration of the monuments of Egypt, Chaldæa, Assyria, Asia Minor, Greece, and Magna Grecia, was chromatic, yet, saving in the case of Egypt, how little of the actual colour has survived. It is only those who are the first to enter a hitherto sealed tomb that can fully realise the freshness and vividness of the palette of the Egyptian artists. Few, however, have these opportunies, which can only occur by a fortunate accident, while the Louvre in these Persian friezes has given to all the world examples of what there is every reason to believe were the masterpieces of colour produced by the artists of antiquity."

The Assyrian and Phœnician Museum fills six rooms on the eastern side of the quadrangle, and a vestibule on the northern side. It contains valuable specimens of Assyrian sculpture, disinterred at Nineveh by M. Botta. The other rooms contain Phœnician sarcophagi, and curious sculptures, inscriptions, urns, &c., from Asia Minor. One room is called Salle du Vase de Pergame, from the fine vase with sculptured bas-reliefs discovered at Pergamos.

The Museum of Sculpture of the Middle Ages and of the Renaissance occupies five halls, and consists of several sepulchral monuments which were rescued from churches destroyed in the Revolution, and of works by Michael Angelo, Cellini, Mino du Fiesole, Cousin, Pilon, Michel Colomb, and others. The chief treasures are the two statues called " The Prisoners," executed by Michael Angelo for the tomb of Julius II. The Museum of Modern Sculpture is a collection arranged in five halls, filling the north half of the western side of the quadrangle. It consists chiefly of the works of artists of the French school, though there are a few by foreign artists. Here are Puget's " Milo of Croton devoured by the Lion," " Psyche " by Pajon, and statues by Clodion, Houdon, Pradier and others. Here also is Canova's " Cupid and Psyche."

The famous Great Gallery (Musée des Tableaux des Ecoles Italiennes et Flamandes), contains pictures by the Italian masters. Here are Mantegna, the celebrated Madonna della Vittoria ; Palma Vecchio, a Holy Family ; Sandro Botticelli, a Holy Family ; Raphael, Portrait of a Young Man, the so-called Raphael and his fencing master ; Leonardo da Vinci, " La Belle Ferronière," and St. John Baptist ; with others by Titian, Perugino, Cima da Conegliano, Bonifazio, and Carpaccio. A gallery supported on gilded columns runs round the greater part of it. The western half of the Great Gallery is devoted to the Flemish, Dutch, and German schools. Here are some fine Van Dycks, the " Children of Charles I. "; Holbein, portraits of Nicholas Kratzer, Ruben, (" The Kermesse ") with others by Denner, Bol, Paul Potter, Metza, and Teniers. The most striking contents of the Flemish collection are the twenty-one large paintings by Rubens and his scholars, represent- ing events in the life of Maria di Medici, and of her husband, Henry IV. They were painted to decorate the Luxembourg. Also at the western end of the Great Gallery is a suite of rooms in which have been hung the paintings of the French school of the sixteenth century. On one side of the grand staircase is situated the Musée des Dessins. It consists of fourteen rooms, and comprises some 36,000 specimens of the great masters of nearly all the schools. A number of rooms in the other half of the northern side of the Louvre are devoted to the mediæval collections, the greater part consisting of the Musée Sauvageot, formed by the gentleman whose name it bears, and who left it to the Louvre in 1856. It consists of furniture, wood-carvings, miniatures, Venetian glass and enamels, bronzes, &c. In other rooms of the suite are admirable collections of Palissy ware and other specimens of French pottery; two rooms devoted to Italian faïence or majolica with Della Robbia reliefs. The Musée de la Marine contains models of Oriental boats and vessels, and of the apparatus used in removing the Obelisk or Luxor, now in the Place de la Concorde. Beyond this Museum is the Musée Ethnographique, a collection of articles of domestic use and of manufacture of uncivilised nations, together with Chinese manufactures, and objects from India and elsewhere. There is also an American Museum, consisting of antiquities discovered in Peru, Bolivia, Mexico, Yucatan, &c.; and in another part of this storey are three rooms containing Chinese objects, mostly the plunder of the Emperor's palace at Pekin.

No marked differences either of classification or arrangement between the Louvre and the British Museum are noticeable. What visitors miss are cheap, handy and clear guides such as can be obtained at the British Museum. The official catalogues of the Louvre are bulky volumes, too profuse for the general visitor, and so he has to content himself with his Galignani, Baedeker, or Murray, all of which give good descriptions of the various sections. Many of the Continental Galleries are closed at three o'clock, an unnecessarily early hour, leading often to much dissatisfaction among English visitors. The authorities at the Louvre, however, have for the past few years extended the hours during which it is open till four in winter and five in summer. Other Galleries would do well to follow this example.

The small cost of superintendence in France is surprising. The work of watching and keeping order in the four great Museums, the Louvre, the Luxembourg, Versailles and St. Germains is accomplished by a staff of 158 men; the two chiefs receive only £80 a-year, while 132 of this number are engaged at salaries varying from £54 to £66.

There are many other Museums in France. One point worth naming is that in connection with the porcelain works at Sèvres and other manufactories there are excellent Museums. That at the Government porcelain factory contains many valuable specimens of old Sèvres ware. It may, however, be stated that what has required a Government subsidy in France has been better accomplished in this country by private enterprise. The Museums attached to the works of the Worcester Royal Porcelain Company, and Messrs. Minton's, of Stoke-on-Trent, are quite equal in every respect to that at Sèvres. Mr. R. W. Binns, F.S.A., of the former Company, and Mr. Thomas Minton and his predecessors, of the latter Company, have devoted special attention to these trade Museums.

The Greek Government in July, 1888, created some consternation in French art circles. The French Fine Arts Department were surprised at the representations made to the French Ministry of Justice by the Greek judicial authorities, who claimed the right to seize in the art dealers' shops, and even in the French archæological Museums, the antiquities which might appear to have been illegally exported from Greece. As the matter at present stands the Greek Government has to take steps to make its own laws respected.

The Guille-Allès Library and Museum, Guernsey, is

well known in the Channel Islands. This Museum
comprises local collections and objects of general
interest. It occupies several extensive rooms, and
consists largely of objects formerly belonging to the
Guernsey Mechanics' Institute. These were handed
over in 1883 to the Guille-Allès Library for the benefit
of the public. The collections comprise fine specimens of ethnographical interest from various parts of
the world; birds of almost all the species known to
visit the Channel Islands; also 200 specimens of birds
presented from the East India Museum, London, and a
considerable number from America. Specimens of
conchology occupy several large cases. The Guernsey
shipping at one time visited all parts of the world,
while Guernsey men went out as settlers or traders into
many foreign countries. Many of these sent or brought
home interesting specimens with which they enriched
the Museum, and which include curiosities from Australia, New Zealand, Fiji, Australasia, &c. There is
also a good collection of rocks and minerals, with
many objects of local interest. Mr. Thomas Guille
and Mr. F. M. Allès have added a valuable series of
fossils, principally from the coal measures; also large
specimens of minerals, crystals, cases of insects, and
cabinets of coins. The Museum is now being fitted
up with large wall and other cases, principally at the
cost of the honorary Curator, Mr. Whitehead, in one
of which has been arranged a very complete collection
of local and British shells. When the re-arrangements
now in progress are completed, the Museum will become
a very attractive resort. The Guille-Allès Library and
Museum has been established and maintained entirely
at the cost of the gentlemen whose name the institution
bears, and it is their intention to endow it and present
it to the Guernsey States as a gift to the people. Mr. A.
Cotgreave is at present engaged in cataloguing the books.

CHAPTER XXIV.

THE MUSEUMS OF BELGIUM, HOLLAND AND DENMARK.

NDUSTRIOUS Belgium can boast of a number of capital Museums. The Royal Museum, or Palais de Beaux Arts, in Brussels, forming one of a group of Government buildings, has nothing marked in its exterior architecture. It was formerly an old palace, and used as the residence of the Spanish and Austrian Governors of the Low Countries. Like all adapted buildings, it has had several additions in the form of side Galleries, to contain modern paintings by Belgian artists, and these have not improved its architectural appearance.

The building has four distinct sections, the Picture Gallery, the Sculpture Gallery, the Museum of Natural History, and the Palace of Industry. In the first there are thirteen works by Rubens, but competent critics say that many of these are inferior to the pictures at Antwerp. One portrait of interest to Englishmen is that of Sir Thomas More, by Holbein. There is also a sketch by D. Teniers of exceptional interest, containing the figures of the painter himself, his two daughters, and several servants, while his carriage and house are also conspicuous. The picture is entitled "The Village Wake." Some eighteenth century tapestry forms a capital background for the groups of statuary.

It is claimed that the Museum of Natural History is the most complete in Belgium, but this is hardly to

the credit of that country.   The collection is somewhat
of a conglomeration.   The series of volcanic products
of Vesuvius is perhaps as complete as any out of Italy.
In the Mineralogical collection there are Russian
minerals which add interest to it.

The Palace of Industry, as its name indicates,
is used for occasional exhibitions of arts and
manufactures, and some of these have been of considerable note.   That this part of the building may
not be empty at other times, there are kept in it
models of engines and machinery.   Experts would
not award a first-class place to the Belgian National
Museum, and Brussels has yet many steps to take
before it places itself in line with other leading cities.
The Belgian Government erected the Wiertz building
for the eccentric works of an eccentric artist.   Some
of these are shown through peep-holes—a fact which
explains their character.   There is a further small
Museum at the Porte de Hal, a large Gothic gate-
house, which played an important part during the
religious persecutions of the fourteenth century.   Now
it contains carved ivories and enamels.   Old breech-
loading cannon, helmets, gauntlets, fire-arms, wheel-lock
pistols and guns give it a dash of the military.

In Antwerp there are several Museums worthy of
mention.   The Museum or Academy of Painting
occupies the first place, for here are stored fourteen
works of Rubens and six by Van Dyck.   The description by Sir Joshua Reynolds of these works is well
known to art connoisseurs.   His criticism of the famous
"Crucifixion of Christ, between the two Thieves,"
particularly, would commend any Gallery.   Sir Joshua
says of it that "it is certainly one of the first
pictures in the world, for composition, colouring, and,
what was not to be expected from Rubens, correct-
ness of drawing."   One of the most quaint Museums

on the Continent is that of the Museum of Antiquities in Antwerp. It is in the sixteenth century style of architecture, and the building was originally the city jail. As a Museum of the varieties of human torture it is perhaps unexampled, for here are curious and horrible dungeons and chambers of torture supplied with water through pipes, by means of which the prisoner could be choked or drowned, or the more exquisitely calculated despatchment of dropping of water on the skull; and finally there can be seen the place where the body was dropped through a narrow hole into the river below. Some historic relics, such as arms, armour, furniture, insignia of city guilds, and other similar matters are to be found here.

The Royal Museum, or Picture Gallery, would be visited by anyone going to The Hague. It is almost entirely confined to the works of the Dutch masters, and contains a considerable number of their best productions. The Netherlands Museum houses an interesting collection of objects of art and antiquity. In the same building there are 35,000 coins and medals, and a number of cameos. The Royal cabinet of Chinese and Japanese curiosities is in a small building, and cannot be said to be an important collection. The costumes of China, and the deities of China and Japan in porcelain, are remarkably fine examples of native manufacture.

The Dutch Museum and the Ryke Museum, at Amsterdam, the Museum at Bruges, and the Natural History Museum at Ghent do not contain anything special.

THORWALDSEN'S MUSEUM, COPENHAGEN.

Copenhagen must ever have an attraction for Englishmen for several reasons. The associations of Shakespeare and Nelson with the place would alone be

z

sufficient to awaken memories of a national character, and considering the connection of Thorwaldsen and Hans Andersen with the city, the memories become still stronger and more lasting. Bertel Thorwaldsen was born at Copenhagen in 1770, and where the Museum bearing his name is situated, we are for the present only concerned. The son of a ship's carpenter—wood-carver, say some, on account of the ship's head-pieces which he carved—his early struggles and ultimate success are well known. Hope deferred, after gaining the gold medal which obtained for him the privilege of three years' study abroad, had somewhat saddened him, and he was delaying his stay in Rome, a struggling student with his eye on fame. Whilst in the Eternal City, an Englishman named Hope, in giving the commission for "Jason with the Golden Fleece," in marble, brought, in 1803, the change in the tide of affairs of the young Danish sculptor which led on to fortune. It is fortunate for his memory that he bequeathed all the works of art in his possession to Copenhagen, his native city, to constitute a Museum which was to bear his name, the Corporation finding part of the funds for the building. This is situated by the side of the Christiansborg Palace, destroyed a very few years ago by fire. It is an unattractive-looking building, as will be seen from the sketch. Three sides of it are covered with paintings in crude and unsightly colours, which have been destroyed by the salt air, representing scenes of the joy of the people of Copenhagen when they once more welcomed their celebrated townsman, Thorwaldsen, among them. The building forms the double purpose of tomb and temple, for he was here buried, and here also are most of his greatest works. The sculptor left all his personal estate to be converted into a fund for the conservation of this Museum, with the exception of some bequests to his grandchildren and

THORWALDSEN'S MUSEUM, COPENHAGEN.

their mother. His chief works are " Night and Day,"
Copernicus, Schiller, and a number of groups of bas-
reliefs. It is natural for his countrymen to claim for
him a high position as an artist, but it is doubtful
whether he will continue to hold the rank given to
him by them. Some critics trace a want of ideal
beauty in his works, and say that his treatment of the
female form lacks grace and symmetry of proportion.
His bas-relief, " The Ages of Love," not so well known
as some of his other works, is perhaps the most marked
for the expression of the faces and the softness and
beauty of form in the modelling. The whole conception
is full of thought and vigour. The Museum contains
many relics of Thorwaldsen and his pictures. One
of these is a characteristic picture of himself seated in
his shirt sleeves at dinner, but sketching two children
and a dog that are playing on the floor. All lovers of
Museums will be glad of the existence of Thorwaldsen's
Museum, for copies and reproductions of his works have
enriched numerous other Museums. On the Danes and
Swedes who visit it the Museum is said to exercise a
peculiarly impressive effect. This arises chiefly from
the fact that there is a unity of style about the many
statues and bas-reliefs, and the visitor as he progresses
is gradually educated to an appreciation of the works.

THE FODOR MUSEUM, AMSTERDAM.

The Fodor Museum, Amsterdam, was founded by a
wealthy merchant of that name, who died in 1860. It
consists of a collection of paintings by ancient and
modern masters, preserved in a building erected and
maintained with funds left by the donor for this purpose. For the study of the French masters of the
present century this Gallery occupies a very prominent
place. Meissonier, Decamps, Ary Scheffer, and others
are here represented by admirable works, while the

Gallery also contains numerous fine pieces of the modern Belgian and Dutch schools. The first room contains "Fishing-boats on the Beach," by H. Koekkoek; L. Dubourcq, "Scene in the Campagna"; Ch. Immerzeel, Landscape with Cattle; E. Fichtel, "Chessplayers"; Lindlar, "Lake of Lucerne"; Van Dos, Still Life; H. Koekkoek, Sea-piece; J. Bosboorn, "Administration of the Sacrament in the Groote Kerk at Utrecht"; Gudin, "Fishing Village on the French Coast." The second room contains "Horses at Pasture," by Decamps; Rosa Bonheur, Team of Horses; Meissonier, "The Death-bed"; Pettenhoven, "Procession of Hungarian Peasants"; Gudin, Spanish Coast; Waldorp, "Drawbridge over a Canal"; Verveer, "Fair at Scheveningen"; Decamps, "Turkish School"; Roelofs, Landscape; Decamps, "The Lost Track"; and "Flock of Sheep in Stormy Weather"; Ary Scheffer, "Christus Consolator," a large picture well known from engravings and photographs; J. Beaume, "Rescue by the Monks of St. Bernard," and numerous others.

BOYMAN'S MUSEUM, ROTTERDAM.

A collection of pictures by Dutch masters, which became the property of the town in 1847. Although inferior to the Galleries of The Hague and Amsterdam it is well worthy of a visit. The building was burned down in 1864, and upwards of 300 pictures, besides numerous drawings and engravings, were destroyed. Only 163 were saved, and all were more or less injured. The building was re-erected in 1864-67, and the collection has since been extended by purchase and gift to 350 pictures. Fees are charged for admission. There are, on the ground floor, three rooms which contain drawings, of which the Museum possesses upwards of 2,000. The ground floor also contains the archives of the city; a collection of books,

engravings, and drawings relating to Rotterdam and
its history; and the city Library of 30,000 volumes.
Among the more celebrated pictures are a Van
Dyck, sketch for the large portrait group of Charles I.
and his family at Windsor, in a remarkably easy and
spirited style; above, Frans Snyders, "Boar Hunt"; a
Van Dyck, Group of Saints, a sketch; Esaias van de
Velde, "Skirmish by Night"; J. J. van Vliet, Old
Man (Rembrandt's model); Allart van Everdingen,
Cascade; after Murillo, Three Children, the original
of which is in England; A. Stork, "Dutch Harbour
in Winter"; V. de Hensch, Italian Landscape; Ferd.
Bol, portrait; Esaias van de Velde, Man on Horse-
back (thirteen inches in height). "This little figure,
with its back turned to us, seated squarely and easily
on a dun horse, with flowing mane and tail, has all the
effect of life size, and looks almost like an equestrian
statue," says a critic.

CHAPTER XXV.

THE ITALIAN MUSEUMS.

LTHOUGH not the birthplace of Art, Italy
has for several centuries been one of the
chief homes of beauty, as represented in
her many Museums, Picture Galleries, and
buildings. To wander about these at one's
own sweet will is of itself an education.
The chief Museums of Italy lack clear and
definite labels and good explanatory catalogues. Some of the catalogues in connection with the
Museo Nazionale, in Naples, are disgraceful specimens
of printing. The attempt to translate them into
English has in some cases led to an amusing confusion
of phrases. The guide books in English are better
and more comprehensive than those printed in English
in Italy, and many of those printed in Italian are not
by any means good specimens of typography. They
are too scanty for the student, although, no doubt, full
enough for the tourist à la Cook, but some one familiar
with the Museums and the language would render a
good service by compiling a short series of explanatory
catalogues in English for the benefit of his countrymen
who visit the sunny South.

So far as there is any record the Vatican contains
the oldest of existing Museums, although there must
have been during the time of the Cæsars many
Museums of considerable note. The Vatican Palace is,
as everyone knows, the principal residence of the Pope.
It is situated on the right bank of the Tiber, to whom,

according to our national poet, the ancient Romans prayed, and into whose bed and sluggish current the modern Romans empty their drainage. It is said to be the largest palace in the world, and dates back to about 300 A.D. Charlemagne at one time used it as a residence. Whether the number of rooms in it is 4,000 or 11,000 is immaterial, for the statements vary, but it contains the finest existing collection of marbles, bronzes, frescoes, mosaics, gems, and statues in the world. The most striking rooms open to the general visitor are the Sistine Chapel, built in 1473, and adorned by the genius of Michael Angelo; the Pauline Chapel, dating from 1540; the Loggie and Stanze of Raphael; the Court of the Belvedere; the Library, containing 24,000 MSS. and 50,000 printed volumes; several rich Museums of ancient and modern articles of *vertu* and the mosaic manufactory. A fine staircase, richly adorned with entablatures and columns of marble, granite, and porphyry, leads to the Hall of the Greek Cross. Here are the two immense sarcophagi of red Egyptian porphyry, probably the largest ever made out of that material. These are the sarcophagi of Constantia, the daughter of Constantine, and of the Empress Helena. The Rotonda was built by Pius VI. In the centre is a grand basin in porphyry, forty-one feet in circumference, found in the Baths of Diocletian. On each side of the entrance are two colossal Hermes, found in Hadrian's Villa, representing Tragedy and Comedy. Round the hall are statues and colossal busts of Jupiter, a bronze statue of Hercules, one of the largest of the ancient bronze statues existing, being fifteen feet high, and many others. The Hall of the Animals is divided by a vestibule into two parts, and paved with mosaics chiefly found at Palestrina. The sculptures of animals constitute the finest collection of the kind ever formed, and fully confirm the statement of Pliny respecting the excellence of the Greek sculptors in their representations of animals. It has been with truth called a menagerie in marble. The Gallery of Statues was collected in the halls belonging to the Casino of Innocent VIII. It contains the celebrated recumbent statue of the Ariadne, formerly called Cleopatra, because the bracelet has some resemblance to a serpent. It was found near Lunghezza, and is one of the most interesting draped statues in the Museum. The Hall of the Busts is a continuation of the Gallery of the Statues, and contains a number of colossal busts, the historical portion of which are arranged in chronological order. Two unique representations in marble of the Organs of Respiration are extremely interesting, as showing the knowledge of the ancients in human anatomy. The Belvedere Court, designed by Bramante, is an octagonal room, of unequal sides, surrounded by four open porticos, with four cabinets in the angles, which contain some celebrated examples of ancient sculpture. The porticos contain numerous statues, bas-reliefs, and sarcophagi. The Second Cabinet contains the Belvedere Antinous, found near S. Martino ai Monti, and considered by Visconti to be Mercury. The proportions of this beautiful statue have received unqualified praise: its high finish is combined with elegance of form and with all the gracefulness of youth. Domenichino made it his constant study and declared that he was indebted to it for his knowledge of the beautiful. Poussin declared this to be the statue which, of all others, represents the proportions of the human body in the purest form. A Third Cabinet contains the Laocoon, found in the Vigna de Fredis, on the Esquiline, in 1506, and which was characterised by Michael Angelo as the "wonder of art." The Fourth Cabinet contains the Apollo Belvedere, found in the end

of the fifteenth century. It was purchased by Julius
II., when Cardinal della Rovere, and was one of the
first specimens of ancient sculpture placed in the
Belvedere Palace. This fact constitutes the ground of
the belief that at this point the Vatican Museum
commenced. Some Italian writers describe the
Apollo Belvedere as the work of Agasias of Ephesus,
the sculptor whose name occurs on the Fighting
Gladiator in the Louvre, which was also found at
Antium ; but there is no further evidence to support
this conjecture. This work of art was the admiration
of Raphael, and of Michael Angelo, who is said to
have refused to try the restoration of the left-hand.
The Square Vestibule of the Torso is adorned with
arabesques by Daniele da Volterra, in the reign
of Julius III., and representing histories of the
Old and New Testament, and landscapes. It also contains the famous Torso Belvedere, sculptured by
Apollonius, son of Nestor of Athens, found in the
Campo dei Fiori, near the site of the Theatre of
Pompey, to whose times it is generally referred. This
fragment has commanded the admiration of the first
sculptors of modern times. Michael Angelo declared
that he was its pupil, and was indebted to it for his
power in representing the human form. Few objects
have been made so well-known by models and engravings as this celebrated relic of Republican Rome. The
Museo Pio-Clementino is so-called after Clement XIV.
and Pius VI. ; it is, without exception, the most magnificent Museum of ancient sculpture extant. Pius VI.
contributed more munificently towards its completion
than any of his predecessors, and is said to have
enriched it with more than 2,000 specimens, building
for their accommodation the Hall of the Animals, the
Gallery of the Muses, the Rotunda, the Halls of the
Greek Cross and of the Biga, the Grand Staircase, and

other portions of the building. The Museo Chiaramonti was arranged by Canova. It contains upwards of 700 specimens of ancient sculpture, arranged in thirty compartments. Many are, of course, of secondary interest; but, taken as a whole, the collection in any other place but Rome would be considered a Museum in itself. Opening to the west from the Museo Chiaramonti, the Gallery of Inscriptions is a long corridor, occupied almost exclusively with ancient sepulchral inscriptions and monuments, arranged in classes by Marini. The collection contains some 3,000 specimens. The Pagan inscriptions are classified according to ranks and professions, from divinities to slaves. Nothing is so striking in the Roman inscriptions as the frequent disregard of grammar and orthography. Many of the verses are quite irreconcilable with the laws of metre, showing that the epitaphs of the ancients are as little to be trusted as indications of literary taste as those of our own times.

The Etruscan Museum is a very interesting department, owing its origin to Pope Gregory XVI., whose memory will ever be honoured by the student of Etruscan antiquities for the zeal and liberality with which he added these valuable objects of art to the treasures accumulated in the Vatican by his predecessors. These ancient treasures would doubtless have been dispersed, perhaps irrecoverably lost, if Gregory XVI. had not secured them for the Museum. They have been arranged in thirteen rooms. The Egyptian Museum, although inferior to many similar collections, presents much interest. It was commenced by Pius VII., with a collection purchased from Andrea Gaddi, and with various Egyptian antiquities formerly in the Capitoline and other Museums; numerous additions have been made to it since then. It occupies ten rooms underneath the Etruscan collection.

But very scant justice has been done to the Vatican Museum by this brief sketch. No words could, in fact, convey all that is to be learned from a visit to its various Galleries. There is an effect on the observant mind in wandering through the Galleries which never could be effaced. The Museum devotee will ever be grateful to the Vatican authorities for not placing together objects belonging to every place and time. Wherever one may be in the Vatican buildings, the genius of the classical age surrounds us, and the mind becomes steeped in an awe and reflection which is never exhausted, but renewed again and again as the various Museums are visited.

NEW MUSEO NAZIONALE, FLORENCE.

The Palazzo del Podestà was from 1261, the residence of the chief magistrate of Florence. The building was repeatedly damaged by fire and water during the disturbances of the fourteenth century, but was afterwards restored. From the end of the sixteenth century down to 1859 it served as a prison, and seat of the head of the police. Between 1859 and 1865, the structure was judiciously restored and fitted up for the New National Museum, illustrative of the mediæval and modern history of Italian culture and art. Part of the collection, which is still in course of formation, belongs to the State, and part to private individuals. It contains several admirable works, such as the Renaissance bronzes, formerly in the Uffizi and the Palazzo Vecchio. The ground floor contains a valuable collection of weapons, formerly in the possession of the Medici. There is a picturesque Court, embellished with the armorial bearings of former Podestàs or Mayors, and forming with its fine colonnades a picture of the spirit of the fourteenth century. The colonnades contain a fountain and a marble door of the fifteenth; the walls are painted with the armorial bearings of the different quarters of the town. A small colonnade opposite the Tower Room contains a portal of the Palazzo Pazzi, by Donatello, the "Marzocco" of the same artist, and figures of saints in the style of the Pisani. The Second Saloon contains ancient furniture and crystal, dating from the sixteenth and seventeenth centuries, and the Third Saloon displays a fine collection of faïence, chiefly from the manufactories of Urbino, Gubbio, and Faenza (sixteenth century). Below a coloured relief, attributed to Andrea Pisano, is the entrance to the Fourth Saloon. This was originally a chapel, but for centuries a dingy prison, adorned with frescos by Giotto. Here are mediæval crosses, goblets, episcopal rings, reliquaries, mediæval goldsmiths' work, valuable niellos, enamels, a choir stall of 1493, and an inlaid choir desk of 1498. The Fifth Saloon contains carvings in ivory, consular diptych, two triptychs of the fourteenth century, Madonna in the style of Orcagna, Byzantine casket, a fine crystal of the sixteenth century, and two ivory saddles of the fourteenth century. The Sixth Saloon contains bronzes, among others one by Donatello, of David, a slender youthful figure, noble both in gesture and bearing, one of the two masterpieces of the artist. There is also a relief of a dog by Benvenuto Cellini, together with grotesques in bronze, fountain figures, a peacock, statuettes of Apollo and Juno, of the school of Giovanni da Bologna. In the centre of the Seventh Saloon are Bronzes by Donatello—a Cupid treading on a snake; by Giov. da Bologna, a Mercury, a bold, but thoroughly successful work. The first room on the second floor, has, on the walls, interesting frescoes by Andr. del Castagno, about 1,450, transferred to canvas, the finest being nine portrait figures, formerly in the Villa Pandolfini at Legnaia, and other frescoes. The glass cabinets contain articles of clothing dating from the sixteenth and seventeenth centuries, altar-cloths, and ecclesiastical vestments. The two stained-glass windows, representing the Nativity and the Adoration of the Magi, the latter with the amorial bearings of Leo X., from designs by Luca Signorelli, were formerly in the cathedral at Cortona. In the second room are glazed terra-cotta reliefs, by the Della Robbias. Among other noted objects may be named John the Baptist, by Benedetto da Majano ; Bacchus, by Sansovino ; statue of Apollo, about to take an arrow out of his quiver, unfinished, by Michael Angelo ; and a Bacchus, by Ben. da Majano. The Mask of a Satyr is probably only a copy of that executed by Michael Angelo when in his fifteenth year ; the gap among the teeth was made on the jesting advice of Lorenzo il Magnifico ; two fine busts of children ; portrait bust of Giovanni de Medici ; early Christian sarcophagus, with a representation of Jonah ; a bust of Piero de Medici, of 1453, by Mina da Fiesole, and a relief of the Madonna and Child, by the same master. Below these, Leda, erroneously attributed to Michael Angelo, and a bust of Macchiavelli.

MUSEO NAZIONALE, NAPLES.

The Neapolitan Museum and the Museum in the City of Pompeii are most interesting, and a first visit to them will be a never-to-be-forgotten event in a lifetime. The institution first named was originally commenced in 1586 as a cavalry-barrack, but left unfinished until 1610, when it was assigned to the University, and after the inauguration in 1616 the building was known as the Regii Studii. After the earthquake of 1688 it was used by the Courts, and during the revolution of 1701 it became a barrack. In 1767 it was enlarged and assigned to the Department of Public Instruction, and having been arranged for a public Museum, King

Ferdinand IV., in 1790, removed here the Royal collection of antiquities. After the restoration of the Bourbons they enriched it by additions from time to time, and declared it to be their private property, independent of the Crown, under the name of the Museo Reale Borbonico. Garibaldi, when dictator, proclaimed in 1868 the Museum and the territory devoted to the excavations to be the property of the nation, and increased the endowments and works connected with it. On the consolidation of the kingdom of Italy, Victor Emmanuel reorganised the Museum and included in it the Cumæan and Santangelo collections. The Museo Nazionale is especially rich in bronzes and statues, but its most characteristic feature is the priceless collection of frescoes and paintings, and other objects dug from the ruins of Pompeii and Herculaneum. The large vestibule divides the building in half, and the sixteen cippolino columns which support it are ancient, on modern pedestals. The statue of Alexander Severus and the Genius of the City of Rome were part of the Farnese collection. The Pompeian frescoes and mosaics are, with the exception of painted vases and mosaics, almost the only specimens of ancient painting which have come down to us, and are therefore of great value. They are our sole informants with regard to the ancient style, colouring, and treatment of light and shade. Landscapes, historical and mythological subjects, genre-paintings, architectural drawings, and animal and fruit pieces are included, and many of them are beautifully conceived and executed with an easy, masterly style. But some of the subjects are coarse and repulsive to modern eyes. They show the condition of art before the Christian era, and the methods of decoration in a fashionable Roman town. The rapid, easy execution and absence of minute detail evidence that they were intended for effect and not for close inspection. Their state of preservation varies considerably. To this collection belongs a corridor containing ornamental paintings from Pompeii and Herculaneum, being mural decorations, some of them with raised stucco designs and reliefs. The Gallery of Inscriptions contains upwards of 2,000 Latin inscriptions, others in Oscan, and engraved and painted mural inscriptions from Pompeii. The collection is arranged in accordance with the geographical situation of the different localities of discovery. It consists chiefly of epitaphs, but also includes laudatory and other inscriptions. Among the bronze tables are the celebrated Tables of Heraclea, bearing on one side regulations as to temple lands in ancient Greek, and on the other (inscribed at a later date) the Italian municipal laws promulgated by Cæsar, B.C. 46. In one of the principal rooms is the celebrated group of the Farnese Bull, a work of the Rhodian sculptors Apollonius and Tauriscus, once in possession of Asinius Pollis, and found in 1546 in the Thermæ of Caracalla at Rome. The restoration of the group was superintended by Michael Angelo. Opposite, on the right side of the room, stands the so-called Farnese Hercules, found in 1540 in the baths of Caracalla. Among the Egyptian Antiquities is a celebrated Papyrus, in Greek, which dates from the second or third century of our era, and which is said to have been found in a subterranean building at Memphis, with forty others, enclosed in a box of sycamore wood. The Greek characters are valuable for their antiquity. The manuscript is written in columns, and contains the names of the workmen who constructed the dykes and canals of the Nile. In the glass cases are scarabæi, necklaces, and other ornaments.

The Corridor of the Masterpieces of marble sculptures contains the finest works in the collection, and affords a review of the development of ancient plastic art

from the fifth century B.C. down to the reign of
Hadrian and his successors. This part of the collection supplies an admirable illustration of the history of
ancient art, and includes, moreover, several works of
high merit. The Corridor of Portrait Statues and
Busts contains examples of ancient sculpture. There are
equestrian statues of M. Nonius Balbus and his son.
The Corridor of the Roman Emperors contains statues
and busts in chronological order, of a more or less ideal
character. The Hall of the Flora is so called from the
colossal statue known as the Farnese Flora, found in
Rome at the same time as the Hercules and the Bull.
It is celebrated as a masterpiece of ancient Roman
sculpture. Though upwards of twelve feet in height, it
is finely proportioned and graceful, notwithstanding
its huge proportions. In the centre of this hall is
the mosaic of a Battle Scene, found in 1831 in
the House of the Faun at Pompeii. It is the finest
mosaic yet discovered, and measures more than seventeen feet by eight feet. It is a most spirited and
interesting composition, representing a battle between
Greeks and barbarians, probably the victory of Alexander
over Darius.

The collection of bronzes contains the most renowned
and interesting bronze castings in Italy. Most of them
are from Herculaneum, and a few only from Pompeii;
but both amply illustrate the various epochs of this
art, which was first practised in Egypt, whence it came
probably through Assyria to the Greeks, who perfected
it. The value of the metal excited the cupidity of the
different rulers who swayed the troubled fortunes of
Italy during the period succeeding the fall of the
Roman Empire, and the wars of the Middle Ages; and
we owe the beautiful specimens here collected to the
eruption of Vesuvius, which guarded for a long time,
beneath lava and ashes, the treasures of Herculaneum

and Pompeii. The bronzes of Herculaneum are of a dark, black-green hue, while those of Pompeii, which were much more exposed to moisture, are oxydised and of a light, bluish-green colour. The two rooms, filled with copies of pictures, remains of food and other objects from Pompeii and Herculaneum, are of more than ordinary interest. The former serve to convey an idea of the brilliant colouring of the walls of those ancient cities when they were first discovered. The articles in common daily use 2,000 years ago are thus illustrated in a way to show that so long a lapse of time has done little to alter many things applying to domestic life. The double pan with meat, a bottle with oil, and loaves of bread show this in a way which could scarcely have been so conclusive had there been the records of books alone.

The Library of the Papyri contains rolls discovered in a villa near Herculaneum in 1752. The rolls were completely encrusted with carbonaceous matter, and it was only by slow degrees that the real value of the discovery became known. About 3,000 were discovered, of which 1,800 only have been preserved. The method of deciphering these is unique. On one side of a large magnifying glass, fixed in a frame, the papyrus sheet is placed, and the student has his paper on which he is transcribing placed on the other side. He rarely touches with his fingers the papyri, for were he to do so it would crumble to pieces, and draughts from the doors and windows are carefully excluded for the same reason.

The Picture Gallery contains a splendid collection of paintings of the Italian schools, the Neapolitan excepted, and includes several of the finest works of native artists. The Library embraces about 200,000 volumes and 4,000 MSS.

The gold and silver ornaments and gems are shown

on the first floor, and these include a most valuable collection of objects in gold, silver, rings, cameos, or stones cut in relief, and intaglia, or stones on which the designs recede, which are so placed that the designs are seen through the stone. The Numismatic Collection, which fills five rooms, contains nearly 40,000 specimens, and is particularly rich in metals and coins of Magna Græcia, Sicily, and of the Middle Ages. The Santangelo Collection, which occupies three rooms, is a very important addition to the Museo Nazionale. It was purchased by the city of Naples in 1865, and placed where it now is. It is a rich and valuable collection of antique vases, terra-cottas, small bronzes, mosaics, Greek and Roman armour, ancient glass and lamps, and an extensive series of rhytons, or drinking cups, in the form of heads of animals of every kind.

The Etruscan, or Italo-Greek, vases occupy seven rooms, and are one of the most important collections of the kind in Europe. There are about 4,000 specimens, all from Southern Italy and Sicily—principally of painted vases found in tombs. As Greek vase painting was adopted by the Etruscans and modified according to the national taste, so this branch of art was strongly influenced in Lower Italy by the peculiar character of its inhabitants. The vases are of large dimensions, and the artists, not satisfied with the decoration of painting alone, have frequently superadded reliefs to adorn the necks and handles. Their aim appears to have been to cover, if possible, the entire surface of the vase with the colours. The plan is adopted of placing the most important specimens by themselves. The collection of small bronzes is the finest of its kind in existence. The specimens number nearly 20,000, and are chiefly from Pompeii. They are admirably adapted to convey an idea of the life and habits of the inhabitants of a South Italian city at the beginning of the Christian era. The collection consists chiefly of household utensils, lamps, candelabra, tools of all kinds, musical and surgical instruments, and weapons.

The Italian Government adopt a plan with regard to the duplicates from Pompeii and Herculaneum which sends a shudder through all true lovers of art. Duplicates of the priceless treasures found in the excavations at Pompeii are destroyed by melting down in the case of the bronzes or gold ornaments. This plan is adopted so that the unique character of the Neapolitan Museum may be preserved. If our Government have never yet made representations on this subject it might be well worth while their doing so, and an earnest attempt made to secure these duplicates by purchase for the provincial Museums. The British Museum contains some bronzes and other ornaments from Herculaneum.

There are numerous other Museums in Italy. In Milan the following institutions : The Museo Archaologia, Museo Artistico, Museo Civico, Museo Poldi-Pezzoli. Turin is even better off, for here there are the Museo Civico, Museo Egezio, Museo Lapidario, Museum of Antiquities, and the Natural History Museum.

CHAPTER XXVI.

ORIENTAL MUSEUMS.

ANY of the Museums of Eastern countries present an appearance of repose peculiar to them. It would be fortunate for us if more of the Museum treasures of the East were in this country. The records of ancient times housed in these buildings in the far East would be with us fruit-bearing wealth. If our Government could purchase some of these or get casts of statuary for English Museums, they would render good service. A Government can far better negotiate to buy relics such as are to be found all over the East than can individual Museums. By our Consuls this would be practicable at times when such objects were not being looked for— a very important feature when the East is concerned. If the Turkish Government could be persuaded or bought into permitting further excavations on the sites of Nineveh and Babylon, and the other buried cities of the East, they would render good service to the world. The discoveries of Sir Henry Layard have enriched the British Museum with treasures the value of which cannot be estimated. We should, as a nation, be still more fortunate if a few men of Dr. Schliemann's wealth and love of research would do for us what he has done through his treasure from the site of ancient Troy, now in Athens.

THE CONSTANTINOPLE MUSEUM.

This is located in the gardens of the Seraglio. The Museum building was formerly the Tchinili-Kiosk; in

itself an object of interest as it is said to have been
built A.H. 870 (A.D. 1466), and to have been the first
monument erected by the Turks after their conquest of
Constantinople. It was repaired and embellished A.D.
1590, and is in a beautiful position, is very picturesque
both externally and internally, and is very fairly
lighted.

The collection is not by any means large, but comprises several objects of great interest.   Amongst them
may be noticed a marble sarcophagus splendidly
sculptured with mythical scenes (Ariadne, &c.), and
supposed to be of the time of the Antonines, a large
collection of gold and other objects found by Dr.
Schliemann at Hissarlik, and three terra-cotta sarcophagi found at Clazorneme, which are considered by
the Director to be Assyrian. These sarcophagi have
no covers, but there is a fourth sarcophagus which has
a circular-headed cover.

The Museum possesses, also, one of the serpent heads
of the famous bronze tripod in the Hippodrome, and
two bronze figures of extreme beauty, though somewhat
injured, and assigned by various authorities to the age
of Polycles and Praxiteles,—certainly before Lysippus.
They are said to have been found at Tarsus.
Of these and the other interesting contents of the
Museum there is, unfortunately, no catalogue. In the
same garden is a School of Art.

GREECE.

The Minister of Public Instruction at Athens has
presented to the Greek Chamber a Bill for the foundation of a Museum of casts to be erected in the rear of
the Central Museum on the road to Patissia.   The
casts will embrace copies of all the chief works of
ancient art in foreign Museums. The Greek Syllogos
of Candia, the capital of Crete, have published an

illustrated catalogue of the chief objects of archæological interest contained in their Museum. Amongst the objects illustrated are those recently discovered in the grotto of the Idæan Zeus and in the Temple of Apollo at Gortyna. A new edition of the celebrated inscription discovered by Halbherr and Fabricius at Gortyna is being prepared by Professor Perdikaris, of Candia, in Greek, while a new Italian edition, illustrated by a large plate of the whole monument, is being prepared by Professor Comparetti, of Florence.

THE NEW MUSEUM, TOKIO, JAPAN.

The New Museum in Tokio consists of a ground and upper floor. The contents of the Museum are distributed in the following order :—On the ground floor are thirteen rooms containing Japanese and Chinese books ; a few specimens of early printing facing the door ; European books (chiefly Dutch), modern lacquer, porcelain (Japanese and foreign), carpets, bronzes, and miscellaneous, Agricultural and Forestral section, Natural History section, and Minerals.

There are sixteen rooms on the upper floor, containing respectively the following :—The Mikado's State carriage and State palanquin, oil-paintings and chromo·lithographs, Archæology and Christian relics, Archæology (utensils for Confucian services, coins, old paper money, Buddhist images), Court robes and ancient textiles, armour and weapons, palanquins and screens, musical instruments, tea utensils, masks and theatrical costumes, old lacquer and swords.

The Industries occupy five rooms, devoted to cotton and hemp, glass and lacquer, wood, straw, and basket work, Japanese pottery and porcelain, foreign glass, pottery, &c. In the grounds is an annexe, containing models of bridges and other engineering works, with specimens of building material. An avenue from the left of the Museum gate leads to the Educational Museum, established in 1877. On the ground floor are exhibited toys, models of school appliances, and philosophical apparatus. Upstairs are Japanese and foreign minerals and fossils, botanical models, and a zoological collection, consisting chiefly of native species. Between the Educational Museum and the Temple of Iye-yasu is the entrance to the Zoological Gardens, chiefly containing animals indigenous to Japan.

THE INDIAN MUSEUM, CALCUTTA.

This is an immense building, and from its enormous weight and the want of solidity in the ground on which it is built, the walls have cracked in the centre from top to bottom. It was founded in 1866, but not completed for Museum purposes until 1876. It is governed by Trustees, of whom the Home Secretary, the Accountant-General, the President of the Asiatic Society, and the Superintendent of the Geological Survey are *ex-officio* members. Five other members are nominated by the Viceroy, and four by the Asiatic Society; three are elected by the Trustees. There are on an average 1,170 native visitors a day, and 700 Europeans a month. The Museum is open free to the public on Sundays and on all other days of the week, excepting Thursdays and Fridays, between the hours of ten and four.

On the ground floor is a fine collection of fossils, minerals, and rocks. On the first floor is the Geological Gallery, also very rich in specimens, the Library and offices. A Gallery of Antiquities, particularly those brought from Bharhut, is a valuable section.

Prominent amongst the Siwalik fossil remains are the Hyæna-Bear, the Amphicyon, a dog-like animal as large as the Polar Bear, the Machairodus or sabretooth tiger, whose canine teeth were seven inches long, also the Siwalik cat, which was as large as a tiger. Amongst the American Edentata are the Megalonyx, long-nailed animal, and the Glyptodon, a gigantic armadillo, whose armour was all of one piece, so that it could not roll itself up. America, as all palæontologists are well aware, has been the home of many huge animals the species of which are now extinct. In this Museum there is the skeleton of a Megatherium brought from America, and one of an elephant eleven feet high; also of Hodson's antelope, whose two horns seen in a line were thought to belong to a unicorn. Amongst Siwalik birds are the shank and breast bones of a wading bird as big as an ostrich. These bones are, it is said, the only ones belonging to this species existing in the world. Amongst the reptiles are a Magar, or crocodile, from Matlah, and a snake of the python species, each eighteen feet long. There are also the remains of the Crocodilus crassidens, an extinct species of gigantic dimensions; and a specimen of a gigantic tortoise. All the species and many of the genera of the Siwalik mammals and birds are entirely different from those now inhabiting the earth. All the genera of the reptiles have living representatives in India. The collection of the fossil vertebrata of the Siwaliks is the most comprehensive in the world.

There is also a fine collection of diamonds, chiefly from Bandalkhand and Sambhalpúr; and models of the most celebrated diamonds, such as the Regent, the Koh-i-Noor, the Great Nizam, &c., all of which were obtained in India. Amongst the meteorites is a model of one which fell on January 23rd, 1870, in the Madras Presidency, and which weighed ten pounds; and there is also portion of the original.

There are many of other Museums in India, those in Bombay, Delhi, and Peshâwar being particularly good.

CHAPTER XXVII.

SOME NOTES ON THE MANAGEMENT OF MUSEUMS AND ART GALLERIES.

HEREVER there is a body of men found rendering faithful and good service they are deserving of generous treatment. Take Curators as a body, they are the most enthusiastic of public servants. It requires only a casual acquaintance with them to discover with what pride they look upon the Museum or Art Gallery of which they have charge, and they consider, as a rule, no effort too great when the welfare of their institution is in question. This is an excellent trait in any body of officials, and for their particular work it makes all the difference between incompetence and all-round suitability for the post. Some Curators are much harassed and hindered by the captious and fault-finding tendencies of one or two members of their Committee. It is marvellous how one man in a governing body has the power to make a public servant very uncomfortable. Where this is the case it is unfortunate both for the man and the Museum.

Except in cases where there are specialists in certain departments the Curator will invariably be the best judge of new departures and the general minutiæ of Museum work, and a patient and considerate hearing should be given to his suggestions. Curators do not profess to know everything about a Museum; the man who says he does should be immediately pensioned. One of the drawbacks in Museum work is that owing to so many special departments there is at times a pardonable bewilderment. If one finds, or has given him, an odd-looking coin, such as he has never seen before, or has sent him a comical looking beetle, or a bird, and does not know the value or name of either, he forthwith darts off to the nearest Curator and asks what the coin is worth, or to what class the beetle belongs, or what is the name of the bird. Anything from an old Roman nail to the skeleton of an elephant comes within the category, and it cannot be expected that the Curator shall be able straight off to give chapter and verse for, and a brief disquisition on, whatever is placed before him. Furthermore, a walking encyclopædia at £120 a-year is a commodity which in these days of education ought not to be expected. There is great need for increasing the salaries of some of these patient workers. What does it signify if the Committee receive fifty, seventy, or a hundred applications when they advertise for a Curator? How many of those applying possess one-half of the necessary qualifications? No men better earn their salaries, take them all in all, than do the Curators of Museums and Art Galleries, and it is greatly to be hoped that the immediate future will see them placed on a more satisfactory footing in this respect. For new Museums of limited extent the best and most suitable Curators are to be found among the assistants in provincial and London Museums. They are in training for the higher posts and should be preferred. Some of the best Curators to-day are the men who began life as boys or assistants in country Museums. The ideal Curator is the man absorbed with enthusiasm for his work; in touch with the needs, possibilities, and objects of his Museum; who looks upon himself as the servant of the public, and treats all with unvarying politeness from the wearer of the fustian coat to the wearer of the latest fashion from Regent Street. He must especially be a man of method, or he will soon find confusion worse confounded. One Curator is his own taxidermist, and a very successful one too, and another is no mean picture-framer. Neither are necessary qualifications, but here whatever knowledge a man possesses is sure to come some time or other into use.

It cannot be too strongly impressed upon those who have the management of Museums, Art Galleries, and Public Libraries that a clear and steady light is absolutely essential for continuous reading or seeing to advantage the various objects. The seats may be comfortable and luxurious, the tables and cases admirably constructed, and the supply of specimens or books ample, but if plenty of light be wanting this is a cardinal defect.

The electric light is not only giving a better light, but being less injurious to the contents of cases in Museums or books in a Library. The Chancellor of the Exchequer said it would cost some £30,000 to instal the electric light throughout the British Museum, and would also involve an annual outlay of £7,000. The figures are worth going into again, and must be accepted *cum grano salis*. Government contracts are usually very elastic. The Oldham Free Library and Art Gallery has been lighted by electricity since January, 1888. The dynamo is placed in the gas works 150 yards away, and an insulated cable is carried overhead. The dynamo is driven by an old horizontal engine, which in the daytime does duty for the ordinary requirements of the gas works, and has been in regular work for the last twenty-four years. The dynamo was made, and the whole installation has been carried out by a local firm.

Next in importance is effective ventilation. Some

Museums and Libraries, in the anxiety to exclude dust, are as close and stuffy as if there were a tax on fresh air. This ought not to be. It is impossible to lay down rules, or to say which principle is the best for each building. For heating hot air is considered by most authorities the best. As the ventilating and heating of large public buildings has now been reduced to a science, it is not necessary to do more here than point out the great necessity for giving the best attention to these features.

The little living enemies of Museums create at times terrible havoc, and drive Curators to their wits' ends to know what to do to stop their ravages. The Curator of Colombo Museum, Ceylon, recently sent all the way to England to gain information of any preparation which will destroy the fungus that had attacked the teak cases as well as the specimens in his Museum. Carbolic acid, cyanide of potassium, benzine, have been tried in vain, and even naphthaline seems to have little effect, though it effectually wards off the attacks of mites. The only thing that has been found to check the growth of the fungus is citronella oil. Camphor has been found to hold its own, and it may be doubted if there has yet been found a better preservative. Pure carbolic acid on wool, for the preventive of mould in insect cases, is a good plan.

The discussion of details as to the management of Museums in the Report of the British Association is complete and exhaustive.

Periodical exhibitions are becoming customary at the leading Art Galleries and Museums, and in many instances they are successfully conducted and productive of widespread interest, which causes them to be looked forward to locally from year to year. As a rule there is a commendable willingness on the part of owners to lend pictures, curios, and specimens, for the fear of injury resulting to them has largely disappeared. There is comparatively little risk of mishaps of this nature, for promoters know perfectly well that, to ensure repetitions of loans, the utmost care with exhibits is necessary. A monetary guarantee against injury is not of itself sufficient. Artists are becoming universally willing to send their pictures on loan, for by so doing they not only secure publicity but sales are very frequently effected. As year by year exhibitions are held, this is a matter of importance to many artists. There has, of course, been a rush after loans from South Kensington, but some reorganisation of this department is necessary. There is too much of a stereotyped character about the loans. One Curator when asked whether there had been any loans from South Kensington at his Museum, laconically replied, "Thank God! no; and don't want them." The educational value of these periodical exhibitions is considerable, and as aids in the popularising of the Museum or Art Gallery they can scarcely be over-estimated. The addresses of artists can be obtained from various sources, e.g., the Royal Academy catalogue. Specimens of circulars, catalogues, and guides can readily be had from some of the leading towns, and all information respecting organisation and management is thus easily accessible.

Museums and Art Galleries have not yet by any means reached perfection in their guide-books. Some of these in provincial Museums are crude, and too scanty in their information to be of much service to the visitor, or to convey much instruction. Others are badly arranged and indifferently printed. Illustrations, again, are not sufficiently introduced, and considering that electrotypes can now be had through some of the London publishing firms, engravings of objects should be much more largely adopted. They not only relieve the monotony of a guide-book, but give these publications a better chance of life. The usual price for electrotypes is ninepence per square inch.

It cannot be too seriously impressed upon all who have to do with the management of Museums, that both they and the institution of which they form a part are the servants of the public. A uniform civility and courtesy to all should be a conspicuous feature in the bearing of those whose work lies in these institutions. The great mass of the public want neither patronage nor favours. They simply want to be treated as human beings with minds and feelings, for whose benefit the Museum or Art Gallery exists. The very poor are beginning to use these places far more universally than hitherto. Do not add to their life's burdens by a superciliousness or an official insolence for which there is no need. It is wise to remember that the indifferently dressed boy, with perhaps evidences of ventilation in his clothes and boots, may have capabilities lying dormant which will one day place him high in the estimation of his fellows. Amongst the world's greatest men are those who began life on the lowest rung of the ladder. There are in the cathedrals and old churches of the country many curios hid away which would be seen to better advantage if placed in the nearest Museum. Lincoln Cathedral contains a number of such, and among them a fine amphora, dug up near the city. In many cases the matter need only be courteously represented to the proper authorities, and it will have attention.

There is a very universal feeling among Librarians, Curators, and Committees of Management that the Acts of Parliament relating to these institutions are too confusing, and many points left so uncertain, that a Consolidation and Amendment Act is very requisite. The following necessary features to be embodied in such a Bill are suggested for the consideration of those interested :—

1.—Taking the power out of the hands of the rate-payers for the adoption of the Acts and transferring it to the governing body. The citizens would still have a voice through their representatives. This would save the expense of a poll, and there would be other gains.

2.—That loans be for a period of sixty instead of thirty years.

3.—That loans be permitted for books, works of art, and objects for Museum as well as for sites and buildings.

4.—The power to enforce the rate six months after the adoption of the Acts.

5.—That Committees shall be permitted to make such charges, for renewals of borrowers, cards, &c., as they deem necessary. There is a doubt whether, as the Acts are worded, such charges are legal.

6.—Clauses giving facilities to rural districts to affiliate with the nearest town for the supply of books and general Library work.

7.—The maintaining of the rate at a penny for Free Libraries as at present, and a further penny for Museums and Art Galleries.

N.B.—Any opinions on these or other points, which could with advantage to the progress of the movement be embodied in such a Bill, transmitted to the author, shall have attention.

CHAPTER XXVIII.

STATISTICS.

THIS has been a somewhat difficult section for which to gather material. Many Curators replied immediately to my circular with words of encouragement. Others replied more reluctantly, and some required a second and third application, while from some there has not been any reply at all. This especially applies to Museums supported by subscriptions and fees. It will be noticed that the plan of the Committee appointed by the British Association has not been followed.

The following were the questions asked :—1.—Town? 2.—Name and address of Museum? 3.—When established? 4.—How supported? 5.—Terms of admission? 6.—What governing body controls it? 7.—Average number of visitors per week? 8.—Special features of Museum? 9.—Does it form part of Free Library work or other institution? 10.—Have you Lectures in connection with the Museum? 11.—Is your work extending? 12.—Is the Museum associated with Board or other schools? 13.—Approximate value of gifts since established? 14.—Aggregate annual expenses? 15.—Curator's name and address? 16.—Have you ever had any loan exhibits from South Kensington or elsewhere? 17.—What are the special local features of your Museum? 18.—Have you any special methods of classification? 19.—What do you consider the best means of extending the work of Museums generally, and of increasing their individual utility?

2 B

RATE-SUPPORTED MUSEUMS.

Town & name of Museum	When established	How supported	Terms of admission	Governing body	Average No. of visitors per week	Special features	9	10	11	12	Gifts 13 £	Aggregate expenses £	Loan exhibits from S.K.	Special local features	Curator's name
Birmingham	1885	rate	free	Corporation	18,000	Indus. Art, Italian Art, &c.	yes	yes	yes	no	50,000	3500	yes	Metalwork, glass, lacquer, &c.	Whitworth Wall F.R.G.S.
Birmingham, Aston Hall	1864	rate	free	Corporation	2000	Old Elizabethan Mansion	no	yes	—	no	10,000	1000	yes	Antiq. fur. of Elizabethan & Jacobean periods	A. J. Rodwa F.R.H.S.
Blackburn	1862	rate	free	Corporation	1500	General	yes	no	yes	no	12,000	150	yes	Geology, Nat. History and Antiq.	D. Geddes
Bolton (Chadwicks)	1883	rate	free	Corporation	5000	Geology, Zoology, Ornith.	no	yes	yes	yes	7000	400	yes	Geology of coal measures. Local Textiles, Machinery made and used by Arkwright & Crompton	W. W. Midgl F.R.M.S.
Bootle, Lanc.	1887	rate	free	Corporation	600	Col. of 17,000 European coleoptera	yes	yes	yes	yes	520	—	yes	"Gregson" collection of Economic products	John J. Ogle
Bradford, Yorkshire	1879	rate	free	Corporation	6500	Pictures, Sculpture	yes	yes	yes	no	4000	800	yes	Fossils, Pictures by local artists	Butler Wood
Brighton	1873	rate	free	Corporation	1000	Composed entirely of donations	no	no	yes	no	—	1100	no	Geology & Archæology	Benj. Lomax, F.L.
Burslem (Wedgewood)	1869	rate	free	Corporation	3000	—	yes	yes	yes	yes	—	400	yes	Local pottery from earliest period	Thos. Holme
Canterbury	1823	rate	free	Corporation	700	—	yes	no	yes	no	—	300	yes	Roman and Saxon relics	A. D. Blaxland
Colchester	1855	rate	free	Corporation	250	—	no	yes	gradually	no	—	—	no	Local Roman antiquities	F. Spalding
Darwen, Lanc.	1871	rate	free	Corporation	large	—	yes	no	yes	no	—	375	no	Rocks and Coal	E. Neville
Derby	1872	rate	free	Corporation	5000	—	yes	no	yes	no	large	—	yes	Geology and Mineralogy	W. Crowther
Devonport	1882	rate	free	Corporation	—	Minerals	yes	no	no	no	—	—	no		Chas. R. Rowe
Dover	1838	rate	free	Corporation	400	British birds	no	no	yes	no	large	—	no	Kentish Ornithology	E. Astley, M.D.
Exeter	1908	rate	free	Corporation	100	Local productions	yes	yes	yes	no	large	200	yes	Mammals. Cave remains	James Dallas, F.L.
Folkestone	1870	rate	free	Corporation	700	Pottery	yes	yes	yes	no	—	70	no	Fossils	H. Ullyett, B.Sc.
Hanley	1887	rate	free	Corporation	100	—	yes	no	yes	no	none	40	yes	Old pottery	H. A. Taylor
Hereford	1873	rate	free	Corporation	165	—	yes	—	yes	no	—	—	no	Ornithol., Geol. & Arch.	Alex. Gott
Hindley	1888	rate	free	Corporation	—	—	yes	yes	yes	no	—	—	no		
Ipswich	1847	rate	free	Corporation	1500	Geology, Botany, &c	yes	yes	yes	no	large	500	no	Splendid collec. of Geol.	Dr. J. E. Taylor
Leeds	1884	rate	free	Corporation	1100	—	yes	no	yes	no	none	—	yes	Birds, Geology	James Yates
Leek (Nicholson Institute)	1884	rate	free	Corporation	200	—	yes	yes	yes	no	Building, &c. Thou'nds	—	yes		Wm. Hall
Leicester	1849	rate	free	Corporation	1500	—	yes	yes	yes	no	—	—	yes		Montagu Brown F.Z.S.
Lichfield	1859	rate	free	Corporation			yes			no					

Town	Founded	Support	Management	No.	Principal collection	Art	(a)	Growing	(b)	No.	No.	Free	Special collection / remarks	Curator
Macclesfield	1883	Sch. of Art	Committee	100	Textiles and Manufactures	—	yes	no	yes	—	—	yes	Specimens of silk	Walter Scott
Middlesboro'	1888	rate free	Corporation	—	British birds	no	—	—	no	large	100	—	Lias collection	Dr. W. Y. Veitch
Northwich	1885	rate free	Corporation	100	—	yes	no	yes	no	4000	—	yes	Salt & its manufacture	F. A. Howe
Northampton	1865	rate free *	Corporation	560	Geol. collection	yes	yes	yes	yes	large	225	yes	Land and fresh-water shells, Antiq. Roman Remains	T. J. George, F.G.S.
Nottingham	1872	rate free	Corporation	6000	—	yes	yes	yes	yes	large	1220	yes	Birds, Mam., fish, shells	J. W. Carr, B.A.
Oldham	1885	rate free	Corporation	—	—	yes	no	no	no	—	—	yes	Geology	T. W. Hand
Poole	1830	free	Corporation	—	Local Antiq.	no	—	yes	no	300	—	no	Geol. Nat. His. Sea birds	Wm. Penny, A.L.S.
Preston	1880	rate free	Corporation	350	Natural History	yes	yes	yes	yes	—	—	yes	—	Jonathan Shortt
Reading	1883	rate free	Corporation	1000	Marine and fresh-water shells	yes	yes	yes	yes	Valuable deposits	100	yes	Lepidoptera. Typical Mammalian remains	Joseph Stevens
Salford	1849	rate free	Corporation	7000	Brit. For. Zoology	yes	no	no	no	50,000	small	yes	Portraits of local celeb. Lancs. birds & animals	John Plant, F.G.S.
Sheffield	1875	rate free	Corporation	3000	Tech., Nat. History, Metalwork, &c.	yes	yes	yes	no	large	1000	yes	Hist. col. of Cutlery. Yks. & Derbys. fossils	E. Howarth, F.R.A.S.
Stafford	1879	rate free	Park Com.	600	Botanical	—	no	no	no	150	—	no	Fossils, Birds' eggs, &c.	C. J. Culvert
Staleybridge	1875	rate free	Corporation	large	—	no	yes	yes	yes	—	—	no	Fossils from coal meas.	Wm. Bardsley
Stoke-upon-Trent	1878	rate free	Corporation	1200	Geol., Ethno., old pottery	no	yes	no	no	—	—	yes	Geol. and Mineralogy collection	Alfred Caddie
South Shields	1873	rate free	Corporation	600	Roman Antiq.	yes	no	sl'wly	no	100	12	no	Local Sea birds	Geo. Lyall, F.G.S.
Shrewsbury	1888	rate free	Corporation	—	Bot., Arch., Geol.	yes	—	yes	yes	—	—	—	—	A. C. Phillips
Stockport	1860	rate free	Corporation	600	Zoo., Geol., Art	—	—	—	—	—	—	—	—	John Tym
Sunderland	1880	rate free	Corporation	1800	British birds, mean fossils	—	yes	rapid-ly	no	100	800	yes	Ship Models, Brit. Birds	R. Cameron
Tynemouth	1830	rate free	Corporation	—	—	yes	no	not much	no	—	15	no	Skins of animals, birds, and curiosities brought by sailo's frm for. coun.	No one appointed
Warrington	1888	rate free	Corporation	600	Shells	yes	no	—	yes	—	—	—	—	C. Madeley
Winchester	1847	rate free	Corporation	—	Stone mplts.	yes	no	no	no	—	40	once	Local antiquities	J. T. Burchett
Wolverhampton	1884	rate free	Corporation	3000	Ironwork, Electro-deposits	no	yes	no	no	30,000	400	yes	—	W. J. Wheddon
Watford	—	rate free	Corporation	—	—	yes	yes	no	yes	small	—	yes	—	Dr. A. T. Brett
Worcester	1837	rate free	Corporation	—	Geol., Bot., Arch.	—	—	—	—	—	—	—	—	G. Reece
SCOTLAND.														
Dundee	1874	rate free	Corporation	4000	Arctic Fauna	yes	yes	l'gely	no	Considerable	600	yes	Fossils of old Red sandstone, &c.	J. Maclauchlan
Paisley	1870	rate free	Ten Magistrates	0	Nat. History	yes	yes	yes	yes	Considerable	650	yes	Local Nat. Hist.	Morris Young
WALES.														
Bangor	1871	rate free	Corporation	300	Foreign collection	yes	—	yes	no	—	150	no	—	Peter Williams
Cardiff	1867	rate free	—	—	Fossilised timber	—	—	yes	no	1000	small	once	Antiq. Nat. Hist.	John Storrie
Welshpool	1867	rate free	Corporation	—	—	yes	yes	yes	no	1000	1000	—	—	M. C. Jones

* Mondays free ; one penny other days.

2 R 2.

MUSEUMS SUPPORTED BY SUBSCRIPTIONS, FEES, ETC.

Town & name of Museum	When established	How supported	Terms of admission	Governing body	Average No. of visitors per week	Special features	9	10	11	12	Gifts 13	Aggregate expenses £	Loan exhibits from S.K., &c.	Special local features	Curator's name
Alton, Hants, Curtis Mus.	1855	—	Membrs free, otrs 2d.	Com'tee of Mech.Inst.	very few	Geol., Zoology	no	no	no	no	not known	cann't say	yes	Geology, Antiquities	Wm. Curtis
Andover, Lit. Institute	1863	by insti.	free to membrs	Com'tee of Instit.	10	—	no	no	yes	no	—	—	no	Spec. of Chalk formation, Rom.antiq.	A. W. Smith
Aylesbury, Bucks, Arch. & Archit. So.	1849	subn.	6s. per annum	,,	—	None	no	no	—	no	none	—	no	None	Robert Gibbs, F.S.A.
Bath, Royal Lit.& Sci.In.	1825	,,	6d. each	,,	—	Moore Geol. collection	no	yes	—	no	—	400	no	Herbarium	H. Mitchell
Berwick-on-Tweed	1867	,,	1d.	,,	20	Geol.	no	no	no	no	500	30	no	Birds, Moths' eggs, Fish, Geol. Bot., Arch.	John Scott
Burt'n-on-Tr't	1882	Nat. His Soc.	—	,,	—	Geol.	—	no	—	no	—	20	—	Birds, Geol.	F. E. Lott
Bury St. Ed-munds	1844	gr'nt f'm T'n C'nl of £20	free	Town Coun-cil	30	British fossils	—	no	—	no	—	20	no	Birds, Roman and Saxon antiq.	Hy. Prigg
Bristol Mus'm and Library	1887	sub. 21s. per year subn.	6d. for 3 wk days	Co'ncil elected by subs	240	Geol., Zool., Egypt. Antiq. Roman and Med.	no	yes	sl wly	no	all the collections	—	no	Miner., Land&Fresh Water Shells, Bees	Edwd. Wilson, F.G.S.
Caerleon, Monm'tbsh'e	1849	subn.	—	,,	(*)	Roman and Med. Antiq.	no	no	—	—	—	—	—	—	L. J. Mitchell
Carlisle	1837	Crp'atn pays r'nt and gas	2d.	Corporation Committee	60	Local Roman antiq., Geol.	no	no	—	no	—	20	no	Local Roman antiq., Geol.	R. S. Ferguson, F.S.A.
Chester (Gros-venor)	1886	subns.	free Wedn's-days, 6d oth'r d's	Trustees	60	Archaeological	yes	yes	yes	no	—	180	yes	Nat. Hist.	R. Newstead
Chesterfield	—	—	—	—	—	—	no	no	—	no	—	—	—	—	—
Chichester	1830	subns.	3d.	Council	20	Geol., Arch. Ornith.,Geol., Coins	no	no	slig'ly	no	—	10	no	Fossils, Bot., Flints, Roman interments	Rev. J. M. Mello
Cirencester	1856	instit'n & fees	3d.	Committee	few	Zoo., Geol.	no	no	no	no	—	—	yes	Arch. Roman	Josh. Anderson, Jun.
Coalbrook-dale, Salop	1858	—	small charge	Committee	—	—	no	yes	sl'wly	no	—	—	—	—	C. Bowley
Devizes	1853	subns.	2d.	Committee	30	Geol., Zool. Fossils, &c.	no	yes	sl'wly	no	—	—	yes	Arch.	Isaac Dunbar
Dorchester County Mus.	1848	—	3d.	Trustees	66	—	no	no	no	no	—	—	yes	Dorset antiq., specially good	H. Cunningham H. J. Moule, M.A.
Eastbourne	1872	—	—	Trustees	15 (†)	(†)Geol., Miner., Zool.	no	no	no	no	trifling	—	no	—	No Curator

* Clo ed during the winter months, the attendance is so small. † One hundred and forty-three per week when free.

	Date	Supported by	Admission	Governed by	No. of members	Miscell. collection					No. of specimens	No.		Subject of collection	Curator
Frome	1844	,,	free to membrs 4d.&2d.		100		no	no	no	no	—	—	yes	Shells, Minerals, and Geol.	W. West
Glastonbury	1886	,,		Sci. & Art Society	100		no	yes	no	no	—	—	yes	Local antiq.	G. Lawrence Bullen
Gloucester	1870	subns.& contri.	2d.	Committee	100	Nat. Hist., Geo., Ant.	no	no	no	no	—	—	no	Fossils, Shells, Antiquities	Hon. Curator
Halifax	1631	subn.	1d.	Council	45		no	yes	no	no	—	—	—	Nat. Hist., Geol.	Hon. Curator
Hull	—	—			—		—	—	—	—	—	—	—		
Huntingdon	—	—		Committee	40		—	—	—	—	—	—	—		
Kendal	1840	subn.	free to membrs	Committee	70		no	yes	yes	no	—	—	no	Geology	I. Severs
Keswick	1887	,,	free	Committee	—	Ornith., Geo., Zoo.	no	no	no	no	5000	90	no	Geo., Zoo., Bot.	Jno. Birkett
King's Lynn	1844	,,	free	Committee	100		no	no	no	no	—	—	no	Plants, Mammalia, Birds	Hon. Curator
Lancaster	—	—	—	Council	—	Geol., Zoo.	—	—	—	—	—	—	—		G. Kelland
Launceston	—	,,	free	Council	—	Undergoing reorg'n	—	—	—	—	! !	—	—	Antiq., Flora & Fauna	W. Wise
Leeds, Yorks Architec'l So.	1882	subns.		Council	500	Building and Decorative Appliances	yes	yes	no	yes	—	—	no		L. F. Hicks
Leeds Phil. & Lit. Society	1820	r'nts f'm exh'b'n society	1d.	Council	—	Nat. Hist., Geol.	no	no	no	no	—	300	no	Antiquities	Prof. L. C. Miall
Lewes Castle	1850	adm's'n fees	6d.	Arch. Socy.	50		no	no	no	no	—	—	yes	Arch., Tapestry	R. Crosskey
Ludlow	1842	subns.	3d.		—		no	no	no	no	—	—	no	Salurian Fossils, Birds	C. Fortey
Manchester	'84-6	,,	free	Committee	1200	Oral addresses and conversation	no	yes	yes	yes	7900	300	yes	See chap. vi	Henry Brooke
Malton, Yks.	1880	,,	2/6 & 5/- per ann	Committee	50	Geol, Herbarium	yes	yes	no	no	—	—	no	Sponges fr'm middle chalk, Fish remains	S. Chadwick
Much - Wenlock	1820	,,	6s.pr.an	12 trustees	200 to 300	Free reading-room	yes	no	no	no	7000	50	no	Geol., Fossils	Mrs. S. Landon
Newcastle-on-Tyne	1873	,,	6d.		350	Castle & Blackgate Mus. of Antiq. Soc. Hancock collection of British Birds	yes	—	—	—	—	—	—		R. Blair
Newcastle-upon-Tyne, BarrasBrdge	1829	snbs.& fees	ad'lts 3d childr'n 1d.	Committee	—		no	yes	yes	no	very large	600	no	Amphib. Fishes and Plants, Drawings by Bewick	Richard Howse
Norwich and Norfolk Mus.	1824	subs. & don.	free two days or't d'yssub. orders	Committee	500 to 600	Raptorial Birds, Mammalian Remains	no	no	yes	no	—	320	no	Norwich Chalk and Craig Fossils, Local antiquities	James Reeve
Nottingham Castle	1878	—	fees		4000	Indus. Arch.	—	—	—	—	—	—	—		G. H. Wallis
Penrith	—	—			—		no	yes	—	—	—	—	—		
Penzance Nat. His & An. So.	1839	subns.	free to membrs 6d., Sat. free	Committee	20	Flora and Fauna	no	yes	yes	no	—	—	—	Cornish sepulchral urns, mosses, &c.	John Symons
Plymouth	1889	society	6d., Sat. free	Plymouth Institution	60 to 100	Palæn., Miner.	no	yes	yes	no	considerable	—	yes	Petrology, Ornith., Entom.	J. C. Inglis

MUSEUMS SUPPORTED BY SUBSCRIPTIONS, FEES, ETC.—Continued.

Town & name of Museum	When established	How supported	Terms of admission	Governing body	Average No. of visitors per week	Special features	9	10	11	12	Gifts 13	Aggregate expenses	Loan exhibits from S.K., &c.	Special local features	Curator's name
Peterboro'....	1880	subns.	6d. each	Committee	10	Engrvngs, Norman & French Prison-work	no	yes	yes	no	£—	£50	no	Roman and Saxon Remains	J. W. Bodger
Richm'd, Yks.	1885	,,	subns.	Committee	—	Shells	no	yes	no	no	—	—	no		W. D. Benson
Ripon....	1883	4s. per a. sml en-dow. & to trus-tees, &c.	free on applica-tion.	Natur'st Clb	12 to 30	Antiq. and Geology	—	yes	yes	—	—	—	yes	Antiq., Geo., Entom.	N. Waite
Saff'r'n Wald'n	1832	subns.	3d. each	Trustees	200	British Birds, Antiq.	no	no	yes	no	3000	300	yes	Geology, Archæol., Zool.	G. N. Maynard
Scarbro Arch. & Philos. So.	1824	subns.	free	Council	100	Geol., Ornith., and Conch.	no	no	yes	no	2000	100	no	Geol. and Arch. (has good scientific lib.)	C. F. Strangeways
Southam'pton	1862	endow-ment	4d.	Council	500	Geol., Antiq., Paintings	yes	—	yes	no	1000	—	yes	Etchings & Engrav-ings, Mollusca, &c.	T. W. Shore, F.G.S.
Hartley Inst.		Botanic Gard'ns													W. Fish
Southport....	1876	subn.	6d. subn.	—	2500	Zoo., Geol., Anth.	—	—	—	—	—	—	—		
Stamf'rd, Linc	1842	subn.	2d. & 1d.	Trustees & Committee	—	(Mus. of Lit. & Sci. In) Min., Geol., Arch.	no	yes	yes	no	—	300	yes		H. Mitchell
Taunton, Som'rs't Arch & N. H. Soc.	1874		6d.		100	(Mus. of Royal Instn)	yes	yes	yes	no	—	—	yes	Geol., Cave bones from Mendip Hills	W. Bidgood
Truro....	1818	subns.	str'g'rs 6d.	Council	—	Geol., Lias and New Red Sandstone	no	yes	—	no	valuable	—	—	Birds, Conch., Local Lias	W. Newcombe
Warwick....	1837	subns.	6d.	Council	20 to 30	Bot., Geol.	yes	yes	yes	no	—	—	no		P. B. Brodie, M.A.
Wenlo'k, Sal'p	1840	,,		—	—		—	—	—	—	—	—	—		Mrs. Landon
Whitby	1823	,,		—	—		—	—	—	—	—	—	—		
Windsor	1880	,,	free	Committee	—	Pottery, &c.	no	yes	yes	no	consider-able	—	yes	Pottery, &c.	Joseph Lundy
Albert Inst.				—	—		—	—	—	—	—	—	—		
Wisbeach....	1835	endwmt	6d., one even. 1d	Committee	20	British Fish, Arch., Min'ls, Birds, Shells	no	yes	no	no	specimens chiefly given	—	no	Geology of the Fens	George Oliver
York, Yorks. Philos. Socy.	1822	subns.	membrs £3 & £2 anl.sub.	Council	500	Fine Gardens, Palæn. and Arch. collect'n especially good	no	yes	no	no	large, one gift of £10,000	1100	no	Yorkshire fossils, land and fresh water shells	H. M. Plat-nauer, B.Sc.
LONDON.															
City, Guild-hall	1872	Corpor-ation.	free	Library Committee	2232	Roman remains	yes	no	yes	no	—	—	no	Showing the occupa-tion of Londinium by the Romans	W. H. Overall, F.S.A.
Westminster, Royal Archi-tect. Mus.	1851	subns.	free	Council	70 or 80	4000 casts	no	yes	yes	no	900	600	no	Casts from West-minster Abbey	Edgar John Varley

Town	Date	Maintained by	Admission	Management	No.	Society / Remarks					Specimens	No.		Nature of collection	Name
Armagh, Nat. History and Philos.	1850	subns.	—	Committee	—		—	yes	yes	no	—	—	no	Sharks' teeth	Mrs. Reid
Belfast	1821		6d. & 2d.	Council	yearly 7000	Nat. Hist. & Philos. Society	no	yes	yes	no	10,000	250	—	Fossils, minerals, plants, shells, &c.	W. Darragh
WALES.															
Swansea	1835		1d.			M. of Royal Inst. of South Wales								—	Geo., Zoo., Botany	H. Huxham
Tenby	—		—										—		Ed. Laws
SCOTLAND.															
Alloa	1863	subn.	—			(M. of Society of Nat. Science)	no	no		no		—	—	—	Zoology, Botany, Anth.	J. F. Lyon
Banff																
Dumfries Observatory Museum	1835	charges	6d. & 3d.	Committee	1500	Ancient pottery	no	no		no		60	—	Minerals, fossils, &c.	Miss Locke
Dumfries	1855	free	6d.	Committee	16	Reptilian fossils	no					—	—	Botany, Geol., Zoology	J. Wilson
Elgin	1836	subns.	6d.	Committee	10	Geology, Zoology, Botany					2500	32	—		John Gatherer
Forres	1871	endowmnt. and fees	—	Committee		See chapter xviii					—	—	—	Zoology, Botany	J. D. Davidson
Glasgow, Kelvingrove	—		—										—		James Paton
Greenock	1876	endowmnt	free	Committee	360	Marine Zoology	yes	yes	yes	ne		270	yes	Ships' models, post-Pliocene geology	Thos. Bennie
Hawick	1856	subns.	2d.	Committee		Geology, Ornith., Indian fishes	yes	yes	yes	no		20	yes	Antiq. portraits	James Waugh
Inverness																
Kelso	1833	subns.	—										—		E. Johnson
Kircudbright	1881	subn.	6d.	Committee	25	Fauna, Flora, Archaic Sculptures	no	yes	yes	no	1500	30	yes	Botany, birds' eggs, antiq.	J. McKie
Largo, Fife	1863	free	free	President & Sec. Council	20	(Field 'Naturalists' Society)	no	no	yes	no			no	Conch., Geol., Ornith.	Robt. Smith
Montrose	1837		6d.			(M. of Nat. History and Antiq. Society)							—	Geol., Zoology, Botany	R. Barclay
Perth	1785	subns.	—			(M. of Lit. and Antiq. Society)							—	Geo., Zoo., Bot., Arch.	A. R. Urquhar M.D.
Peterhead	1851	Burgh funds and fees	2d.	Town Council	20	Zoology, Geology, Arch.	no	no		no		50	yes	Shells, Crustacea, Fishes	Alex. Wood
Stirling	1874		—		100	(Stirling M. Smith Inst.)							—	Zoology	James Sword

SCHOOL AND UNIVERSITY MUSEUMS.

Town & name of Museum	When established	How supported	Terms of admission	Governing body	Average No. of visitors per week	Special features	9	10	11	12	Gifts 13	Aggregate expenses	Loan exhibits from S.K., &c.	Special local features	Curator's name
Cambridge Mineralogical	1863	University	free to stude'ts	Museum Syndicate	small	Crystallographic	—	—	yes	—	£ abt. 20,000	£ 150	no	None	Prof. W. J. Lewis
Cambridge Botanical	—	—	free to stude'ts	—	—	—	—	—	yes	—	—	—	—	—	C. C. Babington
Cambridge Woodward'n	1728	endowmt & grants	free to stude'ts	University	—	Specimens collected & arranged to promote orig. research	no	yes	yes	no	two mil. specimens	500	no	Geol. specimens	Hy. Keeping
Cambridge Zoology	—	—	—	—	50	—	—	—	—	—	—	—	—	—	—
Cheltenham College	1887	—	free	Curator	—	Nat. Hist., Geol., Botany Zoo., Geo., Arch.	no	yes	yes	no	considerable	100	no	Fossils, Skulls of stone period Bot., Arch.	C. Pierson
Durham	1833	Council University	free to stude'ts	University	—	—	—	yes	—	—	—	—	—	—	J. Cullingford
Eton College, Windsor Sch.	—	school	,,	—	—	Rocks, Mineral, &c.	—	—	—	—	—	—	—	Under revision and re-building	Frederic Drew
Harrow Sch.	—	—	,,	—	—	—	—	—	—	—	—	—	—	For teaching purposes	A. Hen-ley
Hertford College	—	—	—	—	—	—	—	—	—	—	—	—	—	—	—
Haileybury College	—	—	—	—	—	—	—	—	—	—	—	—	—	—	—
Huddersfield	1884 Yks. Col	—	free	Gov. of Sch.	—	Technical, Scientific Med., Pathy., Anat.	no	no	yes	no	500	small	no	Birds	A. Keen, F.C.S.
Leeds Yks. Col	1830	—	,,	College Council	—	Teaching collection, good col. of Tunicata	—	—	—	—	—	—	—	—	E. H. Jacobs, M.D
Liverpool, Univ. Col.	1881	College	,,	College Council	—	Geo., Zoo., Arch.	—	yes	yes	no	—	—	—	Fauna of Liverpool Bay	Prof. W. A. Herdman, D.Sc.
Malvern	—	Mal. Col.	,,	,,	—	Miner., Geol., Zool., Bot.	—	—	—	—	—	—	—	—	G. E. Mackie
Manchester, Owens Col.	1872	Col. and endowmt subn.	,,	,,	—	Oil & Water-colour paintings, &c.	—	yes	yes	no	large 10,000	1,000	—	Carboniferous Flora	Prof. W. Boyd Dawkins, F.R.S.
Rugby School	1879	subn.	,,	Headmaster &c.	—		—	yes	yes	no	—	—	yes	Work done by schol. drawings esp. good	T. M. Lindsay
SCOTLAND.															
St. Andrew's	1788	University	,,	Museum Committee	—	—	—	yes	yes	no	—	—	no	Local Marine Fauna &c.	Thomas Walker

Place	Date	Managed by	Admission	Governing body	No.	Objects				Cost / Grant	Amount		Speciality	Curator
Galway, Queen's Col.	1849	Government Grant	,,	Council	—	Teaching collection	—	yes	—	no	—	150	yes	Galway Mineral	R. J. Andrews, M.A.
Ryde, Sch. of Sci. and Art.	1850	—	,,	Committee	—	—	no	no	no	no	—	500	yes	Geol., Arch., Flora, Ornithological	Benj. Barnes

ISLE OF WIGHT.

PRIVATE MUSEUMS.

Place	Date	Managed by	Admission	Governing body	No.	Objects				Cost / Grant	Amount		Speciality	Curator
Bakewell, Bingham's Geol.	1873	By owner	free	—	—	County and foreign fossils	—	—	—	—	£12 to £20	—	Minerals, lavas, &c.	L. F. Bingham
Carne, near Penzance	near 1800	By prop. C. C. Ross	free	—	—	—	—	—	—	—	—	—	Cornish Mineral	C. C. Ross
Huddersfield, Beaumont Park	1880	By owner	free	—	20	Insects injurious to farm and garden crops	yes	yes	yes	100	—	no	Fauna and flora	S. L. Mosley
Sheffield, St. George's Museum	1875	St. George's Guild	free	St. George's Guild	50-100	—	no	yes	no	Many thousands of pds. almost entirely by Mr. Ruskin	250	no	Plants, flowers, &c.	Henry Swan
Stratford-on-Avon	1847	—	—	—	—	Shakespeare relics	—	—	—	—	—	—	—	—
Thornhill, Dumfriesshire	1872	Owner	6d.	—	20	—	—	;	—	—	—	—	Arch., Anth.	T. B. Grierson, M.D.

MUSEUMS SUPPORTED BY GOVERNMENT AID.

Place	Date	Managed by	Admission	Governing body	No.	Objects				Cost / Grant	Amount		Speciality	Curator
Edinburgh, Mus. of Sci. and Art	1855	Annual Grant	Free some days and charges on others	Lords of Com. of Council on Education	6500	Nat. Hist., Technology	no	no	yes	—	£12,000	yes	Geology	Col. Sir R. Murdoch Smith
Edinburgh, Nat. Mus. of Antiquities	1780 orig	,,	,,	Trustees & Society of Antiquities	1450	Arch. of Scotland	yes	yes	yes	400	—	yes		Jos. Anderson, LL.D.
Gosport, Haslar Hospital	1859	,,	—	Inspector of Hospital	—	Anat., Nat. History, &c.	—	—	—	—	—	—		Dr. W. Reid, R.N.
Woolwich	1814	,,	—	Sec. of State for War	200	Military appliances	no	yes	no	200	—	no	Engines of War	Mr. Loose
Dublin, Sci. & Art Mus.	1792	,,	free ,,	Council of Education	3903	Natural Hist. and Fine Art	—	yes	—	One-third of entire col.	9000	yes	Irish Zoology, Geology, &c.	Prof. V. Ball, M.A.

MUSEUM LECTURE ON SPARROW-LIKE BIRDS.

The common House Sparrow is very familiar to everybody. but among those who study birds, he is held in especial honour, nearly half the known species being named after him as Passerine birds (*Passer*, L., a sparrow). Some of these, one would not, at first, consider to be very much like a sparrow, and, indeed, there are great differences in size, in form of beak, in coloration, in voice, and in other respects. The points, however, that remain constant are : The horny beak without *cere;* the tarsus covered with thin plates or scales ; three toes directed forward and one backward, with the outer toe and the one next it usually more or less united from the base, or, exceptionally, all four toes directed forwards ; the young are born naked, or nearly so, and helpless. A special vocal apparatus with muscles, is oftener present than absent. Nearly all the birds in this order are of small size, but they fly very well, and rest by preference on trees and bushes. Most of them when on the ground move by hopping. The males are usually true to a single wife, and often the individual kinds associate in large flocks. Many are skilful architects, and make charming nests ; and the wonderful travels which many of them undertake at the migratory season are the admiration of all true naturalists.

When one comes to divide into companies the vast number of the sparrow order, difficulties crowd thick and fast. Shall the singing birds be separated from the shriekers ? Certain naturalists say Yes, others emphatically answer No. Why ? Because if you make separate groups of singers and non-singers some of the first are very much like some of the second in many important respects. Is the possession of a voice, then, to determine the first grand division ? Many of the greatest authorities say not ; and these look to the bill to furnish the principal characters for separation into tribes. This division is here adopted. Tribe number one let us call the light-beaks ; number two the thin-beaks ; number three the cleft-beaks ; number four the toothed-beaks ; and tribe the last the conical-beaks.

Look at one of the Hornbills and tell me if you would reckon him among the light-beaks ? I hardly think you would. His beak seems as big as his body. Yet on examination it proves to be wonderfully light, and so, after all, he is reckoned in the light-beak tribe. The Bee-eaters and the Rollers form a second and a third family of this tribe. There are many interesting facts relating to these which time will not now allow me to

---

* A membranous partial covering.

notice, so by your leave the Kingfisher shall serve to represent to us the whole tribe and its characteristics. The Kingfishers form a fourth family of the light-beaks, of which only one is a genuine British bird. Notice the two outer toes fastened together

Light Beaks.

throughout a great part of their length. This kind of foot is called a *gressorial* foot, and is specially adapted for clinging to branches. Here, too, you have a large, light beak, which is keeled and angular, and does good service to its owner when

1. Beak of Hornbill.
2. Beak of Kingfisher.
3. Foot of Kingfisher.

catching fish, for which he watches, perched on a low over-hanging bough close to the surface of a secluded brook. The large head and short *tarsus*,* besides the short wings and short

---

* Part of the leg from what is usually but wrongly regarded as the knee down to the toes.

tail, are also characteristic. Probably this bird has the most brilliant plumage of any of our natives. It is satisfactory to learn that its numbers are increasing since the passing of the "Small Birds' Protection Act." The Kingfisher and all the light-beaks belong to the group of non-singers, as indeed do most, though not all, of the brilliantly coloured birds.

The thin-beaks include both singing and shrieking birds, with long beaks, and feet with toes all quite free or having the outer toe and the next to the outer toe attached for but a short distance from the base, a type of foot known as *ambulatory*. A long hind toe is usual among the thin - beaks. The first family of the thin - beaks contains the beautifully coloured Hoopoes, one species of which sometimes strays into Britain. The Humming-birds form the next family, and one that need not be ashamed to show itself. The

Thin Beak of
Humming Bird.

Cleft Beak of Goatsucker.

smallness of their size and their metallic lustre will ever gain for them wonder and admiration. The feet are very slender, the beak is long and awl-shaped, the upper beak projects along the edges over the lower beak forming a tube from which a long slit tongue is protruded into the hearts of tropical flowers where the glittering fairy finds her food. Brazil is the home of most of these living gems. There is quite sufficient of interest in their history to serve for a special lecture. The Honey-suckers, which, like the preceding family, find their food in flowers. are small beautiful birds of stout build found principally in Australia and New Guinea. They have a muscular vocal apparatus and so can sing in their way. A long gently curved beak, a long tarsus, and wings of medium length and a long tail are features which assist one to identify the family. The tree creeper is the only thoroughly British bird belonging to this second tribe of the sparrow order ; and the tree creepers form a family, known by their long, slightly-curved beak, pointed horny tongue, metatarsus covered with scales, and long hind toe with a sharp claw. The common creeper may be seen where trees are abundant clinging with its long toes to the branches of hawthorn and other trees spasmodically moving about now above now below the branch examining every crevice for insects, which it captures in much the same way as the woodpecker, who impales his victims with his hard pointed tongue. It is wonderful to see the activity of these little creatures among the boughs of a thorn tree before the leaves come out, and their merry musical note rapidly repeated gives an air of cheeriness to the dingle or woodside where they be.

Now turn to the cleft beaks. The best known of the tribe is the swallow, and almost equally well-known is the sand-martin, which makes its nest in the sandy rock of the railway cuttings in this neighbourhood. In either of these birds you may notice the short neck, flattened head, deeply-cleft beak, long pointed wings and somewhat weak feet characteristic of the tribe. The Swallows and Martins form one family, the Swifts another, and the Goatsuckers a third. In the swift, notice the four toes all pointing forwards, and the long sabre-formed wing. These birds are very good flyers, and indeed very rarely do they rest on the ground, though one may see them clinging near their nests under the eaves of houses and in similar places. Often in the summer evenings their musical squeak may be heard as they fly in companies overhead with mouth wide open and sticky tongue netting, as it were, the flies that gambol in the air. The goatsuckers are non-singers, with an uncommonly flat, triangular beak. They resemble the owls in their soft plumage, which looks like the bark of trees in colour. To see them hawking for moths, on which they feed, one should go by a woodside in the deepening twilight of a summer evening. Their flight is silent as an owl's, indeed they form a sort of connecting link between the family of the owls and the order of the perching birds. As with the swifts, the legs are very weak and short. Nearly all the cleft beaks dwell in warmer climates. The swallow is a rapid traveller. In the autumn, he quits England for the

Sunny South, and finds his way to Northern Africa, and even to Syria.

The tribe of the toothed-bills comes next, and the birds in it are grouped in ten families, nearly all of which are reckoned among the singing birds, though the cawing of a rook would hardly pass for a song with some people. The beak is variously shaped, but in all it is notched on the upper beak near the tip, though sometimes very slightly. Another peculiarity is that the first of the primary wing feathers is small and sometimes absent altogether. The jackdaw, the magpie, the crows, and the jay form a family with strong and thick beaks, somewhat curved near the tip and only slightly notched. The jackdaw's habit of stealing and hiding all manner of things perhaps suggested to somebody the story of the Jackdaw of Rheims. Many of this family are notable talkers when trained. The jay is one of the handsomest of the family. He is disliked by gamekeepers, who accuse him of thieving the eggs of game-birds. The next family includes the celebrated Bird of Paradise, about which there is a tradition that it never settles on the ground. This is untrue. The two middle feathers of the tail in the males of this group are often very long and thin with a little vane at the end. The feet are very strong and the toes large. They are not represented among British birds. The Starlings come next. In these there is a strong beak which is either straight or slightly curved. The point is distinctly notched, and there are none of those stiff hairs near the base of the beak noticeable in some families of birds. The common starling is one of the sober-sided members of the family. There is, however, a rose-coloured starling, and here, as elsewhere, colour is one of the least constant of the characters by which a bird is to be distinguished. Passing over some foreign birds which are doubtfully included with the toothed-bills, the Shrikes next attract attention. The red-backed shrike is the type of the group, and his murderous nature is sufficiently indicated by his hooked, strongly-serrated beak, and tolerably long, sharply-clawed feet. Indeed he approaches the birds of prey in his nature, and his game includes beetles, which he is in the habit of impaling on thorns in the neighbourhood of his nest. From this circumstance he has been called the butcher-bird. The Flycatchers have a short broad beak depressed at the base and narrowed forwards, with a hooked curved point. The spotted flycatcher is a British example. The waxwing belongs to this family, but seldom visits this country, although found native on the Continent. It is quite a showy bird. Then come the Titmice, who are in some respects the most entertaining of birds. They are all small and very active ; of stout build, with sharp, short, almost conical beak. An account of the marsh titmouse, by a witness of its antics, may fitly come in here :—"It was delightful to watch the lively motions of these black-capped, grey-bodied acrobats. Only when one clung to the tip-top branch of a hedgerow, feet uppermost, peering curiously among the starting buds, could the observer be quite sure about his plumage. His activity destroyed the distinctness of his contour, and blended black and grey feathers like the mixed colours of a kaleidoscope."

The Wagtails are known by the slender body and the tolerably long and notched beak. Few things are more interesting than to watch the water wagtail taking his morning bath in a brook or by the side of a river. The elegance of his personal appearance enhanced by his long tail and the grace of his flight are specially noteworthy. In the family of the Warblers one has some singers worthy of the name and some pretty, though not brilliant, birds. The garden warbler may be taken as representative of the family. He is a small bird fairly abundant in country gardens, and from his nest in a gooseberry bush I have heard many a sweet song worth going far to hear. The whitethroat is a near relative, and here one may fitly introduce a quotation of pure poetry from "The Farmer's Boy," of Bloomfield :—

> " The sportive whitethroat on some twig's end borne
> Sang hymns to freedom and the rising morn,
> Stopt in her lay perchance the starting thrush
> Shook a white shower from the blackthorn bush,
> Where dew-drops thick as early blossoms hung,
> And trembled as the minstrel sweetly sung."

The thrush, though in another family, is close akin to the warblers, but before passing to his family, a word should be said of the wren, which is included with the warblers, who may be known by a thin and pointed beak and a tarsus covered with scales in front.

In *The Birds of Sherwood Forest*, by Mr. W. J. Sterland, one may read : "Of the common wren (*Troglodytes Europaeus*) it is hardly necessary to say more than that it is a most familiar and abundant species. Every child knows and delights to see ' little Jenny Wren,' the very picture of vigorous, bustling industry and pert independence ; and its share in the tragic story of ' Who killed Cock Robin? ' will ever make it familiar to our children. It is always interesting to watch the active vagaries of these birds as they half flit, half creep in the bushes and hedges of our gardens ; they are bold little creatures, approaching within a yard or two without fear, but at the same time vigilantly alive to secure their own safety."

The chiff-chaff, one of the first to arrive of our spring migrants, also belongs to the warblers. Now look at the thrush. Notice the tolerably long somewhat compressed beak, which is slightly notched near the tip, and furnished with stiff hairs near the base. The tarsus is long, and has a characteristic arrangement of scales. This family is a brilliant one so far as rank goes, for it includes, besides the thrush, the blackbird, the robin, and the nightingale. He who has heard the nightingale is so much the richer thereby. In the neighbourhood of Nottingham nightingales come every spring, and I have stood for an hour at midnight listening to the loud chorus of two or three birds in a wood. The nightingales sing by day as well as by night, but at night, when all else is still, is the time to hear them. First the song is low, and seems as if the songster were just clearing his voice, gradually it increases in force and tone until the whole wood echoes with the joyous crescendo. It is really difficult not to imagine the bird moved by human feelings of intense joy and love. Lark, thrush, robin, warbler, the notes of all these and its own in addition seem blended and wrought into endless change until words are powerless to describe the music. If ever you hear of a nightingale within ten miles lose a night's rest to hear it. You will be glad you took my advice. The thrush and the robin are well known. Many people think the robin is with us only in winter, but really he is here in the summer too, but then the red of his breast is less conspicuous, and sometimes hardly visible at all.

The fieldfare very much resembles a thrush, but is devoid of the thrush's song.

Toothed Beak of Fieldfare.

The last tribe of the sparrow-like birds is that of the conical beaks. Here you have a thick head, short neck, wings of medium length, and ambulatory feet. The tarsus is short and covered with scales in front. The usual food is corn and seeds, but insects are by no means

Conical Beak of Yellow Hammer.

despised. The first family is that of the Larks, which differ from their fellows in having broad and long wings. The beak is of medium length and the tail short. The skylark is fortunately so well known in England that there is no need to describe his song. The Finches form the next family, and the common house sparrow is their representative. All know the short thick beak with a little swelling at the base. This is found in the yellow hammer, the chaffinch, the bull-finch, the goldfinch, and many other birds. The sparrow is a very pugnacious bird, and on occasion will fight a pigeon even. He is a good bird to study as to variation in colour. White sparrows are not at all infrequently met with, and among twenty or thirty birds in a street one may notice great differences in the markings. Many other birds are thus liable to appear in white or partly white plumage whose ordinary coat is entirely different. There have been found white blackbirds and white crows.

The Weaver-birds are remarkable for the long purse-shaped nests that they build. They live in Africa, East India, and Australia. *Ploceus textor* is the representative of this last family of the conical beaks. The weavers, like most of the conical beaks, live on small fruits and seeds, and do damage in gardens in summer-time. The nest is usually suspended to a tree over running water. Speaking of a remarkable nest it may be well here to say a word or two about other nests of the sparrow-like birds.

The Marquis de Cherville says that he watched a pair of magpies from the beginning of their nest-building to the end. They had fixed themselves in a large poplar, just before M. de Cherville's window, and he watched them from his desk and from his bed, missing hardly anything that they did. The work lasted for forty-seven days, during which, especially in the morning and evening, the two birds carried materials with a feverish activity. In a single day he counted two hundred and eight journeys in quest of material, and this was not the whole.

2 C

The comparative usefulness of our common English birds is but little understood by gardeners. Captain Becher, R.A., a first-rate observer of bird life, says that those birds "that do the most good and least harm are . . . the willow wren, the chiff-chaff, the wagtails, and the common wren," and, perhaps, the long-tailed tit. Next in order of usefulness come "the robin, hedge-sparrow, garden warbler [perhaps], and the other tits." Next again, "the missel thrush, song thrush, and blackbird." "Then next we have those who do most harm and least good . . . the finches, and, lastly, in a class by itself, as doing no good and most harm, the house sparrow." In connection with the small singing birds that so much attract our attention and interest, a few words on the phenomena of migration may well close this lecture.

Rectrices or Tail Quills.

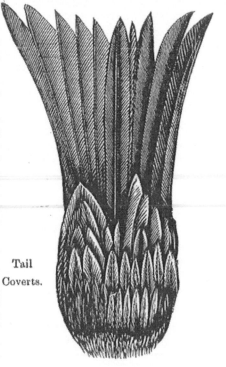

Tail Coverts.

"The migration of birds," says Captain Becher, "is still an unexplained mystery ; the only method of solving it is by registering continued observations. A Committee has been appointed for this purpose by the British Association, schedules for recording observations being sent to various lighthouses and lightships. This migratory instinct is so strong that swallows and other birds will leave their young to die in the nest, some birds having second broods and some three. It is attempted to explain the phenomena of migratory movements of birds by having recourse to the records of former conditions of land and climate. It is a well

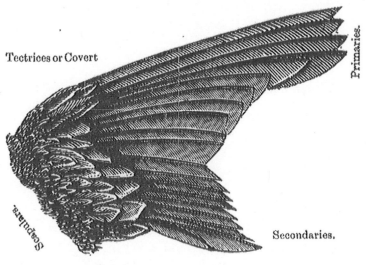

Tectrices or Covert

Primaries.

Scapulars.

Secondaries.

Tectrices or
Coverts.

Method of displaying wings and tail of bird to indicate the parts meant by the technical names occurring in books on Ornithology.

ascertained fact that the young of many birds migrate before their parents, and in separate flocks. These have never travelled before, and how they find their way over some thousands of miles of land and sea seems a very puzzling question, especially as most birds travel by night. I have myself frequently seen them at sea some hundreds of miles from land. In a report of the before-mentioned Committee it says :— ' A great migratory wave moves to and from the nesting quarters of the birds, in the coldest part of their range, north-east in the spring and south-west in the autumn. Quite independent of this there is a continual stream of immigrants, week by week and month by month, to the eastern shores of these islands, coming directly across Europe from east to west, and the reverse in spring.' Many of our commonest birds which we are apt to regard as residents [only] also migrate . . . rooks, blackbirds, thrushes, larks, robins, wrens, and others."

J. J. Ogle, Curator, Bootle Museum.

2 c 2

MUSEUM MEMORANDA.

USEFUL RULES TO KEEP IN MIND ON VISITING A MUSEUM.

1.—Avoid attempting to see too much.
2.—Remember that one specimen or one article *well* seen is better than a score of specimens casually inspected.
3.—Before entering a Museum ask yourself what it is you wish particularly to see, and confine your attention largely to those specimens. Consult the attendant as to what is specially interesting in each room.
4.—Remember that the main object of the specimens is to instruct.
5.—Have a note-book with you and record your impressions, so that on a succeeding visit you may pick up your information where you left off on the previous visit.
6.—Introduce in conversation your impressions of what you see in Museums.
7.—Consult frequently the technical literature on the special subject in which you are interested.
8.—Visit the nearest Museum periodically, and let it be to you an advanced school for self-instruction.
9.—Remember there is something new to see every time you go.
10.—Make a private collection of *something*. Remember that a collection of postage stamps has many uses.
11.—Follow up some special subject of Museum study.
12.—See slowly, observe closely, and think much upon what you see.

WHY SHOULD EVERY TOWN HAVE A MUSEUM ?

1.—Because a Museum and Free Library are as necessary for the mental and moral health of the citizens as good sanitary arrangements, water supply and street lighting are for their physical health and comfort.

2.—Because the rate for their support is very small as compared with other rates, the utmost amount which can ever be charged being one penny in the pound per year on the rateable value.

3.—Because a rate-supported Museum is the town's property, into which any person can enter during the recognised hours without let or hindrance.

4.—Because there is no rate for which there is a more immediate and tangible benefit than the penny rate for the support of a Free Library and Museum.

5.—Because in no town where they have been established is the rate felt as a burden, and is, in fact, often the most cheerfully paid item in the ratepaper.

6.—Because where these institutions have been established in Birmingham, Liverpool, Leeds, Manchester, Derby, and other places they are thoroughly appreciated by the inhabitants.

7.—Because Museums and Art Galleries not only give widespread pleasure, but are, with Free Libraries, the Universities of the working classes.

8.—Because they are open to all classes, rich and poor, and where they exist and are free to all, they are actually used by all classes, from the professional man to the humblest artisan.

9.—Because they are educational institutions for young
and old, and education deepens the sense of
the duties and privileges of citizenship.

10.—Because the existence or absence of a Museum and
Free Library in a town is a standard of the
intelligence and public spirit manifested in
that town.

11.—Because for young people of both sexes they afford
a place for recreation to which they can go,
instead of loitering aimlessly about the public
streets.

12.—Because they bring under one roof priceless gifts
which could not be seen by the public in any
other way.

13.—Because they provide places of reference for specimens of local geology, botany, &c., to which
the citizens in every town should have easy
means of access.

14.—Because they cultivate habits of thought and
conversation, which stimulate reading and
brighten life, and make the home more
cheerful and attractive.

15.—Because Museum and Free Library buildings always
improve the adjoining property. Some trades-
men advertise their business as being within
so many minutes' walk of the Free Library.

16.—Because we do not want Old England to be
behind other countries, and America, France,
Germany, and the Australian Colonies are
setting us an example worthy of imitation.

17.—Because it is said that the workmen of some other
countries are better educated than ours, and
Englishmen are determined that this shall
not be so in time to come, but that our
children after us shall be able to hold their
own in the van of peaceful progress.

APPENDIX.

FREE PUBLIC LIBRARIES AND MUSEUMS ACT.

The earlier Acts having been repealed are not reprinted here.

CAP. LXX.

An Act for further promoting the Establishment of Free Public Libraries and Museums in Municipal Towns, and for extending it to Towns governed under Local Improvement Acts, and to Parishes.

[30th *July*, 1885.]

WHEREAS it is expedient to amend and extend the Public Libraries Act, 1850 : Be it therefore enacted by the Queen's most Excellent Majesty, by and with the Advice and Consent of the Lords Spiritual and Temporal, and Commons, in this present Parliament assembled, and by the Authority of the same, as follows :

I. *13 & 14 Vict. c. 65 repealed.*—The Public Libraries Act, 1850, is hereby repealed; but such Repeal shall not invalidate or affect anything already done in pursuance of the same Act, and all Libraries and Museums established under that Act or the Act thereby repealed shall be considered as having been established under this Act, and the Council of any Borough which may have adopted the said Act of One thousand eight hundred and fifty, or established a Museum under the Act thereby repealed, shall have and may use and exercise all the Benefits, Privileges and Powers given by this Act; and all Monies which have been borrowed by virtue of the said repealed Acts or either of them, and still remaining unpaid, and the Interest thereof, shall be charged on the Borough Rates, or a Rate to be assessed and recovered in the like Manner as a Borough Rate to be made by virtue of this Act.

II. *Short Title of Act.*—In citing this Act for any Purposes whatever it shall be sufficient to use the Expression " The Public Libraries Act, 1855."

III. *Interpretation of Terms.*—In the construction of this Act the following words and Expressions shall, unless there be something in the Subject or Context repugnant to such Construction, have the following Meanings assigned to them respectively ; that is to say, " Parish " shall mean every place maintaining its own Poor; " Vestry " shall mean the Inhabitants of the Parish lawfully assembled in Vestry, or for any of the Purposes for which Vestries are holden, except in those Parishes in which there is a Select Vestry elected under the Act of the Fifty-ninth Year of King *George* the Third, Chapter Twelve, or under the Acts of the First and Second Years of King William the *Fourth,* Chapter Sixty, or under the Provisions of any Local Act of Parliament for the Government of any Parish by Vestries, in which Parishes it shall mean such Select Vestry, and shall also mean any Body of Persons, by whatever Name distinguished, acting by virtue of any Act of Parliament, Prescription, Custom, or otherwise, as or instead of a Vestry or Select Vestry ; " Ratepayers " shall mean all Persons for the time being assessed to Rates for the Relief of the Poor of the Parish ; " Overseers of the Poor " shall mean also any Persons authorised and required to make and collect the Rate for the Relief of the Poor of the Parish, and acting instead of Overseers of the Poor ; " Board " shall mean the Commissioners, Trustees, or other Body of

Persons, by whatever Name distinguished, for the Time being in Office and acting in the Execution of any Improvement Act, being an Act for draining, cleansing, paving, lighting, watching, or otherwise improving a Place, or for any of those Purposes; " Improvement Rates " shall mean the Rates, Tolls, Rents, Income, and other Monies whatsoever which, under the Provisions of any such Improvement Act, shall be applicable for the general Purposes of such Act.

IV. *Town Councils of certain Boroughs may adopt this Act if determined by Inhabitants.*—-The Mayor of any Municipal Borough the Population of which, according to the then last Census thereof, shall exceed Five thousand Persons, shall, on the Request of the Town Council, convene a Public Meeting of the Burgesses of the Borough, in order to determine whether this Act shall be adopted for the Municipal Borough, and Ten Days Notice at least of the Time, Place, and Object of the Meeting shall be given by affixing the same on or near the Door of every Church and Chapel within the Borough, and also by advertising the same in One or more of the Newspapers published or circulated within the Borough, Seven Days at least before the Day appointed for the Meeting; and if at such Meeting Two Thirds of such Persons as aforesaid then present shall determine that this Act ought to be adopted for the Borough, the same shall thenceforth take effect and come into operation in such Borough, and shall be carried into execution in accordance with the Laws for the Time being in force relating to the Municipal Corporation of such Borough: Provided always, that the Mayor, or, in his Absence, the Chairman of the Meeting, shall cause a Minute to be made of the Resolutions of the Meeting, and shall sign the same; and the Resolutions so signed shall be conclusive Evidence that the Meeting was duly convened, and the

Vote thereat duly taken, and that the Minute contains a true Account of the Proceedings thereat.

V. *Expenses of carrying Act into Execution.*—The Expenses incurred in calling and holding the Meeting, whether this Act shall be adopted or not, and the Expenses of carrying this Act into execution in such Borough, may be paid out of the Borough Fund, and the Council may levy by a separate Rate, to be called a Library Rate, to be made and recoverable in the Manner hereinafter provided, all Monies from Time to Time necessary for defraying such Expenses; and distinct Accounts shall be kept of the Receipts, Payments, and Liabilities of the Council with reference to the Execution of this Act.

VI. *Board of any District within limits of any Improvement Act.*—The Board of any District, being a Place within the Limits of any Improvement Act, and having such a Population as aforesaid, shall, upon the Requisition in Writing of at least Ten Persons assessed to and paying the Improvement Rate, appoint a Time not less than Ten Days nor more than Twenty Days from the Time of receiving such Requisition for a Public Meeting of the Persons assessed to and paying such Rate in order to determine whether this Act shall be adopted for such District, and Ten Days Notice at least of the Time, Place, and Object of such Meeting shall be given by affixing the same on or near the Door of every Church and Chapel within the District, and also by advertising the same in One or more of the Newspapers published or circulated within the District, Seven Days at least before the day appointed for the Meeting; and if at such Meeting Two Thirds of such Persons as aforesaid then present shall determine that this Act ought to be adopted for the District, the same shall thenceforth take effect, and come into operation in such District, and shall be carried into effect according to the Laws for the time being in force relating to such Board.

VII. *Expenses of carrying Act into Execution.*— The Expenses incurred in calling and holding the Meeting, whether this Act shall be adopted or not, and the Expenses of carrying this Act into execution in any such District, shall be paid out of the Improvement Rate, and the Board may levy as Part of the Improvement Rate, or by a separate Rate to be assessed and recovered in like Manner as an Improvement Rate, such Sums of Money as shall be from Time to Time necessary for defraying such Expenses; and the Board shall keep distinct Accounts of their Receipts, Payments, Credits, and Liabilities with reference to the Execution of this Act, which Accounts shall be audited in the same Way as Accounts are directed to be audited under the Improvement Act.

VIII. *The Vestry to appoint Commissioners.*— Upon the Requisition in writing of at least Ten Ratepayers of any Parish having such a Population as aforesaid, the Overseers of the Poor shall appoint a Time, not less than Ten Days nor more than Twenty Days from the Time of receiving such Requisition, for a Public Meeting of the Ratepayers in order to determine whether this Act shall be adopted for the Parish; and Ten Days Notice at least of the Time, Place, and Object of the Meeting shall be given by affixing the same on or near the Door of every Church and Chapel within the Parish, and also by advertising the same in One or more of the Newspapers published or circulated within the Parish, Seven Days at least before the Day appointed for the Meeting; and if at such Meeting Two Thirds of the Ratepayers then present shall determine that this Act ought to be adopted for such Parish, the same shall come into operation in such Parish, and the Vestry shall forthwith appoint not less than Three nor more than Nine Ratepayers Commissioners for carrying the Act into execution, who shall be a Body Corporate by the Name of " The Commissioners for Public Libraries and Museums for the Parish of   in the County of   ," and by that Name may sue and be sued, and hold and dispose of Lands, and use a Common Seal: Provided always, that in any Parish where there shall not be a greater Population than Eight thousand Inhabitants by the then last Census, it shall be lawful for any Ten Ratepayers to deliver a Requisition by them signed, and describing their Place of Residence, to the Overseers or One of the Overseers of the said Parish, requiring the Votes of the Ratepayers at such Meeting to be taken according to the Provisions of the Act passed in the Fifty-eighth Year of the Reign of King *George* the Third, Chapter Sixtynine, and the Votes at such Meeting shall thereupon be taken according to the Provisions of the said lastmentioned Act of Parliament, and not otherwise.

IX. *One Third of such Commissioners to go out of Office yearly.*—At the Termination of every Year (the Year being reckoned from and exclusive of the Day of the First Appointment of Commissioners) a Meeting of the Vestry shall be held, at which Meeting One Third or as nearly as may be One Third of the Commissioners, to be determined by Ballot, shall go out of Office, and the Vestry shall appoint other Commissioners in their Place, but the outgoing Commissioners may be reelected; and the Vestry shall fill up every vacancy among the Commissioners, whether occurring by Death, Resignation, or otherwise, as soon as possible after the same occurs.

X. The Commissioners shall meet at least once in every Calendar Month, and at such other Times as they think fit, at the Public Library or Museum or some other convenient Place; and any One Commissioner may summon a Special Meeting of the Commissioners by giving Three clear Days Notice in Writing to each Commissioner, specifying therein the Purpose for which the Meeting is called; and no business shall be transacted at any Meeting of the Commissioners unless at least Two Commissioners shall be present.

XI. *Minutes of Proceedings.*—All Orders and Proceedings of the Commissioners shall be entered in Books to be kept by them for that Purpose, and shall be signed by the Commissioners or any Two of them; and all such Orders and Proceedings so entered, and purporting to be so signed, shall be deemed to be original Orders and Proceedings, and such Books may be produced and read as Evidence of all such Orders and Proceedings upon any judicial Proceeding whatsoever.

XII. *Distinct Accounts.*—The Commissioners shall keep distinct and regular accounts of their Receipts, Payments, Credits, and Liabilities with reference to the Execution of this Act, which Accounts shall be audited yearly by the Poor Law Auditor, if the Accounts of Poor Rate Expenditure of the Parish be audited by a Poor Law Auditor but if not so audited, then by Two Auditors, not being Commissioners, who shall be yearly appointed by the Vestry, and the Auditor or Auditors shall report thereon, and such Report shall be laid before the Vestry by the Commissioners.

XIII. *Expenses of executing Act.*—The Expenses of calling and holding the Meeting of the Ratepayers, whether this Act shall be adopted or not, and the Expenses of carrying this Act into execution in any Parish, to such amount as shall be from Time to Time sanctioned by the Vestry, shall be paid out of a Rate to be made and recovered in like manner as a Poor Rate, except that every Person occupying Lands used as Arable, Meadow, or Pasture Ground only, or as Woodlands or Market Gardens, or Nursery Grounds, shall be rated in respect of the same in the Proportion of One Third Part only of the full net annual Value thereof respectively; the Vestry to be called for the Purpose of sanctioning the Amount shall be convened in the Manner usual in the Parish; the Amount for the Time being proposed to be raised for such Expenses shall be expressed in the Notice convening the Vestry, and shall be paid, according to the Order of the Vestry, to such Person as shall be appointed by the Commissioners to receive the same: Provided always, that in the Notices requiring the Payment of the Rate there shall be stated the Proportion which the Amount to be thereby raised for the Purposes of this Act shall bear to the total Amount of the Rate.

XIV. *Vestries of Two or more neighbouring Parishes.*—The Vestries of any Two or more neighbouring Parishes having according to the then last Census an aggregate Population exceeding Five thousand Persons may adopt this Act, in like Manner as if the Population of each of those Parishes according to the then last Census exceeded Five thousand, and may concur in carrying the same into execution in such Parishes for such Time as they shall mutually agree; and such Vestries may decide that a Public Library or Museum, or both, shall be erected in any One of such Parishes, and that the Expenses of carrying this Act into execution with reference to the same shall be borne by such Parishes in such Proportions as such Vestries shall mutually approve; the Proportion for each of such Parishes of such Expenses shall be paid out of the Monies to be raised for the Relief of the Poor of the same respective Parishes accordingly; but no more than Three Commissioners shall be appointed for each Parish; and the Commissioners so appointed for each of such Parishes shall in the Management of the said

Public Library and Museum form One Body of Commissioners, and shall act accordingly in the Execution of this Act; and the Accounts of the Commissioners shall be examined and reported on by the Auditor or Auditors of each of such Parishes; and the surplus Money at the Disposal as aforesaid of such Commissioners shall be paid to the Overseers of such Parishes respectively, in the Proportion in which such Parishes shall be liable to such Expenses.

XV. *Rates levied not to exceed One Penny in the Pound.*—The Amount of the Rate to be levied in any Borough, District, or Parish in any One Year for the Purposes of this Act shall not exceed the Sum of One Penny in the Pound; and for the Purposes of the Library Rate all the Clauses of the Towns Improvement Clauses Act, 1847, with respect to the Manner of making Rates, to the Appeal to be made against any Rate, and to the Recovery of Rates, shall be incorporated with this Act; and whenever the words "Special Act" occur in the Act so incorporated they shall mean "The Public Libraries Act, 1855"; the Accounts of the said Board and Commissioners respectively with reference to the Execution of this Act shall at all reasonable Times be open, without Charge, to the Inspection of every Person rated to the Improvement Rate or to the Rates for the Relief of the Poor of the Parish, as the Case may be, who may make Copies of or Extracts from such Accounts, without paying for the same; and in case the Board or the Commissioners, or any of them respectively, or any of their respective Officers or Servants having the Custody of such Accounts, shall not permit the same Accounts to be inspected, or Copies of or Extracts from the same to be made, every Person so offending shall for every such Offence forfeit any Sum not exceeding Five Pounds.

XVI. *Power to borrow.*—For carrying this Act into

execution the Council, Board, or Commissioners respectively may, with the Approval of Her Majesty's Treasury, (and as to the Commissioners, with the Sanction also of the Vestry and the Poor Law Board,) from Time to Time borrow at Interest, on the Security of a Mortgage or Bond of the Borough Fund, or of the Rates levied in pursuance of this Act, such Sums of Money as may be by them respectively required; and the Commissioners for carrying into execution the Act of the Ninth and Tenth Years of Her Majesty, Chapter Eighty, may from Time to Time advance and lend any such Sums of Money.

XVII. The Clauses and Provisions of "The Companies Clauses Consolidation Act, 1845," with respect to the borrowing of Money on Mortgage or Bond, and the Accountability of Officers, and the Recovery of Damages and Penalties, so far as such Provisions may respectively be applicable to the Purposes of this Act, shall be respectively incorporated with this Act.

XVIII. *Lands, &c., may be appropriated, purchased.*—The Council of any Borough and the Board of any District respectively may from Time to Time, with the Approval of Her Majesty's Treasury, appropriate for the Purposes of this Act any Lands vested, as the Case may be, in a Borough, in the Mayor, Aldermen, and Burgesses, and in a District in the Board; and the Council, Board, and Commissioners respectively may also, with such Approval, purchase or rent any Lands or any suitable Buildings; and the Council and Board and Commissioners respectively may, upon any Lands so appropriated, purchased, or rented respectively, erect any Buildings suitable for Public Libraries or Museums, or both, or for Schools for Science or Art, and may apply, take down, alter, and extend any Buildings for such Purposes, and rebuild, repair, and improve the same respectively, and fit up, furnish, and supply the same respectively with all requisite Furniture, Fittings, and Conveniences.

XIX. " The Lands Clauses Consolidation Act, 1845," shall be incorporated with this Act; but the Council, Board, and Commissioners respectively shall not purchase or take any Lands otherwise than by Agreement.

XX. The Council, Board, and Commissioners aforesaid respectively may, with the like Approval as is required for the Purchase of Lands, sell any Lands vested in the Mayor, Aldermen, and Burgesses, or Board, or Commissioners respectively, for the Purposes of this Act, or exchange the same for any Lands better adapted for the Purposes; and the Monies to arise from such Sale, or to be received for Equality of Exchange, or a sufficient part thereof, shall be applied in or towards the Purchase of other Lands better adapted for such Purposes.

XXI. The general Management, Regulation, and Control of such Libraries and Museums, Schools for Science and Art, shall be, as to any Borough, vested in and exercised by the Council, and as to any District in and by the Board, and as to any Parish or Parishes in and by the Commissioners, or such Committee as such Council or Board may from Time to Time appoint, the Members whereof need not be Members of the Council or Board or be Commissioners, who may from Time to Time purchase and provide the necessary Fuel, Lighting, and other similar Matters, Books, Newspapers, Maps, and Specimens of Art and Science, for the Use of the Library or Museum, or School, and cause the same to be bound or repaired when necessary, and appoint salaried Officers and Servants, and dismiss the same, and make Rules and Regulations for the Safety and Use of the Libraries and Museums, and Schools, and for the Admission of the Public.

2 D

XXII. *Property of Library, &c., to be Vested in Council.*—The Lands and Buildings so to be appropriated, purchased, or rented as aforesaid, and all other Real and Personal Property whatever presented to or purchased for any Library or Museum established under this Act, or School, shall be vested, in the Case of a Borough, in the Mayor, Aldermen, and Burgesses, in the Case of a District in the Board, and in the Case of a Parish or Parishes in the Commissioners.

XXIII. If any Meeting called as aforesaid to determine as to the Adoption of this Act for any Borough, District, or Parish shall determine against the Adoption, no Meeting for a similar Purpose shall be held for the Space of One Year at least from the Time of holding the previous Meeting.

XXIV. The Lord Mayor of the City of *London* shall, on the request of the Lord Mayor, Aldermen, and Commons of the City of *London*, in Common Council assembled, convene a Public Meeting in manner hereinbefore mentioned of all Persons rated and assessed to the Consolidated Rate in the City of *London*, in order to determine whether this Act shall be adopted in the said City ; and if at such Meeting Two Thirds of such Persons then present shall determine that this Act ought to be adopted for the City of *London*, the same shall thenceforth take effect and come into operation in the City of *London*, and shall be carried into execution in accordance with the Laws for the Time being in force relating to the City of *London* : Provided always, that the Resolution of such Public Meeting, signed by the Lord Mayor, shall be reported to the said Lord Mayor, Aldermen, and Commons, in Common Council assembled, and entered on the Minutes thereof, and that such Entry shall be Evidence ; the Expenses incurred in calling and holding the Meeting, whether this Act shall be adopted or not, and the Expenses of carrying this Act into execution in the City of *London*, shall be paid out of the Consolidated Rate, and the Commissioners of Sewers of the City of *London* may levy a Part of the Consolidated Rate, or, by a separate Rate, to be assessed and recovered in like Manner as the Consolidated Rate, all Monies from Time to Time necessary for defraying such Expenses, and distinct Accounts shall be kept of the Receipts, Payments, and Liabilities of the said Lord Mayor, Aldermen, and Commons with reference to the Execution of the Act.

XXV. *Museums to be Free.*—The Admission to all Libraries and Museums established under this Act shall be open to the Public free of all Charge.

XXVI. This Act shall not extend to *Ireland* or *Scotland*.

PUBLIC LIBRARIES AND MUSEUMS AMENDMENT ACT (ENGLAND AND SCOTLAND), 1866.

CAP. CXIV.

An Act to amend the Public Libraries Act.

[*10th August*, 1866.]

WHEREAS it is expedient to amend the Public Libraries Act, 1855, and to assimilate the Laws relating to Public Libraries in *England* and *Scotland* : Be it therefore enacted by the Queen's most Excellent Majesty, by and with the advice and consent of the Lords Spiritual and Temporal, and Commons, in this present Parliament assembled, and by the authority of the same, as follows :

1. So much of the Section Fifteen of the said Public Libraries Act, 1855, as incorporates with that Act certain Clauses of the Towns Improvement Clauses Act,

1847, shall, so far as the same relates to or concerns Municipal Boroughs, be repealed.

2. Section Five of the said Act, except so much thereof as relates to keeping distinct Accounts, shall be repealed; and the Expenses incurred in calling and holding the Meeting, whether the said Act shall be adopted or not, and the Expenses of carrying the said Act into execution in any Municipal Borough, may be paid out of the Borough Rate of such Borough, or by and out of a Rate to be made and recovered in such Borough, in like Manner as a Borough Rate may be made and recovered therein, but the amount so paid in such Borough in any One Year shall not exceed the Sum of One Penny in the Pound upon the annual Value of the Property in such Borough rateable to a Borough Rate: Provided always, that nothing in this Act shall interfere with the Operation of the Act Twenty-eighth and Twenty-ninth *Victoria*, Chapter One hundred and eight, so far as it relates to the Collection of a Rate for a Public Library in the City of *Oxford*.

3. *In Boroughs Meeting to be called at the Request of Ten Ratepayers.*—The Public Meeting mentioned in Section 4 of the said Public Libraries Act, 1855, shall be called either on the Request of the Town Council, or on the Request in Writing of Ten Ratepayers residing in the Borough.

4. Any Parish, of whatever Population, adjoining any Borough, District, or Parish which shall have adopted or shall contemplate the Adoption of the said Public Libraries Act, 1855, may, with the consent of more than One Half of the Ratepayers thereof present at a Meeting to be convened in manner directed by the said Act with reference to Meetings of Ratepayers, and with the Consent also of the Town Council of such Borough, or the Board of such District, or the Commissioners of such Parish, as the Case may be, determine that such

adjoining Parish shall for the Purposes of the said Act form Part of such Borough, District, or Parish, and thereupon the Vestry of such adjoining Parish shall forthwith appoint Three Ratepayers Commissioners for such Parish, One Third of whom shall go out of Office, and the Vacancies be filled up as provided by the said Act with respect to the Commissioners of a Parish and such Commissioners for the Time being shall for the Purposes of the said Act be considered as Part of such Town Council, Board, or Commissioners, as the Case may be ; and the Expenses of calling the Meeting, and the Proportion of the Expenses of such adjoining Parish of carrying the said Act into execution, shall be paid out of the Poor Rates thereof to such Person as the Commissioners of the said adjoining Parish shall appoint to receive the same.

5. *A Majority of One-Half of the Ratepayers may adopt Act.*—The Majority necessary to be obtained for the Adoption of the said Act or the Public Libraries Act (*Scotland*), 1854, shall be more than One Half of the Persons present at the Meeting, instead of Two Thirds of such Persons as now required.

6. *Act may be adopted whatever Amount of Population.*—The Public Libraries Act (1855) and the Public Libraries Act (*Scotland*) (1854) shall be applicable to any Borough, District, or Parish or Burgh, of whatever Population.

7. So much of Section 6 of the Public Libraries Act (*Scotland*), 1854, as authorizes the demanding of a Poll, and Sections Seven and Eight of the said Act, are hereby repealed.

8. If any Meeting called as provided by the said last-mentioned Act shall determine against the Adoption of the Act in any Burgh, no Meeting for a similar Purpose shall be held for the Space of One Year at least from the Time of holding the previous Meeting.

9. The Clauses and Provisions of the Companies Clauses Consolidation (*Scotland*) Act (1845) with respect to the borrowing of Money upon Mortgage or Bond, and the Accountability of Officers, and the Recovery of Damages and Penalties, so far as such Provisions may respectively be applicable to the Purposes of the said Public Libraries Act (*Scotland*) (1854), shall be respectively incorporated with that Act.

10. *A Library or Museum may be established in connexion with any Museum or Library.*—Wherever a Public Museum or Library has been established under any Act relating to Public Libraries or Museums, or shall hereafter be established under either of the said before-mentioned Acts, a Public Library or Museum, as the Case may be, may at any Time be established in connexion therewith without any further Proceedings being taken under the said Acts.

11. *Short Title.*—This Act may be cited as The Public Libraries Amendment Act (*England* and *Scotland*), 1866, and shall be taken to be Part of the said Public Libraries Act, 1855, and shall be construed accordingly.

ACT FOR ACQUIRING SITES FOR MUSEUMS, 1868.

Cap. XLIV.

An Act for facilitating the Acquisition and Enjoyment of Sites for Buildings for Religious, Educational, Literary, Scientific, and other Charitable Purposes.

[*13th July, 1868.*]

WHEREAS it is expedient to afford greater Facilities for the Acquisition and Enjoyment by Societies or

Bodies of Persons associated together for Religious, Educational, Literary, Scientific, or other like Charitable Purposes, of Buildings and Pieces of Land as Sites for Buildings for such Purposes :

Be it therefore enacted by the Queen's most Excellent Majesty, by and with the Advice and Consent of the Lords Spiritual and Temporal, and Commons, in this present Parliament assembled, and by the Authority of the same, as follows :

1. *Grants of Land for Buildings for Religious and certain other Purposes.*—All Alienations, Grants, Conveyances, Leases, Assurances, Surrenders, or other Dispositions, except by Will, *bond fide* made after the passing of this Act, to a Trustee or Trustees, on behalf of any Society or Body of Persons associated together for Religious Purposes, or for the Promotion of Education, Arts, Literature, Science, or other like Purposes, of Land, for the Erection thereon of a Building for such Purposes or any of them, or whereon a Building used or intended to be used for such Purposes or any of them shall have been erected, shall be exempt from the provisions of an Act passed in the Ninth Year of the Reign of King *George* the Second, and intitled *An Act to restrain the Disposition of Lands whereby the same become unalienable*, and also from the Provisions of the Second Section of an Act passed in the Twenty-fourth Year of the Reign of Her present Majesty, intituled *An Act to amend the Law relating to the Conveyance of Land for Charitable Uses :* Provided that such Alienation, Grant, Conveyance, Lease, Assurance, Surrender, or other Disposition, shall have been really and *bond fide* made for a full and valuable Consideration actually paid on or before the making of such Alienation, Grant, Conveyance, Lease, Assurance, Surrender, or other Disposition, or reserved by way of Rent, Rent-charge, or other annual Payment, or partly paid

and partly reserved as aforesaid, without Fraud or Collusion, and provided that each such Piece of Land shall not exceed Two Acres in Extent or Area in each Case.

2. Provided always, that the Trustee or Trustees of any Deed or Instrument by which any such Alienation, Grant, Conveyance, Lease, Assurance, Surrender, or Disposition shall have been made, or the Trusts thereof declared, may, if he or they shall think fit, at any Time cause such Deed or Instrument to be enrolled in Her Majesty's High Court of Chancery.

3. From and after the passing of this Act it shall not be necessary to acknowledge any Deed or Instrument in order that the same may be enrolled in Her Majesty's High Court of Chancery.

PUBLIC LIBRARIES AMENDMENT ACT, 1871.

CHAP. 71.

An Act to amend the Public Libraries Act, 1855.

[14*th August*, 1871.]

WHEREAS it is expedient to amend and extend the Public Libraries Act, 1855, hereinafter referred to as the "principal Act":

Be it therefore enacted by the Queen's most Excellent Majesty, by and with the advice and consent of the Lords Spiritual and Temporal, and Commons, in this present Parliament assembled, and by the authority of the same, as follows:

1. Every local board, under the Public Health Act, 1848, and the Local Government Act, 1858, or either of them, is empowered, in like manner as a board

under any Improvement Act, to adopt and carry into execution the principal Act.

2. *Interpretation of terms.*—For the purposes aforesaid, the following words in the principal Act shall have the following extended significations ; viz., the word " board " shall mean any such local board as aforesaid ; the words " improvement rate " shall mean the general district rate levied by any such board ; the word " ratepayers " shall mean all persons assessed to and paying such general district rate ; the word " district " shall mean the district in which such local board has authority to levy a general district rate ; the term " Improvement Act " shall mean the Local Government Act, 1858.

3. So much of section fifteen of the principal Act as refers to the Towns Improvement Clauses Act, 1847, shall not apply to rates made by local boards under the principal Act ; but nothing herein contained shall enable local boards to levy or expend for the purposes of the principal Act any greater sum in any year than one penny in the pound.

4. *Provision as to borrowing.*—For carrying into execution the principal Act, every such local board may borrow upon mortgage of the general district rate or any separate rate to be levied under the principal Act ; and such borrowing shall be effected in conformity with the provisions as to borrowing contained in the Local Government Act, 1858, and the Acts incorporated therewith, in lieu of the provisions as to borrowing contained in the principal Act.

5. *Not to apply to certain districts.*—This Act shall not apply to any district the whole or any part of which is within any municipal borough, or within the jurisdiction of Commissioners under any Improvement Act.

6. This Act may be cited for all purposes as "The Public Libraries Act, 1855, Amendment Act, 1871."

PUBLIC LIBRARIES AMENDMENT ACT, 1877.

CHAP. 54.

An Act to amend the Public Libraries Acts.

[14*th August*, 1877.]

WHEREAS by the Public Libraries Acts, 18 & 19 Victoria, c. 40, for Ireland; 29 & 30 Victoria, c. 114, for England; and 30 & 31 Victoria, c. 37, for Scotland, the mode by which the Act is to be adopted is prescribed to be by public meeting, and it has been found that in many cases a public meeting is a most incorrect and unsatisfactory mode, and fails to indicate the general opinion of the ratepayers, and it is desirable to ascertain these opinions more correctly:

Be it enacted by the Queen's most Excellent Majesty, by and with the advice and consent of the Lords Spiritual and Temporal, and Commons, in this present Parliament assembled, and by the authority of the same, as follows:

1. *Ratepayers' opinions may be ascertained by voting papers.*—It shall be competent for the prescribed local authority in any place or community which has the power to adopt one of the above recited Acts, to ascertain the opinions of the majority of the ratepayers either by the prescribed public meeting or by the issue of a voting paper to each ratepayer, and the subsequent collection and scrutiny thereof, and any expense in connexion with such voting papers shall be borne in the same way as the expense of a public meeting would be borne, and the decision of the majority so ascertained shall be equally binding.

2. In addition to the simple vote " Yes " or " No " to the adoption of the Act, such voting paper may stipulate that its adoption shall be subject to a limitation to some lower rate of assessment than the maximum allowed by Act of Parliament in force at the time, and such lower limit, if once adopted, shall not be subsequently altered except by public vote similarly taken.

3. "Ratepayer" shall mean every inhabitant who would have to pay the Free Library assessment in event of the Act being adopted.

4. This Act may be cited as the Public Libraries Amendment Act, 1877.

MALICIOUS INJURIES TO PROPERTY ACT (1861) [ENGLAND AND IRELAND.]

24 AND 25 VICTORIA, CAP. XCVII., § 39.

WHOEVER shall unlawfully or maliciously destroy or damage any Book, Manuscript, Picture, Print, Statue, Bust, or Vase, or any other Article or Thing kept for the purposes of Art, Science, or Literature, or as an Object of Curiosity, in any Museum, Gallery, Cabinet, Library, or other Repository, which Museum, Gallery, Cabinet, Library, or other Repository is either at all Times or from Time to Time open for the Admission of the Public or of any considerable Number of Persons to view the same, either by the permission of the Proprietor thereof or by the Payment of Money before entering the same, or any Picture, Statue, Monument, or other Memorial of the Dead, Painted Glass, or other Ornament or Work of Art, in any Church, Chapel, Meeting House, or other Place of Divine Worship, or in any Building belonging to the Queen, or to any

County, Riding, Division, City, Borough, Poor-Law Union, Parish, or Place, or to any University, or College, or Hall of any University, or to any Inn of Court, or to any Street, Square, Churchyard, Burial Ground, Public Garden or Ground, or any Statue or Monument exposed to Public View, or any Ornament, Railing, or Fence surrounding such Statue or Monument, shall be guilty of a Misdemeanour, and being convicted thereof, shall be liable to be imprisoned for any Term not exceeding Six Months, with or without Hard Labour, and, if a Male under the Age of Sixteen Years, with or without Whipping: provided that nothing herein contained shall be deemed to affect the Right of any person to recover, by Action at Law, Damages for the Injury so committed.

PUBLIC LIBRARIES ACT, 1884.
CHAP. 37.

An Act to amend the Public Libraries Acts.

[*28th July,* 1884.]

BE it enacted by the Queen's most Excellent Majesty, by and with the advice and consent of the Lords Spiritual and Temporal, and Commons, in this present Parliament assembled, and by the authority of the same, as follows:

1. *Power of Council, Board, &c., to Accept Parliamentary Grant.*—Whereas doubts have arisen as to whether authorities acting under the Public Libraries Acts, have power to fulfil the conditions required for a parliamentary grant in aid of the establishment of a school of science and art, and it is expedient to remove such doubts: It is therefore hereby declared and enacted that,—

Where any authority acting under the Public

Libraries Acts accepts a grant out of moneys provided by Parliament from any Committee of the Privy Council on Education towards the purchase of the site, or the erection, enlargement, or repair, of any school for science and art, or school for science, or school for art, or of the residence of any teacher in such school, or towards the furnishing of any such school, such authority shall have power to accept such grant upon the conditions prescribed for the acceptance thereof by the said Committee, and to execute such instruments as may be required by the said Committee for carrying into effect such conditions, and upon payment of the grant shall, together with their successors, be bound by such conditions and instrument, and have power and be bound to fulfil and observe the same.

2. Whereas section eighteen of the Public Libraries Act, 1855, as regards England, and section nine of the Public Libraries Act (Ireland), 1855, as regards Ireland, provide for the erection of buildings "suitable for public libraries, or museums, or both, or for schools for science and art":

And whereas section ten of the Public Libraries Act (Scotland), 1867, provides for the erection of buildings "suitable for public libraries, art galleries, or museums, or each respectively," and doubts are entertained as to the meaning of those provisions: Now, therefore, it is hereby declared and enacted that—

Buildings may under the said sections be erected for public libraries, public museums, schools for science, art galleries, and schools for art, or for any one or more of those objects.

3. (1.) *Power to establish Library, Museum, or School for Science and Art.*—Where any of the following institutions, namely, a public library, a school for science and

art, a school for science, a school for art, or an art gallery has been established either before or after the passing of this Act under the Public Libraries Acts, or any of them, there may at any time be established in connexion therewith any other of the said institutions without any further proceedings being taken under the said Acts.

(2.) Section ten of the Public Libraries Amendment Act (England and Scotland), 1866, and section seventeen of the Public Libraries Act (Scotland), 1867, are hereby repealed, without prejudice to anything done under those sections.

4. In this Act,—

The expression " Public Libraries Acts " means as respects England, Scotland, and Ireland respectively, the Acts mentioned in the first, second, and third parts respectively of the schedule to this Act.

The expression "authority acting under the Public Libraries Acts" means the council, board, magistrates, or commissioners acting in execution of the said Public Libraries Acts.

5. This Act may be cited as the Public Libraries Act, 1884.

The Acts mentioned in the first part of the schedule to this Act may be cited together with this Act as the Public Libraries (England) Acts, 1855 to 1884.

The Acts mentioned in the second part of the schedule to this Act may be cited together with this Act as the Public Libraries (Scotland) Acts, 1867 to 1884.

The Acts mentioned in the third part of the schedule to this Act may be cited together with this Act as the Public Libraries (Ireland) Acts, 1855 to 1884.

FORM OF BEQUEST.

I bequeath out of such part of my personal Estate as may by Law be bequeathed for such purposes, to the Mayor, Aldermen, and Burgesses of the Borough of   in the County of the sum of   , free from Legacy Duty, for the benefit of the Museums and Free Libraries of the said Borough, to be expended in such way as they may deem expedient; and I direct that the Receipt of the Town Clerk of the said Borough shall be an effectual discharge for the same Legacy.

For specimens of other forms see *Free Public Libraries.*

WHAT SOME OF OUR PUBLIC MEN SAY OF MUSEUMS AND FREE LIBRARIES.

THE LATE LORD IDDESLEIGH.

" I heartily wish success in the promotion of Free Libraries. All that I have seen of these institutions is encouraging except the smallness of their number."

SIR JOHN LUBBOCK, M.P.

" It is much to be regretted that so few towns have availed themselves of the Free Libraries Acts."

MR. THOMAS BURT, M.P.

" I attach the greatest importance to the Free Libraries movement. In Newcastle-on-Tyne we had a long and rather severe fight. We won, and at present an excellent institution is established and is doing valuable work."

RIGHT HON. W. E. GLADSTONE, M.P.

" A Free Library is of great importance for maintaining the knowledge and guiding the life of those who can use it, even though they may not represent the entire population."

DUKE OF RUTLAND (LORD JOHN MANNERS).

" I wish that in every town, not only Museums, but Free Public Libraries, were established."

MR. ROBERT GIFFIN, LL.D. (OF THE BOARD OF TRADE).

" The value of a Free Library in a large city is simply incalculable. It does not give bread or clothing to the working man, but it helps to make life sweeter and better, and opens out careers even to the poorest."

RIGHT HON. JOHN BRIGHT, M.P.

" There is no blessing that can be given to an artisan's family more than a love of books. The home influence of such a possession is one that will guard them from many temptations and from many evils. To the young especially this is of great importance, for if there be no seed time there will certainly be no harvest. It is impossible for anybody to confer upon young men a greater blessing than to stimulate them to associate themselves constantly with a Free Library, and draw from it any book they like."

THE LATE EARL OF SHAFTESBURY.

"The Free Library Institution will effect great and lasting good in generations to come."

CHARLES DICKENS.

"The Free Library is a great Free School, inviting the humblest workman to come in and to be a student."

RIGHT HON. JOHN MORLEY, M.P.

"The immense popularity and undoubted usefulness of a Free Library have been amply proved in every place where the experiment has been tried. There can be no greater encouragement to new experiments than the past success of this excellent movement."

THE RIGHT HON. A. J. MUNDELLA, M.P., SAYS —

"I regard Museums and Free Libraries as one of the necessities of the age. No town should be without one."

PROFESSOR HUXLEY SAYS :—

"It was not worth while discussing whether it was absolutely right or absolutely wrong to employ the authority of the community for the payment of those sums which were necessary for the purposes of education. What they must look at was this, that whatever might be the ultimate state of the world, at the present time we were not advanced enough to leave to private enterprise general measures for the public welfare, and if there were no other excuse for State authority in this matter, the very excellent one was sufficient that the existence of these libraries would, more than anything, tend to bring about that state of mind in which compulsion would become less and less necessary, and more opportunities would be given for voluntary effort."

RIGHT HON. JOSEPH CHAMBERLAIN, M.P.

"I am a great believer in the advantages of a miscellaneous reading. I believe that by it we open our minds to new ideas, we widen our sympathies and expand our intellectual and moral horizon, and I know, also, that for the student who desires to

2 E

pursue thoroughly any subject, it is absolutely necessary that he should have access to books, many of which are costly, many of which are very difficult to obtain even to the richest of single individuals, *but which it is in the power of a community to provide for all its members alike.* And in this possession there is no favour conferred: it is a right which is enjoyed by all."

THE LATE PROFESSOR W. STANLEY JEVONS.

" The main *raison d'être* of the Public Libraries, as indeed of Public Museums, Art Galleries, Parks, Town Halls, Public Clocks, and many other kinds of Public Works, is the enormous increase of public utility which is thereby acquired for the community at a trifling cost."

MR. HENRY BROADHURST, M.P.

" Next to elementary education, the ratepayers can scarcely invest their money in a more profitable or more desirable manner than in a Free Library. By means of these institutions written knowledge is brought within reach of the poorest. Up to the present time it has only been in the power of the rich and well-to-do to provide themselves with the best works for the formation of the character and the instruction of the mind. The only superiority that one has over another is in knowledge and character. Free Libraries are therefore a direct aid to the promotion of equality among men. I hope that the working classes of the district will heartily support the undertaking.'

MR. J. A. FROUDE SAYS :—

"Free Libraries, if the right books are in them, and Museums will be of immense value. But we read more and more nowadays for amusement, and the most absurd books are the most popular."

MR. FREDERIC HARRISON :—

" The Free Library and Museum movement is perfectly free from suspicion of belonging to party, class, or sect. Of all the Acts passed in the last fifty years he thought there was none which had done more quiet good with less burden on the country, absolutely without hitch or complaint, than the Free Library Act."

THE MAYOR OF LEEDS.

" The Free Library in this Borough has been established for upwards of fifty years. It has been very successful in its operations, and has proved itself to be one of the most important educational institutions in the Borough."

THE MAYOR OF READING WRITES :—

"I have pleasure in saying that the Free Library in this town has been an unqualified success, and has conferred signal advantages upon the inhabitants."

The MAYOR OF NEWCASTLE-ON-TYNE WRITES :—

"There can be no question that the Public Library in Newcastle has been a great benefit to the inhabitants, and is more used by the citizens of all classes than the Corporation ever contemplated as probable when it was initiated. I think there is only one opinion in the city as to its value."

SIR JOHN LUBBOCK, M.P.

"How much better it is to spend our money on Museums, Libraries and schools than on prisons. Already the Public Libraries Act of 1885 is beginning to tell. To no other cause, I think, can we attribute the gratifying diminution in crime which has taken place, and is taking place."

THE BISHOP OF ROCHESTER.

"Sooner or later you must succeed in what is but the proper completion of the Elementary Education Act of 1870, and the true safe-guarding of that memorable extension of the franchise, from which a new era of English history will assuredly begin. Your effort is but the duty of wise men, who love their country, who do not fear knowledge of any kind, so long as it is exact and complete ; who feel that the education a man gives himself is far more valuable than any other ; who expect, not without reason, that in course of time the trifling additional expense from a penny rate will be more than saved by a diminution of the public charges. The United States have long been ahead of us in this question of Free Libraries, as I well know from personal observation."

Reprinted from " FREE PUBLIC LIBRARIES."

INDEX.